Digital Technologies and Public Procurement

Digital Technologies and Public Procurement

Gatekeeping and Experimentation in Digital Public Governance

ALBERT SANCHEZ-GRAELLS

Professor of Economic Law
University of Bristol Law School

OXFORD
UNIVERSITY PRESS

OXFORD
UNIVERSITY PRESS

Great Clarendon Street, Oxford, OX2 6DP,
United Kingdom

Oxford University Press is a department of the University of Oxford.
It furthers the University's objective of excellence in research, scholarship,
and education by publishing worldwide. Oxford is a registered trade mark of
Oxford University Press in the UK and in certain other countries

First Edition published in 2024

Published in the United States of America by Oxford University Press
198 Madison Avenue, New York, NY 10016, United States of America

British Library Cataloguing in Publication Data
Data available

Library of Congress Control Number: 2023948100

ISBN 978–0–19–886677–0

DOI: 10.1093/oso/9780198866770.001.0001

Printed and bound by
CPI Group (UK) Ltd, Croydon, CR0 4YY

To Mateo and Emma,
mis dos peques

The writing of this book, between September 2022 and July 2023, was funded by the British Academy through a Mid-Career Fellowship for the project 'Digital technologies and public procurement. Gatekeeping and experimentation in digital public governance' (MCFSS22\220033).

The British Academy

Preface

I first came up with the idea of researching the interaction between digital technologies and public procurement in 2015, when I had to formulate my long-term research agenda for my job interview at the University of Bristol Law School. Back then, public sector digitalization was rather patchy and a relatively small field of scholarship—certainly in law, but also in public administration and political science. While digitalization was starting to gain prominence in academic literature, the volume of published works still seemed manageable. Procurement digitalization seemed like a very far frontier given the slowness in the transition towards electronic procurement and the paucity of procurement data. I thought I would have time to get to understand the technologies that were being touted as *disruptive*, and to think about their governance and regulatory implications at my own pace. I made this book project the central plank of my research leave application for 2018/19. If everything had gone to plan, as I saw it in February 2018, this book should have been published in 2019. Then, life decided to get in the way! I have since had the immense privilege of having two children. In 2020/21 there was also a global pandemic that effectively wiped out a year of working time, and because of which I experienced some physical and mental health issues. Researching and writing this book has been a constant start and stop process, and increasingly complicated by the challenges of work-life balance while parenting two pre-schoolers. The pandemic also accelerated public sector digitalization. Developments in digital technologies, and artificial intelligence in particular, have brought their regulation to the forefront of political and public discourse. The literature has exploded. Four years later, this book bears no resemblance to its '2019 self'. Hopefully, it is a better book for it.

My motivation in writing the book arose from claims that data, digitalization, and innovation would overcome all procurement and public governance challenges. I thought that most legal scholarship on procurement digitalization and touting the use of procurement as a regulatory tool to discipline public sector digitalization failed to see the technology for what it was, overestimated the practical power of procurement as a regulatory tool, or both. I often found that scholarship too eagerly jumped on the bandwagon of techno solutionism, fuelled by tech companies generating hype and policymakers unable or unwilling to cut through it. This book is my effort to push back, and to contribute to policymaking that is technology-centred and legally-informed. As I wrote in my funding application to the British Academy, I conducted this research 'aiming to improve public governance and public service delivery in the digital space'. The reader will judge whether I have achieved my goal.

I would like to record my gratitude to the University of Bristol Law School for the period of research leave I enjoyed during 2019, which was at the start rather than the end of this project. I am also grateful to the British Academy for the Mid-Career Fellowship that allowed me to complete the book in 2022/23. Additionally, I wish to express my gratitude to everyone who engaged with my ideas and normative recommendations at several events, as well as through my blog *How to Crack a Nut*. Every interaction helped me to refine my thoughts. I am particularly indebted to Marco Almada, Pedro Cerqueira Gomes, John Coggon, Michèle Finck, Willem A Janssen, Ian Makgill, Yseult Marique, Tony Prosser, Akis Psygkas, Pedro Telles, and Chris Yukins for very useful discussions and for specific comments on earlier versions of the book proposal or specific book chapters. I am also grateful to Alex Flach, Charlotte Kershaw, and the entire team at Oxford University Press, as well to the three anonymous reviewers of the book proposal, who gave me useful suggestions for improvement. Needless to say, despite all this support and input, the book only reflects my own understanding and I am thus responsible for any errors or shortcomings.

I would not have been able to complete this book without the support and daily joy provided by my dear friends and family, especially Jule, Mateo, and Emma.

Albert Sanchez-Graells
Bristol, 11 July 2023

Contents

II. REGULATING PUBLIC SECTOR DIGITALIZATION BY CONTRACT

III. EXPERIMENTING WITH PUBLIC SECTOR DIGITALIZATION

Table of Case Law

EUROPEAN UNION

Table of Legislative Materials

EU Directives

EU Decisions

European Commission Implementing Regulations

European Commission Decisions

European Commission Recommendations

European Commission Legislative Proposals

US LEGISLATIVE PROPOSALS

Abbreviations

AI	Artificial Intelligence
AIPSA	AI in the Public Sector Authority
API	Application Programming Interface
CJEU	Court of Justice of the European Union
DLT	Distributed Ledger Technology
eForms	Standard forms for the publication of notices in the field of public procurement in the EU
ENISA	European Union Agency for Cybersecurity
EU	European Union
GDPR	General Data Protection Regulation
ICT	Information and Communication Technology
IoT	Internet of Things
IPR	Intellectual Property Rights
IT	Information Technology
LLM	Large Language Models
ML	Machine Learning
NLP	Natural Language Processing
OCDS	Open Contracting Data Standard
OCP	Open Contracting Partnership
OECD	Organisation for Economic Cooperation and Development
OJEU	Official Journal of the European Union
R&D	Research and Development
RPA	Robotic Process Automation
TED	Tenders Electronic Daily, a supplement of the Official Journal of the European Union
UK	United Kingdom
UNCAC	United Nations Convention Against Corruption
US	United States of America
WB	World Bank
XaaS	Anything as a Service

PART I
INTRODUCTION

1
Introduction

1. Research Scope, Contribution, Methodology, and Book Structure

1.1 Research Scope and Contribution

This book is about the adoption of digital technologies by the public sector; the so-called public sector 'digital transformation'. It focuses on the role of public procurement—the set of rules, policies, and practices controlling the acquisition of technology by public buyers—in this transition towards new modes of digital public governance.[1]

The digital transformation of the public sector opens significant opportunities to improve its functioning and the provision of public services, including in terms of their effectiveness, accessibility, and personalization.[2] Digital technologies can be used to streamline information exchanges and to simplify the forms required to interact with the public sector for unavoidable tasks, such as discharging tax obligations.[3] Digital technologies can also reduce the costs and increase the effectiveness of fundamental public services, such as healthcare[4]

[1] Digital public governance broadly refers to the adoption of digital technologies by the public sector to discharge its obligations, interact with citizens and provide (or facilitate the outsourced provision of) public services. This phenomenon has been intensely researched and labelled 'digital era governance', primarily through the seminal works of Dunleavy and Margetts: Patrick Dunleavy and others, *Digital Era Governance: IT Corporations, the State, and E-Government* (OUP 2006); Patrick Dunleavy and others, 'New Public Management Is Dead—Long Live Digital-Era Governance' (2006) 16(3) Journal of Public Administration Research and Theory 467; Helen Margetts and Patrick Dunleavy, 'The Second Wave of Digital Era Governance: A Quasi-Paradigm for Government on the Web' (2013) 371(1987) Philosophical Transactions of the Royal Society 1. For an overview, see Jacob Torfing and others, *Public Governance Paradigms. Competing and Co-Existing* (Edward Elgar 2020) 89. While there are some disagreements and terminological differences, as well as nuances, in the public governance literature, this book will not explore them in detail, as the focus will be on the commonly accepted general trend of public sector digitalization. cf Evrim Tan and Joep Crompvoets, *The New Digital Era Governance. How New Digital Technologies Are Shaping Public Governance* (Wageningen Academic 2022).

[2] OECD, 'Recommendation on digital government strategies' (2014) <https://www.oecd.org/gov/digital-government/Recommendation-digital-government-strategies.pdf> accessed 12 June 2023.

[3] ICAEW, 'Digitalisation of tax: international perspectives' (2022) <https://www.icaew.com/technical/technology/technology-and-the-profession/digitalisation-of-tax-international-perspectives> accessed 12 June 2023.

[4] Song-Hee Kim and Hummy Song, 'How Digital Transformation Can Improve Hospitals' Operational Decisions' (*Harvard Business Review*, 18 January 2022) <https://hbr.org/2022/01/how-digital-transformation-can-improve-hospitals-operational-decisions> accessed 12 June 2023.

Digital Technologies and Public Procurement. Albert Sanchez-Graells, Oxford University Press.
 DOI: 10.1093/oso/9780198866770.003.0001

or education.[5] They can be used to deploy new approaches to emergency preparedness or environmental management.[6] Digital technology applications across the public sector and their potential to improve our lives may seem endless.

However, this digital transformation comes with a multitude of risks and the certainty of harms,[7] both of an operational and a governance nature.[8] It is not only that projects of digital transformation can go wrong and result in large losses of public funds.[9] Badly designed and implemented 'digital solutions' can cause significant individual and collective harms[10]—including discrimination, exclusion, and other violations of fundamental rights.[11] They can undermine the functioning of the public sector and its legitimacy,[12] and generate further mistrust from citizens in the operation of the State.[13] The transition towards new modes of digital public governance is quickly accelerating with the emergence of ever more advanced digital technologies that could be used to replace human with algorithmic governance.[14] These technologies create heightened risks of regulatory capture by the powerful economic actors that develop and

[5] UNESCO, 'AI and education: guidance for policy-makers' (2021) <https://unesdoc.unesco.org/ark:/48223/pf0000376709.locale=en> accessed 12 June 2023.

[6] UN Environment Programme, 'How digital technology and innovation can help protect the planet' (17 August 2022) <https://www.unep.org/news-and-stories/story/how-digital-technology-and-innovation-can-help-protect-planet> accessed 12 June 2023.

[7] Dan McQuillan, 'Predicted Benefits, Proven Harms. How AI's Algorithmic Violence Emerged from Our Own Social Matrix' (*Sociological Review*, 6 June 2023) <https://thesociologicalreview.org/magazine/june-2023/artificial-intelligence/predicted-benefits-proven-harms/> accessed 15 June 2023.

[8] See eg Hannah Trittin-Ulbrich and others, 'Exploring the Dark and Unexpected Sides of Digitalization: Toward a Critical Agenda' (2020) 28(1) Organization 3.

[9] See eg in the UK context, House of Commons Committee of Public Accounts, 'Challenges in implementing digital change' (HC 2021-22, 637).

[10] See eg Alexandra James and others, 'From Access and Transparency to Refusal: Three Responses to Algorithmic Governance' (2023) 12(2) Internet Policy Review <https://doi.org/10.14763/2023.2.1691> accessed 12 June 2023.

[11] Such as those established in the Charter of Fundamental Rights of the European Union [2012] OJ C 326/391. See Karen Yeung, 'A Study of the Implications of Advanced Digital Technologies (Including AI Systems) for the Concept of Responsibility within a Human Rights Framework' (2019) Council of Europe DGI (2019)05 <https://rm.coe.int/a-study-of-the-implications-of-advanced-digital-technologies-including/168096bdab> accessed 12 June 2023; Elizabeth M Renieris, *Beyond Data. Reclaiming Human Rights at the Dawn of the Metaverse* (MIT Press 2023).

[12] Ines Mergel and others, 'Study on the Impact of Digital Transformation on Democracy and Good Governance' (2021) Council of Europe CDDG (2021)4 Final <https://rm.coe.int/study-on-the-impact-of-digital-transformation-on-democracy-and-good-go/1680a3b9f9> accessed 12 June 2023.

[13] Balazs Bodo and Heleen Janssen, 'Maintaining Trust in a Technologized Public Sector' (2022) 41(3) Policy and Society 414; Katie Szilagyi, 'Artificial Intelligence & the *Machine*-ation of the Rule of Law' (PhD thesis, University of Ottawa 2022) <http://dx.doi.org/10.20381/ruor-28401> accessed 15 June 2023.

[14] Frank Pasquale, *The Black Box Society. The Secret Algorithms that Control Money and Information* (Harvard UP 2015).

own them.[15] Digital transformation thus also comes with significant risks of regulatory capture and privatization of public sector governance.[16]

Given the evolving nature of those risks and harms, regulating the digital transformation of the public sector is a major challenge[17] and a pressing need. However, it is receiving much less attention than the also urgent and challenging regulation of private digital actors, platforms, and markets.[18] Some of the emerging horizontal instruments of digital regulation, such as rules on data governance, will be applicable to the public sector. However, most vertical instruments target undertakings operating major digital platforms or providing digital services. The regulation of the 'digital public sector' is falling behind. This is progressively widening a regulatory gap that leaves the adoption of digital technologies by the public sector largely unregulated, as well as exposed to regulatory capture and commercial determination. This book focuses on this phenomenon of insufficient regulation of public sector digital transformation, maps the existing but hidden regulatory gap, and makes innovative and specific policy proposals to contribute to closing this gap.

The book concentrates on public procurement as a perceived 'regulatory fix' for the absence of more general regulation of the 'digital public sector'. It is the first to show how, far from solely serving an instrumental or 'back office' function in facilitating technology acquisition, public procurement is assigned the role of regulating public sector digitalization. The discussion will demonstrate how there is an emerging consensus amongst international organizations, domestic policymakers, academics, and think tanks that, as a buyer, the State is in a good position to demand fair, ethical, trustworthy, transparent, and secure technologies. The hope is that, in exercising its buying power, the State will act as a gatekeeper and 'regulate by contract' technologies that it is reluctant or slow to regulate through general legislation. As a 'responsible technology buyer', the State is expected to act as norm-setter and market-shaper and not only steer public sector digitalization, but also influence the (self-)regulation of the tech industry. Procurement is thus expected to be both an instrument

[15] Julie Cohen, *Between Truth and Power: The Legal Constructions of Informational Capitalism* (OUP 2019). The same actors are also increasingly dominating technological research, which further erodes possibilities for contestation and diversification; see eg Nur Ahmed, Muntasir Wahed, and Neil C Thompson, 'The Growing Influence of Industry in AI Research' (2023) 379 Science 884.

[16] See eg Hongfei Gu, 'Data, Big Tech, and the New Concept of Sovereignty' (2023) Journal of Chinese Political Science <https://doi.org/10.1007/s11366-023-09855-1> accessed 12 June 2023.

[17] See eg the breadth of the work undertaken by the Council of Europe in relation to Artificial Intelligence (AI) <https://www.coe.int/AI> accessed 12 June 2023.

[18] For discussion of how market regulation logics are driving the process of digital regulation in the European Union (EU), see Giovanni De Gregorio and Pietro Dunn, 'The European Risk-Based Approaches: Connecting Constitutional Dots in the Digital Age' (2022) 59(2) Common Market Law Review 47 (hereafter De Gregorio and Pietro Dunn, 'The European Risk-Based Approaches').

of public sector self-regulation and a mechanism of meta-regulation of the tech industry.[19] Ultimately, despite the broader underregulation of *both* digital technologies and the new modes of digital public governance they enable, procurement is expected to generate foundational safeguards in the functioning of the digital public sector and therefore protect citizens' rights.[20] Alas, the book demonstrates that procurement is unable to effectively meet these expectations.

By carefully mapping the sources of inadequacy of procurement as a 'regulatory fix', this book dispels the emerging consensus that procurement can (and will) operate as an effective safety net against the adoption of inadequate technologies and technological misuse by the public sector. It shows how relying on procurement as a tool of digital regulation is inadequate and can result in regulatory complacency and inaction. By laying bare the regulatory gap that lies beneath the approach to digital 'regulation by contract', the book raises awareness of the need to pay more regulatory attention and to dedicate more regulatory resources to the quickly accelerating phenomenon of public sector 'digital transformation' to safeguard individual rights and social interests. To inform the necessary legislative reforms, the book advances specific proposals informed by its innovative methodology.

1.2 Methodology

The book uses a transdisciplinary methodology driven by a technology-centred enriched legal method. This methodology is best described as consisting of three components. First, the book builds on critical doctrinal analysis of procurement law, policy, and practice.[21] Second, it builds on a technology-centred analysis of the potential applications of digital technologies in the public sector, which is underpinned by a deep functional understanding of the digital technologies under discussion, as well as their socio-technical implications.[22]

[19] For a conceptual framework describing the interaction between such mechanisms, see Cary Coglianese and Evan Mendelson, 'Meta-Regulation and Self-Regulation' in Robert Baldwin, Martin Cave, and Martin Lodge (eds), *The Oxford Handbook of Regulation* (OUP 2010) 146.

[20] More broadly, then, procurement becomes the conduit for State digital sovereignty; Matthias Leese 'Staying in Control of Technology: Predictive Policing, Democracy, and Digital Sovereignty' (2023) Democratization 1, 4 <https://doi.org/10.1080/13510347.2023.2197217> accessed 19 April 2023. The issue of digital sovereignty will not be discussed in detail. Interested readers can see the connections made by, eg, Luciano Floridi, 'The Fight for Digital Sovereignty: What It Is, and Why It Matters, Especially for the EU' (2020) 33 Philosophy & Technology 369, 371.

[21] See eg Ernst Hirsch Ballin, 'Critical Angles in Legal Research' in Ernst Hirsch Ballin, *Legal Research Methods* (Edward Elgar 2020) ch 2.

[22] On the importance of legal scholars engaging with a proper understanding of the technologies under regulation, and their broader socio-technical interactions, see eg Ryan Calo, 'The Scale and the

Third, the book builds on interdisciplinary insights derived from political economy,[23] political science, and theories of governance and regulation.[24] This methodology produces legal analysis informed by the technology and governance context. This facilitates the formulation of original insights and ensures analytical rigour. Moreover, the analysis in the book is grounded on, and informed by, the practical experiences and insights emerging from the quickly accelerating processes of public sector digital transformation. This is achieved through the integration of knowledge created beyond the academy and, especially, the insights generated by technical and policy reports. This approach not only blends insights stemming from academic disciplines, but also those emerging from practice, to inform legal analysis and proposals for legal reform.

The book was written at a time when the literature has exploded,[25] and there is increasing dynamism in the generation of regulatory proposals, both at global level and in several relevant jurisdictions. Staying on top of policy proposals and scholarly analyses is a challenge that necessitates a selective approach. No piece of research on digital technologies and their regulation can be comprehensive of all scholarly and policy materials being published. This book does not claim to be so. The selection of sources for this book has been driven by an analysis of their rigour and by following a conceptual saturation strategy, where only sources making distinct, or additional, conceptual or contextual contributions are used. The strategy of source selection has also been supported by a concentration on the sub-set of digital technologies most likely to be implemented by the public sector, and in relation to procurement digitalization. The book is not only about Artificial Intelligence (AI), but rather about the adoption by the public sector of a wide variety of digital technologies. However, it often focuses on public sector adoption of AI as the most contested digital technology and the one currently attracting most attention. However, the arguments developed in the book apply to digital technology

Reactor' (SSRN, 15 April 2022) <https://ssrn.com/abstract=4079851> accessed 7 September 2022. This is a different methodological approach to the nascent field of computational legal studies, which deploys digital technologies and data driven techniques to research the law; see eg Ryan Whalen, *Computational Legal Studies. The Promise and Challenge of Data-Driven Research* (Edward Elgar 2020).

[23] This is informed by, but not limited to, law and economics; see eg Alessio M Pacces, 'A Law and Economics Perspective on Normative Analysis' in Sanne Taekema, Bart van Klink, and Wouter de Been (eds), *Facts and Norms in Law. Interdisciplinary Reflections on Legal Method* (Edward Elgar 2016) 171.

[24] See eg Edward L Rubin, 'Law and the Methodology of Law' (1997) 3 Wisconsin Law Review 521.

[25] Trevor Bench-Capon, 'Thirty Years of Artificial Intelligence and Law: Editor's Introduction' (2022) 30 Artificial Intelligence and Law 475; Marco Almada 'What Do We Talk About When We Talk About AI Regulation?' (*RAILS blog*, 9 April 2023) <https://blog.ai-laws.org/what-do-we-talk-about-when-we-talk-about-ai-regulation/> accessed 11 April 2023.

adoption more generally and, to the extent this is appropriate, the book generalizes governance challenges and potential solutions beyond AI and current debates.

A final consideration in relation to the analytical approach of the book is that it is primarily informed by regulatory and policy developments in the European Union (EU) and the United Kingdom (UK)—though with an eye on the United States of America (US). It is thus unavoidable that the book has been influenced by the pace of developments, or the absence of them, in these jurisdictions. Moreover, the legal analysis in the book refers to EU law—which is by and large still UK law in relation to procurement (at least until October 2024),[26] although not in other issues of public sector digitalization. This EU-centric legal analysis can thus generate some friction in post-Brexit UK, but that seems largely unavoidable. To mitigate against this, the analysis in the book is functional, and stresses governance implications above legal ones. A related benefit is that the insights provided by the book are largely projectable to regulatory contexts and jurisdictions other than the EU (and the UK)—although one should be wary of 'digital legal transplants'.

The book presents the author's best understanding of the law and policy developments up to 15 June 2023.

1.3 Book Structure

After this introduction, Chapter 2 lays down the foundations for the analysis in the remainder of the book by providing a detailed account of the emerging digital regulation gatekeeping role assigned to procurement, as well as by framing procurement digitalization as an unregulated site of public sector technological experimentation ripe for a detailed case study.

The book is then divided in two main substantive parts.

Part II focuses on the digital regulation gatekeeping role assigned to public procurement, to dispel its adequacy as a 'regulatory fix' in the context of public sector digital transformation. It shows that procurement is ill-suited to develop a regulatory role that depends on the simultaneous and aligned self-regulation of the public sector and the tech industry. Procurement is the wrong institution, and its tools are inadequate. Chapter 3 shows that procurement can hardly be expected to control public sector decision-making on the adoption

[26] This depends on the future entry into force of the Procurement Bill undergoing parliamentary debate at the time of writing.

of digital technologies—which risks being driven by policy entrepreneurs and captured by the tech industry, capitalizing on the 'policy irresistibility' created by the abstract promises and hype surrounding these technologies. Moreover, as shown in Chapter 4, due to its market-based design and flexible instruments, in buying un(der)regulated digital technologies, procurement risks being the conduit of regulatory privatization through reliance on industry practices and standards.[27] Rather than acting as a gatekeeper, procurement risks being a Trojan horse for the adoption and use of untrustworthy and risky digital technologies by the public sector.[28] In Chapter 5, the book submits that procurement must be discharged of the digital regulation gatekeeping role, and that protecting the public interest and generating trustworthiness in public sector digitalization necessitates reallocating such regulatory role to an independent oversight authority tasked with enforcing new mandatory requirements for public sector digital technology adoption.

The book not only develops its analysis in the abstract, but grounds it on a detailed case study. In Part III, the book focuses on the digitalization of public procurement as a largely unregulated site of public sector technological experimentation. Chapter 6 shows in detail how the digitalization of this area of public sector activity can be driven by the policy irresistibility of 'tech fixes', limited public sector digital capabilities, and specific governance characteristics (such as the policy push for innovation procurement). It also shows that this process can result in excessive experimentation with immature technologies, or in technological experimentation in environments lacking adequate data and technical infrastructures. Chapter 7 shows how a deeper understanding of the technologies, their required enablers, and realistically feasible applications, could mitigate against the hype and allure that surrounds them. Chapter 8 stresses the importance of factoring new governance duties and risks into the decision-making process leading to technological adoption by the public sector. Chapter 9 shows the inadequacy of current regulatory frameworks in the EU and the UK and stresses the need for strengthened modes of digital procurement governance. Throughout this rich case study, Part III stresses risks of regulatory capture and regulatory privatization that pervade procurement digitalization—which justify subjecting the adoption of digital

[27] For broader discussion, see Colin Scott, 'Private Regulation of the Public Sector: A Neglected Facet of Contemporary Governance' (2002) 29(1) Journal of Law and Society 56; and Colin Scott, 'Standard-Setting in Regulatory Regimes' in Robert Baldwin, Martin Cave, and Martin Lodge (eds), *The Oxford Handbook of Regulation* (OUP 2010) 104.

[28] Relatedly, see Nitesh Bharosa, 'The Rise of GovTech: Trojan Horse or Blessing in Disguise? A Research Agenda' (2022) 39 Government Information Quarterly 101692.

technologies to mandatory requirements and external oversight, as advanced in Part II.

The book concludes by bringing together the insights developed in both substantive parts in a combined Conclusion.

* * *

To set the scene for the book, the remainder of this Introduction provides the background for the broader transition towards new modes of digital public governance (Section 2) and sketches the emerging regulatory model in the EU and the UK (Section 3) within which procurement is assigned the role of gatekeeper of public sector digitalization (Section 4). This gatekeeping role, and the context for the choice of procurement digitalization as a useful case study of public sector technological experimentation, are then further explored in Chapter 2.

2. The Un(der)regulated and Accelerating Transition Towards New Modes of Digital Public Governance

The transition towards new modes of digital public governance picked up pace with the turn of the twenty-first century,[29] and significantly accelerated in the aftermath of the COVID-19 pandemic.[30] Increased data availability,[31] technological developments—especially concerning AI[32]—and practical needs, have coalesced to push the process of public sector digitalization over existing blocks and resistances.[33]

[29] See eg OECD, 'The Path to Becoming a Data-Driven Public Sector' (2019) OECD Digital Government Studies <https://doi.org/10.1787/059814a7-en> accessed 7 March 2023.

[30] European Commission, 'AI Watch, Overview of the use and impact of AI in public services in the EU' (2020) <https://data.europa.eu/doi/10.2760/039619> accessed 7 March 2023; European Commission, 'AI Watch, European landscape on the use of artificial intelligence by the public sector' (2022) <https://data.europa.eu/doi/10.2760/39336> accessed 5 September 2022. For discussion, see Renata Gabryelczyk, 'Has COVID-19 Accelerated Digital Transformation? Initial Lessons Learned for Public Administrations' (2020) 37(4) Information Systems Management 303.

[31] This is driving the move towards what Yeung has labelled the 'new public analytics', to stress the risks of datafication as part of the wider phenomenon of public digital governance; see Karen Yeung, 'The New Public Analytics as an Emerging Paradigm in Public Sector Administration' (2022) 27(2) Tilburg Law Review 1 (hereafter Yeung, 'New Public Analytics').

[32] Yeung had previously focused on the technology aspect of the phenomenon, coining the term 'algorithmic regulation', which constitutes new public analytics' 'underpinning form of social ordering and mode of governance', ibid 9. See Karen Yeung, 'Algorithmic Regulation: A Critical Interrogation' (2018) 12(4) Regulation & Governance 429; Lena Ulbricht and Karen Yeung, 'Algorithmic Regulation: A Maturing Concept for Investigating Regulation of and through Algorithms' (2022) 16(1) Regulation & Governance 3.

[33] See eg Davide Giacomini and Caterina Muzzi, 'Promoting Digital Innovation in the Public Sector: Managerial and Organisational Insights from a Case Study' (2021) 8(3) International Journal of

Public sector digitalization is a global phenomenon that is clearly visible in Europe. The Organization for Economic Cooperation and Development (OECD) has documented over 250 'showcase' public sector digital innovations in the period 2019–2022, with over 100 originating in Europe.[34] The 2022 Government AI Readiness Index scored Western European countries above global average for readiness, and eleven European countries (led by the UK) were in the top twenty for public sector AI readiness.[35] A similar picture emerged from the 2021 World Bank's GovTech Readiness Index.[36] However, the European Court of Auditors has highlighted the unequal availability of digital public services across the EU, and criticized some aspects of the 2016 eGovernment Action Plan.[37] There is scope for further penetration of digital technologies in all countries, as well as for EU efforts to 'level up' and to promote EU-wide digitalization. The EU is thus giving public sector digitalization high strategic priority in the Digital Decade Policy Programme 2030.[38] The UK has also developed strategic plans to further public sector digitalization by 2025.[39] This mirrors similar strategic efforts around the globe.

Public sector digitalization indeed needs to be placed in the broader global context. States are not solely seeking to digitalize their public sector and public services with a view to enhance their operation (internal goal).[40] States are also increasingly willing to use the public sector and the construction of public infrastructure[41] as sources of funding[42] and spaces for digital

Public Sector Performance Management 236; Heather Broomfield and Lisa Marie Reutter, 'Towards a Data-Driven Public Administration: An Empirical Analysis of Nascent Phase Implementation' (2021) 25(2) Scandinavian Journal of Public Administration 73.

[34] Including the EEA and UK; see OECD Observatory of Public Sector Innovation <https://oecd-opsi.org/case_type/opsi/> accessed 10 March 2023.

[35] Oxford Insights, 'Government AI Readiness Index 2022' (2022) <https://www.oxfordinsights.com/government-ai-readiness-index-2022> accessed 10 March 2023.

[36] Cem Dener and others, *GovTech Maturity Index: The State of Public Sector Digital Transformation* (World Bank 2021).

[37] European Court of Auditors, 'e-Government actions targeting businesses' (2022) Special Report 24/2022 <https://www.eca.europa.eu/Lists/ECADocuments/SR22_24/SR_e-Government_EN.pdf> accessed 10 March 2023.

[38] Decision (EU) 2022/2481 of the European Parliament and of the Council of 14 December 2022 establishing the Digital Decade Policy Programme 2030 [2022] OJ L 323/4, art 4(1)(4).

[39] Central Digital and Data Office, 'Transforming for a digital future: 2022 to 2025 roadmap for digital and data' (Policy Paper, 9 June 2022) <https://www.gov.uk/government/publications/roadmap-for-digital-and-data-2022-to-2025> accessed 5 September 2022.

[40] For discussion in the Swedish context, see Anthony Larsson and Robin Teigland (eds), *Digital Transformation and Public Services. Societal Impacts in Sweden and Beyond* (Routledge 2020).

[41] See eg Andrea Bastianin and Chiara F Del Bo, 'Public Procurement in Big Science: Politics or Technology? The Case of CERN' (2021) 30(3) Industrial and Corporate Change 740.

[42] OECD, 'Tackling Policy Challenges Through Public Sector Innovation: A Strategic Portfolio Approach' (2022) <https://oecd-opsi.org/> accessed 3 November 2023. See also Mariana Mazzucato

experimentation,[43] to promote broader technological development[44] and boost national industries in a new wave of (digital) industrial policy[45] (external goal). The European Commission clearly seeks to make the 'public sector a trailblazer for using AI',[46] and the UK is exploring ways to make the public sector the 'first customer' of AI innovations to boost investment in AI research and development.[47] The process of public sector digitalization is thus embroiled in the broader race for AI,[48] and this conditions the relevant decision- and policymaking processes as internal and external goals overlap or interact in different ways.[49] Public sector digitalization is far from being solely a 'technical matter' (not that it could ever be), and this conditions the governance of the process.

Relatedly but more generally, the emergence of digital technologies has created regulatory challenges,[50] within a new paradigm of digital

and Gregor Semieniuk, 'Public Financing of Innovation: New Questions' (2017) 33(1) Oxford Review of Economic Policy 24; Mariana Mazzucato, 'Mission-oriented public procurement: lessons from international examples. UCL Institute for Innovation and Public Purpose' (2020) Policy Report IIPP 2020-20 <https://www.ucl.ac.uk/bartlett/public-purpose/pr2020-20> accessed 7 March 2023; Mariana Mazzucatto, *Mission Economy. A Moonshot Guide to Changing Capitalism* (Allen Lane 2021). For discussion, see Albert Sanchez-Graells, 'How to Rethink the Role of Procurement to Foster Economic Recovery and the Green Transition—Re Mazzucato (2021, 2020)' (*howtocrackanut.com*, 6 August 2021) <https://www.howtocrackanut.com/blog/how-to-rethink-procurement-for-economic-and-green-transition-re-mazzucato> accessed 7 March 2023.

[43] This can be labelled GovTech, though the extent to which the public sector props up digital economy sectors is not limited to it. For an overview, see eg Interreg Europe, 'GovTech and digitalising the public sector' (2022) <https://www.interregeurope.eu/find-policy-solutions/webinar/govtech-and-digitalising-the-public-sector> accessed 7 March 2023; European Parliament, 'The digital single market and the digitalisation of the public sector: GovTech and other innovations in public procurement' (2022) <https://data.europa.eu/doi/10.2861/830794> accessed 17 October 2022.

[44] See eg European Commission, 'Coordinated Plan on Artificial Intelligence: 2021 Review' 46–49, Annex to 'Fostering a European approach to Artificial Intelligence' (Communication) COM (2021) 205 final.

[45] See eg Paul Timmers, 'Digital Industrial Policy for Europe' (2022) CERRE <https://cerre.eu/wp-content/uploads/2022/12/Digital-Industrial-Policy-for-Europe.pdf> accessed 7 March 2023. See also House of Lords Committee on Artificial Intelligence, *AI in the UK: Ready, Willing and Able?* (HL 2017–19) 100.

[46] European Commission, 'Fostering a European approach to Artificial Intelligence' (Communication) COM (2021) 205 final, stressing that procurement can 'help stimulate demand and offer of trustworthy and secure AI technologies in Europe' at 46.

[47] Office for Artificial Intelligence, 'Understanding UK Artificial Intelligence R&D commercialisation and the role of standards' (2022) 9 <https://www.gov.uk/government/publications/understanding-uk-ai-rd-commercialisation-and-the-role-of-standards> accessed 7 April 2023.

[48] See eg European Commission, 'Artificial Intelligence: A European perspective' (2018) <https://ec.europa.eu/futurium/en/system/files/ged/ai-flagship-report_online.pdf> accessed 7 March 2023.

[49] For a critical reflection, see eg Regine Paul, 'Can Critical Policy Studies Outsmart AI? Research Agenda on Artificial Intelligence Technologies and Public Policy' (2022) 16(4) Critical Policy Studies 497.

[50] For discussion, see eg Matthijs M Maas, 'Aligning AI Regulation to Sociotechnical Change' in Justin Bullock and others (eds), *Oxford Handbook of AI Governance* (OUP 2022) <https://doi.org/10.1093/oxfordhb/9780197579329.013.22> accessed 7 March 2023.

constitutionalism.[51] Digital technologies, and especially AI, create new sets of risks that are yet to be fully understood[52] and managed—which warrants not only an adaptation of existing regulatory frameworks,[53] but also the development of new or additional ones.[54] However, regulatory developments are constrained by well-known problems in managing uncertainty in technology regulation. Notably, regulatory developments face the *Collingridge dilemma* or pacing problem ('cannot effectively regulate early on, so will probably regulate too late').[55] Different normative positions[56] interact with industrial policy considerations to create regulatory hesitation and side-line anticipatory precautionary approaches.[57]

[51] The literature is too vast and fast-moving to attempt to summarize it here. See Giovanni De Gregorio, *Digital Constitutionalism in Europe. Reframing Rights and Powers in the Algorithmic Society* (CUP 2022); De Gregorio and Dunn, 'The European Risk-Based Approaches' (n 18).

[52] Including, but not exclusively, new systemic risks. See eg Noam Kolt, 'Algorithmic Black Swans' (2023) 101 Washington University Law Review 31; Victor Galaz and others, 'Artificial Intelligence, Systemic Risks, and Sustainability' (2021) 67 Technology in Society 101741. For broader discussion, see eg Artificial Intelligence/Machine Learning Risk & Security Working Group (AIRS), 'Artificial Intelligence Risk & Governance' (undated) <https://aiab.wharton.upenn.edu/research/artificial-intelligence-risk-governance/> accessed 7 March 2023; Camino Kavanagh, 'New Tech, New Threats, and New Governance Challenges: An Opportunity to Craft Smarter Responses?' (2019) Carnegie Endowment for International Peace <https://carnegieendowment.org/files/WP_Camino_Kavanagh___New_Tech_New_Threats1.pdf> accessed 7 March 2023. For discussion in the specific context of the public sector, see Anneke Zuiderwijk, Yu-Che Chen, and Fadi Salem, 'Implications of the Use of Artificial Intelligence in Public Governance: A Systematic Literature Review and a Research Agenda' (2021) 38 Government Information Quarterly 101577; Jean-Bernard Auby, 'Administrative Law Facing Digital Challenges' (2020) 1(1) European Review of Digital Administration & Law 7.

[53] eg in relation with the level of oversight and control to be exerted over private tech providers within the broader context of enforced self-regulation; see Benjamin Farrand and Helena Carrapico, 'Digital Sovereignty and Taking Back Control: From Regulatory Capitalism to Regulatory Mercantilism in EU Cybersecurity' (2022) 31(3) European Security 435; Helena Carrapico and Benjamin Farrand, '"Dialogue, Partnership and Empowerment for Network and Information Security": The Changing Role of the Private Sector from Objects of Regulation to Regulation Shapers' (2017) 67 Crime, Law and Social Change 245.

[54] See eg Andrew Tutt, 'An FDA for Algorithms' (2017) 69 Administrative Law Review 83 (hereafter Tutt, 'FDA for Algorithms'); Gianclaudio Malgieri and Frank Pasquale, 'From Transparency to Justification: Toward Ex Ante Accountability for AI' (2022) Brooklyn Law School Legal Studies Paper No 712 <https://ssrn.com/abstract=4099657> accessed 4 November 2022.

[55] David Collingridge, *The Social Control of Technology* (Pinter 1980). For discussion, see eg Audley Genus and Andy Stirling, 'Collingridge and the Dilemma of Control: Towards Responsible and Accountable Innovation' (2018) 47(1) Research Policy 61; Ryan Hagemann, Jennifer Huddleston Skees, and Adam Thierer, 'Soft Law for Hard Problems: The Governance of Emerging Technologies in an Uncertain Future' (2018) 17(1) Colorado Technology Law Journal 37; Carla Alvial-Palavicino, 'The Future as Practice: A Framework to Understand Anticipation in Science and Technology' (2015) 6(2) Tecnoscienza 135.

[56] See eg Vagelis Papakonstantinou and Paul De Hert, 'The Regulation of Digital Technologies in the EU: The Law-Making Phenomena of "act-ification", "GDPR mimesis" and "EU law brutality"' (2022) Technology and Regulation <https://doi.org/10.26116/techreg.2022.005> accessed 7 March 2023; Jess Whittlestone and Samuel Clarke, 'AI Challenges for Society and Ethics' in Justin Bullock and others (eds), *Oxford Handbook of AI Governance* (OUP 2022) <https://doi.org/10.1093/oxfordhb/9780197579329.013.3> accessed 7 March 2023.

[57] Margot E Kaminski, 'Regulating the Risks of AI' (2023) 103 Boston University Law Review, forthcoming <https://ssrn.com/abstract=4195066> accessed 4 November 2022 (hereafter Kaminski,

The emerging light-touch approach to risk-based self-regulation (see Section 3) is proving slow to adapt to public sector digitalization and there is a regulatory gap[58]—or rather a *laissez faire* environment—whereby the public sector is allowed to experiment with the adoption of digital technologies without clear checks and balances,[59] and without a clear plan on how to close the regulatory gap.[60] The current strategy is by and large one of '*experiment first, regulate later*'.[61] And while there is little to no regulation specifically addressed at governing public sector digitalization, there is significant experimentation and digital technology adoption by the public sector.[62]

As a result of such unregulated experimentation, there is mounting evidence of the problems and harms that come with the adoption of digital technologies by the public sector[63]—notably in relation to the automation of administrative decision-making as a particularly problematic area,[64] but also in broader areas of policymaking.[65] This has started to push for *some form of regulatory*

'Regulating AI'). For broader discussion, Elen Stokes, 'Beyond Evidence: Anticipatory Regimes in Law' (2021) 43(1) Law & Policy 73.

[58] Carlos Ignacio Gutierrez Gaviria, 'The Unforeseen Consequences of Artificial Intelligence (AI) on Society. A Systematic Review of Regulatory Gaps Generated by AI in the U.S.' (2020) RAND <https://www.rand.org/pubs/rgs_dissertations/RGSDA319-1.html> accessed 8 March 2023. This is a generalized problem; see eg Lyria Bennett Moses, 'Recurring Dilemmas: The Law's Race to Keep Up With Technological Change' (2007) 2 University of Illinois Journal of Law, Technology & Policy 239.

[59] See eg Urvashi Aneja, 'Public Sector Procurement of AI Must Take a Principled Approach' (*mint*, 4 December 2022) <https://www.livemint.com/opinion/online-views/public-sector-procurement-of-ai-must-take-a-principled-approach-11670173999072.html> accessed 9 March 2023.

[60] Jose Vida Fernandez, 'Artificial Intelligence in Government: Risks and Challenges of Algorithmic Governance in the Administrative State' (2023) 30(1) Indiana Journal of Global Legal Studies 65, 83 (hereafter, Vida Fernandez, 'Artificial Intelligence in Government').

[61] Which can not only make it difficult to reign in experimentation after the fact, but can also have significant knock-on effects eg in reducing public sector capability; see eg Rosie Collington, 'Disrupting the Welfare State? Digitalisation and the Retrenchment of Public Sector Capacity' (2022) 27(2) New Political Economy 312.

[62] Above (n 30); Yeung, 'New Public Analytics' (n 31) 4–6. For statistics on the UK, see Tussell, 'Artificial Intelligence & the public sector: trends, growth & opportunities' (2022) <https://www.tussell.com/insights/ai-and-the-public-sector> accessed 9 March 2023. For an in-depth analysis in the area of immigration administration, see Jack Maxwell and Joe Tomlinson, *Experiments in Automating Immigration Systems* (Bristol UP 2022) (hereafter Maxwell and Tomlinson, *Experiments in Automating*).

[63] The existing evidence and literature are too vast to even attempt to summarize. For recent discussion, see eg John Croker, 'Law, Artificial Intelligence and Human Rights; Connecting the Dots' (*Law That Shapes Us*, 2 March 2023) <https://www.law.ox.ac.uk/content/article/law-shapes-us-law-artificial-intelligence-and-human-rights-connecting-dots> accessed 7 March 2023.

[64] The literature on automated decision-making (ADM) is also too vast to even attempt to summarize it. See eg Yeung, 'New Public Analytics' (n 31) 2–3; Ryan Calo and Danielle Keats Citron, 'The Automated Administrative State: A Crisis of Legitimacy' (2021) 70(4) Emory Law Journal 797; Cary Coglianese, 'Administrative Law in the Automated State' (2021) 105(3) Daedalus 104; Maciej Kuziemski and Gianluca Misuraca, 'AI Governance in the Public Sector: Three Tales from the Frontiers of Automated Decision-Making in Democratic Settings' (2020) 44(6) Telecommunications Policy 101976; Michèle Finck, 'Automated Decision-Making and Administrative Law', in Peter Cane and others (eds), *The Oxford Handbook of Comparative Administrative Law* (OUP 2020) 656.

[65] See eg Ryan Calo, 'Modeling Through' (2022) 71(6) Duke Law Journal 1391.

response.[66] For example, there is a push for the adaptation of classical mechanisms[67] (such as judicial review) as the outputs of digital public governance are scrutinized and contested.[68] There is also a push to generate new obligations and controls through legislative proposals to ban or regulate some (high-risk) uses of digital technologies by the public sector—notably in the EU,[69] which legislation could become a global regulatory benchmark.[70] However, at the time of writing in late Spring 2023, the effective operation of such new rules remains a relatively distant future possibility—likely to push well past the 2025 horizon. And, in any case, the model currently emerging in the EU and the UK—which could easily crystallize and thus be difficult or impossible to replace in the future—is one of light-touch risk-based self-regulation likely to have limited effects in disciplining and governing public sector digitalization, despite efforts to instrumentalize procurement to that end.

3. Light-Touch Risk-Based Self-Regulation of Digital Technologies

3.1 Risk-Based Approaches to Digital Technology Regulation

There is a regulatory gap concerning the development and use of digital technologies, both generally and by the public sector in particular. Importantly, there is no (temporary) ban on the development or adoption of digital technologies while regulatory issues are thrashed out, and European (and other)

[66] Leading to a race to regulate AI, see Nathalie A Smuha, 'From a "race to AI" to a "race to AI regulation": Regulatory Competition for Artificial Intelligence' (2021) 13 Law, Innovation and Technology 57. For discussion of competing regulatory models, see Michael Veale, Kira Matus, and Robert Gorwa, 'AI and Global Governance: Modalities, Rationales, Tensions' (2023) 19 Annual Review of Law and Social Science <https://doi.org/10.1146/annurev-lawsocsci-020223-040749> accessed 5 June 2023. See also Mark Chinen, *The International Governance of Artificial Intelligence* (Edward Elgar 2023).

[67] Vida Fernandez, 'Artificial Intelligence in Government' (n 60) 93–94.

[68] Which presents significant challenges, see eg Jennifer Cobbe, 'Administrative Law and the Machines of Government: Judicial Review of Automated Public-Sector Decision-Making' (2019) 39(4) Legal Studies 636; Rebecca Williams, 'Rethinking Administrative Law for Algorithmic Decision Making' (2022) 42(2) Oxford Journal of Legal Studies 468.

[69] Proposal for a Regulation of the European Parliament and of the Council laying down harmonised rules on Artificial Intelligence (Artificial Intelligence Act) and amending certain union legislative acts, COM (2021) 206 final (hereafter EU AI Act).

[70] See Charlotte Siegmann and Markus Anderljung, 'The Brussels Effect and Artificial Intelligence' (2022) Centre for the Governance of AI <https://www.governance.ai/research-paper/brussels-effect-ai> accessed 10 March 2023. On the global propagation of EU regulatory standards, see eg Anu Bradford, *The Brussels Effect. How the European Union Rules the World* (OUP 2020) 131 ff; Elaine Fahey, *The EU as a Global Digital Actor. Institutionalising Global Data Protection, Trade, and Cybersecurity* (Hart Publishing 2022) 82 ff.

jurisdictions are engaged in regulatory discussions contemporaneously with the accelerating adoption of digital technologies described above (Section 2). Effectively, current processes of public sector digitalization are taking place in a largely unconstrained way. This means that, by the time any new rules or regulatory requirements enter into force, a significant stock of 'legacy' technological adoptions will already exist, which will pose additional regulatory challenges—such as whether to grandfather them, or how to transition towards regulatory compliance, including considerations on the discontinuation or replacement of technological deployments that cannot be brought into compliance.

However, as also mentioned, given the mounting evidence of the risks resulting from the use of digital technologies—and perhaps a heightened awareness that regulatory intervention is urgent—there are increasing efforts to form regulatory responses. Before providing an overview of the regulatory trends in the EU and the UK (Section 3.2), it is worth reflecting on some broader implications of the dominant regulatory strategy, which follows a risk-based logic.[71] This will highlight the unaddressed regulatory issues implicit in the models emerging in the EU and UK.

The regulation of digital technologies, and AI in particular, is indeed quickly taking the shape of risk regulation, or risk-based regulation.[72] The first point to note is that this is not a value- or consequence-free regulatory approach.[73] The most immediate implication is that relying on risk regulation leading to risk mitigation and management, rather than strict precaution,[74] carries an assumption that 'a technology will be adopted despite its harms'[75]—which necessarily means accepting (part of) the dangers inherent to the technology and the related future harms.[76] Taking a risk regulation approach thus accepts that technological solutions may (or will) generate (some) negative impacts on public and private interests, even if it is not known when or how those harms

[71] This approach has been advocated by prominent scholars; see eg Julia Black and Andrew Douglas Murray, 'Regulating AI and Machine Learning: Setting the Regulatory Agenda' (2019) 10(3) European Journal of Law and Technology 1.

[72] For broader discussion, which however tends to bend the boundaries and obscure the implications of the different models—in particular the labelled 'emergent model' and the risk regulation model, see Nicolas Petit and Jerome De Cooman, 'Models of Law and Regulation for AI' in Anthony Elliott, *The Routledge Social Science Handbook of AI* (Routledge 2022) 199 (hereafter Petit and De Cooman, 'Models of AI Regulation').

[73] Kaminski, 'Regulating AI' (n 57).

[74] There is, however, considerable overlap between both approaches. Precaution is taken in its maximalist form here (eg implying a technological ban in the face of uncertainty concerning future harms); see ibid 22–25. Advocating for a strict precautionary approach, at least for the time being, see Maxwell and Tomlinson, *Experiments in Automating* (n 62) 82–83.

[75] Kaminski, 'Regulating AI' (n 57) 4.

[76] Kaminski, 'Regulating AI' (n 57) 9.

will arise,[77] or how extensive they will be. This does not seem to be sufficiently acknowledged in current regulatory discussions, which tend to present the risks of digital technologies as 'future risks',[78] disregarding the fact that there is a real and quickly growing stock of 'embedded risks' in already implemented 'legacy' technology deployments, including those in the public sector.

The relevance of such existing stock of risks is particularly acute in relation to AI. AI risks are unique because they are 'long-term, low probability, systemic, and high impact', and because 'AI both poses "aggregate risks" across systems and low probability but "catastrophic risks" to society'.[79] This should thus trigger careful consideration of the ultimate implications of embracing risk-based strategies of AI regulation, and certainly advocates in favour of taking a robust regulatory approach.[80] Importantly, this should factor more heavily in considerations whether to adopt specific digital technologies, and AI in particular, to replace existing modes of governance—especially in the public sector—as the comparison should not solely involve a one-for-one analysis of, for example, performance or accuracy,[81] but also take into account the systemic and aggregate risks that the technology entails. This may require an adaptation of existing approaches to, for example, risk assessment, to significantly broaden and tighten them up.

The logical corollary to the acceptance of future harms under a risk-based regulatory approach must be the design and implementation of robust measures seeking to reduce them.[82] Such measures could include variations on a set of precautionary tactics, such as licensing[83] or regulatory sandboxing,[84]

[77] Tutt, 'FDA for Algorithms' (n 54) 86–90.

[78] Jenna Burrell, 'Artificial Intelligence and the Ever-Receding Horizon of the Future' (*Tech Policy Press*, 6 June 2023) <https://techpolicy.press/artificial-intelligence-and-the-ever-receding-horizon-of-the-future/> accessed 15 June 2023.

[79] Kaminski, 'Regulating AI' (n 57) 57, by reference to the US National Institute of Standards and Technology, 'AI risk management framework concept paper' (13 December 2021) <https://www.nist.gov/system/files/documents/2021/12/14/AI%20RMF%20Concept%20Paper_13Dec2021_posted.pdf> accessed 4 November 2022. This makes the classification of AI risks particularly complicated, which undermines attempts at simplification and the singling out of particular types of AI risks, such as the category of 'existernalities' coined by Petit and De Cooman, 'Models of AI Regulation' (n 72) 209 to refer to 'existential threats and opportunities created by AIs and robotic applications'.

[80] Kaminski, 'Regulating AI' (n 57) 75 ff.

[81] cf Cary Coglianese and Alicia Lai, 'Algorithm vs. Algorithm' (2022) 71(6) Duke Law Journal 1281.

[82] Kaminski, 'Regulating AI' (n 57) 23–24. See also OECD, 'Risk-based regulation' in OECD Regulatory Policy Outlook 2021 (2021) 182 (hereafter OECD, 'Risk-based regulation').

[83] Tutt, 'FDA for Algorithms' (n 54) 91 and 111.

[84] Kaminski, 'Regulating AI' (n 57) 27. See Jon Truby and others, 'A Sandbox Approach to Regulating High-Risk Artificial Intelligence Applications' (2022) 13 European Journal of Risk Regulation 270. For discussion and criticism of sandboxing, see Sofia Ranchordas, 'Experimental Regulations and Regulatory Sandboxes—Law Without Order?' (2021) Law and Method <https://doi.org/10.5553/REM/.000064> accessed 7 November 2022. More broadly, see Gabriel Domenech-Pascual, 'Thought Experiments in Law' (2021) Law and Method <https://doi.org/10.5553/REM/.000053> accessed 7 November 2022.

measures of risk assessment and mitigation,[85] as well as post-market and other ongoing measures.[86] These could be complemented by guidelines and advice, which could be developed by regulators engaging private industry.[87] A combination of those precaution and knowledge-support tactics would seek to achieve a reduction in future harms—but it should be stressed that it would not imply a strategy to suppress or entirely avoid future harms, as a strict precautionary approach would.[88]

Importantly, assessing risks requires quantification and leads to cost-benefit analysis. However, not all risks are quantifiable or can be known.[89] This has further implications for the adoption of a risk-based regulatory approach,[90] especially if the analysis is skewed by informational barriers to assessing the potential benefits and harms resulting from the technology, which tends to be the case.[91] The regulatory approach must thus be evidence-led and include elements of information disclosure to facilitate the proper functioning of risk-based techniques.[92] There should also be clear guidance on how to address risks which measurement is impossible.

Finally, it should be stressed that 'risk-based regulation' does not entail a single approach,[93] but rather encompasses different (sub)models, including varying institutional designs in relation to the agents in charge of identifying and managing risks. There are clear differences (and varying expected levels of effectiveness) between models premised on external assessments (either by a regulator, or a certifying third party) and those based on self-assessment (eg enterprise-level self-certification).[94] Institutional design will be crucially important in ensuring the effectiveness of the risk-based approach.[95]

[85] There can be some overlap with licensing regimes, eg if licensing is conditioned on risk mitigation or on meeting a performance standard, Kaminski, 'Regulating AI' (n 57) 28.

[86] ibid 29.

[87] Tutt, 'FDA for Algorithms' (n 54) 111.

[88] As aptly summarized, 'risk regulation … entails mitigating harms while avoiding unnecessarily stringent laws, while the precautionary principle emphasizes avoiding insufficiently stringent laws', Kaminski, 'Regulating AI' (n 57) 24.

[89] ibid 8.

[90] ibid 33.

[91] ibid 59. See Chapter 6 for discussion of the disproportionate importance that the potential benefits of digital technologies, especially in terms of reduction of the administrative burden, can play in the process of technological experimentation and adoption.

[92] OECD, 'Risk-based regulation' (n 82) 193.

[93] This opens a myriad of diverse implications resulting from varying approaches, eg in relation to the transparency of self-assessments, which could have a 'risk management chilling effect', Kaminski, 'Regulating AI' (n 57) 38.

[94] ibid 30.

[95] For discussion, see Florentin Blanc, 'Tools for Effective Regulation: Is "More" Always "Better"?' (2018) 9(3) European Journal of Risk Regulation 465.

Therefore, there can be variation in risk-based approaches to digital technology (and AI) regulation. At the most stringent end of the spectrum, regulatory approaches will imply mandatory risk assessment and risk mitigation strategies enforced by an independent regulator. At the other end, most permissive approaches will be based on voluntary risk assessment and risk mitigation strategies left to voluntary compliance and self-assessment. There are multiple possible combinations in between. Therefore, even accepting the pragmatic inevitability of the overarching risk-based regulatory approach, jurisdictions have a broad array of decisions to make in establishing the (sub)model better suited to controlling the adoption and use of digital technologies, especially by the public sector.

Against this background, the following section will sketch the emerging models of regulation in the EU and the UK,[96] which will be further explored and critiqued in the remainder of the book. The succinct analysis provided here evidences the way in which soft self-regulation approaches can easily lead to the instrumentalization of public procurement to try and strengthen them (see Section 4). Procurement can thus be seen as a tool deployed to move very permissive regulatory systems towards the more prescriptive end of the regulatory spectrum, at least where the technology is to be adopted by the public sector. This could be seen as a flexible regulatory strategy capable of generating two tiers of risk-based approaches: one (more permissive) for the general economy, and another one (more restrictive) for the public sector. It could also be seen as a mode of incremental or experimental regulation, at least to the extent that more stringent procurement practices were replicated or propagated to the general economy as 'golden standards' or 'best practices'. However, the analysis in the remainder of the book (Part II in particular) will show that this is not a viable or effective regulatory strategy and that, despite its intuitive appeal, it can conceal the lack of effective regulation of public sector digitalization. Permissive models cannot be strengthened through procurement without the seemingly more stringent requirements leading back to mechanisms of industry self-regulation (eg via technical standards) and self-assessments carried out by tech providers as functional delegates of the public buyers. Procurement operates as a mere conduit of soft forms of risk-based regulation and cannot effectively alter the permissiveness resulting from (the absence of) general regulatory requirements, checks, and balances.

[96] These are explored in detail in Chapter 9, in relation to the digitalization of procurement. For further details and additional references, see that analysis.

3.2 The Emerging Model in the EU and the UK

At the time of writing, the UK government does not intend to promote any new rules or the creation of any new regulators.[97] AI use is to be subjected to existing regulatory frameworks and existing sectoral regulators are tasked with providing guidance on how a set of general principles of AI regulation are to be followed within their regulatory remit.[98] This leaves the adoption of digital technologies, including AI, by the public sector unregulated[99]—other than by pre-existing regulatory mechanisms, which are primarily those of general administrative law, and some sectoral regulation regimes, such as data protection, where applicable.[100] There is, however, a body of soft-law guidelines that promotes voluntary engagement by public authorities with measures such as algorithmic impact assessments, on a self-assessed basis.[101] There is also a voluntary framework for the disclosure of some details of AI use by the public sector,[102] although its current uptake is minimal.[103]

[97] Department for Science, Innovation and Technology and Office for Artificial Intelligence, 'AI regulation: a pro-innovation approach' (CP 815, 2023) (hereafter DSIT, 'AI regulation: a pro-innovation approach'). For critical analysis, see Huw Roberts and others, 'Artificial Intelligence Regulation in the United Kingdom: A Path to Good Governance and Global Leadership?' (2023) 12(2) Internet Policy Review <https://policyreview.info/articles/analysis/artificial-intelligence-regulation-united-kingdom-path-good-governance> accessed 15 June 2023. See also Andrew Charlesworth and others, 'Response to the UK's March 2023 White Paper "A pro-innovation approach to AI regulation"' (SSRN, 19 June 2023) <https://ssrn.com/abstract=4477368> accessed 22 June 2023.

[98] These include the five 'values-focused cross-sectoral principles' of: Safety, security and robustness; Appropriate transparency and explainability; Fairness; Accountability and governance; and Contestability and redress, see DSIT, 'AI regulation: a pro-innovation approach' (n 97) para 48.

[99] Albert Sanchez-Graells, 'UK's "Pro-Innovation Approach" to AI Regulation Won't Do, Particularly for Public Sector Digitalisation' (*howtocrackanut.com*, 31 March 2023) <https://www.howtocrackanut.com/blog/2023/3/31/uk-pro-innovation-ai-regulation-wont-do> accessed 6 April 2023.

[100] See eg Information Commissioner's Office, 'Guidance on AI and data protection' (2023) <https://ico.org.uk/for-organisations/guide-to-data-protection/key-dp-themes/guidance-on-ai-and-data-protection/> accessed 12 April 2023.

[101] Office for Artificial Intelligence, 'A guide to using artificial intelligence in the public sector' (2019) <https://www.gov.uk/government/collections/a-guide-to-using-artificial-intelligence-in-the-public-sector> accessed 8 November 2022; and Office for Artificial Intelligence, 'Guidelines for AI procurement' (2020) <https://www.gov.uk/government/publications/guidelines-for-ai-procurement> accessed 8 November 2022.

[102] Central Digital and Data Office and Centre for Data Ethics and Innovation, 'Algorithmic transparency recording standard hub' (2023) <https://www.gov.uk/government/collections/algorithmic-transparency-recording-standard-hub> accessed 12 April 2023.

[103] At the time of writing, only six use cases of AI in the public sector have been published. Central Digital and Data Office and Centre for Data Ethics and Innovation, 'Algorithmic transparency reports' (last updated 13 January 2023) <https://www.gov.uk/government/collections/algorithmic-transparency-reports> accessed 12 April 2023. Interestingly, the Tracking Automated Government (TAG) Register developed by the Public Law Project contains a larger number of use cases; Public Law Project, 'The Tracking Automated Government register. A new tool lifting the lid on secretive government algorithms' (2023) <https://publiclawproject.org.uk/resources/the-tracking-automated-government-register/> accessed 9 March 2023. This seems to be a quite telling indication of the reluctance to engage with the government's official voluntary standard.

The EU's approach is more complicated, or at least nuanced, as it distinguishes between digital technologies and between uses of those technologies. There is no proposal to regulate the adoption and use of digital technologies other than AI.[104] In relation to the latter, the proposed EU AI Act would prohibit some uses,[105] and impose regulatory requirements in relation to high-risk uses[106]—including requirements on risk management systems, data and data governance, technical documentation, record-keeping, transparency, accuracy, and robustness and cybersecurity. Compliance with such obligations would be verified through mechanisms of conformity assessment, which could involve third parties, and would be generally overseen by a designated market surveillance authority in each Member State.

However, such high-risk uses would be established in a closed list that covers an important but limited range of public sector uses,[107] and classification is far from automatic,[108] which creates uncertainty over the future scope of covered public sector uses. Therefore, most permitted uses of digital technologies by the public sector would remain unregulated and subject only to voluntary engagement with measures of risk-based regulation on a self-assessed basis.[109] It is important to stress that the regulation of high-risk uses would also be strongly reliant on self-assessments by tech providers, although they would be mandatory and scrutinized by regulatory bodies.[110]

Overall, then, with the notable exception of prohibited and high-risk uses under the EU AI Act, the emerging model in the UK and the EU is one of light-touch risk-based self-regulation of the adoption of digital technologies by the public sector. Moreover, even where specific mandatory requirements can be

[104] EU AI Act (n 69); although the definition of AI is contentious.

[105] ibid art 5.

[106] ibid arts 8–15.

[107] ibid arts 6 and 7 and Annex III.

[108] appliedAI, 'AI Act: risk classification of AI systems from a practical perspective' (2023) <https://aai.frb.io/assets/files/AI-Act-Risk-Classification-Study-appliedAI-March-2023.pdf> accessed 14 April 2023.

[109] Subject to further regulation at Member State level, which permissibility under the EU AI Act is contested. The position taken here is that the EU AI Act does not entirely exclude Member State regulatory activity other than in relation to high-risk uses, which therefore allows for the development of additional requirements, both in relation to formal checks (eg permissioning or licencing of AI use) and substantive requirements. This is based on the legal competence of the EU AI Act (Treaty on the Functioning of the European Union (TFEU), art 114) and the limits resulting from Protocol (No 25) TFEU, especially in relation to the principle of administrative self-organization. The reasoning is the same as that developed in Albert Sanchez-Graells, 'The Emergence of Trans-EU Collaborative Procurement: A "Living Lab" for European Public Law' (2020) 29(1) Public Procurement Law Review 16, 27–33. For further discussion of the additional requirements that are considered compatible, see Chapter 5, Section 3.

[110] See eg Jonas Schuett, 'Risk Management in the Artificial Intelligence Act' (2023) European Journal of Risk Regulation <https://doi.org/10.1017/err.2023.1> accessed 12 April 2023.

expected to emerge—that is, in relation to high-risk uses under the EU AI Act—those requirements are still dependent on self-assessment and a set of enterprise-level regulatory mechanisms, and will be carried out by reference to standards driven by the tech industry.[111] Crucially, thus, both jurisdictions are placing the effectiveness of their regulatory approach in self-assessments and in commitments to demanding regulatory and technical standards by tech providers. Promoting the effectiveness of this approach would require the development of a culture of strong compliance,[112] and the setting of norms and practices leading to demanding self-assessments moving away from box ticking exercises.[113]

4. Plugging the Regulatory Gap Through Procurement?

Given its strong reliance on self-assessment by tech providers, the emerging regulatory approach in the EU and the UK lends itself to using public procurement to reinforce the effectiveness of risk-based regulation in public sector digitalization. In this regulatory context, procurement can be seen as a tool to promote self-regulation by the public sector as a 'responsible technology buyer' through the dissemination and embedding of 'best practices' of digital technology procurement. In this regard, decisions about which technologies to procure and how to govern their deployment could be used by the public sector to commit to voluntary standards of digital technology regulation and to promote robust risk-based governance by imposing such standards on tech providers, for example through risk assessments, risk mitigation strategies, or requirements for (external) verification or audit. This would simultaneously be a mechanism of meta-regulation to promote self-regulation by the tech industry by creating market incentives for tech providers to demonstrate engagement with those voluntary standards and practices of risk-based regulation to secure public contracts. What the legislator would not have imposed

[111] Michael Veale and Frederik Zuiderveen Borgesius 'Demystifying the Draft EU Artificial Intelligence Act—Analysing the Good, the Bad, and the Unclear Elements of the Proposed Approach' (2021) 22(4) Computer Law Review International 97.

[112] For discussion of the importance of cultural elements, see eg Julia Black and Robert Baldwin, 'Really Responsive Risk-Based Regulation' (2010) 32(2) Law & Policy 181.

[113] See eg Mohammad Moniruzzaman, 'Risk of Regulatory Failure of "Risk-Based Regulation" While Using Enterprise Risk Management as a Meta-Regulatory Toolkit' (2022) 6(1) Asian Journal of Economics and Banking 103. See also the broader framework developed in Julia Black and Robert Baldwin, 'When Risk-Based Regulation Aims Low: Approaches and Challenges' (2012) 6(1) Regulation & Governance 2; and Julia Black and Robert Baldwin, 'When Risk-Based Regulation Aims Low: A Strategic Framework' (2012) 6(2) Regulation & Governance 131.

through mandatory requirements, the public buyer would impose through procurement mechanisms. Procurement best practices could then propagate throughout the economy. As mentioned above (Section 3.1), this could be seen as way of strengthening the generally very lax and permissive approach underpinning current regulatory trends in the EU and the UK.

Indeed, to plug the current gap resulting from the absence of general legislation on the development and use of digital technologies—or smaller gaps left by future rules on high-risk AI use by the public sector[114]—proposals have started to emerge to use public procurement as a tool of digital regulation.[115] Or, in other words, to use the acquisition of digital technologies by the public sector as a gateway to the 'regulation by contract' of their use and governance. For example, the UK's 2021 National AI Strategy stressed how the government had taken steps 'to inform and empower buyers in the public sector, helping them to evaluate suppliers, then *confidently and responsibly procure AI technologies for the benefit of citizens*'.[116] Similarly, the European Commission is promoting the development of contractual clauses for the acquisition of AI by public organizations,[117] which seek to generate a framework of risk-based contractual regulation of public sector AI use.

Such leveraging of public expenditure for purposes of digital 'regulation by contract' to cover the gaps left by—or promote compliance with—emerging models of risk-based regulation of public sector digitalization assigns a gatekeeping role to procurement. Procurement is given this role due to its position as the touchstone or contact point between the public sector and the technology sector, with the expectation that such gatekeeping will have broader norm-setting and market-shaping effects because the State will, through tender and contract requirements linked to the increasing volumes of expenditure in digital technologies, generate compliance with the otherwise voluntary (soft) tools of risk-based regulation. Put more simply, under this approach, procurement would be a 'regulatory fix' to address the regulatory gap left by the permissive general regulatory regimes emerging in the EU and UK.

[114] eg in relation to non-high risk uses under the EU AI Act (n 69).

[115] For a short overview, see Ravit Dotan and others, 'How to Manage AI Procurement in Public Administration' (*World Economic Forum blog*, 5 July 2023) <https://www.weforum.org/agenda/2023/07/how-to-manage-ai-procurement-in-public-administration/> accessed 6 July 2023.

[116] Department for Digital, Culture, Media and Sport, 'National AI strategy' (CP 525, 2021) 47, emphasis added.

[117] Living-In EU, Proposal for standard contractual clauses for the procurement of artificial intelligence by public organizations, version 0.9 (2022) <https://living-in.eu/sites/default/files/files/Draft%20AI%20Clauses_1.pdf> accessed 21 October 2022.

The remainder of this book shows that this regulatory approach cannot be effective and that an alternative, more stringent (sub)model of risk-based regulation of public sector digitalization is needed. Before detailing this analysis in Part II and evidencing it with the case study of procurement digitalization developed in Part III, Chapter 2 further explores the dual role of procurement in gatekeeping and experimentation with public sector digitalization.

2
The Two Roles of Procurement in the Transition Towards Digital Public Governance

1. Introduction

Against the background provided in Chapter 1, this chapter explores the position of public procurement and its roles in the broader transition towards digital public governance. First, in Section 2, it describes how, within the emergent model of risk-based regulation in the EU and the UK, procurement is being assigned a *gatekeeping role* to discipline the adoption and use of digital technologies by the public sector and to promote goals such as transparency, trustworthiness, or explainability. In more detail, Section 2 also explores the extent to which selected putative goals of digital regulation pose challenges for implementation through procurement, which will be assessed in detail in Part II. Section 3 then frames procurement as a *site of technological experimentation*, as procurement is itself an area of public sector activity currently undergoing digitalization. Digital procurement thus offers a useful case study to understand the broader challenges, issues, and limitations in the leveraging of procurement to regulate public sector digitalization—which will be developed in Part III. This chapter thus lays the foundation for the analysis of the gatekeeping and experimentation roles of procurement in the transition towards digital public governance, in the remainder of the book.

2. Procurement, Gatekeeping, and Digital 'Regulation by Contract'

Given the absence, or limitations, of general rules governing public sector digitalization, procurement is gaining prominence as one of few levers to regulate

Digital Technologies and Public Procurement. Albert Sanchez-Graells, Oxford University Press.
 DOI: 10.1093/oso/9780198866770.003.0002

the acquisition and use of digital technologies by the public sector[1]—with personal data protection as another primary lever in relation to automated administrative decision-making.[2] Public procurement is increasingly expected to play a crucial gatekeeping role in the adoption of digital technologies for public governance and the delivery of public services. Public contracts and other arrangements for the development and acquisition of digital solutions are the entry point into the public sector for these innovations. Procurement rules governing the award of public contracts can be either a catalyst or a hindrance to co-production and experimentation with digital public governance solutions. Procurement is progressively expected to ensure that the public sector only acquires and adopts trustworthy technologies, and that (private) tech providers adhere to adequate technical, legal, and ethical standards.

Think tanks,[3] non-governmental organizations (NGOs),[4] and academics[5] alike have stressed that the 'rules governing the acquisition of algorithmic systems by governments and public agencies are an important point of intervention in ensuring their accountable use',[6] and that procurement 'is a central

[1] See eg World Economic Forum, 'AI Procurement in a Box' (2020, updated May 2022) <https://www.weforum.org/reports/ai-procurement-in-a-box> accessed 9 March 2023; Digital Catapult, 'Challenges to responsible AI adoption in industry' (2021) <https://www.digicatapult.org.uk/wp-content/uploads/2021/11/Digital_Catapult_Challenges_to_Responsible_AI_Adoption_Report_Juy_2021.pdf> accessed 9 March 2023.

[2] The role and limitations of data protection as a tool of digital regulation will not be explored in detail. However, on the interaction between data protection and procurement as regulatory tools, see Chapter 5.

[3] See eg Kapila Perera, 'Buying Better Technology in Government' (*doteveryone*, 22 May 2020) <https://doteveryone.org.uk/wp-content/uploads/2020/05/Buying-better-technology-in-government.pdf> accessed 9 March 2023; BILETA, 'Written Evidence Submitted to the House of Commons Science and Technology Committee Inquiry on the Governance of Artificial Intelligence' (2022) GAI0082, 6 <https://committees.parliament.uk/writtenevidence/113846/pdf/> accessed 7 March 2023; Policy Connect, 'An Ethical AI Future: Guardrails & Catalysts to Make Artificial Intelligence a Force for Good' (2023) <https://www.policyconnect.org.uk/research/ethical-ai-future-guardrails-catalysts-make-artificial-intelligence-force-good> accessed 22 June 2023.

[4] See eg Liberty, 'Written evidence submitted to the House of Commons Science and Technology Committee Inquiry on the governance of artificial intelligence' (2022) GAI0081, para 20 <https://committees.parliament.uk/writtenevidence/113845/pdf/> accessed 7 March 2023.

[5] See eg Ryan Calo, 'Artificial Intelligence Policy: A Primer and Roadmap' (2017) 51(2) UC Davis Law Review 399, 429; Cary Coglianese and Erik Lampmann, 'Contracting for Algorithmic Accountability' (2021) 6 Administrative Law Review Accord 175; Lavi M Ben Dor and Cary Coglianese, 'Procurement as AI Governance' (2021) 2(4) IEEE Transactions on Technology and Society 192; Lavi M Ben Dor and Cary Coglianese, 'The Procurement Path to AI Governance' (*Regulatory Review*, 27 June 2022) https://www.theregreview.org/2022/06/27/ben-dor-coglianese-procurement-path-to-ai-governance/ accessed 7 March 2023; David S Rubenstein, 'Acquiring Ethical AI' (2021) 73(4) Florida Law Review 747; David S Rubenstein, 'Retooling the Acquisition Gateway for Responsible AI' (*Regulatory Review*, 28 June 2022) <https://www.theregreview.org/2022/06/28/rubenstein-retooling-the-acquisition-gateway-for-responsible-ai/> accessed 7 March 2023; Carlos Ignacio Gutierrez, 'Procurement as an AI Governance Change Agent' (*Regulatory Review*, 6 July 2022) <https://www.theregreview.org/2022/07/06/ignacio-gutierrez-procurement-as-an-ai-governance-change-agent/> accessed 7 March 2023.

[6] Ada Lovelace Institute, AI Now Institute and Open Government Partnership, 'Algorithmic accountability for the public sector' (2021) 33 <https://www.opengovpartnership.org/documents/algorithmic-accountability-public-sector/> accessed 7 March 2023.

policy tool governments can deploy to catalyse innovation and influence the development of solutions aligned with government policy and society's underlying values'.[7] Procurement is thus seen as a mechanism of 'regulation by contract'[8] whereby the public buyer can impose requirements to achieve goals of digital regulation,[9] such as transparency, trustworthiness, or explainability,[10] or to operationalize more general 'AI ethics' frameworks.[11] For example, in the UK, it has been stressed that:

> Government should use its purchasing power in the market to set procurement requirements that ensure that private companies developing AI solutions for the public sector appropriately address public standards. This should be achieved by ensuring provisions for ethical standards are considered early in the procurement process and explicitly written into tenders and contractual arrangements.[12]

In more detail, the Council of Europe has recommended[13] using procurement to: (1) embed requirements of data governance to avoid violations of human rights norms and discrimination stemming from faulty datasets used in the design, development, or ongoing deployment of algorithmic systems;[14] (2) 'ensure that algorithmic design, development and ongoing deployment processes

[7] Carlos Santiso, 'Artificial Intelligence in the Public Sector: An Engine for Innovation in Government … If We Get It Right!' (*OPSI blog*, 6 July 2022) <https://oecd-opsi.org/blog/ai-an-engine-for-innovation/> accessed 9 March 2023.

[8] See Chapters 3 and 4.

[9] In relation to human rights compliance, see eg David Leslie and others, 'Artificial Intelligence, Human Rights, Democracy, and the Rule of Law. A Primer' (2021) Council of Europe and Alan Turing Institute <https://rm.coe.int/primer-en-new-cover-pages-coe-english-compressed-2754-7186-0228-v-1/1680a2fd4a> accessed 9 March 2023.

[10] See Albert Sanchez-Graells, 'Some Further Thoughts on Setting Procurement up to Fail in "AI Regulation by Contract"' (*howtocrackanut.com*, 27 January 2023) <https://www.howtocrackanut.com/blog/2023/1/27/setting-procurement-up-to-fail-in-ai-regulation-by-contract> accessed 8 February 2023.

[11] This is the approach of the City of Amsterdam on which the European Commission seeks to build through the development of standard contractual clauses for the procurement of ethical AI, see <https://living-in.eu/groups/solutions/ai-procurement> accessed 7 March 2023. See also Gry Hasselbalch, Birgitte Kofod Olsen, and Pernille Tranberg, 'White Paper on Data Ethics in Public Procurement of AI Based Services and Solutions' (2021) <https://www.nist.gov/system/files/documents/2021/08/23/ai-rmf-rfi-0043.pdf> accessed 9 March 2023 (hereafter Hasselbalch, Olsen, and Tranberg, 'Data Ethics in Public Procurement'); and Timo von Behr and Pekka Abrahamsson, 'AI Governance and Ethics in Public Procurement: Bridging the Gap Between Theory and Practice' (2022) IEEE 28th ICE/ITMC & 31st IAMOT Joint Conference <https://ieeexplore.ieee.org/document/10033173> accessed 1 June 2023.

[12] Committee on Standards in Public Life, 'Artificial Intelligence and public standards' (2020) 51 <https://assets.publishing.service.gov.uk/government/uploads/system/uploads/attachment_data/file/868284/Web_Version_AI_and_Public_Standards.PDF> accessed 7 March 2023.

[13] Council of Europe, Recommendation of the Committee of Ministers to member States on the human rights impacts of algorithmic systems (8 April 2020) CM/Rec(2020)1.

[14] ibid Appendix, Part B, principle 2.2.

incorporate safety, privacy, data protection and security safeguards by design';[15] (3) require 'public, consultative and independent evaluations of the lawfulness and legitimacy of the goal that the [procured algorithmic] system intends to achieve or optimise, and its possible effects in respect of human rights';[16] (4) require the conduct of human rights impact assessments;[17] or (5) promote transparency of the 'use, design and basic processing criteria and methods of algorithmic systems'.[18]

The Council of Europe has also stressed States' responsibility to use procurement 'with full regard to the need to maintain oversight, know-how, ownership and control over the use of algorithmic systems and their interaction with each other';[19] as well as advocated for the use of (preferential) procurement as an incentive for 'the development of algorithmic systems and technologies that enhance equal access to, and enjoyment of, human rights and fundamental freedoms'.[20] Relatedly, UNESCO has recommended the use of procurement as a driver of gender equality, in particular through the inclusion of gender-related options in the tendering requirements of contracts concerning public service digitalization.[21]

These proposals have in common that they seek to use procurement rules and practice as a filter of the types of digital technologies and tech providers that enter the public sector, as well as a tool to impose specific obligations in the deployment of those technologies. However, different proposals take varying approaches, with some seeking to incentivize 'responsible AI (artificial intelligence) procurement', and others seeking to ban the adoption of 'untrustworthy AI' by the public sector (and several hybrid or intermediate approaches). Some proposals seek to rely on existing rules (perhaps re-interpreting them), while others seek to put procurement in the position of rule-maker. In that regard, it is important to highlight the difference between seeking to ensure that existing obligations are complied with throughout the procurement process and in the

[15] ibid Appendix, Part B, principle 3.2. For discussion of the use of 'by design' requirements from a regulatory theory perspective, see Marco Almada, 'Regulation by Design and the Governance of Technological Futures' (2023) European Journal of Risk Regulation, First View <https://doi.org/10.1017/err.2023.37> accessed 17 May 2023 (hereafter Almada, 'Regulation by Design'); and Marco Almada, 'Regulating Machine Learning by Design' (2023) CPI TechREG Chronicle <https://ssrn.com/abstract=4367025> accessed 7 March 2023.

[16] Recommendation CM/Rec(2020)1 (n 13) Appendix, Part B, principle 3.3.

[17] ibid principle 5.2.

[18] ibid principle 4.1.

[19] ibid principle 5.6.

[20] ibid principle 6.1.

[21] Recommendation 16, UNESCO/EQUALS, 'I'd blush if I could: closing gender divides in digital skills through education' (2019) <https://unesdoc.unesco.org/ark:/48223/pf0000367416> accessed 7 March 2023.

execution of public contracts,[22] on the one hand, and the use of procurement for the creation of those obligations *ex novo*, on the other.

Given the absence of generally applicable mandatory requirements in the development and use of digital technologies by the public sector, the gatekeeping role of procurement in digital 'regulation by contract' would mostly involve the creation of such self-standing obligations—or at least the enforcement of emerging non-binding norms, such as those developed by (voluntary) standardization bodies or, more generally, by the technology industry.[23] It is important to stress that the related challenges are different than those in the (deceitfully) seemingly close area of Information and Communication Technology (ICT) procurement,[24] where there is more limited or no need for such rule-making role.[25] It is also important to note that there are differences between creating procedural obligations seeking to boost alignment with regulatory goals (eg obligations to document or audit) and defining those regulatory goals (eg what is 'responsible AI') in an actionable way.[26] This makes the proposals to use procurement as a means of digital 'regulation by contract' prone to procedural rather than substantive implementation.[27] In turn, this raises questions on the likely effectiveness of such proposals where procurement outputs are subjected to undefined or incommensurable tests,[28] or where the choice between alternative (regulatory) approaches or options is affected by such incommensurability.[29]

[22] In relation to compliance with data protection, see eg European Data Protection Board, 2022 Coordinated Enforcement Action, Use of cloud-based services by the public sector (2023) <https://edpb.europa.eu/system/files/2023-01/edpb_20230118_cef_cloud-basedservices_publicsector_en.pdf> accessed 7 March 2023.

[23] This would create a risk of commercial capture that will feature prominently throughout the book.

[24] Keegan McBride and others, 'Towards a systematic understanding on the challenges of procuring Artificial Intelligence in the public sector' (2021) <https://doi.org/10.31235/osf.io/un649> accessed 7 March 2023; Merve Hickok, 'Public Procurement of Artificial Intelligence Systems: New Risks and Future Proofing' (2022) AI & Society <https://doi.org/10.1007/s00146-022-01572-2> accessed 27 October 2022.

[25] Certainly from a digital constitutional perspective and in relation to the incommensurable goals of digital regulation, as well as in relation to the protection of fundamental rights and freedoms, as the risks arising from ICT technologies are different in nature to those arising from digital technologies, and AI in particular.

[26] For discussion, see Cary Coglianese and David Lazer, 'Management-Based Regulation: Prescribing Private Management to Achieve Public Goals' (2003) 37(4) Law & Society Review 691. This is related to discussions on the evolution of regulation from centralized command-and-control mechanisms to models of decentred enforced self-regulation, or meta-regulation. See Chapter 4.

[27] For related discussion on the difficulties of implementing performance-based (ie output or result) regulation, see Cary Coglianese, 'Performance-Based Regulation: Concepts and Challenges' in Francesca Bignami and David Zaring (eds), *Comparative Law and Regulation* (Edward Elgar 2016) 403; Cary Coglianese, 'The Limits of Performance-Based Regulation' (2017) 50(3) University of Michigan Journal of Law Reform 525.

[28] See Almada, 'Regulation by Design' (n 15) 3–6.

[29] For broader discussion, see Mireille Hildebrandt, 'Privacy as Protection of the Incomputable Self: From Agnostic to Agonistic Machine Learning' (2019) 20(1) Theoretical Inquiries in Law 83; and Matthew Adler, 'Law and Incommensurability: Introduction' (1998) 146(5) University of Pennsylvania Law Review 1169.

To further flesh out the issue, it is worth exploring some of the putative regulatory goals in the use of procurement for digital 'regulation by contract', such as: trustworthiness or responsibility; explainability or intelligibility; technological neutrality, openness, and interoperability; cybersecurity; transparency; or (perhaps more controversially) AI minimization.[30] The analysis of the different goals will stress how procurement is differently placed in relation to them.

The analysis focuses on goals of digital regulation that are generally put forward in current regulatory debates. It has been rightly stressed that this approach can obscure a more basic need to ensure functionality and fitness for purpose, and that most regulatory interventions presume AI functionality too readily.[31] This must be acknowledged, and a core goal of digital technology regulation must be to ensure such functionality. It has been proposed that this can be done through procurement.[32] In that regard, it is submitted that most of the difficulties in operationalizing 'technical goals' (such as cybersecurity or technological neutrality, interoperability, and openness) also apply to that more fundamental or basic goal of ensuring functionality. It will therefore not be discussed separately.

2.1 Trustworthiness or Responsibility

Trustworthiness or responsibility in the adoption of AI can have several meanings,[33] and defining what is 'trustworthy AI' or 'responsible AI' is in itself contested[34]—as is the related issue of algorithmic fairness.[35] This creates a risk

[30] This is not intended as an exhaustive list. Environmental sustainability in particular is a key (ethical) consideration. However, to keep analytical focus, the discussion is limited to 'digital' technological attributes. For an alternative list of relevant goals or principles, see Hasselbalch, Olsen, and Tranberg, 'Data Ethics in Public Procurement' (n 11) 22–26. See also National Institute for Standards and Technology, 'Artificial Intelligence Risk Management Framework (AI RMF 1.0)' (2023) <https://www.nist.gov/itl/ai-risk-management-framework> accessed 7 April 2023. The AI RMF considers that the 'characteristics of trustworthy AI systems … include valid and reliable, safe, secure and resilient, accountable and transparent, explainable and interpretable, privacy enhanced, and fair with their harmful biases managed', at 2–3, see also 12–18 for details.

[31] Inioluwa Deborah Raji and others, 'The Fallacy of AI Functionality' (2022) FAccT proceedings 959.

[32] ibid 968.

[33] And some of them are strongly influenced by broader socio-political considerations; see eg Martin Beraja and others, 'AI-tocracy' (2023) 138(3) The Quarterly Journal of Economics 1349.

[34] Or even whether AI can be trusted; see eg Mark Ryan, 'In AI We Trust: Ethics, Artificial Intelligence, and Reliability' (2020) 26 Science and Engineering Ethics 2749.

[35] See eg Shira Mitchell and others, 'Algorithmic Fairness: Choices, Assumptions, and Definitions' (2021) 8 Annual Review of Statistics and Its Application 141; Fabian Beigang, 'Reconciling Algorithmic Fairness Criteria' (2023) 51(2) Philosophy & Public Affairs 166.

of imprecision or generality,[36] which could turn 'trustworthiness' or 'responsibility' into mere buzzwords[37]—as well as exacerbate the problem of AI ethics washing.[38] In the EU context,[39] 'trustworthiness' is intended to cover three requirements for lawful,[40] ethical, and robust AI.[41] However, the interaction between those different elements is not clear or unproblematic,[42] and each of them break down into more detailed or operationalizable requirements.[43] The point to be made here is that 'trustworthiness' and 'responsibility' are incommensurable regulatory goals, and that procurement (as many other regulatory tools) is not well suited to pursue them without a clear breakdown and concretization allowing for more targeted analysis and enforcement.[44]

Whether procurement can contribute to the broader generation of trustworthiness or responsibility in the adoption of AI and other digital technologies by the public sector is the object of analysis in this book, and requires an assessment of narrower or more clearly defined regulatory goals, such as demands concerning the explainability or transparency of algorithmic solutions, the minimization of their adoption, or 'technical' characteristics

[36] See eg Karen Yeung, 'Recommendation of the Council on Artificial Intelligence (OECD)' (2020) 59(1) International Legal Materials 27.

[37] See eg Luke Munn, 'The Uselessness of AI Ethics' (2022) AI and Ethics <https://doi.org/10.1007/s43681-022-00209-w> accessed 11 November 2022.

[38] For discussion, see eg Karen Yeung, Andrew Howes, and Ganna Pogrebna, 'AI Governance by Human Rights-Centered Design, Deliberation, and Oversight: An End to Ethics Washing' in Markus D Dubber and others (eds), *Oxford Handbook of Ethics of AI* (OUP 2020) 76.

[39] High-Level Expert Group on AI, 'Ethics guidelines for trustworthy AI' (2019) <https://digital-strategy.ec.europa.eu/en/library/ethics-guidelines-trustworthy-ai> accessed 7 March 2023.

[40] The content of such requirement is meant to evolve over time, especially if/when legislative proposals such as the EU AI Act are adopted; Proposal for a Regulation of the European Parliament and of the Council laying down harmonised rules on Artificial Intelligence (Artificial Intelligence Act) and amending certain union legislative acts, COM (2021) 206 final. However, this creates a moving target and assessing at this stage whether legal requirements will suffice does not seem productive. Legal requirements for AI development and use will be relevant to the discussion in this book, in particular in relation to the proposal for the generation of mandatory requirements in Chapter 5.

[41] See eg Luciano Floridi, 'Establishing the Rules for Building Trustworthy AI' (2019) 1 Nature Machine Intelligence 261; Nathalie A Smuha, 'The EU Approach to Ethics Guidelines for Trustworthy Artificial Intelligence. A Continuous Journey Towards an Appropriate Governance Framework for AI' (2019) 20(4) Computer Law Review International 97.

[42] See eg Charly Derave, Nathan Genicot, and Nina Hetmanska, 'The Risks of Trustworthy Artificial Intelligence: The Case of the European Travel Information and Authorisation System' (2022) 13(3) European Journal of Risk Regulation 389.

[43] Perhaps unsurprisingly, signalling trustworthiness to improve citizen trust in AI projects has been shown to be ineffective; Bjorn Kleizen and others, 'Do Citizens Trust Trustworthy Artificial Intelligence? Experimental Evidence on the Limits of Ethical AI Measures in Government' (2023) Government Information Quarterly, forthcoming <https://doi.org/10.1016/j.giq.2023.101834> accessed 12 June 2023.

[44] See more generally David Leslie, 'Understanding Artificial Intelligence Ethics and Safety: A Guide for the Responsible Design and Implementation of AI Systems in the Public Sector' (2019) Alan Turing Institute <https://doi.org/10.5281/zenodo.3240529> accessed 9 March 2023.

such as neutrality, interoperability, openness, or cybersecurity, as discussed below.[45]

2.2 Explainability, Intelligibility, or Interpretability

One of the most contested issues in the adoption of digital technologies, and especially AI, concerns the extent to which their operation and the underlying reasons for the decisions or recommendations they make, or support, are (or should be) visible and understandable for humans—or, in other words, their explainability, intelligibility, or interpretability.[46] The concerns surrounding the deployment of unintelligible digital technologies increase with the technical complexity of the algorithmic solutions,[47] and relate in particular to 'black box' algorithms that are by definition (directly) unexplainable—although they can be subject to post-hoc explanation techniques.[48]

Crucially, there is no such thing as '*the explanation*' that is required in relation to an algorithmic system, as explanations are (technically and legally) meant to serve different purposes and consequently; the design of the explainability of an AI deployment needs to take into account factors such as the timing of the explanation, its (primary) audience, the level of granularity (eg general or model level, group-based, or individual explanations), or the level of risk generated by the use of the technical solution.[49] Moreover, there are different (and emerging) approaches to AI explainability,[50] and their suitability may well be contingent upon the specific intended use or function of the explanation.[51] The provision of explanations is particularly constrained under administrative

[45] However, the attribute of 'trustworthiness' will still be referred to as shorthand in other parts of the book.

[46] Royal Society, 'Explainable AI: The Basics' (2019) Policy Briefing <https://royalsociety.org/-/media/policy/projects/explainable-ai/AI-and-interpretability-policy-briefing.pdf> accessed 9 March 2023.

[47] Though it has been argued that this may be eschewing the discussion towards the internal mechanisms of the algorithm, rather than the type of pragmatical explanations demanded from human decision-makers, see John Zerilli and others, 'Transparency in Algorithmic and Human Decision-Making: Is There a Double Standard?' (2019) 32 Philosophy & Technology 661.

[48] Ronan Hamon, Henrik Junklewitz, and Ignacio Sanchez, 'Robustness and Explainability of Artificial Intelligence—From Technical to Policy Solutions' (2020) <https://data.europa.eu/doi/10.2760/57493> accessed 9 March 2023.

[49] See eg Ronan Hamon and others, 'Impossible Explanations? Beyond Explainable AI in the GDPR from a COVID-19 Use Case Scenario' (2021) <https://ssrn.com/abstract=3774114> accessed 9 March 2023.

[50] See eg Andreas Holzinger and others, 'Explainable AI Methods—A Brief Overview' in Andreas Holzinger and others (eds), *xxAI—Beyond Explainable AI* (Springer 2022) 13.

[51] See eg Sebastian Bordt and others, 'Post-Hoc Explanations Fail to Achieve their Purpose in Adversarial Contexts' (2022) FAccT Proceedings 891.

law.[52] And there are attributes or properties influencing the interpretability of a model (eg clarity) for which there are no evaluation metrics (yet?).[53]

This stresses the need to craft requirements of explainability or interpretability—and the related technical requirements and applicable metrics—to the specific context in which a technological solution will be deployed, with some of the relevant determinants having either a legal or ethical dimension (eg where an explanation would be desirable but not legally mandated), and most likely being open to contestation. Not least, because demands of explainability are not zero-sum, to the extent that more explainable or easily understandable technologies may have lower levels of performance.[54] It thus seems unavoidable that legal demands for an explanation impose technical trade-offs.[55]

This makes a moving target of the goal of ensuring explainability in the adoption of technological solutions by the public sector—particularly by means of procurement, to the extent that it can relate to exploratory, experimental, or pilot solutions which (future) explainability may be hard or impossible to assess prior to awarding the public contract.[56]

2.3 Transparency

While explainability has a bearing on the level of transparency related to the adoption of digital technologies by the public sector,[57] the demands for transparency or disclosure in the adoption of digital technologies by the public sector usually concern two related but distinct issues.[58]

[52] Melanie Fink and Michele Finck, 'Reasoned A(I)administration: Explanation Requirements in EU Law and the Automation of Public Administration' (2022) 47(3) European Law Review 376.

[53] See eg Aniek F Markus, Jan A Kors, and Peter R Rijnbeek, 'The Role of Explainability in Creating Trustworthy Artificial Intelligence for Health Care: A Comprehensive Survey of the Terminology, Design Choices, and Evaluation Strategies' (2021) 113 Journal of Biomedical Informatics 103655.

[54] See eg Diane Coyle, 'The Tensions Between Explainable AI and Good Public Policy' (*Tech Stream*, 15 September 2020) <https://www.brookings.edu/techstream/the-tensions-between-explainable-ai-and-good-public-policy/> accessed 9 March 2023; Diane Coyle and Adrian Weller, '"Explaining" Machine Learning Reveals Policy Challenges' (2020) 368(6498) Science 1433.

[55] For discussion, see Blazej Kuzniacki and others, 'Towards EXplainable Artificial Intelligence (XAI) in Tax Law: The Need for a Minimum Legal Standard' (2022) 14(4) World Tax Journal 573.

[56] See Chapter 4, Section 3.2.1.

[57] Miriam C Buiten, 'Towards Intelligent Regulation of Artificial Intelligence' (2019) 10(1) European Journal of Risk Regulation 41. See also Ida Koivisto, 'Thinking Inside the Box: The Promise and Boundaries of Transparency in Automated Decision-Making' in Deirdre Curtin and Mariavittoria Catanzariti (eds), *Data at the Boundaries of European Law* (OUP 2023) 66. cf Madalina Busuioc, Deirdre Curtin, and Marco Almada, 'Reclaiming Transparency: Contesting the Logics of Secrecy Within the EU AI Act' (2023) 2(1) European Law Open 79.

[58] For discussion of the many senses in which transparency is used in relation to digital regulation, see eg Colin Gavaghan and others, 'Government Use of Artificial Intelligence in New Zealand' (2019)

First, there are demands for disclosure of the fact that an algorithmic system is used *at all* by the public sector, coupled with (high-level) descriptions of relevant details of its functioning, underpinning data, etc.[59] Given that there is currently no mandatory requirement for such disclosure to take place, the adoption of AI in the public sector is clouded in opacity, which undermines general trustworthiness.[60] Procurement rules can be of partial assistance, to the extent that they require, for example, mandatory publication of contract awards, which could provide an indication that a digital technology has been acquired (and, presumably, will soon be put into use). However, even if no part of the standard content of those notices is withheld on, for example, commercial confidentiality grounds (which can be a common occurrence, see below), procurement-related notices as they currently exist are not suited to providing meaningful information for the purposes of algorithmic transparency—for example, they would not include details on how the technology operates, data-related issues, etc. Increasing this type of procurement-adjacent transparency seems relatively straightforward and there are emerging models, for example in the UK,[61] of algorithmic transparency standards that could be used—even to make them mandatory,[62] at least in relation to the acquisition of digital solutions from tech providers. Given that most digital technologies are not developed in-house, this could cover the majority instances of public sector digitalization.[63]

Second, there are demands for access to the details of the workings of the algorithmic system and, primarily, access to algorithmic source code.[64] Given that

41–43 <https://ourarchive.otago.ac.nz/bitstream/handle/10523/9372/NZLF%20report.pdf> accessed 5 April 2023. The discussion here concerns some aspects of the inspectability of public sector digital technology adoption.

[59] However, the effects of transparency, in particular of data processing, on citizens' trust in government are not linear; see Bjorn Kleizen and Wouter Van Dooren, 'Is Everything Under Control? An Experimental Study on How Control Over Data Influences Trust in and Support for Major Governmental Data Exchange Projects' (2023) 28(2) Information Polity 277.

[60] See eg Public Law Project, 'The Tracking Automated Government register. A new tool lifting the lid on secretive government algorithms' (2023) <https://publiclawproject.org.uk/resources/the-tracking-automated-government-register/> accessed 9 March 2023.

[61] See Central Digital and Data Office and Centre for Data Ethics and Innovation, 'Algorithmic Transparency Recording Standard Hub' (2023) <https://www.gov.uk/government/collections/algorithmic-transparency-recording-standard-hub> accessed 9 March 2023.

[62] This was the original approach in the recommendation that led to the development of the UK standard; see recommendation 16 in the Centre for Data Ethics and Innovation, 'Review into bias in algorithmic decision-making' (2020) <https://www.gov.uk/government/publications/cdei-publishes-review-into-bias-in-algorithmic-decision-making> accessed 8 November 2022.

[63] See Chapter 5, Section 3.2.

[64] However, this is a complicated issue in itself and some forms of algorithmic transparency may not yield any meaningful accountability; see eg Arvind Narayanan, 'Twitter Showed Us Its Algorithm.

algorithmic opacity can have its origin not only in the technical configuration of the solutions (see Section 2.2 re explainability), but also in their commercial secrecy, there is an expectation that procurement rules (or public buying power) will be used to demand access to the source code, and the EU has started to adapt its approach to, for example, international trade law to facilitate this possibility.[65] The primary demand is however not for access to the source code by the public buyer, or a limited circle of (directly) interested agents (eg in the context of the tendering of public contracts[66]), but a demand for general or unlimited access as a matter of public accountability. Here, the rules on the protection of commercially sensitive information in procurement raise some issues.

Ultimately, the main issue with using procurement to foster algorithmic transparency in the two senses mentioned above is that the standards and constraints relating to the protection of confidential, commercially sensitive, and other information subjected to the rights of others (eg information protected by intellectual property rights) is a contested issue in procurement regulation.[67] This should make clear that extending the existing rules on procurement-related transparency to issues of algorithmic transparency or other aspects of digital technology governance would also transfer ongoing debates around the limits on procurement-related disclosure. This is thus an area where procurement mechanisms could be used, but this would not necessarily ensure a specific regulatory output (eg maximum or total transparency).

2.4 AI Minimization

Given the issues relating to the adoption and use of complex digital technologies by the public sector, and especially AI in automated decision-making

What Does It Tell Us?' (*Knight Institute blog*, 10 April 2023) <https://knightcolumbia.org/blog/twitter-showed-us-its-algorithm-what-does-it-tell-us> accessed 12 April 2023.

[65] See eg Kristina Irion, 'Algorithms Off-limits? If Digital Trade Law Restricts Access to Source Code of Software Then Accountability Will Suffer' (2022) FAccT proceedings 1561; Albert Sanchez-Graells, 'Ensuring Algorithmic Transparency Through Public Contracts?' (*Digital Constitutionalist*, 24 November 2022) <https://digi-con.org/ensuring-algorithmic-transparency-through-public-contracts/> accessed 20 December 2022.

[66] Albert Sanchez-Graells, 'Public Procurement and [AI] Source Code Transparency, a (Downstream) Competition Issue (Re C-796/18)' (*howtocrackanut.com*, 20 June 2022) <https://www.howtocrackanut.com/blog/2022/6/20/public-procurement-and-ai-source-code-transparency> accessed 7 October 2022.

[67] See eg the contributions to Kirsi-Maria Halonen, Roberto Caranta, and Albert Sanchez-Graells (eds), *Transparency in EU Procurements: Disclosure Within Public Procurement and During Contract Execution* (Edward Elgar 2019). See also Chapter 9, Section 2.1.2, for related discussion.

contexts, a possibility to promote 'responsibility' (in the sense of caution) would be to impose compliance with a principle or goal of 'AI minimization' through procurement. This could require the public buyer to, for example, explicitly consider technical solutions that did not require AI, or that relied on less complex or more explainable models, as a pre-requisite to the eventual award of contracts involving complex (black box) systems where no other (functionally equivalent) simpler technical solutions were available. The adoption of such a principle would run contrary to current policy approaches to instrumentalizing public sector digitalization as a site of AI experimentation and would require a diametrical change of approach and a decoupling of procurement from the 'race for AI'.[68] An implementation of such a principle without changes in broader industrial policy would generate difficult tensions that would probably render the procurement requirement meaningless. Beyond that, the difficulties would be manifold.

First, it would be impossible to operationalize the principle in a technology-neutral way as it would in fact seek to deter use of specific types of technologies—while those types of technologies are not necessarily classifiable in neatly defined boxes but rather sit on a continuous scale that could make their delineation difficult, especially if a specific technological application combined different types of technologies within a single algorithmic assemblage.[69] Moreover, the issue of technological neutrality is important not only because it is a fundamental principle of (EU) procurement law, but also because such a type of technology-specific approach to procurement may not be adequate or efficient.[70] Second, and perhaps more important, the application of the principle would require comparative assessment of potentially substitutable technologies implementing metrics and evaluations that can be impossible to sufficiently specify (eg in relation to explainability, see Section 2.2). Third, there can be other relevant factors, such as feasibility, cost, technical debt, etc that would be difficult to factor into a single assessment, with the trade-offs between those factors being themselves susceptible of contestation

[68] See Chapter 1, Section 2.

[69] More generally, technologies cannot be assessed in the abstract, but need to be embedded in the broader institutional and social context, which could also make it difficult to assess different applications with different potential socio-technical interactions. For related discussion, see Howard Rosenbaum, 'Algorithmic Neutrality, Algorithmic Assemblages, and the Lifeworld' (2020) AMCIS 2020 Proceedings 6 <https://aisel.aisnet.org/amcis2020/philosophical_is/philosophical_is/6> accessed 9 March 2023.

[70] For related discussion, see Natalia Fabra and Juan-Pablo Montero, 'Technology-Neutral Versus Technology-Specific Procurement' (2023) 133(650) The Economic Journal 669.

(and manipulation). If an 'AI minimization' principle was to be implemented, it does not seem that public procurement would be well-placed to enforce it.

2.5 Technological Neutrality, Openness, and Interoperability

A different aspect of technological neutrality concerns the avoidance of technological lock-in effects through the award of public contracts.[71] It is well known that early contracts for new technological solutions can have such an effect where the technology is proprietary. Procurement could thus be used either to ban the acquisition of proprietary technologies by mandating acquisition of open-source technologies only,[72] to impose, for example, broad licensing requirements to ensure that proprietary technologies are however widely available and open to other (public sector) users,[73] or to impose interoperability requirements between procured technologies (whether proprietary or not).[74] These are relatively well-defined goals but the main difficulty in their implementation lies in the fact that a single approach is unlikely to work in all cases. There will be several (competing) technical, organizational, and economic considerations whether to acquire proprietary technologies and, if so, how to design the relevant licensing agreements.[75] In the absence of mandatory requirements or limitations, it can be difficult for the procurement function to commit to such regulatory goals, in particular in relation to AI.[76] Moreover, the move to open source AI can, for example, exacerbate some risks of unethical use, which generates a tension between commitments to open source

[71] See eg Bianca Sjoerdstra, 'Dealing with Vendor Lock-in' (2016) 7th IBA Bachelor Thesis Conference <https://essay.utwente.nl/70153/1/Sjoerdstra_BA_BMS.pdf> accessed 9 March 2023. See also Central Digital and Data Office, 'Managing technical lock-in in the cloud' (2019) <https://www.gov.uk/guidance/managing-technical-lock-in-in-the-cloud> accessed 9 March 2023.

[72] This is by no means a new issue, see eg European eGovernment Services, 'Guideline on public procurement of Open Source Software' (2010) <https://joinup.ec.europa.eu/sites/default/files/document/2011-12/OSS-procurement-guideline%20-final.pdf> accessed 9 March 2023.

[73] See eg European Commission, 'Open Source Licensing and Reuse of Commission Software' (Decision) C (2021) 8759 final; and European Commission, 'Open source software strategy 2020–2023. Think Open' (Communication) C (2020) 7149 final.

[74] Albert Sanchez-Graells, 'Interoperable Europe Act: Quick Procurement Annotation' (*howtocrackanut.com*, 5 January 2023) <https://www.howtocrackanut.com/blog/2023/1/5/interoperable-europe-act-quick-procurement-annotation> accessed 9 March 2023.

[75] For related discussion, see Maha Shaikh and Tony Cornford, 'Strategic Drivers of Open Source Software Adoption in the Public Sector: Challenges and Opportunities' (2012) ECIS 2012 Proceedings 237.

[76] See European Parliament, 'Challenges and Limits of an open Source Approach to Artificial Intelligence' (2021) <https://www.europarl.europa.eu/RegData/etudes/STUD/2021/662908/IPOL_STU(2021)662908_EN.pdf> accessed 9 March 2023.

within public sector use, and broader issues of ethical AI regulation beyond the purview of procurement.[77]

2.6 Cybersecurity

Procurement can also be used to impose compliance with specific cybersecurity requirements. Given that cybersecurity (technical and organizational) standards are quite developed, and compliance is increasingly mandatory, this could seem like a relatively straightforward issue, as the role of procurement could be limited to checking compliance with those (external) standards. However, there are limitations in this approach because the relevant standards are themselves open-ended and their interpretation and application require technical judgements, but also because there are difficult to assess systemic risks for which procurement processes are ill-suited.[78]

2.7 Recapitulation

The theoretical appeal of leveraging procurement as a tool of digital 'regulation by contract' needs to be assessed against the likelihood that it would effectively deliver or promote the desired regulatory goals. Such likelihood is in good part determined by the nature of those goals and the ways in which they can be operationalized through procurement.[79] The analysis of some selected such goals here has shown how there are three types of difficulties that raise questions on the likely effectiveness of this approach.

First, some of the putative goals of digital 'regulation by contract', such as trustworthiness or responsibility are generally incommensurable regulatory goals for which procurement is not geared. Further, some of the related goals into which they can be broken down, such as explainability or a potential principle of AI minimization, raise related issues of incommensurability. In relation

[77] See eg David Gray Widder and others, 'Limits and Possibilities for "Ethical AI" in Open Source: A Study of Deepfakes' (2022) FAccT proceedings 2035.

[78] eg systemic issues evidenced in the so-called Solar Winds attack; see Jeferson Martinez and Javier M Duran, 'Software Supply Chain Attacks, a Threat to Global Cybersecurity: SolarWinds' Case Study' (2021) 11 International Journal of Safety and Security Engineering 537.

[79] Of course, it is also determined by issues concerning resourcing and digital capabilities, which will be a running consideration in the book. See eg David Chinn and others, 'The Future Is Now: Closing the Skills Gap in Europe's Public Sector' (2020) McKinsey <https://www.mckinsey.com/industries/public-and-social-sector/our-insights/the-future-is-now-closing-the-skills-gap-in-europes-public-sector> accessed 9 March 2023.

to these regulatory goals, the main difficulties reside in the absence of metrics or agreed modes of assessment, as well as the contextual dependency of their application.

Second, some putative goals of a seemingly more technical or concrete/operationalizable nature, such as transparency, technological neutrality, openness, and interoperability, or cybersecurity, raise issues regarding their concrete application. The operationalization of such requirements in a procurement context will be dependent on a range of considerations, such as judgements on the need to keep information confidential, judgements on the state-of-the-art or what constitutes a proportionate and economically justified requirement, the generation of systemic effects that are hard to evaluate within the limits of a procurement procedure, or trade-offs between competing considerations.

This relates to the third source of difficulty, which concerns trade-offs between digital regulation goals, such as, for example, open source and ethical AI uses, or trade-offs between regulatory and operational goals, such as, for example, explainability and performance.[80] Some of these difficulties relate to the broader issues with the regulation of AI in general—and, therefore, pose difficulties regardless of the chosen regulatory instrument[81]—but are particularly pertinent to an assessment of the suitability of procurement to deliver such goals. The extent to which procurement can deliver digital regulatory outcomes depends on its position as a regulatory actor and the tools available to it.

This book will argue that the emerging approach to digital 'regulation by contract' cannot work well because the procurement function is badly placed to develop the two-sided regulatory gatekeeping role it is intended for (Chapter 3), and because existing procurement tools cannot effectively operationalize digital regulation goals, either at all, or without simply transferring regulatory decisions to economic operators (Chapter 4). The analysis will show how, despite expectations to the contrary, procurement is not a suitable point of regulatory intervention except in relation to the enforcement of pre-existing requirements. The analysis will also show that procurement lacks the independence required of a gatekeeper and is exposed to risks of regulatory capture that require additional checks and balances. In view of these findings, the book will make alternative regulatory proposals for independent external oversight and the imposition of mandatory requirements in the adoption of

[80] This is, in fact, a rather straightforward or textbook analysis. See eg John Zerilli and others, *A Citizen's Guide to Artificial Intelligence* (MIT Press 2021) 162–64.

[81] For discussion, see Roel Dobbe, Thomas Krendl Gilbert, and Yonatan Mintz, 'Hard Choices in Artificial Intelligence' (2021) 300 Artificial Intelligence 103555.

digital technologies by the public sector (Chapter 5), to minimize the demands on the procurement function as a tool of digital regulation.

3. Procurement Digitalization as a Case Study of Experimentation with Digital 'Regulation by Contract'

The theoretical analysis of the use of procurement as a tool of digital 'regulation by contract' will be enriched and further developed with an in-depth case study of its practical operation in a discrete area of public sector digitalization. Given that the public sector is digitalizing practically all areas of activity, there would be many potential options. The choice of a case study depends on the specific focus of analysis.[82] Part II of this book makes the core argument that procurement is an inadequate tool of digital 'regulation by contract'. To further test and justify this submission, it is important to identify an area of public sector digitalization which is primarily or solely left to 'regulation by contract' through procurement—to isolate it from the interaction with other tools of digital regulation. It is also important for the chosen area to demonstrate a sufficient level of experimentation with digitalization, so that the analysis is not a mere concretization of theoretical arguments but rather grounded on empirical insights.

Public procurement is itself an area of public sector activity undergoing digitalization.[83] The European Commission conceptualizes procurement digitalization as a process of fundamental rethinking of its regulation,[84] and has placed it amongst its top strategic priorities.[85] The Organization for Economic Co-operation and Development (OECD) has stressed how procurement digitalization 'can significantly enhance visibility about how public money is spent, help fight corruption and increase the efficiency of public procurement. [It can] save money and time by reducing administrative burdens and potential mistakes that might arise during public procurement cycles.'[86] Indeed, *public procurement practice or implementation is a primary field for experimentation*

[82] See eg Helen Simons, 'Case Study Research: In-Depth Understanding in Context' in Patricia Leavy (ed), *Oxford Handbook of Qualitative Research* (2nd edn, OUP 2020) 676.

[83] See eg Nataliya Synyutka, Oksana Kurylo, and Mariya Bondarchuk, 'Digitalisation of Public Procurement: The Case Study of Ukraine' (2019) 53(3) Annales Universitatis Mariae Curie-Skłodowska 61.

[84] European Commission, 'Digital procurement' <https://single-market-economy.ec.europa.eu/single-market/public-procurement/digital-procurement_en> accessed 7 September 2022.

[85] European Commission, 'Making Public Procurement work in and for Europe' (Communication) COM (2017) 572 final.

[86] OECD, 'Government at a Glance 2021' (2021) 166.

with digital technologies. The potential of innovations such as robotic process automation (including through the internet of things), embedded legal compliance, blockchain-based data management, big data analytics, recommender systems, or algorithmic screening in reducing corruption, collusion, and wastage in the expenditure of public funds makes procurement a prime site for the deployment of a wide variety of digital technologies.[87]

The adoption of digital tools is seen as a potential source of improvement and efficiency in the expenditure of public funds through procurement,[88] especially through the adoption of digital technology solutions developed in the context of supply chain management and other business operations in the private sector (or 'ProcureTech'),[89] but also through the adoption of digital tools tailored to the specific goals of procurement regulation, such as the prevention of corruption[90] or collusion[91] ('GovTech').[92] There is emerging evidence of experimentation in procurement digitalization,[93] which is shedding light on regulatory risks and challenges.

In view of its strategic importance and the current pace of procurement digitalization, this book chooses procurement as a *site of public sector experimentation*, to explore the shortcomings of the approach to digital 'regulation by contract'. Procurement is an adequate case study because, being a 'back-office' function, it does not concern (likely) high-risk uses of AI or other digital technologies,[94] and it is an area where data protection regulation is unlikely to

[87] World Bank, 'Disruptive Technologies in Public Procurement' (2021) <http://documents.worldbank.org/curated/en/522181612428427520/Disruptive-Technologies-in-Public-Procurement> accessed 8 September 2022.

[88] See eg Jessica Tillipman, 'Using AI to Reduce Performance Risk in U.S. Procurement' (*Regulatory Review*, 29 June 2022) <https://www.theregreview.org/2022/06/29/tillipman-using-ai-to-reduce-performance-risk-in-u-s-procurement/> accessed 15 September 2022; Dan Chenok, 'How Can Governments Use AI to Improve Procurement?' (*Regulatory Review*, 30 June 2022) <https://www.theregreview.org/2022/06/30/chenok-how-can-governments-use-ai-to-improve-procurement/> accessed 7 March 2023.

[89] For contextual discussion, see World Economic Forum, 'Adopting AI Responsibly: Guidelines for Procurement of AI Solutions by the Private Sector' (June 2023) <https://www3.weforum.org/docs/WEF_Adopting_AI_Responsibly_Guidelines_for_Procurement_of_AI_Solutions_by_the_Private_Sector_2023.pdf> accessed 22 June 2023.

[90] See eg Albert Sanchez-Graells, 'Procurement Corruption and Artificial Intelligence: Between the Potential of Enabling Data Architectures and the Constraints of Due Process Requirements' in Sope Williams and Jessica Tillipman (eds), *Routledge Handbook of Public Procurement Corruption* (Routledge forthcoming) <https://ssrn.com/abstract=3952665> accessed 30 June 2023.

[91] See eg Albert Sanchez-Graells, '"Screening for Cartels" in Public Procurement: Cheating at Solitaire to Sell Fool's Gold?' (2019) 10(4) Journal of European Competition Law & Practice 199.

[92] European Parliament, 'The Digital Single Market and the Digitalisation of the Public Sector: GovTech and Other Innovations in Public Procurement' (2022) <https://data.europa.eu/doi/10.2861/830794> accessed 17 October 2022.

[93] Deloitte, 'Study on up-take of emerging technologies in public procurement. Final report' (2020) <https://ec.europa.eu/docsroom/documents/40102> accessed 7 September 2022.

[94] Thus limiting the (future) relevance of legislative initiatives such as the EU AI Act (n 40).

provide a comprehensive regulatory framework (eg for decision automation) because the primary interactions are between public buyers and corporate institutions. Procurement therefore currently represents an *unregulated digitalization space* in which to test and further explore the (in)effectiveness of the 'regulation by contract' approach to governing the transition to a new model of digital public governance. Moreover, the current state of procurement digitalization is not necessarily more advanced than digitalization in other areas of the public sector, and the fact that procurement is a cross-cutting public sector activity makes it comparable with public sector digitalization in areas not subjected to sectoral regulation.

The case study in Part III is structured as follows: first, it focuses on how digital technologies and the abstract potential contribution they could make to improving procurement governance and management create an aura of 'policy irresistibility'[95] that generates risks of regulatory capture and commercial determination that leave the public buyer exposed to excessive experimentation and risk-taking (Chapter 6). Second, to moderate the expectations resulting from their 'policy irresistibility', the case study provides a technology-centred assessment of the enabling requirements and the potential benefits that could result from the adoption of digital technologies to draw a feasibility boundary for procurement digitalization (Chapter 7). Third, the analysis explores the main governance risks and legal obligations arising from the adoption of digital technologies, which revolve around data governance, algorithmic transparency, technological dependency, technical debt, cybersecurity threats, the risks stemming from the long-term erosion of the skills base in the public sector, and difficult trade-offs due to the uncertainty surrounding immature and still changing technologies within an also evolving regulatory framework (Chapter 8). This evidences the type of regulatory risks and challenges likely to emerge in most projects of public sector digitalization. Finally, the analysis shows how existing controls on the adoption of digital technologies by the public sector under EU and UK law are insufficient to protect against the risks of regulatory capture and commercial determination identified in preceding chapters, which aligns with the need for external regulatory mechanisms advanced in Part II (Chapter 9).

[95] For critical analysis, see Dan McQuillan, *Resisting AI. An Anti-fascist Approach to Artificial Intelligence* (Bristol UP 2023) 10–26.

PART II

REGULATING PUBLIC SECTOR DIGITALIZATION BY CONTRACT

3

Regulating Public and Private Interactions Through Procurement

1. Introduction

Chapter 2 detailed how public procurement is erected as the gatekeeper of the public sector's digital transformation and thus positioned as a digital technology regulator. Procurement is expected to ensure that the public sector only adopts trustworthy technologies, and that (private) tech providers adhere to the technical, legal, and ethical standards required to ensure this is the case. Unpacking procurement's gatekeeping role requires moving past the general level of abstraction in which such proposals are formulated and analysing them by focusing on the actors, processes, and tools involved, as well as the expected outcomes.[1] To start this focused analysis, the chapter concentrates on procurement as a regulatory actor. It explores the role of the procurement function[2] in mediating interactions between the public and private actors involved in the adoption of digital technologies by the public sector. Chapter 4 will assess the suitability of procurement tools, both procedural and substantive.

This chapter starts by using agency theory to map the logic of the interactions between the public sector entities seeking to adopt the technology, the (private) economic operators seeking to provide it, and the procurement function as gatekeeper. In addition to the well-known 'weak public buyer' problem, this mapping will evidence the difficulties of the 'two-sided' gatekeeping that procurement is expected to carry out to discipline not only the behaviour of the tech provider, but also that of the adopting public entity. This will show the heightened potential for tensions and governance challenges in the process

[1] Along the same lines, stressing the importance of such analysis to ensure policy implementation and, therefore, effectiveness, see Bob Hudson, David Hunter, and Stephen Peckham, 'Policy Failure and the Policy-Implementation Gap: Can Policy Support Programs Help?' (2019) 2 Policy Design and Practice 1.

[2] 'Procurement function' is used as shorthand for the carrying out of public procurement procedures at an operational level; on this use, see OECD/SIGMA, 'Organising central public procurement functions' (2013) <https://www.sigmaweb.org/publications/Brief26_CentralPPFunctions_2013.pdf> accessed 6 February 2022.

Digital Technologies and Public Procurement. Albert Sanchez-Graells, Oxford University Press.
 DOI: 10.1093/oso/9780198866770.003.0003

of procuring un(der)regulated technologies, where procurement's agency and gatekeeping roles are overlaid. This situation is not unique to the procurement of *digital* technologies, but it is particularly acute in this setting due to the existing legislative and regulatory gap.[3] The chapter concludes with a first sketch of a proposal to discharge procurement of this newest regulatory gatekeeping role through mandatory requirements and external oversight, which will be developed in more detail in Chapter 5.

As discussed in Chapter 2, under an emerging consensus, procurement is expected to ensure that the public sector only acquires and adopts trustworthy technologies, and that (private) tech providers adhere to adequate technical, legal, and ethical standards to ensure that this is the case.[4] Procurement is expected to operate as a lever for the propagation of (soft) regulatory tools—such as independently set technical standards or codes of conduct—to promote their adoption and harness market dynamics to generate effects beyond the public sector (ie market-shaping). Even further, where such standards are not readily available or independently set, the procurement function is expected to formulate specific (contractual) requirements to ensure compliance with the overarching regulatory goals identified at higher levels of policymaking.[5] The procurement function is thus expected to leverage the design of public tenders and public contracts as tools of digital technology regulation to plug the regulatory gap resulting from the absence of binding requirements.[6]

From this perspective, procurement is thus not only expected to simultaneously align the behaviour of all relevant public and private actors towards compliance with a growing set of goals and standards in the adoption of digital technologies, but also to set those standards where they do not result from other legislative or regulatory sources. Procurement is thus: (1) erected as a gatekeeper of the public interest in the process of public sector digitalization; (2) leveraged as a catalyst or multiplier of the effects of other regulatory interventions; and (3) assigned a (residual, temporary) digital technology

[3] See Chapter 1. For discussion focused on procurement digitalization, see Chapter 9.

[4] For a tentative overview of some of the proposals, see Albert Sanchez-Graells, 'Some Further Thoughts on Setting Procurement up to Fail in "AI regulation by contract"' (*howtocrackanut.com*, 27 January 2023) <https://www.howtocrackanut.com/blog/2023/1/27/setting-procurement-up-to-fail-in-ai-regulation-by-contract> accessed 8 February 2023.

[5] These can derive from eg national AI strategies, such as in the UK, or from the implicit logic and effects of legislative measures, such as the EU's AI Act. See Chapter 2, Section 2 for details on putative regulatory goals.

[6] This approach to leveraging procurement as a regulatory tool is by no means a new phenomenon; see nn 27 and 31. This is also not limited to issues of technological regulation, but the approach is also applied to broader issues of digital regulation, such as data governance; see eg Laurens Vandercruysse, Caroline Buts, and Michael Dooms, 'Public Procurement as a Safeguard for Competition: The Case of Smart City Services' (2021) 5 European Competition and Regulation Law Review 102.

regulatory role.[7] This adds to the existing roles of procurement as an instrument of economic regulation and governance—which already include, to varying degrees, other gatekeeping, market-shaping, and regulatory functions. However, these new technological regulatory roles are currently underspecified and underregulated and, perhaps more importantly, insufficiently debated and understood.

As discussed in Chapter 1, as the touchstone between tech providers and adopting public entities, procurement is seen as a suitable regulatory 'entry point' or lever to discipline the development and adoption of digital technologies.[8] While this abstract view makes intuitive sense, such high-level intuition requires careful analysis. A first step towards ascertaining the adequacy and likely effectiveness of leveraging procurement for digital technology gatekeeping and 'regulation by contract' requires a more nuanced understanding and a higher level of concretization. To begin with, it necessitates some clarification of what is meant by the 'procurement function' *as a regulatory actor*. While this label[9] can be helpful as shorthand for 'the use of public procurement law and policy' in general, a focus on the implementation phase of this regulatory approach requires an understanding of the multiplicity of roles assigned to the procurement function, as well as of the institutional setting in which the regulatory gatekeeping of public sector digitalization would take place.

This chapter understands the 'procurement function' in a narrow sense, so that it comprises the preparatory activities leading to the award of a public contract.[10] While there are procurement rules on contract compliance and implementation, modification, and termination,[11] for the purposes of this analysis, the *regulatory role* of procurement is considered largely finished once the public contract is in place, as the management of that contract is

[7] For the purposes of this chapter, gatekeeping is meant as the function of enforcing externally determined rules and standards, whereas regulation is meant as the determination of such rules and standards. Where those rules and standards are *both* expected to be set and applied by the procurement function, the chapter emphasizes this interaction through the label 'regulatory gatekeeping'. Sometimes the boundary between regulation and gatekeeping will be blurred, such as when the procurement function can choose between different externally determined rules or standards for the purposes of its gatekeeping, which implies a certain degree of regulatory power. However, this chapter will not engage with such boundary cases.

[8] David S Rubenstein, 'Acquiring Ethical AI' (2021) 73(4) Florida Law Review 747, 797.

[9] Alternative labels will be used to avoid repetition, such as 'procurement' or the 'public buyer'. Where those expressions are used in this chapter or other parts of the book, they should be understood with the same meaning given to the 'procurement function'.

[10] With the same narrow approach, see Sue Arrowsmith, *The Law of Public and Utilities Procurement. Regulation in the EU and UK*, vol 1 (3rd edn, Sweet & Maxwell 2014) 1.

[11] Some jurisdictions also have rather developed governance frameworks for contract implementation and monitoring, at least for specific types of contracts. However, the analysis concentrates on tender design and contract formation phases for the reasons provided in the main text (ie fit with the theoretical model).

assigned to the adopting public entity as an actor (notionally) separate from the procurement function.[12] In this view, the procurement function interacts with the adopting public entity and all potential tech providers during the tender stage, and designs the public (regulatory) contract that will govern the interaction between the adopting public entity and the chosen tech provider post-award.

The fact that, in this approach, the public buyer is not involved in the implementation and monitoring of the contract has important implications from a regulatory analysis perspective. First, it requires careful consideration of the modified applicability of theories of incomplete and relational contracting,[13] as the relational aspects of co-producing decisions during contract implementation solely concern the adopting entity and the tech provider. The regulatory aspects of the contract designed by the procurement function should be enforced over *both of these actors*.[14] This creates the situation where both actors are expected to interact under a contractual framework they have not (jointly) designed.[15] Second, functionally, this brings the use of public contracts rather close to other regulatory instruments and, at least tendentially, generates the same governance challenges that require different tools and institutional arrangements in regulated markets.[16]

Developing an understanding of whether the procurement function can act as an effective regulatory gatekeeper of the public interest in public sector digitalization requires analysing: (1) the position of the procurement function amongst the public and private actors involved in the process; (2) the governance implications of the procurement function's institutional embeddedness; and (3) the likely (in)effectiveness of public contracts in disciplining

[12] See Sections 2.2 and 2.3.

[13] See Oliver D Hart, 'Incomplete Contracts and the Theory of the Firm' (1988) 4(1) Journal of Law, Economics, & Organization 119; Oliver D Hart, 'Incomplete Contracts and Control' (2017) 107(7) American Economic Review 1731.

[14] At a minimum, this would require a high level of rigidity in the relational contracts, and may even exclude their applicability altogether. For discussion, see Marian W Moszoro, Pablo T Spiller, and Sebastian Stolorz, 'Rigidity of Public Contracts' (2016) 13(3) Journal of Empirical Legal Studies 396; Jean Beuve, Marian W Moszoro, and Stephane Saussier, 'Political Contestability and Public Contract Rigidity: An Analysis of Procurement Contracts' (2019) 28(2) Journal of Economics & Management Strategy 316.

[15] Joint contract design is implicit in theories of relational contracting, including the most recent proposals for open-ended and principles-based relational contracting; see David Frydlinger and Oliver Hart, 'Overcoming Contractual Incompleteness: The Role of Guiding Principles' (2023) Journal of Law, Economics, and Organization, forthcoming <https://doi.org/10.1093/jleo/ewac027> accessed 2 February 2023 (hereafter Frydlinger and Hart, 'Overcoming Contractual Incompleteness').

[16] See Victor P Goldberg, 'Regulation and Administered Contracts' (1976) 7(2) Bell Journal of Economics 426; Keith J Crocker and Scott E Masten, 'Regulation and Administered Contracts Revisited: Lessons from Transaction-Cost Economics for Public Utility Regulation' (1996) 9(1) Journal of Regulatory Economics 5.

private and public behaviour, as well as behaviour that is mutually influenced or coproduced by public and private actors during the execution of public contracts.

To generate that understanding, Section 2 maps the logic of different sets of interactions in the process of public sector digitalization, stressing the different rationales and presumptions embedded in the regulation of public-private, public-public, and decentred interactions,[17] taking the institutional embeddedness of the procurement function into account. It shows that, in addition to potentially being exposed to the well-known 'weak public buyer' problem, and the challenges resulting from risks of policy entrepreneurialism and regulatory capture, procurement finds itself subject to competing or irreconcilable demands under what this chapter labels 'two-sided' gatekeeping. Section 3 then stresses how such irreconcilable demands jeopardize the attainment of the relevant regulatory goals. The analysis identifies the need to discharge procurement from crucial aspects of its newest regulatory gatekeeping role where they are irreconcilable or difficult to align within its structural agency relationship. Section 4 points at ways in which such discharge could be implemented. This would bring the process of digital technology procurement back under the umbrella of agency-based regulation and reduce the expected dysfunctionality in leveraging procurement as a tool of digital technology gatekeeping through increased coherence in the regulatory logic.

2. Mapping the Logic of Public and Private Interactions in the Procurement of Digital Technologies

The regulation of procurement is primarily concerned with public-private interactions,[18] and with the creation of procedures and contractual mechanisms seeking to ensure that such interactions between the public buyer and market actors achieve public interest goals.[19] Procurement rules create a toolkit to facilitate and discipline public-private interactions throughout the process of identifying, shaping, and delivering solutions to satisfy public sector

[17] This classification of interactions stems from the theoretical framing of agency and gatekeeping, which is explored in Sections 2.1 and 2.2.

[18] Public-public interactions are generally exempted from procurement rules; see Willem A Janssen, *Public Procurement Law and Self-Organisation: A Nexus of Tensions and Reconciliations* (Eleven Publishers 2018).

[19] What the public interest exactly means or what it encompasses in this context is debatable and debated. For discussion, see Chapter 6, Section 2.

needs.[20] At one end of the spectrum, some procurement rules are rigid and create highly formalized processes with limited public-private interaction that is focused on a highly specified transaction (eg open procedures with detailed technical specifications). At the other end of the spectrum, some procurement rules are flexible and create adaptable spaces for rather unstructured and exploratory public-private collaboration and interaction (such as competitive dialogues or innovation partnerships), and for the public sector to interact with the market in largely unregulated and non-binding ways (eg market consultations).[21]

The public buyer's ability to extract advantages in its interaction with market actors depends on its capabilities and market power,[22] and on the extent to which it is able to generate meaningful competition for the public contract.[23] Procurement rules have increasingly sought to facilitate the aggregation or centralization of procurement to leverage more capabilities and to concentrate buying power so that the public buyer reaps more benefits from its market interactions,[24] or at least can exercise countervailing power where it confronts strongly positioned or dominant market agents.[25] Given the different types of public-private interactions and the different possible balances of power between the public buyer and market actors, procurement rules create a set of generally applicable safeguards that seek to ensure that the public interest is preserved in all types of market interactions (be they rigid or flexible). The primary logic in the regulation of procurement is thus oriented towards the protection of the public interest in the context of market-based economic transactions. In general, procurement rules presume the public buyer's ability to dictate the terms of the interaction, and to use tender and contract design to

[20] Along the same lines, with a critical view on this approach, see Karen Yeung, 'The New Public Analytics as an Emerging Paradigm in Public Sector Administration' (2022) 27(2) Tilburg Law Review 1, 27–28 (hereafter Yeung, 'New Public Analytics').

[21] See eg Elvira Uyarra and others, 'Barriers to Innovation Through Public Procurement: A Supplier Perspective' (2014) 34(10) Technovation 631.

[22] Which, relatedly, can generate important distortions in market dynamics and competition; see Albert Sanchez-Graells, *Public Procurement and the EU Competition Rules* (2nd edn, Hart Publishing 2015) 60–77 (hereafter Sanchez-Graells, *Public Procurement and Competition*).

[23] Sanchez-Graells, *Public Procurement and Competition* (n 22) 37 ff; Kirsi-Maria Halonen, 'Is Public Procurement Fit for Reaching Sustainability Goals? A Law and Economics Approach to Green Public Procurement' (2021) 28(4) Maastricht Journal of European and Comparative Law 535, 539.

[24] For discussion, see eg Albert Sanchez-Graells and Ignacio Herrera Anchustegui, 'Impact of Public Procurement Aggregation on Competition: Risks, Rationale and Justification for the Rules in Directive 2014/24' in R Fernandez and P Valcarcel (eds), *Centralizacion de compras publicas* (Civitas 2016) 129.

[25] This can be particularly important in digital technology industries; see Section 2.1.2. For broader discussion of countervailing market power, see Ignacio Herrera Anchustegui, *Buyer Power in EU Competition Law* (Concurrences 2017) 455–512.

foster the public interest—save in exceptional circumstances of market failure or absence of competition for other reasons.[26]

This regulatory logic has a relatively natural extension in the leveraging of procurement to pursue related public interests that go beyond the specific public-private interaction or transaction, such as the use of procurement to enforce environmental or social standards.[27] This adds or overlays a gatekeeping function in procurement regulation.[28] The public buyer is then not only expected to interact with the market in a way that adequately satisfies the identified public sector need, but also to use its market power to enforce other rules or standards or to create incentives for specific behaviours by the market actors with which it interacts.[29] This logic also rests on a presumption of superiority, as the public buyer is expected to be able to dictate the terms of the interaction with the market.[30] Generally, then, the addition of a gatekeeping or market-shaping function aimed at influencing the behaviour of market agents follows a similar logic to that of market-based interactions.

[26] This logic will create a potential 'weak public buyer' problem in some cases; see Section 2.1.2.

[27] Peter Trepte, *Regulating Procurement. Understanding the Ends and Means of Public Procurement Regulation* (OUP 2004) 13–14 (hereafter Trepte, *Regulating Procurement*). For detailed analysis, see Christopher McCrudden, *Buying Social Justice. Equality, Government Procurement, & Legal Change* (OUP 2007); Sue Arrowsmith and Peter Kunzlik (eds), *Social and Environmental Policies in EC Procurement Law. New Directives and New Directions* (CUP 2009); Roberto Caranta and Martin Trybus (eds), *The Law of Green and Social Procurement in Europe* (DJØF Publishing 2010); Albert Sanchez-Graells (ed), *Smart Public Procurement and Labour Standards. Pushing the Discussion after RegioPost* (Hart Publishing 2018).

[28] For discussion of the potential negative effects arising from such expansion of procurement's regulatory remit, see eg Pedro Telles, 'Applying Tirole's Socially Responsible Agencies Thesis to Public Procurement' (*telles.eu*, 11 May 2023) <http://www.telles.eu/blog/2023/5/11/applying-tiroles-socially-responsible-agencies-thesis-to-public-procurement> accessed 11 May 2023,with reference to Jean Tirole, 'Socially Responsible Agencies' (2023) 7(4) Competition Law & Policy Debate 171.

[29] There are points of contact between this approach, in particular the leveraging of market power to induce specific types of (non)market behaviour and the more general use of conditionality mechanisms for the purposes of EU governance through budgetary allocations 'with strings attached'; see Antonia Baraggia and Matteo Bonelli, 'Linking Money to Values: The New Rule of Law Conditionality Regulation and Its Constitutional Challenges' (2022) 23(2) German Law Journal 131. More narrowly, one of the conditions used by the EU to promote good governance in the expenditure of public funds concerns compliance with EU procurement law in the context of EU-funded projects, see Viorica Vita, 'The Rise of Spending Conditionality in the EU: What Can EU Learn from the U.S. Conditional Spending Doctrine and Policies?' (2017) EUI Working Papers LAW 2017/16, at 18 <https://cadmus.eui.eu/handle/1814/48644> accessed 6 February 2023. See also European Commission, 'Public Procurement Guidance for Practitioners on Avoiding the Most Common Errors in Projects Funded by the European Structural and Investment Funds' (2018) <https://ec.europa.eu/regional_policy/sources/wikiguidance/brochure_public_procurement_guidance_for_practitioners.pdf> accessed 6 February 2023.

[30] This will not always be the case and procurement rules tend to have exceptions to general gatekeeping requirements, such as the possibility of waiving exclusion grounds when there is only one potential supplier or an overriding public interest in the award of the contract to an otherwise excluded supplier; see Pascal Friton and Janis Zoll, 'Article 57—Exclusion Grounds' in Roberto Caranta and Albert Sanchez-Graells (eds), *European Public Procurement. Commentary on Directive 2014/24/EU* (Edward Elgar 2021) 588, 605 (hereafter Caranta and Sanchez-Graells, *Commentary*).

This general logic also underpins the related use of procurement as a tool of 'regulation by contract', whereby contractual requirements are imposed on economic operators to achieve specific goals in the implementation of the public contract.[31] This approach is heavily oriented towards disciplining the behaviour of economic operators, which are expected to be at the receiving end of unilaterally established tender conditions and contractual requirements. This setting thus also presumes public buyer (bargaining) superiority. This regulatory logic and its implications are further explored in Section 2.1.

The main claim in this section is that the proposals to leverage procurement to regulate public sector digitalization, which seek to use public sector market power and its gatekeeping role to enforce standards of technological regulation by embedding them in public contracts, are bound to generate significant dysfunction due to a break in regulatory logic. The proposals uncritically promote the extension of the above regulatory logic premised on vertical relationships where the public buyer holds a (presumed) superiority to an institutional setting where the procurement function has a different position. The proposals seem to presume that the public buyer can mandate not only the behaviour of the market agents providing the technology, but also the behaviour of the adopting public entity. The need to ensure adherence to the regulatory standards embedded in public contracts by the public sector entities seeking to adopt the technology is omitted in the proposals, perhaps on the presumption that they will have fully internalized the (public interest) regulatory goals entrusted to procurement as gatekeeper. This is far from a certainty, though.[32] The adopting public entity can have diverging goals, be captured, or more simply be

[31] There is a rich literature on regulation by contract, or government by contract, which are the two primary labels attached to this phenomenon in the UK. It should be noted that a significant part of this scholarship focuses on public law issues rather than the commercial determination of private behaviour. See eg Colin Turpin, *Government Contracts* (Penguin 1972) 244–59; Terence Daintith, 'Regulation by Contract—The Third Prerogative' (1979) 32(1) Current Legal Problems 41; Mark Freedland, 'Government by Contract and Public Law' [1994] Public Law 86; Hugh Collins, *Regulating Contracts* (OUP 1999) 303–20; Peter Vincent-Jones, *The New Public Contracting: Regulation, Responsiveness, Relationality* (OUP 2006) (hereafter Vincent-Jones, *New Public Contracting*); Anne CL Davies, *The Public Law of Government Contracts* (OUP 2008). For comparative considerations, see Jean-Bernard Auby, 'Contracting Out and "Public Values": A Theoretical and Comparative Approach' in Susan Rose-Ackerman, Peter L Lindseth, and Blake Emerson (eds), *Comparative Administrative Law* (2nd edn, Edward Elgar 2017) 552.

[32] For discussion on the drivers of technology adoption by the public sector and the limited or non-existent role of public values in that context, see eg Rohit Madan and Mona Ashok, 'A Public Values Perspective on the Application of Artificial Intelligence in Government Practices: A Synthesis of Case Studies' in Jose Ramon Saura and Felipe Debasa (eds), *Handbook of Research on Artificial Intelligence in Government Practices and Processes* (IGI Global Publishing 2022) 162. For broader discussion, see eg Theresa Züger and Hadi Asghari, 'AI for the Public. How Public Interest Theory Shifts the Discourse on AI' (2022) AI & Society <https://doi.org/10.1007/s00146-022-01480-5> accessed 3 February 2023.

unable to manage the complexity of those regulatory goals.[33] Moreover, the (in)ability of the procurement function to ensure adherence to the overarching goals of digital regulation where the public entity sought to deviate from them during the contract implementation phase is also largely ignored. These omissions pose a problem because the regulatory logic described above does not necessarily or easily extend to interactions between the procurement function and the adopting public sector entities.

Notably, the public buyer is rarely, if ever, in a position of superiority over other public sector entities. To the contrary, the regulatory logic underpinning procurement regulation presumes a subordination of the public buyer to a principal, as will be explored in Section 2.2. Moreover, the regulatory logic breaks down where procurement's gatekeeping function is not (solely) expected to generate effects through market interactions, but rather to influence the behaviour of other actors. Notably, that of entities in the public sector with which it does not interact through market-based mechanisms, but rather based on hierarchical principles or related mechanisms of inter-administrative collaboration. In that regard, considering the institutional embeddedness of the procurement function, either within a bureaucratic hierarchy or one step removed but still within the larger public sector (eg in the case of central purchasing bodies, or ad hoc collaborative procurement projects) is highly relevant. A lack of independence of the procurement function will immediately raise questions about its suitability for a gatekeeping role.[34] Additionally, there are important timing and commitment issues in that procurement is not geared towards disciplining behaviour that results from the future interaction between the adopting public sector entity and the tech provider under the regulatory contract,[35] as discussed in Section 2.3.

It is submitted that this breakdown in regulatory logic is at the root of an expected dysfunctionality in leveraging procurement as a tool of digital technology 'regulation by contract'. The position that promotes the leveraging of procurement to that end seems to be based on a presumption that the only behaviour that requires disciplining is that of the technological provider. Implicitly, under that view, imposing stringent contractual obligations on the tech provider is presumed to suffice to ensure the attainment of the desired

[33] These issues are not unique to the use of procurement for the purposes of digital regulation, but can affect any instances of gatekeeping through procurement where the goals are contested or complex, and there is thus a risk of goal conflict or capture of the public sector entity along the lines discussed here.

[34] For discussion of *dependent* gatekeepers in the context of corporate finance, see Arthur B Laby, 'Differentiating Gatekeepers' (2006) 1 Brooklyn Journal of Corporate, Financial & Commercial Law 119.

[35] See n 10 and accompanying text.

regulatory goals. Setting aside for now the difficulties in specifying such (contractual) obligations (see Chapter 4), the analysis in this section will show that this is far from the case. Effective regulation by contract of public sector digitalization does not only require disciplining the behaviour of the public contractor, but also and crucially that of the adopting public sector entity. As Section 2.2.2 will show, risks of policy entrepreneurship and regulatory capture highlight the importance of constraining the behaviour of the public entity seeking to adopt a digital technology. It is important because the public sector entity will be able to influence the interpretation and enforcement of the contract on the tech provider at a stage where the procurement function has no possibility of affecting the outcome.[36]

To provide more detailed analysis, this section explores the roles of procurement in the context of public-private, public-public, and decentred interactions. It shows how they follow the different regulatory logics of agency and gatekeeping. In doing so, the section also considers the potential 'weak public buyer' problem, risks of policy entrepreneurship and regulatory capture, and the impact of different modes of institutional embeddedness of the procurement function on such interactions. Section 3 will then explore the implications of the overlay of roles and the tension between competing logics in 'two-sided gatekeeping'.

2.1 Public-Private Market Interactions, and the 'Weak Public Buyer' Problem

2.1.1 Public-private market interactions

Given that the public sector will rarely develop digital technologies in-house, pragmatically, public sector digitalization involves interactions with economic operators seeking to provide technological solutions and related services to support that process.[37] This is the type of market-based interactions that frame

[36] For consideration of how the institutional embeddedness of procurement can alter this analysis, especially where the same organization (or individual/s) are tasked with procurement and contract administration, see n 84 and accompanying text. Given that this book will propose discharging procurement from the regulatory gatekeeping goal (see Section 4 and Chapter 5), this issue does not require more detailed analysis.

[37] In cases where the public sector did develop such solutions, the public sector tech provider would take the position of the private provider in our model. In the absence of specific rules governing this type of inter-administrative relationship, the governance challenges would be similar, although the peculiarities of the market position of the in-house provider would need assessing. A detailed analysis of such issues exceeds the scope of this chapter. This chapter can also not address in detail the complexities that arise from digital supply chains and will presume interaction with the tech provider closest to the public buyer only. For analysis of regulatory challenges concerning digital supply chains, see Ian

procurement regulation.[38] As mentioned above, the public buyer is meant to use tenders and negotiations leading to the award of public contracts, and the design of those public contracts, as mechanisms to generate value for money in public expenditure. Procurement rules provide a toolkit for the public buyer to design and manage such market interactions, while imposing a set of requirements aimed at implementing good governance standards to foster the integrity, efficiency, and objectivity of the procurement process.[39] Given known risks of malfunctioning and capture of this market-based mechanism, procurement rules include specific safeguards, such as rules on conflicts of interest, or pro-competitive requirements.[40] These safeguards and requirements ultimately seek to ensure that procurement is carried out at arms' length and objectively, and that its outcomes reflect market conditions as a key public interest guarantee. This conceptualization of procurement is generally based on a vertical understanding of the public-private interaction, with the public buyer on top, holding control over significant aspects of tender and contract design.[41]

This same position of (presumed) superiority of the public buyer underpins the gatekeeping role assigned to the procurement function.[42] In that role, procurement is expected to act as a check on the (general, past) behaviour of economic agents through differential access to public tenders.[43] Such a check can concern, for example, compliance with social, labour, and environmental legislation, compliance with tax, social security, and legislation closely linked to the public sector's financial interests, or legislation (eg criminal law) and professional standards with a bearing on the reliability of the economic operators or with implications for the intended market signalling by the public sector as a 'responsible buyer' imposing specific standards of behaviour as

Brown, 'Allocating Accountability in AI Supply Chains' (2023) Ada Lovelace Institute Expert Explainer <https://www.adalovelaceinstitute.org/resource/ai-supply-chains/> accessed 30 June 2023.

38 Sanchez-Graells, *Public Procurement and Competition* (n 22) 37 ff.

39 See n 19.

40 These requirements have been enshrined at all levels of procurement regulation, and feature prominently in the United Nations Convention Against Corruption (art 9). See UNCITRAL, 'United Nations Convention against Corruption: implementing procurement-related aspects' (2008) <https://digitallibrary.un.org/record/623202> accessed 7 February 2023. See also OECD, 'Recommendation on public procurement' (2015) <https://www.oecd.org/gov/public-procurement/recommendation/>, and OECD, 'Recommendation on fighting bid rigging in public procurement' (2012) <https://legalinstruments.oecd.org/en/instruments/OECD-LEGAL-0396> both accessed 7 February 2023.

41 See Section 2.1.2 for discussion of the potential 'weak public buyer' problem under this regulatory logic.

42 See n 27.

43 Generally, on gatekeeping, see Reiner H Kraakman, 'Gatekeepers: The Anatomy of a Third-Party Enforcement Strategy' (1986) 2 Journal of Law, Economics and Organization 53; see also John C Coffee, *Gatekeepers: The Professions and Corporate Governance* (OUP 2006).

'soft' regulation. Under this approach, the procurement function is expected to monitor the level of compliance with general or sectoral (non-procurement) legislation and to sift compliant from non-compliant economic actors as a matter of, for example, qualitative selection leading to access to (or exclusion from) the public tender.[44]

In most cases, this gatekeeping role does not comprise an independent regulatory dimension, in the sense that the public buyer is solely expected to check compliance with pre-existing (and clearly defined legal) standards that can (or should) be attested through documentary evidence. Procurement is not expected to set those standards.[45] In that regard, procurement can be seen as a complementary enforcement mechanism to reinforce (or, in some cases, substitute for) those specific to the relevant legislative or regulatory framework. Where there are complexities in the obtention, (translation), and interpretation of the documentation, or where discharging the gatekeeping role requires burdensome duties of investigation, the desirability and effectiveness of this approach can be doubted.[46] However, this approach is still premised on the vertical understanding of the relationship between public buyer and economic operators.

The same type of vertical (transactional) interaction underpins the approach to leveraging procurement as a tool of 'regulation by contract',[47] with procurement processes and the ensuing public contracts expected to mandate (specific, future) behaviour on the part of the economic agents engaged as public contractors—especially within the confines of the execution of a given public contract, but sometimes more generally in their market activities. When this role includes a regulatory component—whereby the public buyer independently sets the relevant standards or norms—this is also premised on the presumed vertical nature of the relationship.

[44] See eg Pascal Friton and Janis Zoll, 'Article 56—Choice of Participants and Award of Contracts' in Caranta and Sanchez-Graells, *Commentary* (n 30) 565, 574–76.

[45] As mentioned above (n 7) there will be circumstances where procurement may be *de facto* setting standards in relation with its gatekeeping role, eg when there are several standards from which a choice can be made, or where procurement develops requirements that clarify or build on higher-level requirements or standards. However, this issue is closely linked to the extent to which procurement can be prescriptive in setting those requirements and will thus be assessed in Chapter 4.

[46] For discussion, see Pedro Telles and Grith Skovgaard Ølykke, 'Sustainable Procurement: A Compliance Perspective of EU Public Procurement Law' (2017) 12 European Procurement & Public Private Partnership Law Review 239; Albert Sanchez-Graells, 'Truly Competitive Public Procurement as a Europe 2020 Lever: What Role for the Principle of Competition in Moderating Horizontal Policies?' (2016) 22(2) European Public Law Journal 377; Albert Sanchez-Graells, 'Regulatory Substitution Between Labour and Public Procurement Law: The EU's Shifting Approach to Enforcing Labour Standards in Public Contracts' (2018) 24(2) European Public Law Journal 229.

[47] See n 31.

Overall, despite the different lenses used in market-based, gatekeeping, and 'regulation by contract' approaches, public-private interactions are conceptualized as vertical, in the sense that the public buyer is presumed to hold a position of (functional) superiority. This vertical logic is intrinsic to the use of procurement as a means of 'regulation by contract' and will be key to the assessment of overlaid agency and gatekeeping duties in Section 3. However, the effectiveness of these approaches depends on the ability of the public buyer to mandate, scrutinize, and monitor the general (market, past) and specific (contractual, future) behaviour of the public contractor. This creates a potential 'weak public buyer' problem.

2.1.2 The 'weak public buyer' problem

Section 2.1.1 has evidenced that the regulatory logic underpinning procurement rules aimed at public-private interactions rests on the public buyer's ability to dictate the terms of such market interactions and the ensuing contractual relationships. Where the public buyer is not in such position, the effectiveness of this regulatory approach is undermined. A 'weak public buyer' may be unable to extract many (or any) benefits from its interaction with the market when it faces agents with strong or dominant market positions,[48] when there is no competitive supply for the desired (regulated) supplies,[49] or when the public buyer is at such an informational disadvantage that it cannot meaningfully exercise its buying power.[50]

In the context of the leveraging of procurement for digital technology regulation, it seems that there are two main potential sources of weakness in the public buyer's position. The first one concerns the market power of digital tech providers. Digital technology industries, and in particular the Artificial Intelligence (AI) industry, show a tendency towards concentration.[51] These are also industries where a quickly growing thicket of intellectual property rights and protected know-how can generate (apparent) exclusivity of specific

[48] Gale Raj-Reichert, Cornelia Staritz, and Leonhard Plank, 'Conceptualizing the Regulator-Buyer State in the European Union for the Exercise of Socially Responsible Public Procurement in Global Production Networks' (2022) 60(3) Journal of Common Market Studies 759, 773.

[49] ibid 775.

[50] For discussion of the importance of information, knowledge, and expertise in procurement's market-shaping role, see Fiona A Miller and Pascale Lehoux, 'The Innovation Impacts of Public Procurement Offices: The Case of Healthcare Procurement' (2020) 49(7) Research Policy 104075. This also relates to the public buyer's capability to effectively design digital regulation for the purposes of putting the existing tools and processes into play, which is explored in Chapter 4.

[51] Federico Boffa and others, 'Industry Dynamics in Digital Markets' (2022) 49(3) Journal of Industrial and Business Economics 401.

technological applications, leading to a deactivation of procurement rules seeking to generate competition for the public contract.[52] This can place the public buyer in a weak (relative) position and turn it into a rule-taker, rather than a rule-maker.[53] The second source of weakness concerns information asymmetries exacerbated by a gap in the public sector's digital capability,[54] which can not only reduce the effectiveness of the public buyer's bargaining position, but also weaken its ability to effectively design tender and contractual requirements to channel the overarching regulatory goals into actionable implementation measures. Both sources can, of course, interact and generate combined weaknesses in the public buyer. In the digital technology space, there have already been clear examples of such a situation, including in relation to the public buyer's ineffectiveness in altering the general terms and conditions offered by tech providers.[55]

By itself, the 'weak public buyer' problem raises an important challenge for the use of procurement as a tool of digital regulation. Some governance measures can be implemented to minimize it, such as (further) procurement centralization and the investment in a significant digital upskilling of the (centralized) procurement function. However, those measures would generate additional governance challenges[56] and, in general, seem unlikely to sufficiently (or efficiently) address the potential market power imbalance and information asymmetries between the procurement function and tech providers. The questions that arise about the likely effectiveness of procurement's regulatory gatekeeping and market-shaping role in relation to public-private interactions already point to the need for an alternative regulatory approach, which will be explored in Section 4. That notwithstanding, for analytical purposes, the remainder of Section 2 and Section 3 leave aside the 'weak public buyer' problem.

[52] For discussion, see Chapter 4, Section 2.3.

[53] For related discussion, see Sandra G Hamilton, 'Public Procurement—Price-Taker or Market-Shaper?' (2022) 18(4) Critical Perspectives on International Business 574; Trepte, *Regulating Procurement* (n 27) 112–18.

[54] See Chapter 6, Section 5.3. See also Albert Sanchez-Graells, 'Procuring AI Without Understanding It. Way To Go?' (*howtocrackanut.com*, 4 April 2023) <https://www.howtocrackanut.com/blog/2023/3/31/uk-pro-innovation-ai-regulation-wont-do> accessed 7 April 2023.

[55] Kevin McGillivray, *Government Cloud Procurement. Contracts, Data Protection, and the Quest for Compliance* (CUP 2022) 196 ff.

[56] Those would result from the institutional dynamics governing decision-making by the centralized purchasing body or similar entity, which depend on its organizational design, funding model, etc and would further compound the issues discussed in Section 2.2.3. For discussion, see Albert Sanchez-Graells, 'Competition Implications of Procurement Digitalisation and the Procurement of Digital Technologies by Central Purchasing Bodies' (2023) <https://ssrn.com/abstract=4376037> accessed 12 April 2023.

2.2 Public-Public Interactions, Capture, and Procurement's Institutional Embeddedness

2.2.1 Public-public interactions

Section 2.1 has explored the logic of public-private interactions. This section turns its attention to the perhaps less visible public-public interactions taking place in the background of the procurement of digital technologies, between the public entity seeking to adopt a digital technology and the procurement function.[57] Such interactions are best framed in terms of agency relationships,[58] and are also conceptualized as vertical. From this perspective, the public buyer acts as the agent of a higher-level principal—in our model, the adopting public entity. In this understanding, agency theory places the public buyer in a subordinated position and explains the governance challenges in aligning the agent's incentives to the principal's goals,[59] as well as the governance difficulties that arise from any misalignment between the (policy) interests of principal and agent.[60] Agency theory is concerned with the agent's discretion, a primary focus of procurement regulation.[61]

The added complexity in the context of the procurement of digital technologies is that the regulatory gatekeeping role assigned to the agent (the public buyer) unavoidably encompasses the disciplining of (future) aspects of public sector behaviour and decision-making by its principal (the adopting public entity)—for example, in relation to decisions on data governance or technology management frameworks related to the deployment of the required digital technology.[62] This would place the public buyer in a position of (functional) superiority, in that it would (be expected to) be able to dictate

[57] As mentioned above in text accompanying n, for the analysis of the governance of public sector digitalization, it is useful to (at least notionally) separate the public buyer or procurement function as a distinct agent, acting on behalf of the public sector entity seeking to adopt a given digital technology (but see Section 2.2.3 on institutional embeddedness).

[58] Trepte, *Regulating Procurement* (n 27) 70–111; Christopher R Yukins, 'A Versatile Prism: Assessing Procurement Law Through the Principal-Agent Model' (2010) 40(1) Public Contract Law Journal 63; Sanchez-Graells, *Public Procurement and Competition* (n 22) 56–58.

[59] Conceptually, this can be framed in terms of the theory of delegation. For a law and economics assessment, see Robert D Cooter and Michael D Gilbert, *Public Law and Economics* (OUP 2022) 265 ff.

[60] The issue is parallel to the tensions arising within other forms of contractualized governance where there is a misalignment between central and devolved government units, when the latter is entrusted with the procurement or contracting out of public services. For discussion, see Peter Vincent-Jones, 'The New Public Contracting: Public Versus Private Ordering?' (2007) 14(2) Indiana Journal of Global Legal Studies 259, 269 (hereafter Vincent-Jones, 'Public Versus Private Ordering?').

[61] See Xavier Groussot, Jörgen Hettne, and Sanja Bogojevic (eds), *Law and Discretion in EU Public Procurement* (Hart Publishing 2019).

[62] It is possible that some of these decisions are conditioned by other (non-procurement) frameworks, eg of technological assessment. However, this issue is not explored in detail because any constraints derived from those frameworks would still be external to procurement.

(some of) the terms of the technological adoption. Thus, gatekeeping implicitly requires a reversal of positions within the vertical relationship between the adopting public entity and the public buyer, and flips agency theory on its head.[63]

Ultimately, both public-public interactions between the public buyer and the adopting public entity are conceived in a vertical fashion, but agency and gatekeeping frameworks operate on an opposite understanding of which actor holds a predominant position. Under agency theory, the public buyer is the agent and thus subject to the instructions of the public entity that will ultimately adopt the digital technology. The public buyer is thus mainly tasked with procuring what the entity requires for its operations in the best possible market terms. Conversely, under gatekeeping theory, the public buyer is the (independent) guarantor of a set of goals or attributes in public sector digitalization projects and is thus tasked with ensuring compliance therewith. This could require, for example, directing the public entity to revisit and modify, or even abandon, a digitalization project where the planned implementation falls short of ensuring compliance with the required goals and attributes.

This generates structural tensions, conflicts of interest,[64] and governance challenges that procurement rules are not well-prepared for—as procurement law is primarily designed on the paradigm of a market-based mechanism (see Section 2.1), rather than as an internal tool of public sector governance. It is unclear, for example, whether the procurement function can query (or stop) a digitalization project, for example because of the inadequate content of the impact assessments carried out by the adopting public sector entity, or on the basis of the inadequate management of other digital tools already deployed. The public-public relationship between the adopting public entity and the public function is not regulated by the procurement rules,[65] which places the procurement function in an awkward position when tasked with ensuring compliance with specific standards or expectations by public sector actors for which it is simultaneously expected to function as agent.

[63] Or, at the very least, requires a horizontal repositioning, if the gatekeeping function is meant to be collaborative.

[64] With implications in many different dimensions; see eg the discussion of structural conflicts of interest in relation to second party assurance mechanisms in Chapter 9, Section 3.2.

[65] This is due to a lack of a legal or (explicit) contractual framework. For general discussion of the use of contractual governance to regulate public-public relationships, see Vincent-Jones, *New Public Contracting* (n 31) 141–66 and 321–23. It is possible that several different types of rules, ranging from eg general administrative law to budgetary law, could apply to the public-public relationship. However, such an analysis exceeds the scope of this chapter.

2.2.2 The adopting public sector entity as a potentially captured principal

As mentioned in Section 2.1, the potential conflict between the procurement function and the adopting public sector entity is usually not acknowledged as a regulatory challenge. This could result from a presumption that, as the goals of digital regulation are concerned, both actors are in full alignment because, after all, they are both embedded within the public sector and should thus share a commitment to such goals. However, this is a problematic presumption because existing theories of governance—and in particular garbage can theory[66]—show us that the adopting public sector entity is particularly exposed to risks that would trigger a deviation from such regulatory goals, due to the allure and 'policy irresistibility' that digital technologies generate in a context of policy- and decision-making characterized by top-down pressures, reinforcing effects between different policy strands in the digitalization of the public sector, and limited institutional capacity.[67] Combined with insights from policy entrepreneurship[68] and regulatory capture theory,[69] this subsection highlights governance risks in this setting that underpin the potential for conflict between the procurement function and the adopting public sector entity.

Garbage can theory explains the institutional dynamics of 'organized anarchies'. These are organizations with a combination of: (1) problematic preferences, that is, 'a variety of inconsistent and ill-defined preferences'[70] whereby the organization 'discovers preferences through action more than it acts on the basis of preferences';[71] (2) unclear technology, whereby the organization 'operates on the basis of simple trial-and-error procedures, the residue of learning from the accidents of past experience, and pragmatic inventions of necessity';[72] and (3) fluid participation, whereby participants in decision-making 'vary in the time and effort they devote to different domains'[73] and change capriciously for any particular kind of choice. It is submitted that most public sector institutions, and especially those with a policymaking remit related to public

[66] Michael D Cohen, James G March, and Johan P Olsen, 'A Garbage Can Model of Organizational Choice' (1972) 17 Administrative Science Quarterly 1 (hereafter Cohen and others, 'Garbage Can').

[67] This is explored, in detail, in the case study on procurement digitalization. See Chapter 6.

[68] Michael Mintrom, 'Policy Entrepreneurs and Dynamic Change' in M Ramesh and others (eds), *Cambridge Elements in Public Policy* (CUP 2020) <http://www.cambridge.org/9781108461467> accessed 7 September 2022.

[69] Andrea Saltelli and others, 'Science, the Endless Frontier of Regulatory Capture' (2022) 135 Futures 102860.

[70] Cohen and others, 'Garbage Can' (n 66) 1.

[71] ibid.

[72] ibid.

[73] ibid 1.

sector digitalization,[74] are examples of such organized anarchy. This is due to the complexity and lack of clarity on how to balance competing goals, the lack of clarity on how public sector digitalization should proceed, as well as the fluid participation of several actors in multi-level governance settings.

The 'garbage can process is one in which problems, solutions and participants move from one choice opportunity to another in such a way that the nature of choice, the time it takes, and the problems it solves all depend on a relatively complicated intermeshing of elements';[75] where 'decision-making in the public sector ... reflects the serendipitous, and almost accidental, confluence of streams of problems, solutions, opportunities and actors'.[76] In other words, it is a model of decision-making where 'solutions go looking for problems with which to link'.[77] As extended to policymaking, the model stresses the importance of 'windows of opportunity' for policy formulation and implementation, when there is alignment between the parallel movements of problems and solutions.[78] When those policy windows open, 'policy entrepreneurs must be prepared to exploit the opportunities'.[79]

Relatedly, such policy entrepreneurs can be either internal, or external. First, where a window of opportunity is seized by an internal policy entrepreneur, there is a risk that the views of that individual (or small group) will determine the decisions of the institution. In the context of digitalization, there is a clear risk that decisions are in this way determined by those with higher levels of digital expertise, which may hold idiosyncratic views on the overarching regulatory goals and their importance. Given the specific motivations of those policy entrepreneurs, there is scope for conflict between such motivations and the overarching regulatory goals—for example, a results-driven policy entrepreneur could minimize the relevance of regulatory constraints that affected the technical performance of a given technological deployment, or more simply 'cut corners' to deliver a specific functionality. Second, windows of opportunity can be exploited by external agents, and especially by tech providers

[74] The applicability of the model to EU policymaking generally supports this approach; Jeremy Richardson, *Policy-Making in the EU. Interests, Ideas and Garbage Cans of Primeval Soup* (Taylor & Francis 1996).

[75] Cohen and others, 'Garbage Can' (n 66) 16.

[76] B Guy Peters, 'Governance: A Garbage Can Perspective' (2002) Vienna Institute for Advanced Studies, Political Science Series Num 84, 13 <https://aei.pitt.edu/347/1/wp_84.pdf> accessed 8 September 2022 (hereafter Peters, 'Garbage Can').

[77] Cary Coglianese and Daniel E Walters, 'Agenda-Setting in the Regulatory State: Theory and Evidence' (2016) 68 Administrative Law Review 93, 97.

[78] John W Kingdon, *Agendas, Alternatives and Public Policies* (Harper Collins 1984) 21.

[79] Peters, 'Garbage Can' (n 76) 13. Ryan Hagemann, Jennifer Huddleston Skees, and Adam Thierer, 'Soft Law for Hard Problems: The Governance of Emerging Technologies in an Uncertain Future' (2018) 17(1) Colorado Technology Law Journal 37, 107–10.

seeking to be awarded public contracts for the provision of technology solutions. Where the potential provider manages to persuade the public sector entity that its solution is the best that can do what is required, or that it is the only possible solution, there is clearly scope for clashes between the public sector entity and the procurement function. There are also more subtle ways in which the public sector entity can be captured to steer its decision-making towards specific forms of digitalization.

Therefore, there is significant scope for deviation from the overarching regulatory goals by the public sector entity, either as a result of policy entrepreneurship, regulatory capture, or other sources of friction (eg operational requirements, budgetary constraints, etc). This stresses the need for the procurement function not solely to discipline the behaviour of the tech provider, but also that of the adopting public sector entity. In other words, this stresses that the regulatory gatekeeping is challenging in relation to public-public interactions, as much as in public-private interactions.

2.2.3 Procurement's institutional embeddedness

At this point, it is important to consider the institutional embeddedness of the procurement function. The structural conflict identified in Section 2.2.1 and the challenges outlined in Section 2.2.2 can be exacerbated by organizational structures. Despite considering the public buyer as a separate agent for the purpose of isolating its *regulatory role*, in reality, it is hardly ever the case that procurement is carried out by an entirely separate organization. Procurement is usually carried out by a unit or team within the public entity seeking to adopt the technology, which places it within a hierarchical organization and thus with limited (functional) independence.[80] As a result of the process of procurement centralization, or in the context of collaborative procurement, it is possible for procurement to be carried out by a separate organization. However, in that case, the organizational relationship will still be highly dependent on the interests of the adopting public entity. In the case of collaborative procurement, the governance of the arrangement will generally be subject to veto by the adopting public entity. In the case of centralized procurement, barring the mandatory use of centralized frameworks or

[80] This scenario can be further complicated where the procurement is outsourced to consultants, which would add an additional layer of principal-agent issues in the functioning and decision-making of the adopting public entity. If anything, such a structure could be expected to amplify the risks identified in Section 2.2.2. Therefore, this specific (sub)scenario does not require further assessment, especially in view of the proposals advanced in Section 4—which would mitigate against such heightened risks by imposing external oversight and mandatory requirements that would bind the consultants carrying out the outsourced procurement.

other procurement vehicles, the adopting entity retains the decision whether to partake in any centralized or collaborative procurement procedure. And, in any case, it generally retains discretion for the organization of relevant aspects of the tender (call-offs or mini-competitions) and, possibly, of the negotiation of specific aspects of the resulting public contract. This reduces the possibility for the centralized or collaborative procurement function to dictate the terms to the adopting public entity,[81] which generally retains discretion to conduct a separate procurement or, at the very least, to tailor the use of the centralized tools.

The implication of such institutional embeddedness is that, where the procurement function sits within the same administrative unit or organization as the adopting entity, the gatekeeping role will be substantially affected and potentially jeopardized, if not neutralized, by the hierarchical functioning of that unit—and it can well be that the gatekeeping role is thus driven by policy entrepreneurship or commercial capture. In any such case, a lack of independence of the procurement function undermines the integrity and likely effectiveness of the gatekeeping. Similarly, where the procurement function is detached from the adopting public entity—for example in the case of a central purchasing body or collaborative procurement—the discretion retained by the adopting entity and competing commercial interests can erode the integrity of the gatekeeping function, even if a lower level of dependence can be expected. Simultaneously, other institutional aspects (eg centralization and thus standardization of requirements) can also reduce the effectiveness of the gatekeeping through blanket measures incapable of sufficient adaptation to the case at hand. This can be particularly relevant in the process of adoption of digital technologies given the potentially very high levels of customization required at the point of deployment.

An additional consideration is that the institutional embeddedness of the procurement function needs to be understood in its decentralized context. There is no single procurement function or public buyer, but rather a large multiplicity of them, embedded within different institutional contexts and, importantly, with large variations in terms of (digital) capacity, experience, specialization, inter- and intra-institutional dynamics, etc. This raises further questions on the ability of the procurement function to discipline the behaviour of its principal in any given institutional setting, as it will be highly context dependent.

[81] Moreover, there are additional governance challenges and competing (commercial) incentives that detract from the ability of the central purchasing body to act as an independent regulator; see n 56.

This institutional reality evidences the breakdown in regulatory logic mentioned at the start of Section 2. The lack of functional independence and the atomization of the procurement function raise important questions on the likely effectiveness of the approach to regulate public sector digitalization through procurement, at least as the *public sector side* of the transaction is concerned, which adds to the potential 'weak public buyer' problem. Overall, despite the common vertical conceptualization of public-public interactions, there is a structural tension between agency and gatekeeping approaches in this setting, which will be key to the assessment of overlaid agency and gatekeeping duties in Section 3. Such tension also needs to be considered in relation to decentred interactions between the adopting entity and the tech provider, as analysed in Section 2.3.

2.3 Decentred Interactions

Indeed, a further complication from the perspective of the regulatory logic of procurement is that it presumes the centrality (or at least the direct participation) of the public buyer in the relevant public-private and public-public interactions. The procurement function is conceptualized as the principal, agent, or gatekeeper (or given multiple roles) and is always present in the understanding of the interactions that underpins the relevant rules. However, in leveraging procurement to regulate by contract public sector digitalization, the system would be creating decentred (public-private) interactions. In those, the public sector entity and the public contractor would be jointly shaping the effective deployment of the technological solutions in a way that cannot be monitored or adequately influenced by the procurement function.[82]

This is not only the direct result of the impossibility of regulating technological development and deployment through rigid rules and the unavoidable use of open-ended and/or under-specified standards (to varying degrees).[83] It is also the result of the impossibility of forcing commitment to a strict (or demanding) interpretation of those standards by both the adopting entity and the tech provider at the contract implementation phase, coupled with the retraction or entire disappearance of the procurement function from that contractual

[82] This is the case because the regulatory remit of procurement rules and procedures largely finish at the point of contract award. See Section 1.

[83] See Chapter 4, Section 3.2.1. See also Hadrien Pouget, 'The EU's AI Act Is Barreling Toward AI Standards That Do Not Exist' (*Lawfare*, 12 January 2023) <https://www.lawfareblog.com/eus-ai-act-barreling-toward-ai-standards-do-not-exist> accessed 2 February 2023.

regulatory space. Usually, the involvement of the procurement function ceases with the award of the contract. And, even if there is ongoing involvement of the procurement function in contract execution due to the specific organization of the relevant public sector entity, conflicting (operational and commercial) interests are likely to condition or preclude effective continuous oversight from a gatekeeping perspective.[84] Given the adopting entity's interest in the deployment of the technology, it (and a procurement function embedded within it) is not in an adequate position to effectively perform a gatekeeping role.[85]

This decentring of decision-making creates a significant element of uncertainty (or rather, a moving target) for the procurement function, as regulatory gatekeeper, at the point of choosing specific tools to foster compliance with the regulatory contract.[86] As specific goals or obligations can straddle the public/private divide, it may not be easy, or possible, to identify the appropriate setting or mechanism to regulate them. In the specific context of digital technology adoption, the procurement function may be unable, at the point of designing the contract for the development and deployment of the technology, to ascertain how the adopting entity will take decisions with a significant bearing on the outcome of the process of digitalization and its compliance (or not) with the desired attributes and goals underpinning the gatekeeping function. This will be the case where, for example, the procurement is launched at an early stage of exploration of technological alternatives. Notably, it will also be the case in all (common) instances where the deployment of the technology requires significant tailoring to the specific context and needs of the adopting entity, with crucial decisions on, for example, transparency or explainability left to later stages or, potentially, to decisions of the tech provider.[87]

In theory, the procurement process could result in a contract that imposed obligations on both the adopting entity and the tech provider—indeed, the uncertainty mentioned above would likely push for a rigid contractual design. However, in practice, it will not be possible to come up with operationally adequate strict rules and the (contractualized) regulation of the technology will need to remain standards-based (see Chapter 4). This implies that compliance with such obligations will depend on the willingness of the adopting entity and

[84] In fact, where the same organization (or individual/s) is tasked with carrying out the procurement and overseeing contract implementation, the anticipated conflict of goals resulting from tender and contract design 'in the shadow' of implementation concerns would further weaken the gatekeeping role, independently of the public/private interaction issue.

[85] This relates to the issue of second party assurance mechanisms discussed in Chapter 9, Section 3.2.

[86] See Chapter 4, Section 4.

[87] This raises further risks of commercial determination where such aspects cannot be determined at tender stage and depend on implementation decisions. See Chapter 4, Section 3.2.

the tech provider to abide by the contract as interpreted or expected by the public buyer (as regulator). This is not necessarily a given outcome.

It is indeed by no means clear that the adopting public entity will have the right incentives (or resources) to adhere to the overarching regulatory goals and the desirable goals and attributes of the technological deployment,[88] or that the tech provider will have the incentives (or resources) to force such adherence on the part of the adopting public entity.[89] Moreover, even if the adopting entity was in principle committed to the relevant (contractualized) regulatory goals, its behaviour can be (partly or totally) influenced, determined, or functionally delegated to the tech provider. This is especially the case where compliance with the regulatory goals depends on decisions to be taken during the execution of the public contract (eg on the specific mechanisms to operationalize the explainability requirements of the specific technical solution chosen to perform the contract), or depend on self-assessments by the tech provider. Further, it is possible that both the adopting entity and the tech provider find it in their common interest to ignore or bypass the contractual obligations and deviate from the regulatory goals (eg through the implementation of a less than fully explainable technological solution), in which case the question arises of who would have the incentives and effective possibility of enforcing the contractual terms on both the adopting public entity and the tech provider. This is a rather different enforcement challenge than that of the 'standard' understanding of the use of 'regulation by contract', as the latter presumes that the interests of the contracting parties are opposed, and thus not usually susceptible of alignment contrary to contractual terms, because those terms have been imposed by the principal or result from a common approach under more relational understandings of contracting.[90]

This points to a difficult interaction between the tools that the public buyer can deploy to try to impose specific behaviour on the tech provider through the public contract, and the unregulated and institutionally-driven nature of the public-public interaction, which can leave the procurement function with no

[88] Not least due to risks of capture; see Trepte, *Regulating Procurement* (n 27) 82–83. See Section 2.2.2. For further discussion of the specific risks attached to the 'policy irresistibility' of digital solutions, see Chapter 6. See also Yeung, 'New Public Analytics' (n 20) 29.

[89] This is compatible with the understanding that economic operators generally have an embedded interest in monitoring and seeking enforcement of procurement rules and contracts, as that will only happen when such enforcement is aligned with their own interests; see Trepte, *Regulating Procurement* (n 27) 18.

[90] For discussion of the need to inculcate the contractual agent with elements of institutional morality in the discharge of public functions, thus presuming a clear contrast between the interests of principal and agent in most contractualized governance regimes, see eg Vincent-Jones, 'Public Versus Private Ordering?' (n 60) 273, and Peter Vincent-Jones, 'Citizen Redress in Public Contracting for Human Services' (2005) 68 Modern Law Review 887, 918.

means to effectively influence decision-making by the adopting public entity once the procurement is completed. This is important because the adopting entity is bound to become the principal of the regulatory contract. Differently from other types of 'regulation by contract' where the obligations are solely incumbent upon the public contractor as agent, in this setting the obligations would (also) be incumbent on the contractual principal and thus, potentially seen as an unwanted constraint on the way it digitalizes (and thus, carries out) its operations.[91] The next section will further the analysis and reflect on the interactions and tensions between the overlaid agency and gatekeeping duties incumbent on the procurement function.

3. Overlaid Agency and Gatekeeping Duties: Two-Sided Gatekeeping?

By placing the focus on the multiple public and private interactions that take place in the regulation of public sector digitalization by contract, the analysis in Section 2 has shown how, in addition to the well-known potential 'weak public buyer' problem, the emergent approach to digital technology 'regulation by contract' creates what can be labelled as a 'two-sided gatekeeping' challenge. This challenge encapsulates the difficulties for the procurement function to effectively influence regulatory outcomes where it needs to discipline both the behaviour of tech providers and adopting entities in the public sector, and where contract implementation depends on the decentred interaction of those two actors with the procurement function as a (toothless) bystander. To recapitulate, this challenge stems from two main characteristics of the model that do not fit with the need for the procurement function to simultaneously align the behaviour of the relevant public and private actors.

First, procurement (presumptively)[92] holds a position of superiority in the vertical relationship with market agents that allows it to dictate the terms of tender procedures and to impose contractual obligations to regulate (future) behaviour. However, this does not align with the position of subordination

[91] This shows that, eg, the use of contract performance clauses as a regulatory tool can be largely ineffective where the behaviour of the economic operator can be dictated or influenced by the adopting public entity, over which the public buyer has no control. This is evidence of the limitations of the use of procurement to 'regulate by contract' (which are further explored in Chapter 4), especially as the public-public interaction is concerned and in the absence of other regulatory mechanisms to bind the adopting public entity.

[92] See Section 2.1.2.

of procurement as agent of the public entity seeking to adopt a given digital technology. In this also vertical relationship, the subordination of procurement as agent also runs counter to the functional need for superiority (or at least independence) in the exercise of the gatekeeping function. The unregulated nature of the relationship between the procurement function and the adopting public entity raises questions on the effectiveness of the gatekeeping role, which are exacerbated by the institutional embeddedness of the procurement function.

Second, the timing of intervention and the toolkit available to the procurement function are inadequate to regulate by contract decentred interactions between adopting entity and tech provider. Given that both actors can have convergent incentives to deviate from the terms of the regulatory contract designed by the procurement function, there are also questions about the effectiveness of the gatekeeping function in this two-sided setting. This is not least because the potential impossibility of disciplining the adopting entity can nullify the efforts to embed contractual obligations in the relevant contract when that entity replaces the procurement function and becomes the contractual principal. In the absence of an effective external enforcement mechanism, it is highly problematic that the contractual relationship is established between the two entities whose behaviour it seeks to discipline. The regulatory contract is not a self-executing mechanism and leaving its implementation to the parties that can benefit from (surreptitiously) deviating from it is a risky regulatory approach, to say the least.

Functionally, then, the emerging approach cannot properly function where the adopting public entity is not entirely committed to maximizing the goals of digital regulation that are meant to be enforced by contract, and where the public contractor has a concurring interest in deviating from those goals by reducing the level of demand of the relevant contractual clauses.[93] In the setting of digital technology regulation, this seems a likely common case, especially if we consider that the main regulatory goals (eg explainability, trustworthiness) are open-ended,[94] and thus the question is not really whether the goals in themselves are embraced *in abstracto* by the adopting entity and the tech provider, but the extent to which effective (and costly or limiting) measures are put in place to maximize the realization of such goals.

[93] This evidences that the risk of 'shirking' takes a peculiar two-sided dimension, different from the standard in relational contract theory; see eg Frydlinger and Hart, 'Overcoming Contractual Incompleteness' (n 15).

[94] See Chapter 2, Section 2.

Overall, this shows that gatekeeping and 'regulation by contract' may only be an effective approach where the procurement screening and contractual obligations are aimed at disciplining the behaviour of the tech provider, or to ensure compliance with external legal requirements that bind the tech provider or/and the adopting public entity. In such case, the role of the procurement function and the role of the principal under the contract are aligned towards compliance with the legal obligations, and so the gatekeeping role can straddle the public/private and the tendering/contractual implementation divides. However, this does not necessarily hold where there is a potential tension between the roles and incentives of the procurement function (as regulatory gatekeeper) and the adopting entity as the principal under the regulatory contract. It also does not necessarily hold where the contract cannot set rules but rather needs to rely on standards, which makes the assessment of compliance with contractual obligations particularly difficult and necessitating external oversight.

In view of these insights, the next section explores ways in which the procurement function may be discharged from the emerging role of digital technology regulation by contract, which could instead be implemented by mandatory requirements and external oversight. Those would preclude or constrain the discretion of the procurement function in its gatekeeping role, eliminate its (residual) regulatory role, realign the incentives of the adopting public entity throughout the procurement lifecycle (including contract implementation), and thus bring the procurement of digital technologies back under the umbrella of agency-based regulation.

4. Bringing the Procurement of Digital Technologies Back to an Agency Logic

The analysis so far has shown how agency and gatekeeping theory point towards a dysfunction in the leveraging of procurement to regulate public sector digitalization by contract. There are two main points of tension or rupture with the regulatory logic.

First, the regulatory approach cannot effectively operate in the absence of a clear set of mandatory requirements to bind the discretion of the procurement function during the tendering and contract formation phases, as well as the discretion of the adopting public entity during contract implementation phase.

Those requirements should also be enforceable on the tech provider regardless of the terms of the contract. At a minimum, such absence creates difficulties in disciplining the behaviour of the adopting entity,[95] which can then transfer to difficulties in disciplining the behaviour of the tech provider during contract implementation. The enactment of such mandatory requirements would impose an alignment of the incentives of all actors towards regulatory compliance and would thus facilitate gatekeeping at procurement phase and during contract implementation by having a predefined benchmark. Of course, it is difficult to design such mandatory requirements, as they would have to involve substantive standards and procedural mechanisms to specify the measures required to attain a high level of compliance with the regulatory goals.[96] But even then, the existence of a clear set of standard requirements would address issues of dispersed or atomized (and duplicative) experimentation and facilitate lesson learning.

Second, the regulatory approach cannot effectively operate in the absence of an independent actor capable of enforcing those standards and monitoring continuous compliance during the lifecycle of technological adoption and use by the public sector entity. As things stand, the procurement function is affected by structural and irresolvable conflicts between its overlaid roles. Moreover, even if the procurement function was not caught by the conflicting logics and requirements of agency and gatekeeping (eg as a result of the adoption of the mandatory requirements mentioned above), it would still not be in an adequate position to monitor and discipline the behaviour of the adopting public entity—and, relatedly, of the tech provider—after the conclusion of the procurement phase. Compliance would also be strengthened by external verification at the point of procurement, especially given the impossibility of using rules-based regulation. This supports the need for external independent monitoring and enforcement by an independent regulator.

The combined effect of both interventions would be to free up the procurement function from its newest regulatory gatekeeping role in the context of public sector digitalization. This would bring digital technology procurement

[95] The absence also creates a risk of differential interpretation of the specific requirements to be derived from the general regulatory goals or standards by different public buyers, which is a result of the atomization of the procurement function discussed in Section 2.2.3. It also generates potential problems where a 'weak public buyer' is unable to independently create and enforce equivalent requirements, as discussed in Section 2.1.2.

[96] See Chapter 5.

back into the logic of agency theory. While this would not completely resolve all issues and challenges in the regulation of the adoption of digital technologies by the public sector, it is submitted that it would be a much preferable regulatory approach due to its higher logical coherence. This is explored further in Chapter 5.

4

Procurement Tools for Digital 'Regulation by Contract'

1. Introduction

This chapter continues unpacking the gatekeeping role assigned to the procurement function. After the analysis of procurement as a regulatory actor in Chapter 3, the focus is now put on the procedural and substantive procurement tools that could be used for digital 'regulation by contract' to assess their suitability for the task.[1] The chapter takes a cradle-to-grave view of the mechanisms and principles of procurement that could be activated to create or enforce digital regulation requirements. It primarily seeks to ascertain whether procurement tools could effectively operationalize digital regulation goals without simply transferring regulatory decisions to economic operators—as the primary purpose of the gatekeeping role is to discipline their behaviour and to operate as a market-shaping or norm-setting mechanism. The chapter shows that, in the absence of externally determined mandatory requirements, limitations in the permitted prescriptiveness of procurement requirements significantly raise the complexity or simply make it impossible to use procurement tools effectively for digital regulation purposes.

Using procurement tools for digital regulation by contract raises several challenges. Some of those challenges result from the logic, purpose, and design of the rules themselves, as well as their interpretation in the existing case law. These *legal* challenges will be the core focus of this chapter. Other challenges

[1] The analysis builds on that relating to the use of procurement to deliver other regulatory goals, such as sustainability or human rights compliance requirements. On the latter, see eg Albert Sanchez-Graells, 'Public Procurement and "Core" Human Rights: A Sketch of the EU Legal Framework', in Olga Martin-Ortega and Claire M O'Brien (eds), *Public Procurement and Human Rights: Risks, Dilemmas and Opportunities for the State as a Buyer* (Edward Elgar 2019) 96 (hereafter Sanchez-Graells, 'Procurement and Human Rights'). The analysis will thus draw from previous work on the use of procurement as a regulatory tool more generally.

Digital Technologies and Public Procurement. Albert Sanchez-Graells, Oxford University Press.
 DOI: 10.1093/oso/9780198866770.003.0004

result from the complexity inherent in the exercise of technical discretion to use those tools for regulatory purposes.[2] Those *practical* challenges influence or compound legal challenges and should be acknowledged from the outset. An effective use of procurement tools for the purposes of digital regulation would not only require of the public buyer objectivity and independence (as discussed in Chapter 3), but also sufficient technical capacity.[3] Such technical capacity would encompass both the digital and commercial skills required to understand the digital technologies being procured and the processes influencing technological design and deployment (as the object of regulation),[4] and the skills required to understand the procurement rules themselves (as regulatory tools). Effectively exercising such capacity would also presuppose the existence of sufficient information[5] and the time required to process it and embed the relevant insights into the decision-making process.

Gaps in the required digital and commercial skills, on the available information, or the time required to process it, will jeopardize the use of procurement for regulatory purposes. There are also other sources of potential failure in the use of procurement as a regulatory tool, such as disruption or (repeated) change in the regulatory approach before a policy can be embedded and its effects can be observed, measured, and evaluated; changes in regulatory goals; or inadequate funding and risk allocation structures leading to the abandonment of procurement projects—particularly those of a (regulatory) experimental character.[6] However, except for digital skills,[7] such challenges are not unique to the use of procurement as a tool of *digital* regulation. Rather, they generally constrain the effectiveness of the procurement function. Therefore, these issues are set aside for the purposes of this chapter, so that the analysis can concentrate on the *legal* issues that raise challenges to the use of procurement as a tool of digital regulation. However, that is not to minimize their practical importance, and the issue of capability will necessarily condition the extent to

[2] For related discussion, see Mona Sloane and others, 'AI and Procurement. A Primer' (2021) NYU <https://archive.nyu.edu/bitstream/2451/62255/2/AI%20and%20Procurement%20Primer%20Summer%202021.pdf> accessed 9 March 2023.

[3] For discussion regarding procurement digitalization, see Chapter 6, Section 5.3, and Chapter 8, Section 4.

[4] For discussion, see Albert Sanchez-Graells, 'Procuring AI Without Understanding It. Way To Go?' (*howtocrackanut.com*, 4 April 2023) <https://www.howtocrackanut.com/blog/2023/3/31/uk-pro-innovation-ai-regulation-wont-do> accessed 7 April 2023.

[5] Which stresses the importance of uncertainty in this context, as will be apparent in the analysis.

[6] For broader discussion, see Shirley Kempeneer and Frederik Heylen, 'Virtual State, Where Are You? A Literature Review, Framework and Agenda for Failed Digital Transformation' (2023) Big Data & Society <https://doi.org/10.1177/20539517231160528> accessed 12 April 2023.

[7] Though this could be generalized to *technical* skills, not just *digital* skills.

which legal issues can be resolved, especially where they refer to limitations or requirements in dealing with complexity.[8]

Focusing on *legal* challenges, this chapter examines the extent to which procurement rules can be used to operationalize the regulatory goals discussed in Chapter 2,[9] such as ensuring that the adoption of digital technologies by the public sector meets certain requirements of transparency, explainability, cybersecurity, ethical and legal compliance leading to trustworthiness, etc. This regulatory function of procurement can encompass two different (but interrelated) approaches. First, procurement can be seen as a tool of 'command and control' regulation, whereby the public buyer imposes specific prohibitions on tenderers, or specific restrictions on the content of their tenders. This approach manifests in some of the tools used to implement procurement's gatekeeping role, such as the exclusion of tenderers or the rejection of tenders that fail to meet specific legal requirements.[10] Second, procurement can be seen as a tool of 'responsive regulation'—be it labelled decentred regulation,[11] enforced self-regulation,[12] meta-regulation,[13] or a type of management-based regulation[14]—whereby the public buyer creates incentives for tenderers to adopt certain behaviours or include specific attributes in their tenders. This could, for example, involve the use of qualitative selection criteria to generate incentives for specific types of general corporate behaviour,[15] or award criteria to generate incentives to shape tenders in line with the public buyer's interests.[16]

[8] Sanchez-Graells, 'Procurement and Human Rights' (n 1) 111–14; Albert Sanchez-Graells, 'Regulatory Substitution between Labour and Public Procurement Law: The EU's Shifting Approach to Enforcing Labour Standards in Public Contracts' (2018) 24(2) European Public Law Journal 229, 252–53.

[9] For a similar analysis, see Gry Hasselbalch, Birgitte Kofod Olsen, and Pernille Tranberg, 'White Paper on Data Ethics in Public Procurement of AI Based Services and Solutions' (2021) <https://www.nist.gov/system/files/documents/2021/08/23/ai-rmf-rfi-0043.pdf> accessed 9 March 2023.

[10] eg in relation to tenderers or tenders that fail to ensure compliance with environmental or labour law. See eg Directive 2014/24/EU of the European Parliament and of the Council of 26 February 2014 on public procurement and repealing Directive 2004/18/EC [2014] OJ L 94/65, arts 18(2), 56(1), 57(4)(a) *in fine*, 69(3) *in fine*, and Annex X.

[11] Julia Black, 'Decentring Regulation: Understanding the Role of Regulation and Self-Regulation in a "Post-Regulatory" World' (2001) 54(1) Current Legal Problems 103, 126.

[12] John Braithwaite, 'Enforced Self-Regulation: A New Strategy for Corporate Crime Control' (1982) 80(7) Michigan Law Review 1466.

[13] Peter Grabosky, 'Meta-Regulation' in Peter Drahos (ed), *Regulatory Theory. Foundations and Applications* (ANU Press 2022) 149, 153.

[14] Neil Gunningham and Darren Sinclair, 'Trust, Culture and the Limits of Management-Based Regulation: Lessons from the Mining Industry' in Peter Drahos (ed), *Regulatory Theory. Foundations and Applications* (ANU Press 2022) 711, 721.

[15] See eg David Mosey and others, 'White Paper on Procurement Strategies for Incentivizing Collaborative Delivery to Optimize Whole-Life Outcomes' (2022) <https://www.cdbb.cam.ac.uk/files/white_paper_on_procurement_strategies.pdf> accessed 21 February 2023.

[16] eg in relation to accelerated delivery; see Gregory Lewis and Patrick Bajari, 'Procurement Contracting with Time Incentives: Theory and Evidence' (2011) 126(3) Quarterly Journal of Economics 1173.

While there can be some space for a 'command and control' use of procurement as a tool of digital regulation, in the absence of clear (rules-based) regulatory benchmarks and legally-established mandatory requirements, the responsive approach to the use of procurement as a tool to enforce self-regulatory mechanisms seems likely to be predominant[17]—in the sense that procurement requirements are likely to focus on the tenderers' commitment to sets of practices and processes seeking to deliver (to the largest possible extent) the relevant regulatory attributes by reference to (technical) standards. For example, it is hard to imagine the imposition of an absolute requirement for a digital solution to be 'digitally secure'. It is rather more plausible for the tender and contract to seek to bind the tech provider to practices and procedures seeking to ensure high levels of cybersecurity (by reference to some relevant metrics, where they are available), as well as protocols and mechanisms to anticipate and react to any (potential) security breaches. The same applies to other desirable regulatory attributes in the procured digital technologies, such as transparency or explainability, which will most likely be describable (or described) by reference to technical standards and procedures, or to general principles, such as ethical or trustworthy AI, also requiring proceduralized implementation.[18] In this context, procurement can be seen as a tool to promote co-regulation or (responsible) self-regulation both at tenderer and industry level, for example in relation to the development of ethical or trustworthy AI.[19]

This approach raises questions not only on the legal competence,[20] but also on the legitimacy of the public buyer to instrumentalize procurement in this manner.[21] However, the focus in this chapter is not on the desirability or legitimacy of this approach, but on its feasibility or deliverability. The question is whether procurement *could effectively operationalize digital regulation goals without simply transferring regulatory decisions to economic operators*, either directly through tender design or the awarded public contract, or indirectly through the incorporation by reference or reliance on commercially

[17] This also aligns with the increasing role of compliance in procurement, as stressed in relation to green procurement; see Pedro Telles and Grith Skovgaard Ølykke, 'Sustainable Procurement: A Compliance Perspective of EU Public Procurement Law' (2017) 12 European Procurement & Public Private Partnership Law Review 239.

[18] See Chapter 2, Section 2.

[19] See eg David S Rubenstein, 'Acquiring Ethical AI' (2021) 73(4) Florida Law Review 747 (hereafter Rubenstein, 'Acquiring Ethical AI'). See also Cary Coglianese and Erik Lampmann, 'Contracting for Algorithmic Accountability' (2021) 6 Administrative Law Review Accord 175.

[20] For related discussion, see Albert Sanchez-Graells, *Public Procurement and the EU Competition Rules* (2nd edn, Hart Publishing 2015) 182–85 (hereafter Sanchez-Graells, *Public Procurement and Competition*).

[21] See eg Julia Black, 'Constructing and Contesting Legitimacy and Accountability in Polycentric Regulatory Regimes' (2008) 2(2) Regulation & Governance 137.

determined standards and practices.[22] The need to prevent a transfer or delegation (ie a privatization) of regulatory decisions as a result of the operation of the procurement rules is crucial,[23] as tech providers are the primary target in proposals to use procurement for digital regulation by contract.[24] It would be self-defeating for the regulatory tool chosen to discipline the behaviour of tech providers to end up transferring the relevant regulatory decisions to their self-regulation, as tech providers would have effective control over the meta-regulatory instrument meant to discipline their self-regulation in the first place. The regulatory intervention would then be circular and most likely ineffective.

The functional goal is thus for the procurement function to prevent the acquisition of digital technologies (from providers) that fail to meet the relevant regulatory requirements, and to promote the acquisition of digital technologies (from providers) that maximize those regulatory goals. Taking this perspective, the chapter analyses the procurement tools available at the phases of tender preparation and design (Section 2), tender execution (Section 3), and contract design and implementation (Section 4). The analysis stresses those areas where the existing rules (and their underlying logic) prevent the imposition of rigid regulatory requirements or demands for compliance with prespecified standards (to the exclusion of alternative ones). The chapter shows that, in the absence of a set of externally determined mandatory requirements (discussed in Chapter 5), such limitations in the permitted prescriptiveness of procurement requirements significantly raise the complexity or simply make it impossible to effectively use procurement tools for digital regulation purposes—either as 'command and control' or responsive regulation.[25]

[22] It should also be noted that, 'In rapidly changing fields, agreed standards may be nonexistent or disputed, and so the idea of "best practices"—whether for regulated entities or for the auditors purporting to supervise them—may mean very little', which would further reduce the effectiveness of such approach even if the commercial determination of the standards was not seen as a major governance problem; see Julie Cohen, *Between Truth and Power: The Legal Constructions of Informational Capitalism* (OUP 2019) 191. This creates issues of legitimacy equivalent to those posed by regulation by design approaches; see Marco Almada, 'Regulation by Design and the Governance of Technological Futures' (2023) European Journal of Risk Regulation, First View <https://doi.org/10.1017/err.2023.37> accessed 17 May 2023, 7–8.

[23] Deirdre K Mulligan and Kenneth A Bamberger, 'Procurement as Policy: Administrative Process for Machine Learning' (2019) 34(3) Berkeley Technology Law Journal 773.

[24] See eg Rubenstein, 'Acquiring Ethical AI' (n 19) 797 ff. Chapter 3 already discussed why this is a partial and unsatisfactory approach, and why the behaviour of the public entity seeking to adopt the technology also requires disciplining. However, this chapter sets aside the issue of two-sided gatekeeping for simplicity.

[25] With the same intuition, see Lord Tim Clement-Jones, 'Government AI Procurement Needs Ethical and Data Compliance Obligation' (blog, 30 July 2022) <https://www.lordclementjones.org/2022/07/30/government-ai-procurement-needs-ethical-and-data-compliance-obligation/> accessed 9 March 2023.

2. Tender Preparation and Design

As a preliminary step, the public buyer tasked with the digital regulatory gatekeeping function could consider how to design the tender procedure to maximize the likelihood of achieving high levels of compliance with the relevant regulatory goals.[26] The public buyer could carry out market consultations[27] with a view to gaining a better understanding of, for example, current industry best practices and the state of the art in relation to specific aspects of the technology to be procured—as a way of ascertaining the level of regulatory demand likely to be met by the existing offer. Or it could be interested in market-testing the approach it intends to implement to, for example technical evaluation of data governance mechanisms, or ethical approvals. Similarly, the public buyer may be interested in gauging whether the identified functionality can be provided by existing 'off-the-shelf' technical solutions,[28] with or without modest adaptations that could be secured through limited negotiations,[29] or whether achieving the desired functionality would require more intense innovation necessitating the use of a different procedure, such as a competitive dialogue,[30] or an innovation partnership.[31]

These are important strategic considerations with clear impacts on the likelihood of successful leveraging of procurement for digital regulation, and involve decisions constrained by the public buyer's asymmetry of information (which will increase with reduced digital capability and limited independent market research efforts). The existing regulatory framework controlling market consultations and the choice of procurement procedures creates some constraints, which the public buyer (and industry) may be tempted to sidestep through exclusivity claims allowing for the direct award of (negotiated) contracts.[32]

This section focuses on these issues and stresses how the closer the interactions between the public buyer and the potential tech providers—which is precisely what the relevant mechanisms try to facilitate—the higher the risk of commercial determination of regulatory decisions through attempts of

[26] This is different from carrying out technology risk assessments, which may be highly dependent on specific choices to be made during the tender procedure (eg where different technological solutions could satisfy the same functional need) and thus not susceptible of reliable completion at this early stage. cf Rubenstein, 'Acquiring Ethical AI' (n 19) 799.

[27] Directive 2014/24/EU (n 10) art 40.

[28] Thus, leading to open or restricted procedures; see Directive 2014/24/EU (n 10) arts 27 and 28.

[29] ibid art 29.

[30] ibid art 30.

[31] ibid art 31.

[32] ibid art 32.

capture, or via direct negotiations, where the tech provider can have the upper hand, especially in situations of (claimed) exclusivity. This raises questions as to the compatibility of the flexibility of the procurement rules with the regulatory gatekeeping role the public buyer is expected to carry out, as further explored in Section 5.

2.1 Preliminary Market Consultations

Preliminary market consultations could be used as a way of designing or fine-tuning the procurement requirements leading to compliance with the relevant regulatory goals. For example, the public buyer could consult on how to design the tender in line with a principle of 'AI minimization',[33] thus targeting the consultation to gathering information on technical solutions that could deliver the required functionality with a minimal level of technical complexity (eg by avoiding the use of Artificial Intelligence (AI) altogether, or through simple and easily explainable algorithmic solutions rather than 'black box' solutions). There is obvious difficulty in formulating the relevant problem, the intended functionality (in a technology neutral way), and providing detailed information on the enabling factors (eg legacy systems, available data) required to design the solution.[34] Additionally, the existing regulatory framework creates significant difficulties through the requirement that market consultations do not result in the public buyer adopting received advice that has 'the effect of distorting competition' or 'result[s] in a violation of the principles of non-discrimination and transparency'.[35] This is coupled with a duty to level the playing field by disclosing the exchanged information, with the alternative being an obligation to exclude the economic operator having provided the relevant advice where there are no other means to observe the principle of equal treatment.[36]

[33] See Chapter 2, Section 2.4.

[34] See Oana P Voda and Carolien Jobse, 'Rules and Boundaries Surrounding Market Consultations in Innovation Procurement' (2016) 11(3) European Procurement & Public Private Partnership Law Review 179.

[35] Directive 2014/24/EU (n 10) art 40 *in fine*. See European Commission, 'Guidance on Innovation Procurement' (Notice) C (2021) 4320 final, 26 and 37–39; Dacian C Dragos, 'Article 40—Preliminary Market Consultations' in Roberto Caranta and Albert Sanchez-Graells (eds), *European Public Procurement. Commentary on Directive 2014/24/EU* (Edward Elgar 2021) 448 (hereafter Caranta and Sanchez-Graells, *Commentary*).

[36] Directive 2014/24/EU (n 10) art 41. See Dacian C Dragos, 'Article 41—Prior Involvement of Candidates or Tenderers' in Caranta and Sanchez-Graells, *Commentary* (n 35) 456. See also Sanchez-Graells, *Public Procurement and Competition* (n 20) 373–78.

These are adequate safeguards to prevent preliminary market consultations becoming a lightly regulated space where procurement decisions are made and then simply forced through a strategically designed tender which outcome is predetermined. However, this makes preliminary market consultations difficult to manage and limits their functionality where market dynamics rely on the protection of commercial secrecy and can thus disincentivize information exchange to protect commercial know how (as is notoriously the case of digital technologies).[37] Consultations are also difficult to manage where markets operate in the absence of clear industry standards and the adoption for the purposes of the tender of the specific approach advanced by an economic operator (eg to AI ethics assessments or algorithmic performance evaluation) could be seen to confer an undue advantage. It is also difficult to gauge the level of detail in which market consultations can go, with general approaches unlikely to provide operational insights for the public buyer, and very detailed consultations possibly putting an excessive burden on (otherwise) participating economic operators—which, again, can be reluctant to disclose commercially sensitive information.

Given the regulatory role expected of procurement, another potential use of preliminary market consultations would be to focus them on aspects of digital governance that the public buyer would seek to embed in the contract. In that regard, it seems that economic operators are not in the best position, and lack the incentives, to engage with (public) consultation of elements of the governance of the technological deployment over which they can gain no competitive advantage (eg in the design of a data governance system that would be imposed on any tech provider as a non-negotiable contract clause). This indicates that economic operators will be more prone to participate in such consultations to the extent that they perceive an opportunity to commercially determine (or capture) regulatory approaches[38]—which runs contrary to the overarching gatekeeping goal being pursued. Relatedly, some of the entities that could have an interest in commenting on the proposed procurement and its conditions may well be non-market agents (eg non-governmental, civil society, or research organizations). However, procurement preliminary market consultations are not geared for that broader consultative purpose—starting with the

[37] See eg Wolfgang Sofka, Pedro de Faria, and Edlira Shehu, 'Protecting Knowledge: How Legal Requirements to Reveal Information Affect the Importance of Secrecy' (2018) 47(3) Research Policy 558.

[38] The risk is well understood in the context of regulatory consultations; see OECD, 'Regulatory Consultation. A MENA-OECD practitioners' guide for engaging stakeholders in the rule-making process (2017) 36 <https://www.oecd.org/mena/governance/MENA-Practitioners-Guide-%20EN.pdf> accessed 22 February 2023.

lack of advertisement with which they can be carried out, or the absence of any obligation on the public buyer to take submissions into account or (publicly) justify how they feature in its decision-making.[39]

On balance, it seems unlikely that preliminary market consultations can work as an effective means of (detailed technical) information gathering for the public buyer where secrecy matters, or as a mechanism to legitimately and effectively (co-)produce regulatory requirements that would substitute for (non-existent) industry standards while upholding overarching regulatory goals in a way that is not commercially driven or determined (ie while avoiding a risk of regulatory capture). Conversely, (informal) preliminary market consultations could exacerbate the 'exclusivity temptation' discussed in Section 2.3. Therefore, a public buyer seeking to acquire digital technologies should be particularly careful in the way it engaged with preliminary market consultations as a substitute for other sources of market intelligence or in-house expertise. Or, in other words, preliminary market consultations cannot eliminate the need for advanced digital skills on the public buyer, including to design market consultations on the basis of previous market intelligence and to target them to specific elements of the future competition for the contract.

2.2 Choice of Procedure

A related issue concerns the need for the public buyer to have a good understanding of the level of innovation required to achieve the desired functionality through digital technologies. While it may be possible to acquire some off-the-shelf solutions for some digital technologies, it seems that the more the planned deployment needs to be integrated with legacy systems and use data held by the public buyer or a third party, the more plausible it will be that a successful procurement will require a degree of technical dialogue and/or negotiations, or possibly the co-production of the required (innovative) technological solution.[40] The difficulty is that, until economic operators have access to rather detailed information, it will be difficult for them (and the public buyer) to have a clear view of the level of customization or further development of existing solutions required to deliver the intended functionality. The theoretical way out

[39] Save under an expansive interpretation of the duty to create an internal paper trail of all decisions concerning the procurement, which could fit Directive 2014/24/EU (n 10) art 84(2). Pedro Cerqueira Gomes, 'Article 84—Individual Reports' in Caranta and Sanchez-Graells, *Commentary* (n 35) 869, 873.

[40] Similarly, Rubenstein, 'Acquiring Ethical AI' (n 19) 813–15.

of this chicken and egg problem would be a preliminary market consultation but, for the reasons given in Section 2.1, it seems unlikely to be a productive approach. If that is the case, the public buyer will find itself in a situation where it needs to opt for a procedure that allows a sufficient degree of flexibility to deal with this uncertainty.

Under the EU rules, the theoretical expectation would then probably be that the public buyer would opt for a competitive dialogue,[41] or possibly an innovation partnership,[42] as these procedures were designed with this type of issue in mind.[43] However, evidence on the (limited) use of these procedures shows that contracting authorities have a strong preference for competitive procedures with negotiations[44]—which partially share the same grounds for use.[45] From the regulatory perspective taken in this chapter, this should immediately raise some concerns due to the risk of commercial determination or capture via negotiations, as this type of procedure is flexible and significantly deregulated. The only safeguards against such risk are in scoping which of the elements of the future contract are open to negotiations (and which are non-negotiable), and in establishing how the outcome of such negotiations will be evaluated, which depends on a (seemingly) unilateral determination by the public buyer.[46]

Indeed, under the EU rules, public buyers

> shall identify the subject-matter of the procurement by providing a description of their needs and the characteristics required of the supplies, works or services to be procured and specify the contract award criteria. They shall also indicate which elements of the description define the minimum requirements to be met by all tenders.[47]

[41] Pedro Telles, 'Article 30—Competitive Dialogue' in Caranta and Sanchez-Graells, *Commentary* (n 35) 324, 327.

[42] Pedro Cerqueira Gomes, *EU Public Procurement and Innovation. The Innovation Partnership Procedure and Harmonization Challenges* (Edward Elgar 2021) 121 ff.

[43] Pedro Telles and Luke A Butler, 'Public Procurement Award Procedures in Directive 2014/24/EU' in François Lichere, Roberto Caranta, and Steen Treumer (eds), *Modernising Public Procurement: The New Directive* (DJØF Publishing 2014) 131 (hereafter Telles and Butler, 'Award Procedures').

[44] Pedro Telles, 'Reflecting on 18 Years of Competitive Dialogue' in Carina Risvig Hamer and others (eds), *Into the Northern Light—In Memory of Steen Treumer* (Ex Tuto Publishing 2022) 193, 210 (hereafter Telles, 'Competitive Dialogue').

[45] Directive 2014/24/EU (n 10) art 26. Telles, 'Competitive Dialogue' (n 44) 205; Christoph Kronke, 'Article 26—Choice of Procedures' in Caranta and Sanchez-Graells, *Commentary* (n 35) 287, 290 ff.

[46] Roberto Caranta, 'Article 29—Competitive Procedure with Negotiation' in Michael Steinicke and Peter L Vesterdorf (eds), *Brussels Commentary on EU Public Procurement Law* (Hart Publishing 2018) 400, 402 and 404 (hereafter Steinicke and Vesterdorf, *Brussels Commentary*).

[47] Directive 2014/24/EU (n 10) art 29(1)II.

It is further clarified that the 'minimum requirements and the award criteria shall not be subject to negotiations',[48] and that the public buyer cannot modify them during the procedure.[49] This could enable public buyers to impose high minimum thresholds, in particular concerning the regulatory requirements to be embedded in the contract, which could be ringfenced as non-negotiable.

However, in practice, it seems plausible that public buyers will have difficulties in setting those minimum requirements (be they as technical specifications, or otherwise, see Section 3.2) because of the same uncertainties affecting their choice of procedure (ie how much innovation is required and where to set the minimum threshold in that regard), their information asymmetry (eg about the existence of different technical solutions or approaches to dealing with uncertainty and regulatory risks),[50] and the unavoidable difficulties in formulating regulatory requirements other than by reference to standards that will still need to be interpreted, specified, and operationalized as a result of the negotiations (or during contract implementation, see Section 4). A public buyer seeking to avoid a risk of tender cancellation due to the imposition of excessive minimum requirements that no economic operator can meet will have incentives to reduce them.[51] However, this will expose the public buyer to a higher risk of capture by extending the 'negotiable surface' of the contract, which also runs contrary to the overarching gatekeeping goal being pursued. The mandatory existence of minimum requirements in this type of procedure with negotiations will also generate incentives for economic operators to seek to sidestep them through exclusivity claims that would allow for unconstrained negotiations, as below.

2.3 Exclusivity Claims

The previous two sections have shown how there are limitations in the use of preliminary market consultations as a mechanism for the public buyer as regulatory gatekeeper to reduce its information asymmetry, and how there is a strong preference for negotiations as a mechanism to resolve the related uncertainty. It was also pointed out that the public buyer may face hold up problems[52]

[48] ibid art 29(3)II.
[49] ibid art 29(5).
[50] Telles and Butler, 'Award Procedures' (n 43) 159–60.
[51] Piotr Bogdanowicz, 'Article 29—Competitive Procedure with Negotiation' in Caranta and Sanchez-Graells, *Commentary* (n 35) 315, 318.
[52] Benjamin E Hermalin and Michael L Katz, 'Information and the Hold-Up Problem' (2009) 40(3) The RAND Journal of Economics 405.

when economic operators seek to protect their commercial interests through (algorithmic) secrecy—which (confidential) negotiations could alleviate to the extent that they reduced information disclosure and provided a higher likelihood of being awarded the contract. Economic operators also have incentives both to use preliminary market consultations to capture the public buyer, and to seek ways of bypassing the guardrails of mandatory minimum requirements in competitive procedures with negotiations. In this context, it seems that both parties have the (wrong) incentives to entertain exclusivity claims that could bypass the procurement process by allowing the public buyer to engage in a negotiated procedure without prior publication.

Current EU rules would only permit this either: (1) when this is justified by the absence of competition due to technical reasons,[53] such that there is a 'near technical impossibility for another economic operator to achieve the required performance or the necessity to use specific know-how, tools or means which only one economic operator has at its disposal';[54] or (2) due to the need to protect exclusive rights, including intellectual property rights,[55] which include trade secrets. In both cases, there must be no reasonable alternative or substitute, and the absence of competition must not be the result of an artificial narrowing down of the parameters of the procurement. This must be interpreted strictly.[56] The difficulty with this situation is that, despite the apparent stringency of the legal test, there are strong incentives to rely on this exclusion.[57]

Moreover, this constraint only applies for contracts above the relevant value thresholds,[58] which may not capture a potentially large number of 'exploratory' contracts directly awarded on the basis of claimed technical exclusivity or know how, which can then be a gateway for the commercial determination or capture of deployment decisions down the line.[59] The current rules on the

[53] Directive 2014/24/EU (n 10) art 32(2)(b)(ii).

[54] ibid Recital (50).

[55] ibid art 32(2)(b)(iii).

[56] Piotr Bogdanowicz, 'Article 32—Use of the Negotiated Procedure without Prior Publication' in Caranta and Sanchez-Graells, *Commentary* (n 35) 350, 355–57; Roberto Caranta, 'Article 32—Use of the Negotiated Procedure without Prior Publication' in Steinicke and Vesterdorf, *Brussels Commentary* (n 46) 428, 433–36.

[57] A search in the TED database indicates that this exception is being relied on strongly in some jurisdictions, such as Norway. Absence of transparency on the reliance in other jurisdictions should not be interpreted as this not taking place.

[58] Directive 2014/24/EU (n 10) art 4. It should be noted that this will be less of an issue in jurisdictions that have extended the relevant requirements to contracts of a lower value as a matter of domestic law.

[59] Arguably, this situation could be controlled on the basis of the rules on prior involvement in Directive 2014/24/EU (n 10) art 41. However, establishing the relevant connection becomes more difficult as the prior involvement potentially morphs into an incumbency issue, or determines technical decisions from which the initial consultant does not directly stand to benefit, while still creating a potential deviation from the overarching regulatory goals (eg by predetermining the need to use less or non-explainable solutions).

calculation of contract values[60] can also generate perverse incentives to avoid regulated procurement procedures on the basis of, for example, using access to public (data) assets or allowing the tech provider to retain exclusivity rights on developments or improvements of the (co-created) deployed digital solutions as remuneration. This raises a governance risk that should in principle be mitigated by existing transparency requirements, but which does not square well with the fact that (non-)compliance with the relevant requirements is controlled by the public buyer and that such lack of transparency can raise significant obstacles to the detection of the existence of this type of awards—which then creates a potential governance gap where a public buyer is captured by the tech provider. Alternatively, an obligation to obtain external approval for all projects involving the adoption of digital technologies would mitigate this issue, as discussed in Chapter 5.

3. Tender Execution

This section continues with an analysis of decisions concerning the implementation of the tender procedure that could be taken to maximize the likelihood of achieving high levels of compliance with the relevant regulatory goals. It focuses on the two main decisions the public buyer needs to make: tenderer selection and tender evaluation. The expectation is that in these areas the public buyer can exercise elements of 'command and control', for example through tenderer exclusion decisions as well as by setting demanding qualitative selection thresholds, or through the setting of mandatory technical specifications and the use of award constraints. However, the analysis will show that the existing rules and the associated constraints and regulatory burden, as well as the open-endedness of the relevant standards, significantly erode the regulatory potential of these decisions by the public buyer.

This is not to say that there is no possibility of embedding some regulatory requirements in the tender process, but rather to stress the difficulty and complexity of doing so, as well as the need to consider that alternative (equivalent) approaches to compliance with the requirements set by the public buyer will almost always need to be taken into consideration and potentially accepted.[61]

[60] Directive 2014/24/EU (n 10) art 5(1), which focuses on 'total amount payable'. Even if this has been interpreted widely to include revenue received from third parties, the role of other types of economic transfers is not entirely clear and practice may vary. See eg Pawel Nowicki, 'Article 5—Methods for Calculating the Estimated Value of Procurement' in Negotiation' in Caranta and Sanchez-Graells, *Commentary* (n 35) 48, 51–52.

[61] Sanchez-Graells, 'Procurement and Human Rights' (n 1) 103–07.

This creates a situation where the regulatory requirements set by the public buyer can become *one of several* ways of seeking to comply with the over-arching regulatory goals. At a minimum, this creates uncertainty and imposes additional demands on a regulatory gatekeeper incapable of prescribing *the way* it considers regulation should be implemented. It can also reduce regulatory effectiveness where equivalence is hard to establish, or the effects of different approaches are only observable with significant delay.

3.1 Tenderer Selection

A public buyer seeking to exercise effectively its digital regulatory gatekeeping role would focus on selecting tenderers that could demonstrate high levels of commitment to the relevant regulatory goals. This could be done through a dual approach. First, by excluding tech providers with a previous track record of activity falling short of the relevant regulatory goals. Second, by incentivizing or recompensing high levels of positive commitment to the regulatory goals, demonstrated, for example, through a track record of implementation of specific practices and processes. Both approaches raise significant challenges.

First, proactively seeking to ban 'untrustworthy' tech providers[62] from participating in the relevant tenders implies the need to rely on the possibility of excluding economic operators 'guilty of grave professional misconduct, which renders [their] integrity questionable',[63] and/or those that have 'shown significant or persistent deficiencies in the performance of a substantive requirement under a prior ... contract, ... which led to early termination of that prior contract, damages or other comparable sanctions'.[64] The latter ground would be particularly relevant where the earlier performance deficiencies concerned technology governance-related contractual requirements. In addition to the general difficulties in applying these exclusion grounds,[65] as well as the need to make explicit that the contracting authority seeks to use these grounds as they relate to digital governance behaviour,[66] the added difficulty here is that

[62] This is used as shorthand.

[63] Directive 2014/24/EU (n 10) art 57(4)(c).

[64] ibid art 57(4)(g).

[65] Which analysis exceeds the scope of this chapter. For discussion, see Pascal Friton and Janis Zoll, 'Article 57—Exclusion Grounds' in Caranta and Sanchez-Graells, *Commentary* (n 35) 588, 611–13 and 616–17.

[66] Case law has been restrictive of the possibility of incorporating qualification requirements by reference or to deem them implied, which puts pressure on their specific definition in tender documentation; see *Pizzo* [2016] ECLI:EU:C:2016:404, para 51; *NV Construct* [2023] ECLI:EU:C:2023:47, para 68 (hereafter *NV Construct*).

the framework to assess professional duties in the development of digital technologies is less than settled.[67]

In the absence of clear benchmarks of what can be considered a responsible or ethical digital technology practice, it is not clear, for example, whether a tech provider that had supported the deployment of a technology that was later found to infringe on fundamental rights (eg due to discriminatory outcomes of algorithmic data processing resulting from insufficiently interrogated source data provided by the public buyer) would immediately and inescapably be caught by this provision. At least where decisions leading to the inappropriate outcome are co-determined by (other) public buyers managing previous contracts, where the outcome can be ascribed to a misuse of the technology beyond the tech provider's control, or in areas of high technical uncertainty, there will be difficult questions for the regulatory gatekeeper to answer before proceeding to exclusion—for example, about whether the economic operator was at least negligent[68]—and this will take place with a real prospect of litigation of exclusion decisions. Moreover, a public buyer cannot automatically rely on the findings of another one, as the current EU rules require each contracting authority to come to its own view on the reliability of the economic operator.[69] This raises the burden of engaging with exclusion based on these grounds,[70] which may put some public buyers off, especially if there are complex technical questions on the background. Such judgements may require a level of expertise and available resources exceeding those of the public buyer, which could, for example, justify seeking to rely on third-party certification instead.

Indeed, a complement (or alternative) to the proactive screening of 'trustworthy' tech providers consists of the use of qualitative selection criteria incorporating the findings of third-party certification mechanisms, for example in relation to quality assurance.[71] This can also be done through the use of official lists of approved economic operators, or third-party certification strictly speaking.[72] In both instances, the third-party certification relies on (European) standards which, in the specific field of digital technologies, currently creates a regulatory vacuum and, even when the standards emerge in the future, will create a risk of commercial determination or capture through

[67] The ongoing debates on AI ethics far exceed the scope of this chapter but suffice it to point out that there is no universally accepted benchmark against which to assess the relevant behaviour. See Chapter 2, Section 2 for related discussion.

[68] *Forposta and ABC Direct Contact* [2012] ECLI:EU:C:2012:801, para 30.

[69] *Delta* [2019] ECLI:C:2019:826, paras 28–29.

[70] Which, of course, would also require consideration of any claims of self-cleaning under Directive 2014/24/EU (n 10) art 57(6).

[71] ibid art 62.

[72] ibid art 64.

the setting of the standards themselves.[73] There are also indirect ways of creating such lists, such as by establishing dynamic purchasing systems,[74] in particular if they are created by a central purchasing body,[75] which however have to comply with the general rules on qualitative selection.[76]

In all these cases, from the regulatory perspective taken here, the practical difficulty will be that the public buyer will either see its regulatory function conditioned or precluded by the (commercially determined) standards underlying third-party certification, or else face a significant burden if it seeks to directly scrutinize economic operators. The regulatory burden will to some extent be unavoidable even where the public buyer seeks to rely on certification mechanisms because all the above-mentioned mechanisms foresee that economic operators that do not have access to the relevant certification or are under no obligation to register in the relevant list must be given the opportunity to demonstrate that they meet the relevant (substantive) qualitative selection criteria by other (equivalent) means.[77]

Moreover, in some cases, it may not be possible to obtain the relevant certification ahead of the award of the contract and its implementation,[78] which would ban the option of requiring the certificate at tender stage.[79] It should also be borne in mind that the requirement for certification will be subject to a proportionality assessment, and could even be precluded by other sources of EU digital law.[80] There will also be additional challenges in ensuring that the relevant vetting of economic operators is properly applied where the digital technology solution relies on a long (technical) supply chain or assemblage, without this necessarily involving any (formal) relationship or subcontracting

[73] For further discussion, see Chapter 9, Section 3.

[74] Directive 2014/24/EU (n 10) art 34.

[75] ibid art 37.

[76] This would also generate further governance issues due to potentially excessive centralization, which analysis exceeds the scope of this chapter. See Albert Sanchez-Graells, 'Competition Implications of Procurement Digitalisation and the Procurement of Digital Technologies by Central Purchasing Bodies' (2023) <https://ssrn.com/abstract=4376037> accessed 12 April 2023.

[77] The circumstances under which this needs to happen vary, but the requirement is clear in Directive 2014/24/EU (n 10) arts 62(1), 64(6) and (7).

[78] This could be the case of eg new entrants, or innovative technology deployments for which there is no existing standard.

[79] *Sanresa* [2021] ECLI:EU:C:2021:556, para 62; *NV Construct* (n 66) para 65.

[80] Notably, in relation to AI only, the proposed EU AI Act, to the extent that it imposed maximum harmonization that crowded out regulatory action at Member State level. For discussion, see Michael Veale and Frederik Zuiderveen Borgesius, 'Demystifying the Draft EU Artificial Intelligence Act—Analysing the Good, the Dad, and the Unclear Elements of the Proposed Approach' (2021) 22(4) Computer Law Review International 97, 108 ff. However, as mentioned in Chapter 2, Section 3.2, the position taken here is that the EU AI Act does not entirely exclude Member State regulatory activity other than in relation to high-risk uses, which therefore allows for the development of additional requirements, both in relation to formal checks (eg permissioning or licensing of AI use) and substantive requirements. For further discussion, see Chapter 5, Section 3.

between the tech provider to be contracted and the developers of parts of the technical assemblage.[81] This points at the significant burden that the public buyer may have to overcome in seeking to use qualitative selection rules to 'weed out' tech providers which (general, or past) behaviour is not aligned with the overarching regulatory goals.

Second, a more proactive approach that sought to go beyond exclusion or third-party certification, for example to promote adherence to voluntary codes of conduct, or to require tech providers to justify how they generally 'contribute to the development and deployment of trustworthy digital technologies' for instance, would also face significant difficulties. Such requirements could be seen as unjustified and/or disproportionate,[82] leading to an infringement of EU procurement law. Under current rules, such requirements seem to exceed the permitted scrutiny of an economic operator's technical ability[83]—though it could be argued that such technology governance-oriented requirements could hold a closer link to the 'technical facilities and measures used by the economic operator for ensuring quality'[84] than in the leading precedent, which concerned much broader social policies.[85] As the law stands, where the public buyer wants to ensure adherence to specific practices or behaviours, it may try to embed them within the contract, as contract performance requirements (Section 4).

The difficulties identified here stress that using procurement qualitative selection *in lieu* of a licensing or authorization system generates significant legal hurdles and that procurement may not have the right tools to develop this regulatory function—to which Section 5 will return. Ultimately, this insight mirrors the fact that procurement from industries that require heavy regulation relies on external systems of licensing or authorization and procurement

[81] eg where a customized solution is to be developed on the basis of an off-the-shelf solution licensed from a third party by the tech provider. This type of interaction would make it difficult to apply the existing rules on qualitative selection, as they presume the existence of mechanisms for the reliance on third-party capacities or subcontracting mechanisms that may not easily transfer to digital markets, at least not without a rather strained functional interpretation. See eg Directive 2014/24/EU (n 10) arts 63 and 71(6). For related discussion, see Ian Brown, 'Allocating accountability in AI supply chains' (2023) Ada Lovelace Institute Expert Explainer <https://www.adalovelaceinstitute.org/resource/ai-supply-chains/> accessed 30 June 2023.

[82] Of course, it depends on the intensity and specificity of the requirements. At the opposite extreme, some of the qualitative selection approaches can be ineffective, eg where tenderers are simply asked to indicate whether they would be willing to engage with the relevant code of conduct; Rubenstein, 'Acquiring Ethical AI' (n 19) 808.

[83] Directive 2014/24/EU (n 10) Annex XII.

[84] ibid Annex XII, Part II (c).

[85] *Commission v Netherlands (Max Havelaar)* [2012] ECLI:EU:C:2012:284, paras 107–08. For discussion and a criticism of the current approach in the context of sustainable procurement, see Marta Andhov and others, 'Sustainability Through Public Procurement: The Way Forward—Reform Proposals' (2020) 40 <https://ssrn.com/abstract=3559393> accessed 23 February 2023 (hereafter Andhov and others, 'Reform Proposals').

simply checks that such authorizations or licences are in place.[86] Stretching the gatekeeping role of procurement beyond that implies using procurement as a *de facto* licensing or authorization mechanism, which it clearly is not designed to do.[87]

3.2 Tender Evaluation

As mentioned above, the possibility of setting demanding technical specifications and minimum requirements for tender evaluation through award constraints in principle seem suitable tools of digital regulation. The public buyer could channel its regulatory gatekeeping role by focusing on the technical solutions and embedding the desired regulatory attributes (eg transparency, explainability, cybersecurity) and regulatory checks (on data and technology governance, eg in relation to open source code or interoperability, as well as in relation to ethical assessments) in the technical specifications. Award criteria could generate (further) incentives for regulatory performance, perhaps beyond the minimum mandatory baseline. This section will point out difficulties on these fronts—to which Section 5 will return.

3.2.1 Technical specifications and minimum technical requirements

The primary difficulty in using technical specifications as a regulatory tool relates to the challenge of clearly specifying the desired regulatory attributes. Some or most of the desired technological attributes are difficult to observe or measure, the processes leading to their promotion are not easy to establish. The outcomes of those processes are not binary and determining whether a requirement has been met cannot be subject to strict rules, but rather to (yet to be developed) technical standards with an unavoidable degree of indefinition,[88] which may also be susceptible of iterative application in, for example, agile methods, and thus difficult to evaluate at tender stage. Moreover, the desired attributes can be in conflict between themselves or with the main functional specifications for the digital technology deployment.[89] There is, for example, a

[86] Directive 2014/24/EU (n 10) art 58(2)II.
[87] Note that this refers to licensing of the activities of the tech providers, not the activities of the public sector entities seeking to adopt the technological deployment, which are discussed in Chapter 5, Section 3.
[88] Hadrien Pouget, 'The EU's AI Act Is Barreling Toward AI Standards That Do Not Exist' (*Lawfare*, 12 January 2023) <https://www.lawfareblog.com/eus-ai-act-barreling-toward-ai-standards-do-not-exist> accessed 2 February 2023.
[89] See Chapter 2, Section 2.

growing understanding of the incompatibility (or unavoidable trade-off) between requirements for explainability and AI performance, in the sense that non-explainable AI solutions tend to have high levels of functional performance.[90] Negotiating those trade-offs is complex and subject to non-technical decisions (eg how much more accurate must a solution be to justify a reduction in explainability?).[91] Additionally, other incompatibilities or tensions between goals of digital regulation may be more difficult to identify and balance out, especially if the results of a technological deployment can only be observed and assessed with a significant time lag.

This issue of the definitional difficulties and the incommensurability of some or most of the regulatory goals also relates to the difficulty of establishing minimum technical requirements as an award constraint, for example to require that no contract is awarded unless the tender reaches a specific threshold in the technical evaluation in relation to all or selected requirements (such as explainability). While the imposition of minimum technical requirements is permitted,[92] it is difficult to design a mechanism to quantify or objectify the evaluation of some of the desired technological attributes, which will necessarily require a complex assessment.[93] In conducting such assessment the public buyer cannot have unrestricted freedom of choice.[94] This will require clarifying at the outset the criteria and thresholds that would justify rejecting the tender. This could become a significant sticking point, especially where the public buyer is unable to pre-determine one, and only one, way for tenderers to justify compliance with the required (minimum) technical specifications (as below).

In that regard, it should be stressed that it may be easier to use technical specifications as regulatory tools in relation to some goals (eg those geared towards avoiding technological lock-in, as it is relatively simpler to establish

[90] The debate is particularly complex concerning medical AI applications; see eg Jon Rueda and others, '"Just" Accuracy? Procedural Fairness Demands Explainability in AI-Based Medical Resource Allocations' (2022) AI & Society <https://link.springer.com/article/10.1007/s00146-022-01614-9> accessed 22 February 2023; cf Sabine N van der Veer and others, 'Trading off Accuracy and Explainability in AI Decision-Making: Findings from 2 Citizens' Juries' (2021) 28(10) Journal of the American Medical Informatics Association 2128.

[91] Roel Dobbe, Thomas Krendl Gilbert, and Yonatan Mintz, 'Hard Choices in Artificial Intelligence' (2021) 300 Artificial Intelligence 103555.

[92] Even in open procedures, see *Montte* [2018] ECLI:EU:C:2018:752.

[93] This mirrors the difficulties in assessing quality in procurement, as some of the regulatory requirements will not be strictly 'technical' in the sense of susceptible of detailed description as other types of technical specifications. For discussion, see eg Abby Semple, 'Article 67—Contract Award' in Caranta and Sanchez-Graells, *Commentary* (n 35) 705, 710–11. Along the same lines, Karen Yeung, 'The New Public Analytics as an Emerging Paradigm in Public Sector Administration' (2022) 27(2) Tilburg Law Review 1, 27.

[94] By analogy with Directive 2014/24/EU (n 10) art 67(4).

whether the source code is open access) than others (eg trying to establish if the solution likely to be developed will be 'sufficiently' explainable). Designing technical specifications to capture whether a digital technology is 'ethical' or 'trustworthy' seems particularly challenging.[95] These are meta-attributes or characteristics that refer to a rather broad set of principles in the design of the technology, but also of its specific deployment, and tend to proceduralize the taking into account of relevant considerations (eg what impact will the deployment have on the population affected?).

Additionally, in some respects, the extent to which a technological deployment will be ethical or trustworthy is out of the hands of the tech provider (eg this may depend on decisions of the entity adopting the technology, on how it is used, say). And, in some other respects, it depends on specific decisions and choices made during contract implementation that may be difficult to anticipate, or in which the tech provider may deviate from any commitments made at tender stage (eg where such deviation is non-observable or unlikely to be sanctioned). This could make it impossible to verify *at the point of the tender* whether the end result will or not meet the relevant requirements. Or, in other words, whether the technological deployment will be ethical or trustworthy (as demanded by the technical specifications). This issue relates to a generic problem of verification of forward-looking requirements.[96] Including requirements that cannot be effectively verified prior to award would most likely breach current legal limits.[97] This can create an incentive to push some of the regulatory requirements that cannot be easily described or that have a strong (future-looking) procedural component to contract design and implementation, in particular as contract performance clauses (see Section 4).

Finally, it is worth stressing that the challenge of using technical specifications for regulatory purposes also extends to specifying the attributes in a technology-neutral manner solely based on performance indicators,[98] or by reference to (not yet existing) standards.[99] In the latter case, however, economic

[95] However, see eg the attempt by IEEE, 'GET Program for AI Ethics and Governance Standards' (undated) <https://ieeexplore.ieee.org/browse/standards/get-program/page/series?id=93> accessed 20 April 2023.

[96] *EVN and Wienstrom* [2003] ECLI:EU:C:2003:651, para 52.

[97] *VAR and ATM* [2018] ECLI:EU:C:2018:568, paras 28–34.

[98] Directive 2014/24/EU (n 10) art 42(3)(a); stressing that performance requirements are often used in Information and Communication Technology (ICT) contracts, see Carina Risvig Hamer, 'Article 42—Technical Specifications' in Caranta and Sanchez-Graells, *Commentary* (n 35) 462, 470 (hereafter Risvig Hamer, 'Technical Specifications').

[99] Directive 2014/24/EU (n 10) art 42(3)(b).

operators must be given the possibility of demonstrating that their solutions 'satisfy in an equivalent manner the requirements defined by the technical specifications'.[100] This imposes on the public buyer the burden of retaining the ability to evaluate tenders functionally (or on a performance basis) in all circumstances.[101] While it is possible under the rules to specify the characteristics of the 'process or method of production or provision of the requested works, supplies or services',[102] the public buyer cannot rely on a specific process of production save in exceptional circumstances and, even in those cases, needs to accept equivalent solutions.[103] The same constraint applies to the possibility to offload technical requirements by reference to compliance with labels,[104] and systems of third-party certification.[105] Similarly to what was discussed in relation to tenderer selection (Section 3.1), these mechanisms also require (in some circumstances) giving the economic operator the opportunity to demonstrate compliance by equivalence.[106]

Ultimately, the rules on technical specifications and related mechanisms need to 'afford equal access of economic operators to the procurement procedure and shall not have the effect of creating unjustified obstacles to the opening up of public procurement to competition'[107] and, under these rules, 'it should be possible to submit tenders that reflect the diversity of technical solutions[,] standards and technical specifications in the marketplace'.[108] Recent case law has stressed that 'the more detailed the technical specifications, the higher the risk of favouring the products of a given manufacturer will be',[109] and that it is necessary to assess whether the level of detail in the technical specification 'complies with the principle of proportionality ... [and] is necessary to achieve the desired objectives'.[110] Overall, this limits the potential prescriptiveness of the technical specifications that can be developed by the public buyer, at least in relation to some of the desired technological attributes, which will

[100] ibid art 42(5) *in fine*; Risvig Hamer, 'Technical Specifications' (n 98) 472–73.

[101] Sanchez-Graells, *Public Procurement and Competition* (n 20) 334–35.

[102] Directive 2014/24/EU (n 10) art 42(1)II.

[103] ibid art 42(4).

[104] ibid art 43. For discussion, see Marta Andhov, 'Article 43—Labels' in Caranta and Sanchez-Graells, *Commentary* (n 35) 474, 478–80.

[105] Directive 2014/24/EU (n 10) art 44. For discussion, see Carina Risvig Hamer, 'Article 44—Test Reports, Certification and Other Means of Proof' in Caranta and Sanchez-Graells, *Commentary* (n 35) 482, 484–85.

[106] Directive 2014/24/EU (n 10) arts 43(1)IV and 44(2).

[107] ibid art 42(2).

[108] ibid Recital (74).

[109] *Roche Lietuva* [2018] ECLI:EU:C:2018:865, para 37 (hereafter, *Roche Lietuva*).

[110] ibid para 41.

always be constrained by their nature of standards rather than rules (or metrics) and the duty to consider equivalent modes of compliance.[111] This erodes the practical scope for using technical specifications as regulatory instruments.

3.2.2 Award criteria

Using award criteria to pursue regulatory goals also presents some difficulties. There is no legal impediment *in principle* to the use of qualitative criteria linked to the subject matter of the contract,[112] including qualitative criteria concerning factors in the process of production of goods or the provision of a service, even if such factors do not form part of their material substance.[113] Such criteria can comprise the quality, including technical merit, or innovative characteristics of the goods or services,[114] as well as organizational aspects relating to the staff assigned to the performance of the contract.[115] However, the operationalization of such qualitative criteria *in practice* is subject to some constraints.

First, award criteria shall not have the effect of conferring an unrestricted freedom of choice on the contracting authority and must ensure the possibility of effective competition.[116] Award criteria 'must be applied objectively and uniformly to all tenderers'.[117] Where the award criteria involve professional judgements concerning the evaluation of factual matters that will be only known in the future (as could be the case with some of the desired attributes of the digital technology implementation, such as explainability, or trustworthiness, but also cybersecurity, especially if the tender evaluation was outsourced), case law requires that 'the professional opinion is based in all essential points on objective factors regarded in good professional practice as relevant and appropriate to the assessment made'.[118] Even where it is accepted that quality can be assessed on the basis of less than objective factors, the case law still requires that

> [W]here … the contracting authority establishes award criteria intended to measure the quality of the tenders, those criteria cannot merely refer to

[111] This provides an argument for the acceptance of variants as a matter of course, despite the need to specify minimum requirements for those variants, which will generate similar difficulties; Directive 2014/24/EU (n 10) art 45; Albert Sanchez-Graells, 'Article 45—Variants' in Caranta and Sanchez-Graells, *Commentary* (n 35) 486, 490–92.

[112] Directive 2014/24/EU (n 10) art 67(2).

[113] ibid art 67(3).

[114] ibid art 67(2)(a).

[115] ibid art 67(2)(b).

[116] ibid art 67(4).

[117] *SIAC Construction* [2001] ECLI:EU:C:2001:553, para 44 (hereafter *SIAC*).

[118] *SIAC* (n 117) para 45.

> the design of the projects to be performed under the public contract and the manner of performance of that contract described by the tenderer, but *must be accompanied by indications which allow a sufficiently concrete comparative assessment* ... to be made ... [W]here the quality criteria correspond, in total, to 60% of the points that may be allocated for the purposes of awarding the tender, it is all the more important, in order to guarantee an objective comparison and to eliminate the risk of arbitrary treatment, that those criteria be clearly set out.[119]

Such indications can take the form of, for example, sub-criteria.[120] This seems to exclude the mere use of award criteria such as 'trustworthy and ethical design', or 'responsible deployment', and poses a clear challenge for the definition of award (sub-)criteria that relate to some of the difficult to define attributes that were also ill-fitting as technical specifications (Section 3.2.1), or over which there is significant technical complexity. It can be difficult to establish an objective or sufficiently concrete way of, for example, assessing procedures leading to maximizing the trustworthiness or the ethical approach in the design of a solution, with a view to comparing different approaches taken by tech providers, without the specificity of the award (sub-)criteria in fact determining how those assessments need to be carried out (technological determinism), or creating an advantage for specific economic operators.[121]

In part, the problem stems from the absence of clear standards or benchmarks to be followed in such an assessment, as well as the need to ensure the possibility of alternative compliance (eg with labels,[122] Section 3.2.1). This can be seen, for example, in relation to AI explainability. It would not suffice to establish that the solutions need to be explainable. It would be necessary to establish sub-criteria, such as: 'the solution needs to ensure that an individualized explanation for every output is generated' (ie requiring local explainability rather than general explainability of the model).[123] This would still need to be further specified, as to what type of explanation and containing which information, etc. The difficulty is that there are multiple approaches to local

[119] *ANTEA POLSKA and Others* [2022] ECLI:EU:C:2022:888, para 92 (hereafter *ANTEA POLSKA*), emphasis added.

[120] ibid para 93.

[121] In breach of Directive 2014/24/EU (n 10) art 18(1), in addition to the specific rule on award criteria.

[122] For criticism, see Andhov and others, 'Reform Proposals' (n 85) 46.

[123] See Christoph Molnar, *Interpretable Machine Learning. A Guide for Making Black Box Models Explainable* (2nd edn, 2022) <https://christophm.github.io/interpretable-ml-book/scope-of-interpretability.html> accessed 24 February 2023.

explainability and most of them are contested, as is the general approach to post hoc explanations in itself.[124] This puts the public buyer in the position of having to solve complex technical and other principled issues in relation to this award criterion alone. In the absence of standard methodologies, this is a tall order that may well make the procedure inviable or not used.[125] However, the development of such methodologies parallels the issues concerning the development of technical standards. Once more, when such standards, benchmarks, or methodologies emerge, reliance on them can thus (re)introduce risks of commercial determination, depending on how they are set. However, even if other standards and methodologies were created (see Chapter 5), due to their unavoidable open-texturedness,[126] there would still be some difficulties in operationalizing them.

Second, award criteria must also be accompanied by specifications that allow the information provided by the tenderers to be effectively verified to assess how well the tenders meet them.[127] This comes to exclude the use of non-verifiable attributes of the tender, in the same way as discussed for technical specifications (Section 3.2.1).

Third, where more than one criterion is used, they need to be weighted or, where weighting is not possible, at least prioritized.[128] This not only raises an additional challenge in view of the incommensurability of some of the desired technological attributes (Section 3.2.1), but also raises the question of the weighting that should be adopted between quality (ie regulatory) and cost/price considerations, which would implicitly create a 'price tag' for lower levels of regulatory compliance where minimum technical requirements cannot be established (Section 3.2.1).[129]

[124] Sebastian Bordt and others, 'Post-Hoc Explanations Fail to Achieve Their Purpose in Adversarial Contexts' (2022) FAccT proceedings 891.

[125] There is a clear parallel with the difficulties related to the absence of standard methodologies to assess lifecycle costing under Directive 2014/24/EU (n 10) art 68. Andhov and others, 'Reform Proposals' (n 85) 46; Marta Andhov, 'Article 68—Life-Cycle Costing' in Caranta and Sanchez-Graells, *Commentary* (n 35) 721, 726–28.

[126] For discussion, see Joost Jacob Vecht, 'Open Texture Clarified' (2020) Inquiry <https://doi.org/10.1080/0020174X.2020.1787222> accessed 23 February 2023.

[127] Directive 2014/24/EU (n 10) art 67(4).

[128] ibid art 67(5).

[129] Sanchez-Graells, 'Procurement and Human Rights' (n 1) 106–07. Relatedly, the rules on abnormally low tenders would be difficult to apply where there seemed to be a disconnect between the technical characteristics of the proposed solution and associated costs, especially if there is no clear method to assess the cost impacts that different levels of compliance with overarching regulatory goals *should* have. cf Directive 2014/24/EU (n 10) art 69(2). For discussion of the difficulties in getting to the bottom of technical justifications for specific cost structures, see Grith Skovgaard Ølykke and Christian Clausen, 'Article 69—Abnormally Low Tenders' in Caranta and Sanchez-Graells, *Commentary* (n 35) 729, 733–34.

4. Contract Design and Implementation

The analysis so far has shown how the difficulties in treating some regulatory requirements as either qualitative selection (Section 3.1), technical specifications (Section 3.2.1), or award criteria (3.2.2), could push them to the design of the contract and, in particular, to their treatment as contract performance conditions.[130] In that regard, it should be stressed that the public buyer does not necessarily need to opt for an approach over the others, as the EU rules do 'not preclude the consideration of technical requirements simultaneously as selection criteria relating to technical and professional ability, as technical specifications and/or as conditions for the performance of the contract'.[131] It is also possible to take some technical aspects into consideration as award criteria where they relate to the organization, qualification, and experience of staff assigned to performing the contract, where the quality of the staff assigned can have a significant impact on the level of performance of the contract,[132] with some organizational aspects also being susceptible of treatment as contract performance conditions. It is thus likely that contract performance clauses will be considered as a tool of digital regulation, in particular to create procedural obligations seeking to maximize attainment of the relevant regulatory goals during contract implementation (eg to create specific obligations to test, audit, or upgrade the technological solution in relation to specific regulatory goals, with cybersecurity being a relatively straightforward candidate), or to pass on, 'back-to-back', mandatory obligations where they result from legislation (eg to impose transparency obligations).[133]

A relevant limitation of this approach to embedding (self-standing) regulatory requirements in contract compliance clauses is that 'compliance with the conditions for the performance of a contract is not to be assessed when a contract is awarded'.[134] Therefore, at award stage, all that can be asked is for tech providers to commit to such requirements as (future) contractual obligations—which creates the risk of awarding the contract to the best liar.[135]

130 Directive 2014/24/EU (n 10) art 70.

131 *Klaipėdos regiono atliekų tvarkymo centras* [2021] EU:C:2021:700, para 84 (hereafter *Klaipėdos*); *NV Construct* (n 66) para 63.

132 Directive 2014/24/EU (n 10) art 67(2)(b).

133 This is the approach followed in the piloting of standard contract clauses, which establish some specific documentary and procedural obligations (mirroring those to be included in the proposed EU AI Act). See Living-In EU, Proposal for standard contractual clauses for the procurement of artificial intelligence by public organisations, version 0.9 (2022) <https://living-in.eu/sites/default/files/files/Draft%20AI%20Clauses_1.pdf> accessed 21 October 2022.

134 *Klaipėdos* (n 131) para 89.

135 Sanchez-Graells, 'Procurement and Human Rights' (n 1) 110–11; Albert Sanchez-Graells, 'Using "Cultural Fitness" as Evaluation Criteria Breaches EU and UK Public Procurement Law'

The first thing to note is that this significantly shifts the focus of the regulatory role of procurement. While other procurement tools would be effective prior to the award of the contract and thus align with an anticipatory or precautionary approach to the regulatory gatekeeping role, contract performance conditions operate *ex post* once the tech provider is under contract and performing it. It may be possible to include some anticipatory obligations, such as the need to obtain specific permission or approval from the entity adopting the technology in relation to identified decisions with a bearing on some of the desired attributes. However, this may not always be possible and would in any case significantly raise the burden of contract administration. It can also be that a breach of the relevant condition is only observable with a delay, which can then complicate the adoption of remedial actions.

Moreover, contract performance conditions will require interpretation by the contractual parties and, in case of dispute, independent adjudication. In both instances, interpretation is complicated by the absence of clear external benchmarks and accepted practices.[136] The uncertainty and potential disagreements on the interpretation of the relevant obligations (which will be more likely in relation to open-textured requirements, such as explainability or trustworthiness, than in relation to proceduralized obligations, such as transparency obligations) could create significant delays in the implementation of the relevant requirements and, absent an agreement or injunction to stop contractual performance, disputes could either be resolved extemporaneously or simply translate into compensation claims.

More generally, the effectiveness of contract performance clauses will depend on the contractual remedies attached to them and, in relation to some of the desirable attributes of the technologies, it may well be that there are no adequate contractual remedies or that the potential damages are disproportionate to the value of the contract. It is thus difficult to assess the likely effectiveness of contract performance clauses as regulatory tools in the abstract, but it seems clear that there will be difficulties in their use where obligations can be difficult to specify, where negative outputs and effects are difficult to observe or can only be observed with delay, and where contractual remedies are inadequate. It

(*howtocrackanut.com*, 1 March 2017) <https://www.howtocrackanut.com/blog/2017/3/1/using-cultural-fitness-as-evaluation-criteria-breaches-eu-and-uk-public-procurement-law> accessed 23 February 2023.

[136] In addition to this being the most problematic situation from the perspective of the institutional challenges discussed in Chapter 3. See in particular Chapter 3, Section 2.3 on decentred interactions, pointing out the risk of incentive alignment between the adopting public entity and the tech provider to deviate from the contract.

should be stressed that the embedding of regulatory requirements as contract performance clauses can have the effect of converting non-compliance into (mere) money claims against the tech provider. And, additionally, that contractual termination can be complicated or require a significant delay where the technological deployment has created operational dependency that cannot be mitigated in the short or medium term.[137] This does not seem to be aligned with the regulatory gatekeeping role, as it can be difficult to create the adequate financial incentives to promote compliance with the overarching regulatory goals in this way—in contrast with, for example, the possibility of sanctions imposed by an independent regulator, as mentioned in Chapter 5.

5. Conclusion

This chapter has assessed whether procurement *could effectively operationalize digital regulation goals without simply transferring regulatory decisions to economic operators*. The chapter considered a range of tools covering the following phases of the procurement cycle: tender preparation and design, tender execution, and contract design and implementation.

The analysis in Section 2 has shown how there are significant risks of regulatory capture in the conduct of preliminary market consultations and how technological uncertainty can lead the public buyer to choose minimally regulated negotiated procedures, including procedures without prior publication justified on grounds of (claimed) technical exclusivity. This shows that the phase of tender preparation and design is vulnerable to risks of regulatory capture that are particularly relevant when the procurement function is expected to develop a regulatory role. This indicates that existing flexible mechanisms of market engagement can be a source of regulatory risk, rather than a useful set of regulatory tools.

Similarly, the analysis in Section 3 has shown how the effectiveness of tools of 'command and control' regulation such as the possibility to exclude tenderers or to reject tenders that fail to meet regulatory requirements is likely more limited than could be expected. Section 3.1 has shown that excluding untrustworthy tech providers would be complicated by the absence of accepted industry practices and benchmarks, and by the potentially difficult technical and organizational issues to be clarified prior to exclusion. It would not be easy to offload the screening of tech providers' reliability due to the absence (and

[137] See Chapter 8, Section 2.2.2, for discussion in relation to procurement digitalization.

expected open-endedness) of some of the standards underlying third-party certification, as well as the need to allow for alternative means of proof in relation to qualitative selection criteria. Moreover, reliance on such industry-driven standards would also create a risk of commercial determination of the criteria used to screen tech providers. A more proactive approach seeking to, for example, foster adherence to codes of conduct would likely breach current EU law. This indicates that there are limits in the regulatory role that procurement can carry out, and it is a poor substitute for a separate licensing mechanism where the risks associated with a given activity are such that carrying it out requires a level of scrutiny similar to that expected from the regulatory role assigned to procurement in relation to digital technologies.

The analysis in Section 3.2 has shown equivalent difficulties in the use of technical specifications and minimum technical requirements for regulatory purposes due to definitional difficulties and the incommensurability of some or most of the regulatory goals involved in the procurement of digital technologies, with ethical and trustworthiness-related requirements posing heightened challenges.[138] Technical assessments based on performance or standards will be riddled with difficulties in ensuring the comparability or equivalence of alternative approaches to those specified by the public buyer which, however, must be allowed in a broad array of circumstances. And reliance on standards will once again create a risk of commercial determination of the criteria used to screen tenders. Ultimately, there are limits to the potential prescriptiveness of the technical specifications that can be developed by the public buyer, at least in relation to some of the desired technological attributes, and this erodes the practical scope of using technical specifications as regulatory instruments. The same applies to the use of award constraints seeking to ensure minimum levels of technical compliance, and award criteria seeking to evaluate the regulatory requirements qualitatively. The requirements of objectivity, or at least of sufficient structuring and level of detail in qualitative criteria, make it difficult to establish methods of assessment not based on standard requirements and methodologies—which emergence can once more create a risk of commercial determination of the criteria used to evaluate tenders.

A common difficulty in relation to qualitative selection, technical specifications, and award criteria is that they are ill-suited (and legally impermissible) to assess requirements that will only apply at contract implementation stage. Given that some of the regulatory goals can only be effectively checked at the point of deployment, Section 4 focused on the possibility of using contract

[138] See also Chapter 2, Section 2.

performance clauses. The analysis has shown that such an approach alters the anticipatory regulatory approach expected of procurement and that its effectiveness depends on the possibility of creating clear contractual obligations, breach of which triggers adequate contractual remedies. In that regard, breaches of the system of digital regulation by contract may simply translate into (mere) money claims against the tech provider, which could be a poor substitute for, for example, sanctions imposed by an independent regulator.

Overall, the analysis shows that it is either not easy, or not possible at all, to use procurement tools to embed regulatory requirements in the tender procedure and public contracts, or that those tools are highly likely to end up being a conduit for the direct or indirect application of commercially determined standards and industry practices. This supports the claim that using procurement for digital regulation purposes will either be highly ineffective or, counterintuitively, put the public buyer in a position of rule-taker rather than rule-setter and market-shaper—or perhaps both. In the absence of non-industry led standards and requirements formulated by, for example, an independent regulator, on which procurement tools could be leveraged, each public buyer would either have to discharge a high (and possibly excessive) regulatory burden, or be exposed to commercial capture.

At this point, it is worth going back to two institutional insights. First, that the procurement function is not well-placed to act as a two-sided gatekeeper and that such position has a particular bearing on the (un)suitability of procurement tools, such as contract performance clauses[139] or award criteria, to the extent that the public entity adopting the technology will be able to influence how they are selected, designed, or applied. Second, that the theoretical analysis carried out in this chapter had, for analytical purposes, set aside the issue of practical constraints on the use of complex procurement rules, such as a public buyer's digital and commercial capability. In that regard, it should be stressed that the difficulties in mobilizing procurement tools for regulatory purposes that is intrinsic to their legal design and some specific requirements[140] can only be compounded by constraints and shortcomings in public buyers' capability.[141] The chapter provided a view of difficulties in using the tools by sophisticated and well-resourced buyers. The difficulties facing other public buyers can only be higher. And shortcomings in public

139 See Chapter 3, Section 2.3.

140 eg the duty to allow for compliance by equivalent, but also more general requirements, such as the duty to provide reasons or to facilitate judicial review, which have remained implicit in the analysis.

141 Sanchez-Graells, 'Procurement and Human Rights' (n 1) 111–14.

buyer capability can only exacerbate the risks of commercial determination and capture.

Ultimately, it is submitted that the analysis in Chapter 3 and in this chapter evidences the inadequacy of the emerging approaches to the digital regulation by contract described in Chapter 2. This provides the basis for the alternative approach proposed in Chapter 5.

5
Discharging Procurement of the Digital Regulation Role

1. Introduction

Chapter 3 showed that the procurement function is not well-placed to act as a two-sided gatekeeper and thus unable to effectively 'regulate by contract' the behaviour of the public entities seeking to adopt digital technologies and tech providers offering to deliver them. Additionally, Chapter 4 showed that, given in-built flexibility in the procurement tools, the procurement function is unable to develop prescriptive mandatory requirements for the screening of technology vendors and technological solutions in pursuit of the digital regulation goals discussed in Chapter 2. The analysis stressed that, were the procurement function to rely on externally determined (technical) standards, and those standards be industry-developed, mobilizing procurement would transfer regulatory decisions to economic operators. This would imply the privatization of regulatory power[1]—which runs contrary to the primary aim of digital regulation by contract. This led to the tentative conclusion that it is necessary to discharge procurement of that digital regulation role, and that this should be done by developing mechanisms of external oversight of the adoption of digital technologies by the public sector, as well as a suite of mandatory requirements binding *both* public entities seeking to adopt digital technologies and tech providers.

This chapter develops these proposals by first focusing on the design and role of an external regulator of the process of public sector digitalization, the 'AI in the Public Sector Authority' (AIPSA), and then concentrating on

[1] Which is, of course, not a novel problem, but not less problematic for that. For discussion of how parallel approaches in other areas of EU risk-based regulation entrench the power of economic operators at the detriment of public interest, see Marta Morvillo and Maria Weimer, 'Who Shapes the CJEU Regulatory Jurisprudence? On the Epistemic Power of Economic Actors and Ways to Counter It' (2022) 1 European Law Open 510 (hereafter Morvillo and Weimer, 'On the Epistemic Power of Economic Actors'). See also Carolyn Abbot and Maria Lee, 'Economic Actors in EU Environmental Law' (2015) 34(1) Yearbook of European Law 26.

Digital Technologies and Public Procurement. Albert Sanchez-Graells, Oxford University Press.
 DOI: 10.1093/oso/9780198866770.003.0005

minimum mandatory requirements, both in relation to the digital technologies to be adopted by the public sector and the applicable governance framework. Detailed analysis of these issues would require much more extensive treatment than this chapter can offer. The modest goal here is simply to stress the key attributes and functions that each of these two regulatory interventions should have to make a positive contribution to governing the transition towards a new model of public digital governance.

As stressed in Chapter 1, there is no (longer a) question that digital technologies—and Artificial Intelligence (AI) in particular—require *some* regulation. However, the timing, intensity, and form this regulation should take are highly contested.[2] There are many disputed aspects of digital regulation, with the balance between precaution and risk-management being a prime site of contention.[3] Institutional aspects of the required regulatory architecture are less often explored,[4] despite their crucial relevance for the effectiveness of *any* substantive regulatory requirements.[5]

Chapter 2 showed how, in the absence of an alternative institutional architecture (or while it is put in place), procurement is expected to develop a regulatory gatekeeping role in relation to the adoption of digital technologies by the public sector, which is in turn expected to have norm-setting and market-shaping effects across the economy. This could be seen as a way of bypassing or postponing decisions on regulatory architecture. However, the analysis in Chapters 3 and 4 has also shown that the procurement function is not the right institution to which to assign a digital regulation role, as it cannot effectively discharge such a duty.

[2] For general discussion and a specific proposal based on a liability (tort) law system, see Matthew U Scherer, 'Regulating Artificial Intelligence Systems: Risks, Challenges, Competencies and Strategies' (2016) 29(2) Harvard Journal of Law & Technology 353.

[3] See eg Margot E Kaminski, 'Regulating the Risks of AI' (2023) 103 Boston University Law Review, forthcoming <https://ssrn.com/abstract=4195066> accessed 4 November 2022 (hereafter Kaminski, 'Regulating AI').

[4] For an exception in the EU context, see Michael Veale, 'A Critical Take on the Policy Recommendations of the EU High-Level Expert Group on Artificial Intelligence' (2020) 11(1) European Journal of Risk Regulation 1. See also Bernd Carsten Stahl and others, 'A European Agency for Artificial Intelligence: Protecting Fundamental Rights and Ethical Values' (2022) 45 Computer Law & Security Review 105661.

[5] This is stressed in the context of the broader discussion of alternative regulatory models, their strengths and weaknesses, in Colin Gavaghan and others, 'Government Use of Artificial Intelligence in New Zealand' (2019) 50–73 <https://ourarchive.otago.ac.nz/bitstream/handle/10523/9372/NZLF%20report.pdf> accessed 5 April 2023 (hereafter Gavaghan and others, 'Government Use of AI'). See also Gianclaudio Malgieri and Frank Pasquale, 'From Transparency to Justification: Toward Ex Ante Accountability for AI' (2022) Brooklyn Law School Legal Studies Paper No 712, 14 <https://ssrn.com/abstract=4099657> accessed 4 November 2022 (hereafter Malgieri and Pasquale, 'Ex Ante Accountability for AI').

The analysis so far highlights the existence of an institutional deficit in the process of public sector digitalization, as well as in relation to digital technology regulation more broadly. An alternative approach to institutional design is required.[6] Setting aside the contentious issue of whether there should be a general AI regulator, a network of sectoral regulators, or a mixed approach,[7] the first part of this chapter will concentrate on key features of an independent regulator of the use of digital technologies by the public sector. This will be discussed around a notional authority (AIPSA) that could be integrated into a broader network of sectoral regulators, or which role could be absorbed by a broader AI regulator with compatible institutional features, for example through a dedicated public sector unit. The analysis will focus on regulatory coherence, independence, and expertise (Section 2).[8]

Chapters 3 and 4 have shown how there are pervasive risks of regulatory capture and commercial determination of the process of public sector digitalization stemming from reliance on standards and benchmarks created by technology vendors or by bodies heavily influenced by the tech industry.[9] Therefore, one of the main roles for AIPSA would be to control the process of standardization and to neutralize such risks by ensuring that the public interest is protected in the way the general goals of digital regulation are operationalized and embedded into such standards and related practices.[10] The other main goal would be to ensure that decisions on the adoption of digital technologies by the public sector are not driven by 'policy irresistibility', but rather that they are supported by clear governance structures and draw on sufficient resources, and that adherence to the goals of digital regulation is sustained throughout the implementation and use of digital technologies by the public sector and subject to proactive transparency requirements (Section 3).

[6] Kaminski, 'Regulating AI' (n 3) 75 ff. The alternative approach put forward in this chapter draws from earlier proposals by Andrew Tutt, 'An FDA for Algorithms' (2017) 69 Administrative Law Review 83 (hereafter, Tutt, 'FDA for Algorithms'); and Gavaghan and others, 'Government Use of AI' (n 5).

[7] For related discussion, see Matt O'Shaughnessy and Matt Sheenan, 'Lessons From the World's Two Experiments in AI Governance' (*Carnegie Endowment for International Peace*, 14 February 2023) <https://carnegieendowment.org/2023/02/14/lessons-from-world-s-two-experiments-in-ai-governance-pub-89035> accessed 6 April 2023.

[8] The latter are two of the most prominent features in designing a regulatory body to address issues of regulatory capture; see Liam Wren-Lewis, 'Regulatory Capture: Risks and Solutions' in Antonio Estache (ed), *Emerging Issues in Competition, Collusion, and Regulation of Network Industries* (CEPR 2011) ch 7.

[9] This is further explored in the case study developed in Part III, and the shortcomings of the emerging approach are explored in detail in Chapter 9, Section 3.

[10] Similarly, Gavaghan and others, 'Government Use of AI' (n 5) 76. This is to guard against both direct and more subtle influences on the setting of the relevant standards and benchmarks, as well as broader conceptualizations of what the 'public interest' means in this context; see Wendy Y Li, 'Regulatory Capture's Third Face of Power' (2023) 21(2) Socio-Economic Review 1217 (hereafter Li, 'Regulatory Capture's Third Face of Power').

The chapter will conclude by summarizing how these two regulatory interventions would discharge procurement of the digital regulatory gatekeeping role (Section 4).

2. Creating External Oversight: A Notional 'AI in the Public Sector Authority'

The adoption of digital technologies in the process of public sector digitalization creates regulatory challenges that require external oversight. A particularly relevant issue concerns whether such oversight should be entrusted to a *new regulator*, or whether it would suffice to assign *new regulatory tasks* to existing regulators.[11] To some extent, the answer depends on the existing regulatory landscape in any given jurisdiction as, for example, the second option may not exist. However, it is possible to approach the issue in abstract and functional terms contrasting, on the one hand, a narrow approach to addressing the regulatory challenges posed by public sector digitalization through assignment of new tasks to existing regulators and, on the other, the creation of a new regulator as a broad approach.

A narrow approach could result from a focus on some of the most problematic instances of public sector digitalization—notably, automated decision-making—and advocate for a strengthening of the role of data protection authorities. This would be particularly in line with the existence of statutory rights in relation to automated decision-making, such as under the EU's General Data Protection Regulation (GDPR).[12] However, it is submitted that this would be too narrow an approach because it would concentrate on the protection of individual rights and could thus miss broader social impacts.[13] Especially in relation to areas of public sector activity with no direct bearing on the individual rights of data subjects as defined for the purposes of data

[11] There is also a third potential (private) option involving the creation of audit mechanisms. However, it is highly unlikely that such a mechanism would be created without a link to either an existing or new regulator. Therefore, this possibility is not explored as a self-standing alternative. For discussion of how auditing could be used to complement regulatory controls, see Section 3.2.

[12] Regulation (EU) 2016/679 of the European Parliament and of the Council of 27 April 2016 on the protection of natural persons with regard to the processing of personal data and on the free movement of such data, and repealing Directive 95/46/EC (General Data Protection Regulation) [2016] OJ L 119/1.

[13] Similarly, Gavaghan and others, 'Government Use of AI' (n 5) 61. The reasoning is the same applicable in relation to data protection risks; see Lilian Edwards and Michael Veale, 'Slave to the Algorithm? Why a "Right to an Explanation" Is Probably Not the Remedy You Are Looking for' (2017) 16(1) Duke Law & Technology Review 18; Margot E Kaminski, 'Binary Governance: Lessons from the GDPR's Approach to Algorithmic Accountability' (2019) 92 Southern California Law Review 1529.

protection legislation,[14] or that are unregulated under current rules.[15] The more diffuse collective interests at stake in the process of transition to a new model of public digital governance would require a different set of analyses.[16] Of course, the regulatory remit and goals of data protection authorities could be broadened to encompass a wider variety of issues of digital regulation, but this would alter their nature and strain their resources (unless they were increased proportionately to the workload that would come with the extended remit). Any decisions to pivot data protection regulators into general digital regulators would require an assessment of whether this would create undesirable path dependency or knock-on effects—for example, a reduction of the effectiveness of data protection due to reduced resources for its enforcement, especially in non-digital markets, or excessive concentration on already well-known data protection risks compared to more diffuse and hard to assess algorithmic risks.[17]

A variation of this narrow approach could be to assign the oversight of public sector digitalization to existing (quasi-)regulators with a 'close enough' remit in Information and Communication Technology (ICT),[18] or to those that have emerged as a result of early experimentation with the creation of, for example, centres of expertise on digital technologies[19]—which could absorb some of the

[14] The GDPR only applies to information relating to an identified or identifiable natural person; GDPR (n 12) art 4(1). This would primarily exclude areas of public sector activity addressed to undertakings, of which public procurement is a prime example. See generally Howard Yu, 'GDPR Isn't Enough to Protect Us in an Age of Smart Algorithms' (*The Conversation*, 29 May 2018) <https://theconversation.com/gdpr-isnt-enough-to-protect-us-in-an-age-of-smart-algorithms-97389> accessed 21 November 2022.

[15] See eg Rainer Mühlhoff, 'Predictive Privacy: Collective Data Protection in the Context of Artificial Intelligence and Big Data' (2023) Big Data & Society <https://doi.org/10.1177/20539517231166886> accessed 19 April 2023.

[16] For discussion of cognate harms, see Digital Regulation Cooperation Forum, 'The benefits and harms of algorithms: a shared perspective from the four digital regulators' (23 September 2022) <https://www.gov.uk/government/publications/findings-from-the-drcf-algorithmic-processing-workstream-spring-2022/the-benefits-and-harms-of-algorithms-a-shared-perspective-from-the-four-digital-regulators> accessed 22 November 2022.

[17] See eg the clear privacy focus of the European Data Protection Board and European Data Protection Supervisor, Joint Opinion 5/2021 on the proposal for a Regulation of the European Parliament and of the Council laying down harmonised rules on artificial intelligence (Artificial Intelligence Act) (18 June 2021) paras 56–60 <https://edpb.europa.eu/system/files/2021-06/edpb-edps_joint_opinion_ai_regulation_en.pdf> accessed 21 November 2022.

[18] This could be the case, for example, of Italy, where the Agency for Digital Italy (AgID) already has some roles concerning public sector digitalization; see <https://www.agid.gov.it/en> accessed 6 April 2023. It could also be the case of The Netherlands, where the Advisory Council on IT assessment (AcICT) is in the process of being shaped and given statutory footing; see <https://www.adviescollegeicttoetsing.nl/> accessed 6 April 2023.

[19] This could be the case, for example, of France, which created a 'digital platform expertise for the public' (PEReN); see <https://www.peren.gouv.fr/en/> accessed 6 April 2023. However, the fact that the French data protection authority is also boosting its algorithmic competence raises some questions as to the likely evolution of the regulatory ecosystem; see Commission Nationale de l'Informatique et des Libertés, 'Création d'un service de l'intelligence artificielle à la CNIL et lancement des travaux sur les

new roles and duties deriving from EU law, or those emanating from domestic regulation.[20] Any such possible organic or incremental developments would however also obscure the need to consider aspects of institutional design related to the emerging models of digital regulation in ways that avoid path dependence and undesirable knock-on effects—for example, in relation to the drivers of decision-making by existing bodies, which could be excessively focused on expenditure rationalization or very narrow technical assessments. Moreover, in jurisdictions where there is no separate (quasi-)regulator with a similar role and the governance or steering of technological adoption by the public sector is located within government,[21] a narrow approach that assigned oversight tasks within government would perpetuate the institutional deficit.[22]

A further implication of the narrow approach is that it could create (or perpetuate) regulatory fragmentation if different tasks were assigned to different existing regulators. Given the proliferation of digital regulation initiatives touching upon diverse aspects of digital governance, there is a clear risk of fragmented institutional development, even within the realm of public sector digitalization. This can perhaps be particularly problematic in the EU, where discussion of EU-level institutional aspects is heavily influenced, or even determined, by issues around competence allocation and funding,[23] and where the ultimate decisions on 'on the ground' institutional design belong to the

bases de données d'apprentissage' (2023) <https://www.cnil.fr/fr/creation-dun-service-de-lintelligence-artificielle-la-cnil-et-lancement-des-travaux-sur-les-bases-de> accessed 7 April 2023.

[20] A similar approach underpins a legislative proposal in the US State of Washington; see Washington Bill: SB 5116 <https://lawfilesext.leg.wa.gov/biennium/2021-22/Pdf/Bills/Senate%20Bills/5116-S.pdf> accessed 15 November 2022. For discussion, see Kaminski, 'Regulating AI' (n 3) 64 ff. See also Albert Sanchez-Graells, 'Interesting Legislative Proposal to Make Procurement of AI Conditional on External Checks' (*howtocrackanut.com*, 2 September 2022) <https://www.howtocrackanut.com/blog/interesting-proposal-procurement-ai-gatekeeping-external-checks> accessed 15 November 2022. Related proposals have emerged in other US States, such as Maryland or Connecticut. See Maryland's House Bill 1323 <https://mgaleg.maryland.gov/2021RS/bills/hb/hb1323f.pdf> accessed 6 July 2023. See also Connecticut Senate Bill 1103 <https://legiscan.com/CT/drafts/SB01103/2023> accessed 6 July 2023.

[21] Notably, in the UK, where the Office for Artificial Intelligence and the Centre for Data Ethics and Innovation are part of the Department for Science, Innovation and Technology; see <https://www.gov.uk/government/organisations/office-for-artificial-intelligence>and <https://www.gov.uk/government/organisations/centre-for-data-ethics-and-innovation> accessed 6 April 2023.

[22] Albert Sanchez-Graells, 'UK's "Pro-Innovation Approach" to AI Regulation Won't Do, Particularly for Public Sector Digitalisation' (*howtocrackanut.com*, 31 March 2023) <https://www.howtocrackanut.com/blog/2023/3/31/uk-pro-innovation-ai-regulation-wont-do> accessed 6 April 2023. See also Andrew Charlesworth and others, 'Response to the UK's March 2023 White Paper "A pro-innovation approach to AI regulation"' (SSRN, 19 June 2023) <https://ssrn.com/abstract=4477368> accessed 22 June 2023.

[23] With a clear example in the discussion of the institutional architecture underpinning the EU AI Act and, in particular, opposing and changing views on the creation of the initially proposed European Artificial Intelligence Board or an Artificial Intelligence Office. This issue exceeds the scope of this chapter.

Member States.[24] With recent and proposed instruments of EU digital law leaving it to Member States to assign specific regulatory roles to either a single or multiple domestic regulators, and with potential variation across regulatory instruments, there is a clear risk of fragmentation stemming from a narrow approach. For example, the Data Governance Act,[25] the NIS 2 Directive,[26] the proposed EU AI Act,[27] and the proposed Interoperable Europe Act[28] all require Member States to designate competent authorities, but there is no indication or guarantee that these tasks will be assigned to a single authority in relation to their compliance by the public sector. However, assessing issues around data governance, cybersecurity, compliance with AI requirements for high-risk AI uses or AI uses requiring transparency disclosures, or interoperability may require a joined-up approach, as there are clear interactions and tensions.

Regulatory fragmentation could be avoided through the creation of AIPSA.[29] AIPSA would be an independent authority tasked with regulating the adoption and use of digital technologies by the public sector, whether through in-house development or procurement from tech providers.[30] AIPSA would also absorb regulatory functions in cognate areas, such as the governance of public sector data, and integrate work in areas such as cybersecurity. It would also serve a coordinating function with the data protection authority. AIPSA's statutory function would consist in the promotion of the overarching goals of digital regulation discussed in Chapter 2, as well as in ensuring compliance

[24] Jose Vida Fernandez, 'Artificial Intelligence in Government: Risks and Challenges of Algorithmic Governance in the Administrative State' (2023) 30(1) Indiana Journal of Global Legal Studies 65, 87. For discussion of the Spanish plans to create Europe's first AI oversight agency, see Pablo Jimenez Arandia, 'What to Expect from Europe's First AI Oversight Agency' (*Algorithm Watch*, 1 February 2023) <https://algorithmwatch.org/en/what-to-expect-from-europes-first-ai-oversight-agency/> accessed 7 April 2023.

[25] Regulation (EU) 2022/868 of the European Parliament and of the Council of 30 May 2022 on European data governance and amending Regulation (EU) 2018/1724 (Data Governance Act) [2022] OJ L 152/1. See art 7 on competent bodies.

[26] Directive (EU) 2022/2555 of the European Parliament and of the Council of 14 December 2022 on measures for a high common level of cybersecurity across the Union, amending Regulation (EU) No 910/2014 and Directive (EU) 2018/1972, and repealing Directive (EU) 2016/1148 (NIS 2 Directive) [2022] OJ L 333/80. See art 8 on competent bodies and single points of contact.

[27] Proposal for a Regulation of the European Parliament and of the Council laying down harmonised rules on Artificial Intelligence (Artificial Intelligence Act) and amending certain union legislative acts, COM (2021) 206 final. See art 59 on national competent authorities.

[28] Proposal for a Regulation of the European Parliament and of the Council laying down measures for a high level of public sector interoperability across the Union (Interoperable Europe Act), COM (2022) 720 final. See art 17 on national competent authorities.

[29] However, this label is only intended as shorthand and is not meant to imply that the authority should take a narrow approach to the phenomenon of digitalization and solely concentrate on AI adoption, or the slightly broader issue of adoption of algorithmic systems. While AI is one of the prime areas requiring regulation, a broader analysis and governance of the interaction between digital technologies and of systemic issues, including aspects of risk prevention and management, is required.

[30] In the same terms, see Gavaghan and others, 'Government Use of AI' (n 5) 73 and 76.

with mandatory requirements applicable to the digitalization of the public sector. The specific institutional design of AIPSA would require contextual analysis of the specific jurisdiction and administrative law system within which it would be embedded, but it is submitted that it should seek to achieve three main goals: first, to establish the remit of public sector digitalization as a distinct regulatory field to avoid regulatory fragmentation (Section 2.1); second, to ensure independence from government and from industry in order to promote the public interest (Section 2.2); and, third, to focus efforts to build public sector digital capabilities (Section 2.3).

2.1 AIPSA as a Way to Avoid Regulatory Fragmentation

One of the primary design features for AIPSA should be regulatory coherence. AIPSA's remit should be broad, both in terms of the digital technologies whose use is subject to oversight, and the aspects of digital regulation for which it has competence. Public sector use of AI would clearly be a core issue, as would the governance of public sector-held data required for the development and operation of such AI. However, AIPSA should be able to exercise functions in relation to systemic issues, such as technological debt, intellectual debt, interoperability, and systemic risks. This would require extending its remit to the adoption of all digital technologies, although AIPSA's functions in relation to different technologies would need to be differential and, in particular, the competence for pre-deployment authorization would require modular design to avoid overburdening AIPSA (see Section 3.2). Relatedly, AIPSA may have coordination or collaboration tasks in relation to aspects of digital regulation for which there is a specialist regulator or body, such as cybersecurity or personal data protection. AIPSA should not duplicate the specific activities of those specialist regulators or bodies, but it should have overarching responsibility for the oversight of the relevant issues as they relate to public sector digitalization.

2.2 AIPSA as a Way to Promote the Public Interest

Another of the primary design features for AIPSA should be to put the promotion of the public interest first—especially through the concretization and operationalization of the primary goals of digital regulation seeking to ensure that the public sector only adopts digital technologies that are legal, fair, explainable, transparent, interoperable, or secure—and thus create trust in the process of digitalization and in the new model of digital public governance. The main driver for the creation of AIPSA would be twofold. First, AIPSA would be tasked with preventing the public sector from deploying technological solutions that breach fundamental rights, individual rights, or digital regulation goals or principles (see Chapter 2). Second, and on equal footing, AIPSA would be tasked with avoiding current risks of regulatory capture and commercial determination, to rebalance the current trend of public sector digitalization that is overly reliant on private sector-led technological development and the associated emergence of technical (regulatory) standards.

For AIPSA to be able to play this role, it should be designed with a strong emphasis on two features:[31] independence and digital capability.[32] AIPSA would need to be designed in a way that ensured both political and industry independence.[33] While industry independence could to some extent be strengthened by boosting the regulator's capabilities (Section 2.3), ensuring political independence would require a careful assessment of the composition and conditions of appointment of the members at the top of its leadership. A proposal for AIPSA to have a non-removable single person top management structure (eg a director) seems slightly problematic from that perspective,[34] as it could be easier to target political pressure to an individual than a committee. It is submitted that it is preferable to have a small board of regulators (eg with five members) with different areas of expertise,[35] and with staggered renewals. It would also be necessary to extend regulatory safeguards of AIPSA's independence to the entire organization, much as with entities tasked with audit or control of public sector activity. A particular issue worthy of careful consideration would be the applicable requirements on post-role employment and appointments across the organization.

AIPSA's independence would require developing mechanisms of accountability. In addition to a system of parliamentary appointments (or confirmation

[31] The literature on regulatory agency design is too vast to attempt to summarize it here. The discussion simply aims to stress crucial issues for further consideration.

[32] For discussion on the relevance of these dimensions in ensuring the legitimacy (and effectiveness) of the regulatory infrastructure, see Julia Black, 'Constitutionalising Regulatory Governance Systems' (2021) LSE Law, Society and Economy Working Papers 02/2021, 16 <http://eprints.lse.ac.uk/id/eprint/113670> accessed 7 April 2023.

[33] See eg OECD, 'The governance of regulators. Creating a culture of independence' (undated) <https://www.oecd.org/gov/regulatory-policy/Culture-of-Independence-Eng-web.pdf> accessed 7 April 2023. See also National Audit Office, 'Good practice guidance. Principles of effective regulation' (2021) <https://www.nao.org.uk/wp-content/uploads/2021/05/Principles-of-effective-regulation-SOff-interactive-accessible.pdf> accessed 7 April 2023.

[34] However, this is the preferred structure in the US context; see Tutt, 'FDA for Algorithms' (n 6) 118.

[35] Along the same lines, Gavaghan and others, 'Government Use of AI' (n 5) 63, suggesting that 'expertise in computer science, data analytics, law and ethics seem like obvious inclusions'.

thereof), AIPSA's accountability would need to involve transparency of decision-making, both in relation to strategies and workplans, and in relation to specific decisions—with the latter being subject to judicial review. In that regard, AIPSA's functioning would not create any governance challenges different from those of existing independent regulators in any given jurisdiction and context-specific learning should guide the design of accountability mechanisms.

2.3 AIPSA as a Way to Boost Public Sector Digital Capability

As mentioned, AIPSA's expertise and, in particular, its digital capability should be another of its primary design features. The importance of digital capabilities to effectively exercise a digital regulation role cannot be overemphasized. It is not only important in relation to the active aspects of the regulatory role—such as control of standard-setting or permissioning or licensing of digital technology use, as discussed in Section 3—but also in relation to the passive aspects of the regulatory role and, in particular, in relation to reactive engagement with industry. High levels of digital capability would be essential to allow AIPSA to effectively scrutinize claims from those that sought to influence its operation and decision-making,[36] as well as reduce AIPSA's dependence on industry-provided information.[37] AIPSA's design should thus include elements of centres of expertise or excellence and incorporate strong components of continuous professional development for its workforce, as well as a dedicated unit on horizon scanning and market intelligence.

AIPSA's design should also explicitly address the main obstacles in recruiting and retaining digital professionals. To be sure, these are complicated practical difficulties in boosting the public sector's digital capabilities, but they are unavoidable, with or without AIPSA. The relative advantage of creating AIPSA would be that it would serve to focus efforts to boost public sector capabilities and concentrate the need for expertise,[38] and that it could raise the institutional profile and facilitate the creation of (non-monetary) recruitment and retention incentives through a clear culture of public service in the digital

[36] This is particularly important in relation to long-term approaches to influencing regulatory activities; Li, 'Regulatory Capture's Third Face of Power' (n 10).

[37] This is particularly important to guard against epistemological power imbalances favouring industry influence; see Morvillo and Weimer, 'On the Epistemic Power of Economic Actors' (n 1).

[38] Compared to creating similar capability across a variety of regulators; Tutt 'FDA for algorithms' (n 6) 117.

sphere. In any case, the creation of AIPSA would not bring an end to shortages in public sector digital capability and the role of the regulator in overseeing broader plans for boosting such capability across the public sector should be explored.

3. Mandatory Requirements for Public Sector Digitalization

Regulating the adoption of digital technologies in the process of public sector digitalization requires establishing the substantive requirements that such technology needs to meet, as well as the governance requirements needed to ensure its proper use. Substantive regulation of the technology will depend on standard-setting, which is thus one of the primary functions to be assigned to a digital technology regulator,[39] such as AIPSA. It is also important to establish the degree of bindingness of such standards and other governance requirements. In that regard, regulators can either as soft-touch guidance providers, or as hard-edged regulators.[40] The primary role of a hard-edged regulator in this context would relate to the pre-approval of technological deployments by the public sector. It is submitted that AIPSA would need to act as a hard-edged regulator, as its creation would otherwise be indistinguishable from current soft law approaches to the generation of guidance for the acquisition of digital technologies by the public sector—which are insufficient.[41] Crucially, though, AIPSA's hard-edged regulatory powers would be primarily targeted at the public sector entities seeking to adopt digital technologies, with tech providers effectively opting-in to the (heightened) minimum standards and requirements as a condition for conducting business with the government in areas that can affect the public interest.[42]

AIPSA's role in setting mandatory requirements for public sector digitalization would be twofold. First, as discussed in Section 3.1, through an approval or certification mechanism, it would control the process of standardization to neutralize risks of regulatory capture and commercial determination. Where

[39] Tutt, 'FDA for Algorithms' (n 6) 107–09.

[40] ibid 109–11.

[41] See Chapter 1 and Chapter 9, Section 2.

[42] It should be acknowledged that this can create entry barriers to the provision of digital technologies to the public sector—as compared to the development of technological applications for the private sector if equivalent constraints do not apply. However, it is expected that a proportionate approach to setting those requirements and the specificity of the need to protect the public interest would work as a mitigation.

no standards were susceptible of approval or certification, AIPSA would develop them. Second, as discussed in Section 3.2, through a permissioning or licensing process, AIPSA would ensure that decisions on the adoption of digital technologies by the public sector are not driven by 'policy irresistibility', that they are supported by clear governance structures and draw on sufficient resources, and that adherence to the goals of digital regulation is sustained throughout the implementation and use of digital technologies by the public sector and subject to proactive transparency requirements.

AIPSA's role would need to be supported by a system of sanctions addressed to both public sector entities and tech providers, for example in relation to the use of unapproved technologies or non-compliance with certified standards. However, the design of such system of sanctions would be constrained by contextual legal issues and would probably best follow equivalent approaches under the relevant rules. This issue will thus not be discussed in detail here.

3.1 Standards Tailored to Public Sector Digitalization

The analysis in Chapters 3 and 4 has shown that there are clear risks of regulatory capture or, more simply, of transfer of regulatory decision-making to the technological industry in the way the procurement function is bound to rely on the emergence of industry-led standards and industry practices (or the state-of-the-art). A great variety of standards are quickly emerging,[43] and they are bound to play a particularly relevant role under the proposed EU AI Act,[44] but there is no mechanism to ensure that they reflect the attributes required of technology to be deployed by the public sector—and some of those attributes may be impossible to sufficiently operationalize in a generalizable way through standards.[45] Crucially, the process of standard-setting involves the need to concretize and operationalize abstract normative concepts such as

[43] See European Commission, 'AI watch: artificial intelligence standardisation landscape update' (2023) <https://publications.jrc.ec.europa.eu/repository/handle/JRC131155> accessed 7 April 2023.

[44] Mark McFadden and others, 'Harmonising Artificial Intelligence: The Role of Standards in the EU AI Regulation' (2021) Oxford Commission on AI & Good Governance <https://oxil.uk/publications/2021-12-02-oxford-internet-institute-oxil-harmonising-ai/Harmonising-AI-OXIL.pdf> accessed 7 April 2023; Hadrien Pouget, 'What Will the Role of Standards Be in AI Governance? Why Standards Are at the Centre of AI Regulation Conversations and the Challenges They Raise' (*Ada Lovelace Institute blog*, 5 April 2023) <https://www.adalovelaceinstitute.org/blog/role-of-standards-in-ai-governance/> accessed 7 April 2023 (hereafter Pouget, 'The Role of Standards in AI Governance').

[45] Hadrien Pouget, 'The EU's AI Act Is Barreling Toward AI Standards That Do Not Exist' (*Lawfare*, 12 January 2023) <https://www.lawfareblog.com/eus-ai-act-barreling-toward-ai-standards-do-not-exist> accessed 2 February 2023 (hereafter Pouget, 'Standards That Do Not Exist'). See also Chapter 2, Section 2.

transparency, fairness, and accountability, and thus requires answering 'hard normative questions'[46] that go well beyond 'mere' technical judgement. Or, in other words, creating these standards requires complex value judgements deeply woven into technical decisions.[47] This heightens the risk of privatization of regulatory power around digital regulation, as compared to other areas of technical harmonization.[48]

AIPSA would thus be responsible for neutralizing such risks through the scrutiny of any such standards against the digital regulation goals it is tasked with promoting.[49] Only standards certified or approved by AIPSA could be used in the development or procurement of digital technologies for use by the public sector.[50] This approach would allow AIPSA to avoid having to generate standards from scratch, as it could certify existing standards that met the (heightened) regulatory requirements of the public sector, generate modules to 'top up' the requirements in such standards, or modify some of their requirements. Only where certifiable standards were not independently generated would AIPSA need to create them. It can be expected that this would be a minority of cases. Within the EU context, cross-border collaboration would reduce the burden of certification of the standards.[51]

Additionally, it should be taken into account that standards will hardly be able to generate 'self-executable' criteria.[52] Therefore, even in relation to certified or approved standards, AIPSA should issue binding guidance on how

[46] Johann Laux, Sandra Wachter, and Brent Mittelstadt, 'Three Pathways for Standardisation and Ethical Disclosure by Default under the European Union Artificial Intelligence Act' (SSRN, 20 February 2023) <https://ssrn.com/abstract=4365079> accessed 7 April 2023 (hereafter Laux, Wachter, and Mittelstadt, 'Standardisation and Ethical Disclosure by Default'). See also Roel Dobbe, Thomas Krendl Gilbert, and Yonatan Mintz, 'Hard Choices in Artificial Intelligence' (2021) 300 Artificial Intelligence 103555.

[47] Pouget, 'The Role of Standards in AI Governance' (n 44).

[48] Where it is still problematic, though. See Mariolina Eliantonio and Caroline Cauffman (eds), *The Legitimacy of Standardisation as a Regulatory Technique* (Edward Elgar 2020); Rodrigo Vallejo, 'The Private Administrative Law of Technical Standardization' (2021) 40 Yearbook of European Law 172.

[49] In relation to Laux, Wachter, and Mittelstadt's proposal this would shift the focus from local decision-making to AIPSA; Laux, Wachter, and Mittelstadt, 'Standardisation and Ethical Disclosure by Default' (n 46).

[50] The need for regulators to scrutinize emerging standards to assess their fit with regulatory requirements is stressed in the UK's 'pro-innovation' strategy; see Department for Science, Innovation and Technology and Office for Artificial Intelligence, 'AI regulation: a pro-innovation approach' (CP 815, 2023) Annex A.

[51] To be sure, this is an area where the EU AI Act could generate legal obstacles, as it seeks to regulate standardization as a matter of maximum harmonization. However, this is only the case in relation with 'harmonized standards', which are only mandatory for high-risk AI uses, and may well not cover the relevant issues; see EU AI Act (n 27) art 40. Moreover, given that the primary purpose of this standard certification activity would be to underpin the permissioning or licensing of adoption of digital technologies by the public sector, the extent to which the EU AI Act would prevent such intervention remains to be seen, as it allows for eg the development of codes of conduct and other non-standard requirements; see EU AI Act (n 27) art 69.

[52] Pouget, 'Standards That Do Not Exist' (n 45).

standards have to be implemented where they allow for different approaches, or where compliance with the standard is context-dependent or subject to certain tolerances.[53] This could be done through technical guides and reports. One of the advantages of this type of specific guidance is that it would reduce the need for public sector entities seeking to adopt digital technologies to formulate their own approaches. To avoid excessive prescriptiveness, a set of exceptions could be foreseen in the context of the individualized pre-approvals of specific uses discussed in the next sub-section.

3.2 Governance Requirements for Public Sector Digitalization

To ensure compliance with the goals of digital regulation and adequate digital governance, AIPSA would be tasked with the pre-approval of each specific use of digital technologies by the public sector—and any changes in the use or the technology would require renewal of the approval. Such permissioning or licensing would be separate from (and additional to) any *ex ante* control for the placing of a technology in the market,[54] and would be aimed at the public sector entity seeking to adopt a digital technology.[55] The purpose of this pre-approval would not only be to ensure technical compliance, but also that decisions on digital technology adoption by the public sector are not driven by 'policy irresistibility', are cognizant of the need for the relevant enablers and their implementation is thus feasible,[56] have considered new and modified risks and their mitigation, are supported by clear governance structures and draw on sufficient resources,[57] and that adherence to the goals of digital regulation is sustained throughout the implementation and use of digital technologies and subject to proactive transparency requirements.[58]

This would require AIPSA to verify and approve the existence of an adequate justification for the need to adopt the digital technology and that the data,

[53] This would perhaps be the practical way to specify the heightened needs of the public sector while still in compliance with the maximum harmonization nature of the EU AI Act.

[54] As generally proposed by Tutt, 'FDA for Algorithms' (n 6) 111 and 116–17. Providing additional reasons for *ex ante* approvals by a dedicated regulator where there are high information costs and uncertainty about existing levels of risk, see Eric A Posner and E Glen Weyl, 'An FDA for Financial Innovation: Applying the Insurable Interest Doctrine to Twenty-First-Century Financial Markets' (2015) 107 Northwestern University Law Review 1307, 1349–51. Arguing for a similar *ex ante* licensing scheme for some types of AI used by large firms, see Malgieri and Pasquale, 'Ex Ante Accountability for AI' (n 5).

[55] The same proposal is put forward by Gavaghan and others, 'Government Use of AI' (n 5) 73.

[56] See Chapters 6 and 7.

[57] See Chapter 8.

[58] See Chapter 9.

technological, and governance infrastructure is suited to that technological deployment. This would be an opportunity for AIPSA to provide a 'reality check' on the likely viability and fitness for purpose of the envisaged technological deployment, as well as to enforce principles that are not (easily) susceptible of inclusion in technical standards, such as a principle of AI minimization.[59] It would also allow for a precautionary verification of the risk assessment carried out by the public entity seeking to adopt the technology, which could lead to the imposition of amendments or conditions seeking to improve risk management—or, in extreme cases, lead to a prohibition where AIPSA identified risks that could not be adequately managed. It would also allow AIPSA to ensure that the public sector entity has the digital capability required to understand,[60] use, and control the technology in a sustainable and resilient manner. The process of permissioning would also be a prime gateway for proactive transparency, as all authorized uses would automatically be included in a register of digital technologies used by the public sector.

While AIPSA should have the competence *in principle* to subject all uses of digital technology to pre-deployment authorization—and this creates the default rule of requiring permission, which embeds a precautionary approach[61]—the operation of this system would require modular design to avoid overburdening AIPSA. In that regard, two primary regulatory tools would need to be developed. First, a 'sifting tool' that allowed for the straightforward approval of technology uses that did not raise specific risks meriting closer scrutiny[62]—for example because they are designed in compliance with certified standards (see Section 3.1) and the public entity is able to demonstrate compliance with all additional governance requirements, or because they refer to a modification of the use or the technology that does not alter its overall assessment in a previous approval. The sifting tool would need to be structured around different elements of risk and governance and related thresholds to allow for such screening.[63] These could be refined as AIPSA gained a better

[59] See Chapter 2, Section 2.4, and Chapter 4, Section 2.1.

[60] This is currently far from the case; see Albert Sanchez-Graells, 'Procuring AI Without Understanding It. Way To Go?' (*howtocrackanut.com*, 4 April 2023) <https://www.howtocrackanut.com/blog/2023/3/31/uk-pro-innovation-ai-regulation-wont-do> accessed 7 April 2023.

[61] This is consistent with the precautionary approach advanced here from a normative perspective.

[62] This could be built on efforts at formalizing impact assessments, such as the Privacy, Human Rights and Ethics Framework developed in New Zealand; Gavaghan and others, 'Government Use of AI' (n 5) 71. Another potential foundation on which to build would be the recently released AI RMF; National Institute for Standards and Technology, 'Artificial Intelligence Risk Management Framework (AI RMF 1.0)' (2023) <https://www.nist.gov/itl/ai-risk-management-framework> accessed 7 April 2023.

[63] Granted, developing the sifting tool would not be simple and would require constant review. It should also be acknowledged that there would be a slowing down of the process of AI adoption while exemption based on classes of risk or other technical considerations could be safely developed. The same would apply to new digital technologies. However, once again from a normative perspective, it is

understanding of specific uses of particular technologies in specific contexts, in the same way as mechanisms of block exemption are developed in other areas (notably, competition law). The sifting tool would, however, still have to be used in all cases to facilitate the automatic inclusion of the permissioned use in the register, as well as to give AIPSA visibility of all 'block-exempted' uses and allow it to develop an effective strategy of random audits and inspections in relation to those.

Audits and inspections would be applicable across all categories of use of digital technologies by the public sector—although reporting and audit should be a mandatory part of the approval or licence for high-risk uses and decrease in intensity commensurate with the reduction of risk in different technological uses. It would be possible to exempt some uses based on the creation of *de minimis* or negligible risks. This stresses the point that regulatory requirements should be based on differing levels of risk, and not on other metrics such as, for example, value of the relevant contract, as some low-value contracts could be linked to high-risk uses. It could also be possible to establish reductions in reporting and audit requirements, or to facilitate the approval of some uses, where the adopting public entity met heightened governance and resourcing requirements indicating a lower risk of management of the use of the technology.

A crucial aspect of the auditing requirements would be whether the audits can be entrusted to certified third parties or should be carried out by AIPSA. It is submitted that a mixed approach could be used, whereby technical audits by reference to the certified standards (discussed in Section 3.1)[64] are used when the market is mature,[65] but AIPSA still carries out some of the technical audits (as a quality control on such external audits) and also carries out inspections in relation to broader issues of the governance of the use of the digital technologies.[66]

submitted that the benefits of the *ex ante* permissioned approach outweigh the downsides of the slower technological uptake—at least in the way required for the reversal of the current default rule that all technologies can be adopted unless there is a specific impediment.

[64] This would avoid the issue of the third-party audit replicating the risks of regulatory capture and commercial determination resulting from self-assessment against non-certified standards. See Michael Veale and Frederik Zuiderveen Borgesius, 'Demystifying the Draft EU Artificial Intelligence Act—Analysing the Good, the Bad, and the Unclear Elements of the Proposed Approach' (2021) 22(4) Computer Law Review International 97, 104–05.

[65] For related discussion in the context of data protection impact assessments, see Reuben Binns, 'Data Protection Impact Assessments: A Meta-Regulatory Approach' (2017) 7 International Data Privacy Law 22.

[66] For discussion of the shortcomings of the auditing mechanisms included in the EU AI Act, see Jakob Mokander and others, 'Conformity Assessments and Post-Market Monitoring: A Guide to the Role of Auditing in the Proposed European AI Regulation' (2022) 32 Minds and Machines 241, especially 259.

4. Discharging Procurement of the Digital Regulation Role

Building on the previous analysis in this Part, this chapter has developed two proposals seeking to discharge procurement of the digital regulation role it is unfit to effectively develop. First, the creation of AIPSA as an independent regulator tasked with the oversight of public sector digitalization would solve the issue of lack of competence, independence, and expertise that undermines the procurement function's suitability for a dual gatekeeping role. Second, the generation of a mechanism to certify the standards applicable to the development and acquisition of digital technologies for public sector use and to subject the adoption of digital technologies to pre-approval would ensure the existence of a set of externally determined mandatory requirements that the procurement function could then enforce through, for example, tender requirements and contract compliance clauses.

There can be many objections to the proposals developed in this chapter, which would still require further development. However, most of the objections would likely also apply to the use of procurement as a tool of digital regulation. The functions expected of AIPSA closely match those expected of the procurement function under the approach to digital regulation by contract discussed in Chapter 2. Challenges to AIPSA's ability to discharge such functions would be applicable to any public buyer seeking to achieve the same goals. Similarly, challenges to the independence or need for accountability of AIPSA would be similarly applicable to atomized decision-making by public buyers. Therefore, while the proposal is necessarily imperfect, it is submitted that it would improve upon the emerging *status quo* and that, in discharging procurement of the digital regulation role, it would make a positive contribution to the governance of the transition to a new model of digital public governance. The detailed case study of procurement digitalization developed in Part III will further evidence the need for a change of regulatory approach to the regulation of the public sector's digital transformation.

See also Katerina Demetzou, 'Introduction to the Conformity Assessment under the Draft EU AI Act, and How It Compares to DPIAs' (Future of Privacy Forum, 12 August 2022) <https://fpf.org/blog/introduction-to-the-conformity-assessment-under-the-draft-eu-ai-act-and-how-it-compares-to-dpias/> accessed 15 November 2022; and Luciano Floridi and others, 'capAI—A Procedure for Conducting Conformity Assessment of AI Systems in Line with the EU Artificial Intelligence Act' (2022) <https://artificialintelligenceact.eu/assessment/> accessed 15 November 2022.

PART III

EXPERIMENTING WITH PUBLIC SECTOR DIGITALIZATION

6

The Technological Promise of Digital Governance

Procurement as a Case Study of 'Policy Irresistibility'

1. The Promise of Digital Procurement Transformation

To complement the theoretical analysis carried out in Part II, this Part III focuses on procurement digitalization—that is, the adoption of digital technologies for the conduct of procurement—as a case study of the regulation by contract of the current transition towards new modes of digital public governance.

This chapter takes a governance perspective to reflect on the process of horizon scanning and experimentation with digital technologies. It stresses how digitalization aspirations can drive policy agendas and make them vulnerable to hype, despite technological immaturity and in the face of evidence of the difficulty of rolling out public sector transformation programmes—for example, regarding the ongoing wave of transition to e-procurement. The chapter stresses how delivering on procurement's goals of integrity, efficiency, and transparency requires facing challenges derived from the information intensity and complexity of procurement governance. Digital technologies promise to bring solutions to such informational burden and thus augment decision-makers' ability to deal with that complexity and with related uncertainty. The allure of the potential benefits of deploying digital technologies generates 'policy irresistibility' that can capture decision-making by policymakers overly exposed to the promise of 'tech fixes' to persistent governance challenges.[1] The chapter sets out how this can in turn result in excessive

[1] See Chapter 3, Section 2.2.2. See also Juan Ignacio Criado and others, 'Chief Information Officers' Perceptions About Artificial Intelligence. A Comparative Study of Implications and Challenges for the Public Sector' (2020) 26(1) First Monday <https://doi.org/10.5210/fm.v26i1.10648> accessed 12 April 2023.

Digital Technologies and Public Procurement. Albert Sanchez-Graells, Oxford University Press.
 DOI: 10.1093/oso/9780198866770.003.0006

experimentation with digital technologies for procurement governance in the name of transformation.

As part of the broader transition towards digital government and a new model of public digital governance,[2] policymakers are seeking to digitalize procurement. Digitalization efforts build on earlier attempts at incorporating electronic communications and platforms into procurement governance (e-procurement).[3] At EU level, uptake has consistently remained low,[4] despite policy efforts dating back to at least 1996,[5] e-procurement being a key feature of a 2004 Directive,[6] and despite the advantages related to the adoption of new means of communication being pushed by the European Commission in repeated policies.[7] Accelerating the pace of adoption of e-procurement required a 2014 legal obligation for Member States to fully transition by 2018.[8] The transition to e-procurement has thus been very slow. In fact, at the time of writing in late Spring 2023, it is not yet complete in many Member States, especially at regional or local level.[9] This is not unique to the EU.

[2] The concept and terminology are contested, see Chapter 2, Section 1. For the purposes of this chapter, see Patrick Dunleavy, 'Governance and State Organization in the Digital Era' in Chrisanthi Avgerou and others (eds), *The Oxford Handbook of Information and Communication Technologies* (OUP 2009) 404 (hereafter Dunleavy, 'Digital Era Governance').

[3] This dynamic is shared with the transition from e-government to digital government; Barbara Ubaldi and others, 'State of the art in the use of emerging technologies in the public sector' (2019) OECD Working Papers on Public Governance, No. 31 <https://doi.org/10.1787/932780bc-en> accessed 7 September 2022 (hereafter Ubaldi and others, 'Emerging technologies in the public sector').

[4] PWC, 'E-procurement uptake. Final report' (2015) <https://ec.europa.eu/docsroom/documents/10050/> accessed 12 September 2022; European Parliament, 'Systems and e-procurement—improving access and transparency of public procurement' (Briefing) PE 618.990 (2018) <https://www.europarl.europa.eu/RegData/etudes/BRIE/2018/618990/IPOL_BRI(2018)618990_EN.pdf> accessed 7 September 2022.

[5] European Commission, 'Green paper on public procurement in the European Union: Exploring the way forward' (Communication) COM (96) 583 final.

[6] Timothy Millett, 'Electronic Procurement: Modernising the Public-Private Interface' (2007) 2 European Public Private Partnership Law Review 244.

[7] European Commission, 'Action plan for the implementation of the legal framework for electronic public procurement' (Communication) COM (2004) 841 final; European Commission, 'Green Paper on expanding the use of e-procurement in the EU' (Communication) COM (2010) 571 final; European Commission, 'A strategy for e-procurement' (Communication) COM (2012) 179 final; European Commission, 'End-to-end e-procurement to modernise public administration' (Communication) COM (2013) 453 final. See also PWC, 'E-Procurement Golden Book of Good Practice. Final report' (2013) <https://ec.europa.eu/docsroom/documents/15443/> accessed 7 September 2022. For discussion, see Sangeeta Khorana, Kirsten Ferguson-Boucher, and William A Kerr, 'Governance Issues in the EU's E-Procurement Framework' (2015) 53 Journal of Common Market Studies 292.

[8] Petra Ferk and Bostjan Ferk, 'Article 22—Rules Applicable to Communication' in Roberto Caranta and Albert Sanchez-Graells (eds), *European Public Procurement. Commentary on Directive 2014/24/EU* (Edward Elgar 2021) 236, 240–41.

[9] Petra Ferk, 'Can the Implementation of Full E-Procurement into Real Life Address the Real Challenges of EU Public Procurement?' (2016) 11 European Procurement & Public Private Partnership Law Review 327; Marina Borodina and Mari-Ann Simovart, 'A Qualitative Step from E-Communication to E-Procurement: The Estonian E-Procurement Model' (2017) 2 Ius Publicum 6 <http://www.ius-publicum.com/repository/uploads/09_05_2022_22_14_06_Simovart_Borodina_2017_IUSPUB1.pdf> accessed 7 September 2022.

The difficulties in rolling out e-procurement relate to general issues in the delivery of public sector reform programmes,[10] such as difficulties in: project management, insufficient or defective needs assessments and preparatory work, (dis)continuity and (in)sufficiency of funding, technical debt and shortages in technical skills, other issues related to legacy (proprietary) systems, organizational resistance to change, and so on.[11] This recent experience should offer a cautionary tale about the challenges and difficulties of rolling out an ambitious programme of technological change for procurement governance (and more generally).[12] This should moderate expectations and regulate the importance and priority of digital transformation in policymaking agendas.

However, the accelerating uptake in digital transformation across the public sector, especially in the aftermath of the COVID-19 pandemic,[13] is seen to open the possibility of a more decisive approach to digitalization *this time around*. This places procurement digitalization rather high on the policy agenda. By contrast, there are already early indications that progress will be slow and patchy, especially past initial stages of exploration and piloting.[14] The likely pace of adoption of digital technologies is not the focus of this chapter, though. Rather, the analysis will concentrate on the governance risks resulting from the current impetus and urgency in promoting procurement digitalization—or rather digital procurement *transformation*.

The motivating observation is that, given the *transformative potential* attributed to digital technologies and the hype surrounding digital transformation in the private sector—'ProcureTech', with common claims that '[p]rocurement practices will never be the same and supply chain operations will transform in ways we never imagined'[15]—public buying organizations are keen to engage in horizon scanning and experimentation, even if they are not ready to undertake

[10] Jane E Fountain, *Building the Virtual State: Informational Technology and Institutional Change* (Brookings Institution 2001). Drawing heavily on Fountain's work, see Shirley Kempeneer and Frederik Heylen, 'Virtual State, Where Are You? A Literature Review, Framework and Agenda for Failed Digital Transformation' (2023) Big Data & Society <https://doi.org/10.1177/20539517231160528> accessed 12 April 2023.

[11] Idah Mohungoo, Irwin Brown, and Salah Kabanda, 'A Systematic Review of Implementation Challenges in Public E-Procurement' in Marie Hattingh and others (eds), *Responsible Design, Implementation and Use of Information and Communication Technology* (Springer 2020) 46.

[12] This is of course a well understood phenomenon. See eg National Audit Office, 'The challenges in implementing digital change' (2021) <https://www.nao.org.uk/insights/the-challenges-in-implementing-digital-change/> accessed 7 September 2022.

[13] As discussed in Chapter 1.

[14] European Commission, 'AI watch, European landscape on the use of artificial intelligence by the public sector' (2022) <https://data.europa.eu/doi/10.2760/39336> accessed 5 September 2022 (hereafter European Commission, 'AI watch landscape').

[15] Girish Mutagi, 'Digital Transformation: Next Gen Procurement and Supply Chain' (*IBM Supply Chain and Blockchain Blog*, 25 April 2018) <https://www.ibm.com/blogs/blockchain/2018/04/digital-transformation-next-gen-procurement-and-supply-chain/> accessed 12 September 2022.

digital transformation processes, or there are no clear plans for full rollout.[16] This puts organizations at risk of capture—either by internal policy entrepreneurs, external providers, or both[17]—and translates into a risk of diversion of resources that could be put to better use elsewhere.[18] The normative goal of this chapter is thus to highlight this governance risk, and to point at ways of countervailing it, to be explored in later chapters in this Part III.

1.1 Digital Procurement Governance as Transformation

The transition to e-procurement seeks to achieve several policy goals:

> Countries are harnessing digital technologies to achieve better outcomes and deliver public services more effectively and efficiently ... E-procurement systems can significantly enhance visibility about how public money is spent, help fight corruption and increase the efficiency of public procurement. They save money and time by reducing administrative burdens and potential mistakes that might arise during public procurement cycles.[19]

Embedding Information and Communication Technologies (ICT) in procurement governance is seen as a (partial) solution to some of its most persistent challenges: corruption, inefficiency, and the waste of public money. Technology already has a long track record of being seen as a way of facilitating the achievement of the regulatory goals of procurement, which are discussed in Section 2. However, the transition to e-procurement was largely conceived as an opportunity to 'go paperless', while continuing to administer the same procurement processes of the analogue world (a 'lift and shift' policy intervention). This may partly explain limited motivation to overcome the challenges in its delivery, especially if the expected benefits were considered to be rather marginal.

E-procurement is generally considered a pragmatic pre-requisite for procurement digitalization and the boundary between e-procurement and digital

[16] Albert Sanchez-Graells and Michael Lewis, 'Digital Technologies, Hype, and Public Sector Capability' (*howtocrackanut.com*, 13 July 2022) <https://www.howtocrackanut.com/blog/2022/7/13/digital-technologies-hype-and-public-sector-capability> accessed 12 September 2022.

[17] See Chapter 3, Section 2.2.2.

[18] Albert Sanchez-Graells, 'Data-Driven Procurement Governance: Two Well-Known Elephant Tales' (2019) 24 Communications Law 157 (hereafter Sanchez-Graells, 'Data-Driven Procurement Governance').

[19] OECD, 'Government at a glance 2021' (2021) 166.

procurement is not always clear. It would be possible to conceptualize digitalization as part of the process of developing sophisticated e-procurement systems. In that regard, digitalization could be seen as simply complementary to, or a stretch of, e-procurement programmes, capable of making a gradual and additive (non-transformative) contribution to governance.

However, the European Commission conceptualizes procurement digitalization as:

> rethinking the procurement process with digital technologies in mind. This goes beyond simply moving to electronic tools; it rethinks various pre-award and post-award phases ... It also allows for the integration of data-based approaches at various stages.[20]

Procurement digitalization thus emerges as a policy vision that sees it as a potential catalyst for further and extensive public sector *transformation*:

> New technologies provide the possibility to rethink fundamentally the way public procurement, and relevant parts of public administrations, are organised. There is a unique chance to reshape the relevant systems and achieve a digital transformation.[21]

This more ambitious (but nebulous) strategic view of procurement digitalization as *transformative* has much in common with the emergence of GovTech as a market and policy area where the development of technological solutions to support the operation of government (either in the delivery of public services or the operation of government itself)[22] is seen as a potential governance revolution.[23] This changes the policymaking

[20] European Commission, 'Digital procurement' <https://single-market-economy.ec.europa.eu/single-market/public-procurement/digital-procurement_en> accessed 7 September 2022.

[21] European Commission, 'Making public procurement work in and for Europe' (Communication) COM (2017) 572 final, 11–12. See also the UK's Digital, Data and Technology Profession, 'The Digital, Data and Technology Playbook' (2022) <https://www.gov.uk/government/publications/the-digital-data-and-technology-playbook/the-digital-data-and-technology-playbook> accessed 6 September 2022.

[22] European Parliament, 'The digital single market and the digitalisation of the public sector: GovTech and other innovations in public procurement' (2022) <https://data.europa.eu/doi/10.2861/830794> accessed 17 October 2022 (hereafter Hoekstra and others, 'GovTech and procurement').

[23] Tanya Filer, 'Thinking about GovTech. A Brief Guide for Policymakers' (2020) Bennett Institute for Public Policy <https://www.bennettinstitute.cam.ac.uk/publications/thinking-about-govtech-brief-guide-policymakers/> accessed 7 September 2022; World Bank, 'GovTech: The New Frontier in Digital Government Transformation' (2020) <https://documents.worldbank.org/curated/en/898571612344883836/GovTech-The-New-Frontier-in-Digital-Government-Transformation> accessed 8 September 2022.

narrative,[24] and perhaps activates higher levels of policy engagement than conceptualizing the transition to (advanced or sophisticated) e-procurement as a technical back-office issue. There is a clear trend of techno-centrism in emerging approaches to public sector governance, and procurement in particular. This creates a regulatory environment where technology-based policy entrepreneurship can be quite successful, and where the public sector is highly exposed to capture by technology firms.[25] This is the main preoccupation of this chapter.

1.2 Exploring the Governance Risks of Seeking Transformation

There is no question that digital technologies can positively impact the functioning of public procurement and facilitate higher levels of achievement of its multiple regulatory goals. However, whether digital technologies can be truly *transformative* remains to be seen,[26] and some of the high expectations implicit in some policy visions may easily prove excessive. Not all digital technologies are suitable for deployment as a procurement governance tool. And even those that are suitable require significant adaptive changes to enable their deployment—some of which may be very difficult, costly, or simply undeliverable in practical terms. More importantly, even where they can be deployed, digital technologies cannot create a perfect or unproblematic procurement governance model—not least, because the technologies themselves can create new governance risks.[27] However, these constraints and limitations are not always recognized in digital procurement policy visions, which can result in a large gap between broad high-level strategies and their operational delivery.

[24] Elizabeth A Shanahan, Michael D Jones, and Mark K McBeth, 'Policy Narratives and Policy Processes' (2011) 39 Policy Studies Journal 535; Caroline Schlaufer and others, 'The Narrative Policy Framework: A Traveler's Guide to Policy Stories' (2022) 63 Politische Vierteljahresschrift 249.

[25] See Chapter 3, Section 2.2.2.

[26] cf Juan Carlos Barahona and Andrey M Elizondo, 'The Disruptive Innovation Theory Applied to National Implementations of E-Procurement' (2012) 10 Electronic Journal of e-Government 107.

[27] eg in the way they empower new 'insiders' that have a technological knowledge advantage. This is discussed in Albert Sanchez-Graells, 'Procurement Corruption and Artificial Intelligence: Between the Potential of Enabling Data Architectures and the Constraints of Due Process Requirements' in Sope Williams and Jessica Tillipman (eds), *Routledge Handbook of Public Procurement Corruption* (Routledge forthcoming) <https://ssrn.com/abstract=3952665> accessed 30 June 2023. See also Johnny Prins, Jean-Paul Van Belle, and Marita Turpin, 'Using Information and Distributed Ledger Technologies to Combat Public Procurement Corruption: A South African Perspective' (2022) 32 Annals of Computer Science and Information Systems 223.

Against this background of potentially excessive expectations capable of eschewing policymaking processes, this Chapter focuses on the links between the goals and challenges of procurement regulation and the promises of their digital governance. The Chapter maps the ways in which digital technologies *could* improve procurement governance if the technology could reliably perform the function its developers aspire to. The Chapter concludes by reflecting on how the abstract potential for digital improvements is susceptible to capture decision-making, and by stressing the need to reassess the true potential of digital technologies—and, more importantly, the required enabling mechanisms, likely roadblocks, and new risks—to draw a feasibility boundary for their deployment in the governance of public procurement. Such feasibility boundary should then inform a readjustment of policy priorities and inform and modulate experimentation with digital technologies in procurement governance, as discussed in Chapter 7.

2. Procurement Governance: Goals and Challenges

2.1 Information Intensity and Complexity as Key Governance Challenges

To understand the key challenges of procurement governance as a policy area, first we need to look at the goals of public procurement. This could be a more complex exercise than it may at first seem, as the goals of procurement regulation remain contested.[28] The discussion will be kept functional and high level here. There is a fairly undisputed set of core goals,[29] which primarily relate to ensuring probity in the expenditure of public funds by preventing corruption in the award and administration of public contracts.[30] This usually entails a related transparency goal as an anticorruption tool.[31] A more disputed,[32] but

[28] For discussion, see Steven L Schooner, 'Desiderata: Objectives for a System of Government Contract Law' (2002) 11 Public Procurement Law Review 103; Steven L Schooner, Daniel I Gordon, and Jessica Lynn Wherry, 'Public Procurement Systems: Unpacking Stakeholder Aspirations and Expectations' (2008) GWU Legal Studies Research Paper No 1133234 <https://ssrn.com/abstract=1133234> accessed 6 September 2022.

[29] Stephane de La Rosa and Patricia Valcarcel Fernandez (eds), *Principles of Public Contracts in Europe* (Bruylant 2022).

[30] This is clearly stressed in United Nations Convention Against Corruption (UNCAC), art 9.

[31] Monika Bauhr and others, 'Lights on the Shadows of Public Procurement: Transparency as an Antidote to Corruption' (2020) 33 Governance 495.

[32] Sue Arrowsmith, 'The Purpose of the EU Procurement Directives: Ends, Means and the Implications for National Regulatory Space for Commercial and Horizontal Procurement Policies' [2012] Cambridge Yearbook of European Legal Studies 1; Peter Kunzlik, 'Neoliberalism and the European Public Procurement Regime' [2013] Cambridge Yearbook of European Legal Studies 283.

still broadly accepted, set of goals concerns the use of market-based competitive mechanisms to generate value for money (or efficiency) in the expenditure of public funds.[33] This competition goal has an anti-protectionist element, to the extent that procurement markets need to be (internationally) open, which also facilitates the prevention of corruption.[34] A final set of goals concerns the instrumentalization of public procurement for policy delivery.[35] This can relate to the leveraging of procurement in relation to social, environmental, or innovation goals—as well as the instrumentalization of procurement as a regulatory tool (eg in relation to digital technologies themselves).[36] These goals are more disputed, especially in relation to the unavoidable trade-offs between the 'core' goals of integrity, transparency, and competition, and the 'horizontal' goals of innovation, and environmental or social protection—or now the promotion of trustworthy Artificial Intelligence (AI).[37]

Without seeking to address (again) the issue of procurement goals from a normative perspective,[38] suffice it to establish here that achieving (to any degree) any of the above procurement goals requires addressing two primary challenges: gathering relevant information, which can be very voluminous and originate in a broad array of disparate sources, and dealing with complexity and uncertainty in that information, which can lead to risk management.[39] This applies to each of the putative goals of procurement.

Ensuring integrity requires significant volumes of information of a varying nature, ranging from information on the decision-making process (eg which information did the public buyer take into account and was that information properly and objectively evaluated), to transactional information (eg were payments under a contract correct or excessive, did they respond to the proper implementation of the contract or were they made despite deficiencies in contract execution or compliance), or relational information (eg which personal and

[33] Albert Sanchez-Graells, 'Competition and Procurement Regulation' in Carina Risvig Hamer and others (eds), *Into the Northern Light—In Memory of Steen Treumer* (Ex Tuto Publishing 2022) 65.

[34] UNCAC (n 30) art 9(1). See Robert D Anderson, Alison Jones, and William E Kovacic, 'Preventing Corruption, Supplier Collusion and the Corrosion of Civic Trust: A Procompetitive Program to Improve the Effectiveness and Legitimacy of Public Procurement' (2019) 26 George Mason Law Review 1233.

[35] Sue Arrowsmith, 'Horizontal Policies in Public Procurement: A Taxonomy' (2010) 10 Journal of Public Procurement 149.

[36] See Chapter 3, Section 2.

[37] See Chapter 2, Section 2.

[38] Albert Sanchez-Graells, *Public Procurement and the EU Competition Rules* (2nd edn, Hart Publishing 2015) 101–14.

[39] For discussion in the context of innovation procurement, see Mercedes Bleda and Julien Chicot, 'The Role of Public Procurement in the Formation of Markets for Innovation' (2020) 107 Journal of Business Research 186.

financial relationships exist, if any, between those involved in the decision to award the contract and those owning or managing participating companies).

Promoting competition to drive efficiency also requires both disseminating and collating large volumes of information, and best procurement practice should be based in extensive (and costly) market research and intelligence activities to enable the public buyer to identify potential solutions for its needs in a way that maximizes value for money—as well as horizontal goals of, for example, innovation or green procurement, which are also largely information-based.[40] Moreover, ensuring value for money in the delivery of public contracts also requires gathering and analysing large volumes of information, some of which may require periodic or constant monitoring. Some or all of this information can be made transparent to foster a range of governance goals and public participation, although such disclosure adds additional layers of complexity and value judgement.[41]

This information is complex, tends to require careful analysis (especially as the complexity of the procurement increases), and is always incomplete, which generates the unavoidable need to manage uncertainty and, where appropriate, deploy risk management strategies.[42]

Limitations or failures in achieving the goals of procurement can usually be traced back to information and complexity issues. Corruption and inefficiency can thrive where oversight is ineffective due to a lack of information, or a significant lag between the implementation of public contracts and their audit, or because of the interposition of complex networks of intermediaries. Competition can be impaired where there is insufficient dissemination or collection of information, where the information is not correctly verified or processed, or where complexity exceeds the public buyer's capacity to understand or evaluate information. The same applies to horizontal goals. Resources can also be wasted where the complexity of the procurement system itself prevents desirable outcomes, or where an incorrect interpretation or application of the rules results in, for example, tender cancellations. It is thus clear that procurement is an information-intensive activity and that most of the costs it generates, including opportunity costs and regulatory failure costs, are information costs.[43]

[40] See Chapter 4, Section 2.1.

[41] This is discussed in detail in Chapter 8, Section 2.1.

[42] This is closely related to the conceptualization of the role of legal compliance in procurement by Pedro Telles and Grith Skovgaard Ølykke, 'Sustainable Procurement: A Compliance Perspective of EU Public Procurement Law' (2017) 12 European Procurement & Public Private Partnership Law Review 239.

[43] Peter Trepte, *Regulating Procurement. Understanding the Ends and Means of Public Procurement Regulation* (OUP 2004) 84–93.

It is no surprise that procurement procedures are conceived of as an information revelation mechanism, and that calls to boost the integrity and efficiency of procurement, as well as its effectiveness in delivering horizontal policy goals, highlight the importance of increasing the procurement workforce, and to boost skills development through professionalization programmes[44]—to tackle both aspects of information intensity and complexity. The information dependency, complexity, and resource intensity of procurement governance are thus the core areas of focus of any programme of procurement reform or improvement.

2.2 A 'Tech Fix' for Information-Related Governance Challenges?

Problematized in this way, the primary functional challenges in procurement governance directly map onto the promises of improved performance by digital technologies, which are meant to be able to gather and process volumes of information that far exceed human capabilities (big data), and to identify data patterns and other insights that are too complex for human analysis.[45] In abstract terms, thus, digital technologies could: reduce the burden of gathering, disseminating, and analysing data, and boost the visibility of public sector activities to (near) real time; guarantee the veracity and integrity of the underlying information; distil complexity into actionable policy and operational insights, including in areas of uncertainty through the prediction of future events or the plotting of future trends; and boost public sector productivity by freeing up the workforce from menial, repetitive, and non-value added tasks, as well as avoiding mistakes.

It is this abstract possibility to address the challenges of information intensity and complexity that fuels the ambitious policy visions of transformation discussed in Section 1.1. Problematically, this same abstract potential to contribute to the goals of procurement governance can translate into hype and policy irresistibility, which can in turn underpin an excessive diversion of policy resources towards experimentation with technologies with no

[44] eg Commission Recommendation (EU) 2017/1805 of 3 October 2017 on the professionalisation of public procurement—Building an architecture for the professionalisation of public procurement [2017] OJ L 259/28; see also module four of European Commission, 'ProcurCompEU. European competency framework for public procurement professionals (2020) <https://ec.europa.eu/info/sites/default/files/procurcompeu-ecf_for_pp_en.pdf> accessed 8 September 2022.

[45] See eg Mariusz Maciejewski, 'To Do More, Better, Faster and More Cheaply: Using Big Data in Public Administration' (2016) 83(1) International Review of Administrative Sciences 120.

real, or commensurate, likelihood of generating governance or operational gains.[46] Excessive experimentation can also result from too keen an embrace of emerging calls for 'mission-led' governance approaches.[47] Such excessive experimentation could result from skewed or captured (techno-optimistic) decision-making. This evidences a governance problem in itself, which echoes the broader issue of regulatory pacing:[48] how to guide the process of adoption of digital technologies in a way that avoids such risk of excessive experimentation, without impairing the (transformative) long-term potential of some of those digital technologies?

To start to answer this question, it is useful to explore in more detail what the abstract promises of digital technologies in relation to procurement governance are, to then proceed to understand how those abstract promises can trigger an excessive mobilization of policymaking resources. The following two sections respectively focus on technologies capable of reducing the burden of information intensity and information complexity.

3. Digital Technologies and Procurement Information Intensity

Collecting and exchanging large volumes of information is one of the primary challenges in procurement governance. Deploying digital technologies to tackle this information intensity presupposes the existence of adequate sources, as well as a series of characteristics of that information (such as its machine readability). For the purposes of assessing the technologies' abstract potential, let us assume that such enabling data architecture is in place.[49] In abstract terms, digital technologies could reduce the information burden associated with procurement governance, both in terms of gathering, cross-checking, and exchanging information, and in terms of ensuring its veracity and integrity. Different digital technologies, and combinations thereof, could facilitate these outcomes. The following is a highly stylized and non-exhaustive overview of the technologies and potential applications taking their potential functionalities and advantages at face value.[50] It does not provide a critical

[46] Sanchez-Graells, 'Data-Driven Procurement Governance' (n 18).

[47] See eg Mariana Mazzucatto, *Mission Economy. A Moonshot Guide to Changing Capitalism* (Allen Lane 2021).

[48] See Chapter 2, Section 2.

[49] Which is, however, a big assumption, as discussed in Chapter 7, Section 6.

[50] This is labelled as 'applications in theory' eg in Deloitte, 'Study on up-take of emerging technologies in public procurement. Final report' (2020) <https://ec.europa.eu/docsroom/documents/40102> accessed 7 September 2022 (hereafter Deloitte, 'Emerging technologies in public procurement'); and

assessment of their likely potential contribution to procurement governance, which will be carried out in Chapter 7. The purpose of this overview is to highlight the characteristics that can make these technologies so difficult to resist from a policymaking perspective.

3.1 Automation of Information Retrieval, Cross-Checking, and Exchange

Robotic Process Automation (RPA), or software robotics, is a technology that facilitates the automation of repetitive, information intensive, back-office processes based on clearly defined rules that do not require complex logic[51]—such as establishing matches with specific terms or codes, or checking whether values exceed a specified threshold. RPA can replace manual tasks such as gathering, cross-checking, or exporting information with software 'bots' that conduct them automatically.[52] RPA could thus reduce some information costs in different stages of the procurement process,[53] to the benefit of either potential tenderers, or the procuring entity. RPA could, for example, facilitate a certain degree of customization in the search for contract opportunities where potential tenderers would not rely on a direct examination of the portals where tender notices are published, but RPA software would filter relevant opportunities and bring them to their attention through automated messaging. This could reduce the burden of identifying contract opportunities and generate more competition. Similarly, there are several sub-processes within a procurement that require rules-based verification, such as screening economic operators against debarment or qualification databases or checking specific aspects of their tenders against pre-established values.

The possibility of automation could not only reduce the information burden within procurement procedures for the benefit of the contracting authority, but also allow for the use of more open procedures in situations where other types of procedure are currently used as a way of ensuring that the public buyer has the capacity to screen tenderers or evaluate their tenders—which could also generate a positive effect in terms of competition for the contract.

in World Bank, 'Disruptive technologies in public procurement' (2021) <http://documents.worldbank.org/curated/en/522181612428427520/Disruptive-Technologies-in-Public-Procurement> accessed 8 September 2022 (hereafter World Bank, 'Disruptive technologies').

[51] World Bank, 'Disruptive technologies' (n 49) 17–18.
[52] Deloitte, 'Emerging technologies in public procurement' (n 49) 19.
[53] World Bank, 'Disruptive technologies' (n 49) 41.

Moreover, automation could facilitate the retrieval of information from more sources than are currently used for procurement governance purposes, such as general sources of information on the internet (eg software could be used to gather information from press releases or other sources of publicly-available information to screen for any signs of concern over a tenderer's track record, compliance or other policies). RPA could be deployed to process invoices.[54] RPA could also reduce the burden of information reporting and exchange, such as by automating the creation of specific reports, such as debriefing reports collating the results of other automated checks, and their publication or exchange in near real time.[55] Where connected to Machine Learning (ML) or other forms of AI, RPA can automatically generate decision proposals, or even fully automate decision-making.[56] This could be facilitated by developments in generative AI.[57]

A cursory overview of RPA shows that it holds the abstract promise of automating burdensome and low value-added tasks, which would reduce the cost and time required to complete procurement (sub)processes, as well as potentially freeing up resources that could be redeployed to more value-added tasks. RPA can also reduce error risks and contribute to consistency and reliability in the carrying out of the automated tasks. The advantages of RPA would potentially be larger where existing procurement processes involve the use of many disparate sources of information, or where the same piece of information is used multiple times to verify different aspects of the tenderer or tender. Another abstract potential advantage of RPA is the possibility of speeding up and (endlessly) repeating the automated checks. This generates the additional potential advantage of information update and visibility in (near) real time. This can be particularly helpful in the monitoring of evolving aspects of a procurement process, as well as in ensuring that decisions are adopted based on current information. It can also facilitate early interventions where the relevant automated checks relate to modifiable or evolving parts of a procurement process, or to market dynamics.

The Internet of Things (IoT) refers to technology that automates the collection of information via sensors, as well as facilitating remote interactions

[54] Deloitte, 'Emerging technologies in public procurement' (n 49) 20.

[55] This would be in line with developments in RegTech. For discussion, see Ross P Buckley and others, 'The Road to RegTech: The (Astonishing) Example of the European Union' (2020) 21 Journal of Banking Regulation 26.

[56] The automation of procurement decision-making requires detailed analysis; see Chapter 7, Section 2.

[57] See Section 4; also the panel discussion in Institute for Government, 'What does artificial intelligence mean for government procurement?' (2023) <https://www.instituteforgovernment.org.uk/event/artificial-intelligence-government-procurement> accessed 12 April 2023.

by and with the connected things/sensors. They can be as simple as barcode scanners, or range to more complex sensors designed to capture or measure specific environmental conditions. IoT implementations could substitute traditional information-gathering mechanisms and accelerate information transmission to provide (near) real-time visibility.[58] There could be several implementations in procurement, primarily in relation to contract performance, such as gathering information on demand for specific goods or services. Where combined with RPA or ML, IoT implementations could replace some inspections and checks, as well as trigger automated procurement processes (eg to restock supplies when a pre-determined availability threshold is reached, or to facilitate the execution of 'on demand' or 'pay as you go' contract modalities that can be particularly relevant in models of procurement of anything as a service (XaaS)).[59]

A cursory overview of IoT implementations also shows that, much like RPA, it has the potential to reduce the burden, speed up, and reduce the risk of errors in the retrieval and exchange of information. Both technologies can interoperate between themselves, and both can also interoperate with different elements of AI and ML in forms of intelligent automation. Such intelligent automation would reduce the burden in relation to more complicated (but still rules-based) decisions, along the lines described in Section 4.

3.2 Information Verification and Integrity

Blockchain or, more generally, Distributed Ledger Technology (DLT),[60] is a system of electronic records that

> enables a network of independent participants to establish a consensus around the authoritative ordering of cryptographically-validated ('signed') transactions. These records are made persistent by replicating the data across multiple nodes, and tamper-evident by linking them by cryptographic hashes. The shared result of the reconciliation/consensus process—the 'ledger'—serves as the authoritative version for these records.[61]

[58] World Bank, 'Disruptive technologies' (n 49) 55.

[59] Deloitte, 'Emerging technologies in public procurement' (n 49) 21.

[60] Michel Rauchs and others, 'Distributed Ledger Technology Systems. A Conceptual Framework' (2018) <https://www.jbs.cam.ac.uk/wp-content/uploads/2020/08/2018-10-26-conceptualising-dlt-systems.pdf> accessed 7 September 2022 (hereafter Rauchs and others, 'DLT Conceptual Framework'); Ubaldi and others, 'Emerging technologies in the public sector' (n 3) 13–17.

[61] Rauchs and others, 'DLT Conceptual Framework' (n 59) 24, references omitted.

In other words, DLT allows for new approaches to the storage and exchange of information where 'instead of having one centralised database on which records are stored, this data is stored in a decentralised manner across all of the nodes of the ... network'.[62] DLT is thus an information management technology that can facilitate the decentralization of information verification by ensuring the permanence and tamper-proofness of the records without requiring the intervention of any one given entity, such as the public buyer.[63] It can also facilitate the creation of a trusted, secure, and transparent data backbone[64]—and, in that function, it overlaps with open procurement data efforts.[65] Depending on their specific configuration, DLT systems could ensure the provenance and integrity of information and, in some situations, its veracity (eg where provenance from an authoritative source is established,[66] or where the information is itself automatically generated for inclusion on the DLT, which could be facilitated by an interconnection with IoT or other types of oracle). This could reduce the need to supply the same information for verification on multiple occasions, and thus underpin the implementation of the 'once only principle'. DLT could also facilitate the cross-border exchange of procurement-relevant information.[67] It could prevent or evidence any tampering with such information, as well as help identify the origin of any such information security breach. This is particularly important in relation to the confidentiality of procurement information, as well as, for example, the numerous rules limiting the possibilities to alter or amend tenders. It could also prevent instances of corruption where tenders are modified post-submission, or records are otherwise tampered with.[68]

Moreover, DLT can operate as an infrastructure over which to deploy smart contracts,[69] which are another technology for rules-based automation that

[62] Deloitte, 'Emerging technologies in public procurement' (n 49) 8.

[63] However, it should already be stressed that the likelihood of the public sector implementing a fully decentralized, ie permissionless, form of DLT is very low; Sanchez-Graells, 'Data-Driven Procurement Governance (n 18) 163.

[64] Deloitte, 'Emerging technologies in public procurement' (n 49) 8.

[65] Open data is discussed in detail in Chapter 7, Section 6.1, and in Chapter 8, Section 2.1.1.

[66] World Bank, 'Disruptive technologies' (n 49) 51.

[67] Pedro Telles, 'Existing and Potential Use Cases for Blockchain in Public Procurement' (2022) 17(3) European Procurement & Public Private Partnership Law Review 179; Ramanathan Somasundaram and S M Quamrul Hasan, 'Regional: Development of a Global E-Government Procurement Architecture using Blockchain Technology' (2018) Asian Development Bank Technical Assistance Consultant's Report <https://www.adb.org/sites/default/files/project-documents/47192/47192-001-tacr-en_4.pdf> accessed 8 September 2022.

[68] Deloitte, 'Emerging technologies in public procurement' (n 49) 9; Sope Williams, 'Public Procurement, Corruption and Blockchain Technology: A Preliminary (Legal) Inquiry' (2018) Inaugural Lecture at Stellenbosch University <https://www.sun.ac.za/english/Documents/newsclips/InauguralLecture_ProfSopeWilliamsElegbe_23Oct2018.pdf> accessed 8 September 2022.

[69] Although, in principle, smart contracts could run on platforms other than DLTs, this is the most common technological deployment. For discussion, see Law Commission (England and Wales), 'Smart

could complement or substitute some RPA processes. Smart contracts deployed on a DLT architecture could fully automate (most parts of) the procurement process.[70] Smart contracts could thus, in addition to reducing the administrative burden of carrying out a procurement process, also reduce or exclude the exercise of discretion in procurement, which could have significant anticorruption benefits.[71]

A cursory overview of DLT and smart contracts shows the potential they could have in further reducing information-handling and verification costs, as well as additional potential benefits in terms of ensuring the objectivity (and automaticity) of procurement procedures.

4. Digital Technologies and Procurement Information Complexity

In addition to the potential advantages in relation to the information intensity of procurement procedures, digital technologies could also facilitate the analysis of complex information, as well as support the management of uncertainty, including through risk management systems.

ML is a form of AI that involves 'the use and development of computer systems that are able to learn and adapt without following explicit instructions, by using algorithms and statistical models to analyse and draw inferences from patterns in data'.[72] Functionally, ML can solve classification and prediction problems based on amounts of information (big data) not processable by humans.[73] ML can be deployed for category and spend management,[74] which could support efficiency analysis. ML could also be used to develop synthetic

legal contracts. Advice to Government' (2021) 2.30–2.33 and 2.45–2.47 <https://www.lawcom.gov.uk/project/smart-contracts/> accessed 19 December 2022.

[70] World Bank, 'Disruptive technologies' (n 49) 48–49; Freya Sheer Hardwick, Raja Naeem Akram, and Konstantinos Markantonakis, 'Fair and Transparent Blockchain-based Tendering Framework—A Step Towards Open Governance' (2018) <https://arxiv.org/pdf/1805.05844.pdf> accessed 8 September 2022; Sergi Nin Sanchez, 'The Implementation of Decentralised Ledger Technologies for Public Procurement: Blockchain-based Smart Public Contracts' (2019) 14 European Procurement & Public Private Partnership Law Review 180; Raquel Carvalho, 'Blockchain and Public Procurement' (2019) 6 European Journal of Comparative Law and Governance 187.

[71] Deloitte, 'Emerging technologies in public procurement' (n 49) 10.

[72] Oxford Languages Google Dictionary. This reflects the key elements of the seminar definition provided by Mitchell: 'A computer program is said to learn from experience E with respect to some class of tasks T and performance measure P, if its performance at tasks in T, as measured by P, improves with experience E'; Tom M Mitchell, *Machine Learning* (McGraw-Hill 1997).

[73] Deloitte, 'Emerging technologies in public procurement' (n 49) 14.

[74] ibid 15.

sources of information based on complex and unstructured procurement (and other) information. This could be used, for example, to create reference prices to benchmark the efficiency of procurement procedures; generate (measurable) quality benchmarks; produce predictions of procurement needs or outcomes; or support systems of red flags for a number of procedural or relational aspects of procurement implementation and oversight.[75] For example, from an anticorruption perspective, there are projects seeking to develop new measures to assess risks of conflict of interest and other corrupt practices.[76] ML is also increasingly used to develop screens to detect anticompetitive practices in public procurement.[77]

ML could also be used for Natural Language Processing (NLP)—that is, 'the application of computational techniques to the analysis and synthesis of natural language and speech'[78]—for example to generate standardized procurement documents and draft contracts,[79] or develop decision-making assistants (chatbots) capable of providing (standard) advice or support currently given by specialist members of the procurement workforce. This is a possibility that is attracting significant attention due to rapid advances in the development of generative AI underpinned by Large Language Models (LLM) that can process and generate complex text.[80] Such ML implementation would reduce the need to acquire specialist knowledge to navigate the complex system of rules and regulations applicable to a single procurement exercise. Chatbots could also

[75] Serena Cocciolo, Hunt La Cascia, and Maria Arnal Canudo, 'Strengthening Public Procurement Through Data Analytics' (*Governance for Development*, 20 October 2022) <https://blogs.worldbank.org/governance/strengthening-public-procurement-through-data-analytics-0> accessed 20 December 2022.

[76] Deloitte, 'Emerging technologies in public procurement' (n 49) 16. See also Carlos Santiso, 'Govtech Against Corruption: What Are the Integrity Dividends of Government Digitalization?' (2022) 4 Data & Policy e39; Roberto De Michele and Juan Cruz Vieyra, 'From Fishing to Catching: Developing Actionable Red Flags in Public Procurement to Prevent and Control Corruption' (2022) Inter-American Development Bank Technical Note No IDB-TN-2598 <http://dx.doi.org/10.18235/0004595> accessed 19 December 2022.

[77] Eg Manuel J Garcia Rodriguez and others, 'Collusion Detection in Public Procurement Auctions with Machine Learning Algorithms' (2022) 133 Automation in Construction 104047. For discussion, see Albert Sanchez-Graells, '"Screening for Cartels" in Public Procurement: Cheating at Solitaire to Sell Fool's Gold?' (2019) 10(4) Journal of European Competition Law & Practice 199.

[78] Oxford Languages Google Dictionary.

[79] Deloitte, 'Emerging technologies in public procurement' (n 49) 17.

[80] See OECD, 'AI language models: Technological, socio-economic and policy considerations' (2023) OECD Digital Economy Papers, No 352 <https://doi.org/10.1787/13d38f92-en> accessed 14 April 2023. This is an area of particularly intense hype at the time of writing in late Spring 2023. However, even while taking this technology at face value, it is worth sounding a note of caution about the potential of these models and their inherent costs and risks, which in any case would be affected by the issues concerning the need to control the information they draw from and related issues of legal responsibility discussed in Chapter 7, Section 3.2 in relation to chatbots that could be powered by this technology. For such a cautious approach, see Emily M Bender and others, 'On the Dangers of Stochastic Parrots: Can Language Models Be Too Big?' (2021) FAccT proceedings 610.

be developed to allow tenderers to self-assess compliance with tender requirements before tender submission, thus reducing the scope for mistakes and the submission of non-compliant tenders.[81] Similar techniques could be used to extract and classify information from unstructured sources, and ML could also enable new approaches to procurement due diligence and evaluation based on a larger number of data points, as well as the embedding of forecasts or predictions into procurement evaluation processes.[82] This would allow for the automation of complex decisions that cannot be easily translated into strict rules, for example to enable RPA or smart contract-based automation.[83] ML could also be used to develop recommender systems that facilitate a pre-screening of potential tenderers[84] or products and services, thus potentially reducing the cost and complexity of carrying out market research ahead of procurement exercises. ML could also be used to develop systems of risk indicators, for example in relation to contract non-compliance, supply-chain issues, or other risks of non-performance, which could then inform the deployment of risk management systems.

A cursory overview of ML, including NLP, shows that it has the potential to bridge the complexity of the information relevant from a procurement governance perspective, and that it can augment decision-makers' ability to deal with that complexity and with related uncertainty. This comes with the implicit advantage of automation, as all tasks carried out by ML would be automated. This could minimize the need for human decision-making, or even exclude it altogether.[85]

5. Factors Contributing to Hype and Policy Irresistibility

The superficial technological overview of the last two sections shows that, in abstract terms, digital technologies have the theoretical potential to significantly reduce the burden of information intensity and complexity in procurement governance by a combination of automation and decision-making

[81] Deloitte, 'Emerging technologies in public procurement' (n 49) 15.
[82] World Bank, 'Disruptive technologies' (n 49) 42.
[83] Deloitte, 'Emerging technologies in public procurement' (n 49) 18.
[84] Manuel J Garcia Rodriguez and others, 'Bidders Recommender for Public Procurement Auctions Using Machine Learning: Data Analysis, Algorithm, and Case Study with Tenders from Spain' (2020) Complexity 8858258.
[85] However, the automation of procurement decision-making requires detailed analysis; Chapter 7, Section 2.

support implementations. These could boost the integrity of the procedures, enable heightened competition for public contracts, and reduce administrative costs. Given this theoretical potential to reduce the information and complexity burdens of procurement, it is hardly surprising that the prospect of reaping the gains of the deployment of digital technologies generates significant hype and 'policy irresistibility'. That is, an attractiveness that is likely to bring procurement digitalization to the top of the policymaking agenda, even if its specific benefits and the requirements to unleash them are not very clear, or well understood—not least, as these are immature technologies.

This hype and policy irresistibility are fuelled by the direct mapping of the theoretical functionality of digital technologies onto the primary regulatory challenges in procurement governance, which can obscure the governance embeddedness of digital technology adoption[86] and increase the appeal of 'technological fixes' for governance challenges[87] in a clear example of techno-optimism[88] or techno-solutionism.[89] Moreover, hype and policy irresistibility are also fuelled by governance characteristics such as: multi-level governance, an emphasis on embedding innovation in procurement, and a continued gap in the public sector's digital capability. These characteristics directly connect with the governance risks identified by a combination of garbage can theory, policy entrepreneurship, and policy capture in Chapter 3, Section 2.2.2, as will be further stressed in Section 6.

[86] For discussion, see Juho Pääkkönen and others, 'Bureaucracy as a Lens for Analyzing and Designing Algorithmic Systems' (2020) CHI Conference on Human Factors in Computing Systems <https://doi.org/10.1145/3313831.3376780> accessed 21 April 2023.

[87] This would be a clear instance of technology determinism. Dunleavy, 'Digital Era Governance' (n 2) 404–06. Its exploration in detail exceeds the scope of this chapter. For discussion in relation to blockchain, see Uta Kohl, 'Blockchain Utopia and Its Governance Shortfalls' in Oreste Pollicino and Giovanni De Gregorio (eds), *Blockchain and Public Law. Global Challenges in the Era of Decentralisation* (Edward Elgar 2021) 13. See also H G van der Voort and others, 'Rationality and Politics of Algorithms. Will the Promise of Big Data Survive the Dynamics of Public Decision Making?' (2019) 36 Government Information Quarterly 27. For a useful overview of the relevance and need to contextualize techno-legal interactions by reference to Science, Technology, and Society (STS) studies, see Ryan Calo, 'The Scale and the Reactor' (SSRN, 15 April 2022) <https://ssrn.com/abstract=4079851> accessed 7 September 2022. For an account based on real-life experiences, see Tara Dawson McGuinness and Hana Schank, *Power to the Public: The Promise of Public Interest Technology* (Princeton UP 2021) 57 ff (hereafter Dawson McGuinness and Schank, *Power to the Public*).

[88] For discussion, see Simon Vydra and Bram Klievink, 'Techno-Optimism and Policy-Pessimism in the Public Sector Big Data Debate' (2019) 36(4) Government Information Quarterly 101383.

[89] Karen Yeung, 'The New Public Analytics as an Emerging Paradigm in Public Sector Administration' (2022) 27(2) Tilburg Law Review 1, 16–18 (hereafter Yeung, 'New Public Analytics'); Evgeny Morozov, 'The True Threat of Artificial Intelligence' (*New York Times*, 30 June 2023) <https://www.nytimes.com/2023/06/30/opinion/artificial-intelligence-danger.html> accessed 2 July 2023.

5.1 Multi-Level Procurement Governance

Public procurement is carried out at different levels of government, ranging from local and institutional procurement (eg by universities) to regional and State level, as well as sometimes internationally. There are also increasing trends of centralization and collaboration that alter the traditional structures of procurement governance, including with a cross-border dimension. This implies that some aspects of procurement governance are multi-level, in particular concerning, for example, the establishing of the legal regime or, increasingly, policy priorities. In the EU, the European Commission has been pushing for a set of policy goals that squarely includes innovation,[90] and Member States are systematically monitored for its implementation—although the metrics are never quite clear. At national level, States are also adopting policy frameworks that repeatedly stress the goal of digitalizing procurement, as well as stressing the need to revise procurement processes to ensure that they are innovation-friendly,[91] as discussed in Section 5.2. Translating these high-level policies and goals into operational change is left to the levels of governance closer to the day-to-day operation of procurement, which can generate pressures to adopt digital technologies (or to be able to report doing so), despite the operational needs and framework not necessarily being ready for that. This is reflective of the top-down approach that tends to underlie digital transformation programmes, especially when they are coupled with centralization and standardization, as also discussed in Section 5.3.

5.2 Innovative Procurement (of Innovation)

The use of procurement as an innovation catalyst has been an ongoing policy consideration, and one that has had growing policy relevance over the last decade, especially in the EU.[92] While innovation procurement has mainly focused on the procurement of the process (ie R&D services) and outcomes of innovation,[93] there has been increasing attention to innovative procurement (ie innovation in the way procurement is carried out) as an enabler for the

[90] European Commission, 'Strategic procurement' <https://single-market-economy.ec.europa.eu/single-market/public-procurement/strategic-procurement_en> accessed 5 September 2022.

[91] European Commission, 'AI watch landscape' (n 14) 25.

[92] See eg European Commission, 'Guidance on innovation procurement' (Notice) C(2021) 4320 final.

[93] ibid 5. For discussion, see Pedro Cerqueira Gomes, *EU Public Procurement and Innovation. The Innovation Partnership Procedure and Harmonization Challenges* (Edward Elgar 2021) 41–44.

procurement of innovation.[94] This is perhaps particularly clear in the context of GovTech, where it has been stressed that '[d]elivering digital transformation through GovTech cannot be separated from the purchasing of GovTech'.[95]

Such policy approach creates a conflation between the importance of ensuring that the public sector is benefitting from market innovation as a technological dimension of value for money, on the one hand, and the perception that procurement rules and procedures are inadequate for the purchasing of such innovation, on the other. The perceived inadequacy of procurement rules stems from the touted advantages of less structured and formal processes of information gathering and co-creation of (concept or pilot) solutions, such as hackathons and other challenge-based approaches. The claim is that the full-fledged application of procurement rules could put some of the innovators off, or introduce rigidities that could derail the innovation process.[96] However, there is little evidence that alternative, procurement-compliant approaches would not lend satisfactory results, even if they would be difficult to manage.[97] Regardless, the conflation of the intended procurement outcome and the way it is carried out generates policy pressure 'to do things differently',[98] and to digitalize procurement as part and parcel of adjusting procurement practices to the (perceived) demands of the procurement of innovation. This compounds the effects of other dynamics pushing for the adoption of digital technologies for procurement governance. Some of those dynamics are largely the result of reduced digital capability in the public sector.

5.3 The Public Sector Digital Capability Gap

Most public procurement organizations have limited digital capability.[99] Contrary to what maturity models and other guidelines would

[94] European Commission, 'Guide on public procurement procedures and instruments in support of innovation' <https://ec.europa.eu/docsroom/documents/47179> accessed 5 September 2022.

[95] Hoekstra and others, 'GovTech and procurement' (n 22) 24, emphasis omitted. This is qualified by the possibility of digital transformation being developed fully in-house.

[96] European Commission, 'AI watch landscape' (n 14) 25; Hoekstra and others, 'GovTech and procurement' (n 22) 9 and 28. This is reflected in the OECD, Recommendation of the Council on Digital Government Strategies (2014) para 11.

[97] Hoekstra and others, 'GovTech and procurement' (n 22) 24 ff.

[98] Which is even elevated to the category of principle; see OECD Digital Government Toolkit, Principle 11 <https://www.oecd.org/governance/digital-government/toolkit/principle11/> accessed 5 September 2022.

[99] This is uncontroversial and, to varying extents, a common issue in all jurisdictions. For details on the UK, see eg Central Digital and Data Office, 'Transforming for a digital future: 2022 to 2025 roadmap for digital and data' (Policy Paper, 9 June 2022) <https://www.gov.uk/government/publications/roadmap-for-digital-and-data-2022-to-2025> accessed 5 September 2022 (hereafter CDDO, 'Transforming

recommend,[100] such limited digital capability does not necessarily prevent public sector organizations from engaging—and certainly does not shield them from efforts by the private sector to engage them—in digitalization projects.[101] This digital capability gap creates risks of exploitation of the limited technical knowledge available at public agencies,[102] and 'this dependency risk can become even more significant once modern GovTech solutions replace older government components'.[103] Indeed, limited digital capability opens public buyers up to risks of policy capture,[104] where the private sector determines the 'feasibility boundary' (or art of the possible) and the public sector follows in the award of contracts for the implementation of digital technologies, without properly understanding them,[105] or obtaining sufficient assurances that their abstract benefits will ever be realized.[106]

One way to try to address the digital capability gap is for public organizations to engage consultants and service providers with such knowledge and skills.[107] Such a strategy can provide short-term solutions, but creates medium- and long-term problems, especially as the reliance on outside resources can further the tendency of hollowing out the public sector's capabilities,[108] and extend to core State functions.[109] It can also exacerbate the technical and intellectual debt associated with digital technologies,[110] especially if there is no continuity in

for a digital future'). See also National Audit Office, 'Digital transformation in government: addressing the barriers to efficiency' (HC 2022-23, 1171).

[100] eg Kevin C Desouza, 'Artificial Intelligence in the Public Sector: A Maturity Model' (2021) IBM Centre for the Business of Government <https://businessofgovernment.org/report/artificial-intelligence-public-sector-maturity-model> accessed 8 September 2022.

[101] See n 16.

[102] Dawson McGuinness and Schank, *Power to the Public* (n 87) 1–16.

[103] Nitesh Bharosa, 'The Rise of GovTech: Trojan Horse or Blessing in Disguise? A Research Agenda' (2022) 39 Government Information Quarterly 101692, 8.

[104] OECD, 'Preventing policy capture. Integrity in public decision making' (2017) 39.

[105] Albert Sanchez-Graells, 'Procuring AI Without Understanding It. Way To Go?' (*howtocrackanut.com*, 4 April 2023) <https://www.howtocrackanut.com/blog/2023/3/31/uk-pro-innovation-ai-regulation-wont-do> accessed 7 April 2023.

[106] This links with insights derived from the study of commercial determinants of policymaking. For discussion in the procurement context, see Eleanor Aspey and Richard Craven, 'Regulating Complex Contracting: A Socio-Legal Study of Decision-Making under EU and UK Law' (2018) 81 Modern Law Review 191.

[107] Vera Weghmann and Kyla Sankey, 'Hollowed Out: The Growing Impact of Consultancies in Public Administrations' (2022) EPSU Report <https://www.epsu.org/sites/default/files/article/files/EPSU%20Report%20Outsourcing%20state_EN.pdf> accessed 17 October 2022 (hereafter Weghmann and Sankey, 'Hollowed Out').

[108] Although not specific to digitalization, the analysis is telling in Bridget C E Dooling and Rachel Augustine Potter, 'Regulatory Body Shops' (2022) <https://ssrn.com/abstract=4186402> accessed 8 September 2022. See also H Brinton Milward and Keith Provan, 'Managing the Hollow State. Collaboration and Contracting' (2003) 5 Public Management Review 1.

[109] Sukhdev Johal, Michael Moran, and Karel Williams, 'Breaking the Constitutional Silence: The Public Services Industry and Government' (2016) 87 Political Quarterly 389.

[110] For further discussion, see Chapter 8, Section 2.2.

the engagement of consultants. Such strategy also generates additional risks of conflicts of interest that can become difficult to identify and manage. From a governance perspective, it is thus a less than ideal fix.[111]

Another way to try to address this capability gap is through collaboration and centralization in the procurement of digital technologies.[112] While this can allow for the pooling of expertise and capabilities, it also has governance implications. Centralized procurement in particular, in its drive to standardize needs and create economies of scale (eg the 'buy once, use many times' approach to technology[113]), reduces or completely excludes the chances of operational influence over the procurement process. In other words, it transforms the digitalization of procurement into a top-down process and makes it susceptible to risks of technological-centricity that can generate difficulties in the rollout and adoption of the centrally procured technologies. Moreover, not only the procurement, but also the adoption and continued use of digital technologies at operational level requires digital capabilities. Centralized and collaborative procurement can thus only go so far in alleviating the digital capabilities gap. Finally, centralization of digital technology procurement raises the stakes for potential providers, which can in turn reactivate issues of risk of capture as the reward for influencing technology decisions grows. From a governance perspective, this is also a less than ideal fix.[114]

6. Conclusion

Chapter 3, Section 2.2.2. showed how policy- and decision-making processes are vulnerable to policy entrepreneurship and regulatory capture and that such risks are particularly relevant where confluent developments open a window of opportunity for policy intervention or capture. Given the analysis in this chapter, it is submitted that the current policymaking environment surrounding 'digital transformation' has opened such a window of opportunity for digital technology related policy entrepreneurship, and for attempts at policy capture by (GovTech) entrepreneurs[115]—sometimes under the cover

[111] Weghmann and Sankey, 'Hollowed Out' (n 107). For further discussion, see Chapter 8, Section 4.
[112] As promoted by eg the European Commission, C(2021) 4320 final (n 92) section 2.5.2.
[113] CDDO, 'Transforming for a digital future' (n 99).
[114] Albert Sanchez-Graells, 'Competition Implications of Procurement Digitalisation and the Procurement of Digital Technologies by Central Purchasing Bodies' (2023) <https://ssrn.com/abstract=4376037> accessed 12 April 2023.
[115] Similarly, Yeung, 'New Public Analytics' (n 89) 19–20 and 26–30.

of 'technical decisions'.[116] A couple of additional observations may now be added. Given the limited digital capability in the public sector, it is likely that those with (some) digital skills are internally seen as more capable of leading in digital transformation and, consequently, may enjoy increased opportunities for policy entrepreneurship. Such policy steer can be influenced by the specific vision or relationships of that policy entrepreneur, but those may not be observable to the rest of the organization, which may in any case lack the ability (or incentives) to take a hard look or query specific policies or proposals.[117] Relatedly, for the same reason, there are increased opportunities for capture by tech companies that either have an incumbency advantage (eg they are already providing e-procurement or consultancy services), or otherwise have a strong market position, reputation, or salesforce.[118] It is hard to overstress how standard governance challenges are heightened in the context of a window of opportunity where the allure of digital technologies can serve as sufficient justification for all sorts of policy decisions, including (and perhaps especially) decisions concerning technological experimentation.

Any such instances of policy entrepreneurship or capture, in addition to other significant governance problems, may trigger the investment of excessive or unjustified amounts of resources by policymakers unable to resist the allure of digital technologies and their abstract promises. Beyond excessive experimentation, this can also eventually lead to the adoption of technologies that are not best suited to the procurement function's needs, or technologies that create problems in the medium to long term, such as (further) technical or intellectual debt, or other issues (eg lock-in).[119] This can have clear negative societal impacts.

One of the clear challenges in reducing such risks requires boosting the digital capability of the public sector, to which we will return in Chapter 8.[120] Another challenge is to take a hard look at digital technologies' allure and

[116] For extended discussion, see Karen Yeung and Adam Harkens, 'How Do "Technical" Design Choices Made When Building Algorithmic Decision-Making Tools for Criminal Justice Authorities Create Constitutional Dangers?' Parts I and II (2023) Public Law forthcoming <https://ssrn.com/abstract=4319307> and <https://ssrn.com/abstract=4319319> accessed 8 March 2023.

[117] This further evidences the difficulties resulting from the public-public and decentred interactions discussed in Chapter 3, Sections 2.2 and 2.3.

[118] This clearly risks compounding the 'weak public buyer' problem discussed in Chapter 3, Section 2.1.

[119] For further discussion, see Chapter 8, Section 2.2.

[120] This is a core theme and recommendation eg of the Goldacre Review in the context of health data, which however offers very exportable insights on the challenges of data and technology-related governance reform programmes; Ben Goldacre and Jess Morley, 'Better, Broader, Safer: Using Health Data for Research and Analysis. A Review Commissioned by the Secretary of State for Health and Social Care' (2022) <https://www.goldacrereview.org/> accessed 12 September 2022.

'policy irresistibility' by reassessing their true potential benefits and, more importantly, the required enabling mechanisms, likely roadblocks, and new risks. This would help draw a feasibility boundary for their deployment in procurement and establish what digital technologies could *realistically* bring to procurement governance. This should contribute to a better understanding of the advantages that can arise from procurement digitalization and the associated costs and risks, which should demystify some tech and reduce its 'policy irresistibility'. That will be the object of Chapter 7.

7

Revisiting the Promise

A Feasibility Boundary for Digital Procurement Governance

1. Understanding Digital Technologies in the Procurement Governance Context

Chapter 6 argued that mitigating the allure and policy irresistibility of digital technologies requires reassessing their true potential benefits and, more importantly, the necessary enabling mechanisms, likely roadblocks, and new risks that come with them. This chapter takes a closer functional look at the technologies. This will generate a better understanding of the constraints on their contribution to improving (digital) procurement governance. Such constraints should serve as a counterpoint to the hype that follows superficial or techno optimistic assessments. They should help recentre policy agendas towards establishing proper foundations for digital adaptation in the long term. The chapter will evidence the importance of data availability and quality across technologies. This will lead to an analysis of the difficulties in generating an enabling big data architecture despite efforts led by, for example, the European Commission, or the Open Contracting Partnership (OCP). Such big data architecture will remain the main constraint on the implementation of digital technologies in the near future. Thinking further ahead, the chapter will highlight the displacement, rather than avoidance or resolution, of governance risks that the adoption of digital technologies can generate (which will then be explored in more detail in Chapter 8). The chapter will close with a recapitulation of the feasibility boundary for digital procurement governance.

The importance of embedding a proper understanding of the different technologies—in other words, a distillation of how they work (or could work)—in legal and policy analysis can hardly be overstated.[1] '[T]here is a

[1] See eg David Lehr and Paul Ohm, 'Playing with the Data: What Legal Scholars Should Learn About Machine Learning' (2017) 51 UC Davis Law Review 653 (hereafter Lehr and Ohm, 'Machine Learning for Legal Scholars'); Rembrandt Deville, Nico Sergeyssels, and Catherine Middag, 'Basic Concepts of AI for Legal Scholars' in Jan De Bruyne and Cedric Vanleenhove (eds), *Artificial Intelligence and the Law* (Intersentia 2021) 1 (hereafter Deville, Sergeyssels, and Middag, 'Basic AI Concepts').

Digital Technologies and Public Procurement. Albert Sanchez-Graells, Oxford University Press.
 DOI: 10.1093/oso/9780198866770.003.0007

danger that scholarship not rooted in a technical understanding … may be too speculative to be useful.'[2] This is not at all a novel insight or approach.[3] However, some recent scholarship in digital procurement governance has tended to brush aside the need to move past an intuitive understanding of the technologies, especially in relation to blockchain. This can generate conceptual confusion,[4] or technology optimism biases rooted in too general speculation.[5] At the other end of the scale, legal scholarship can seek to over-theorize the interaction between law and technology,[6] which can also obfuscate the analysis. This chapter seeks to travel a middle path and to engage with the technologies in functional detail sufficient for the analysis of their governance-related deployment.[7]

The chapter will concentrate on a selection of digital technologies, including Robotic Process Automation (RPA) (Section 2); Machine Learning (ML) implementations, such as recommender systems, chatbots, and automated screens, as specific types of Artificial Intelligence (AI) (Section 3); Distributed Ledger Technology (DLT) systems, including smart contracts (Section 4); and the Internet of Things (IoT) and oracles (Section 5). It is submitted that this is the set of digital technologies most likely to be suited to the digitalization of procurement governance. Although some policy reports also address cloud computing as a separate digital technology, this chapter takes the position that cloud technology does not have the potential to significantly alter the governance of procurement, although it can alter (and has been altering) the technological infrastructure used in procurement procedures.[8] The chapter also does not cover 3D printing. Although this could be useful as a mode of delivery

[2] Ryan McCarl, 'The Limits of Law and AI' (2022) 90 University of Cincinnati Law Review 923, 924.

[3] It differs, however, from approaches to law and technology that seek to establish the interaction between both and their respective social constructs. For discussion, see eg Mireille Hildebrandt, *Smart Technologies and the End(s) of Law* (Edward Elgar 2015) 159 ff.

[4] eg Raquel Carvalho, 'Blockchain and Public Procurement' (2019) 6 European Journal of Comparative Law and Governance 187; or Nadia-Ariadna Sava and Dacian Dragos, 'The Legal Regime of Smart Contracts in Public Procurement' (2022) 66 Transylvanian Review of Administrative Sciences 99.

[5] eg Pawel Nowicki, 'Deus Ex Machina? Some Remarks on Public Procurement in the Second Machine Age' (2020) 15 European Procurement & Public Private Partnership Law Review 53; Sope Williams, 'Public Procurement, Corruption and Blockchain Technology: A Preliminary (Legal) Inquiry' (2018) Inaugural Lecture at Stellenbosh University <https://www.sun.ac.za/english/Documents/newsclips/InauguralLecture_ProfSopeWilliamsElegbe_23Oct2018.pdf> accessed 8 September 2022.

[6] eg Thibault Schrepel, 'Law + Technology' (2022) VU University Amsterdam Legal Studies Research Paper Series <https://ssrn.com/abstract=4115666> accessed 13 September 2022.

[7] Of course, this could be challenged on grounds of subjectivity. For a similar approach, see Lehr and Ohm, 'Machine Learning for Legal Scholars' (n 1).

[8] For discussion of the specific challenges in procuring cloud computing services, see Kevin McGillivray, *Government Cloud Procurement. Contracts, Data Protection, and the Quest for Compliance* (CUP 2022).

of procurement contracts,[9] it does not raise issues specific to procurement governance.[10]

2. Robotic Process Automation (RPA)

RPA facilitates the automation of repetitive, information-intensive, back-office processes based on clearly defined rules that do not require complex logic.[11] This means that there are at least three specific requirements for process automation. First, the process has to be rigid and susceptible of entirely detailed description, so that it can be coded into software (ie the 'bot' that carries out the RPA). Second, the process has to involve solely the retrieval, transfer, and cross-checking of information (or some of these tasks) and, implicitly, this information needs to be in machine readable form—or else the automation needs to include a phase of computer vision or Natural Language Processing (NLP) that thus requires integration with ML (see Section 3). Third, the output of the RPA can generally be of a descriptive or reporting nature, and can only imply a 'decision' where the latter is subject to a straightforward and simple rule. Automating the consequences of such 'decision' can only be done through RPA if they involve the inclusion of information on a specific ledger or database. Most often, though, the RPA outcome will require human review or implementation.

Emerging evidence on experimentation with RPA for procurement governance shows that it is mainly being deployed at stages of the procurement procedure that require retrieving and cross-checking information from a disparate range of databases. Some examples include assessing whether a tenderer is included within a list of authorized or pre-screened tenderers, or whether a specific reference is included in a database of previous contracts, to check past performance reports on the tenderer and/or to check that the tenderer is not

[9] See eg Deloitte, 'Study on up-take of emerging technologies in public procurement. Final report' (2020) <https://ec.europa.eu/docsroom/documents/40102> accessed 7 September 2022 (hereafter Deloitte, 'Emerging technologies in public procurement'); and World Bank, 'Disruptive technologies in public procurement' (2021) <http://documents.worldbank.org/curated/en/522181612428427520/Disruptive-Technologies-in-Public-Procurement> accessed 8 September 2022 (hereafter World Bank, 'Disruptive technologies').

[10] Most of those issues relate to intellectual property law and are excluded from the analysis in this chapter. See eg Time.lex and others, 'Legal Review on Industrial Design Protection in Europe', Annex 3 '3D printing' (2016) <https://ec.europa.eu/docsroom/documents/18921/> accessed 15 September 2022.

[11] As advanced in Chapter 6, Section 3.1.

included in a list of debarred, excluded, or sanctioned tenderers.[12] RPA can also be used for back-office purposes requiring a comparison between templates and documents, or between contracts and other documents (eg to automate invoice processing), or processes allowing for automated updates of information in specific databases (eg vendor details in an invoicing database).[13] It is also possible to use RPA to automate some basic screens (eg on compliance with pre-specified deadlines or value ranges), although this type of application can easily require some element of 'intelligent automation',[14] and will thus be discussed in Section 3.3.

The fact that RPA is being deployed in these areas is probably reflective of the three requirements for viable automation through RPA. First, RPA is being deployed to substitute identical manual checks that can be described in full detail. Second, RPA is deployed to overcome an information cost derived from the need to carry out specific, non-discretionary checks. However, the automation mostly does not assign consequences to those checks. Rather, it reports the outcome of the checks, gathering information for human review. Where the automation implies specific consequences, they are primarily limited to the modification of information on a database—the fully automated payment of invoices being the potential exception. Third, RPA is being deployed in areas where procurement information is already digitized through its inclusion in electronic databases and/or an e-invoicing system, and in relation to information that is not only highly standardized and structured, but also follows or is pegged to specific (corporate) identifiers that allow for the relevant cross-checks.

In this type of application, it should be stressed that RPA tends to (completely) discharge the administrative burden and generate time savings in unproblematic cases only. Problematic cases will require human intervention and, potentially, a manual (second) review of the relevant information. RPA will not be able to source information not otherwise available (unless RPA is used to gather information not previously considered due to eg resource limitations), and it will not be able to carry out any analysis of that information. RPA will not be able to deal with open-ended requirements (eg the obligation to accept 'equivalent'

[12] eg the US Truman and the IRS Procurement Office case studies; Deloitte, 'Emerging technologies in public procurement' (n 9) 152 ff and 167 ff, respectively. Broadly the same case is used in World Bank, 'Disruptive technologies' (n 9) 85. For discussion, see Jessica Tillipman, 'Using AI to Reduce Performance Risk in U.S. Procurement' (*Regulatory Review*, 29 June 2022) <https://www.theregreview.org/2022/06/29/tillipman-using-ai-to-reduce-performance-risk-in-u-s-procurement/> accessed 15 September 2022.

[13] eg the Finnish Palkeet case study; Deloitte, 'Emerging technologies in public procurement' (n 9) 162 ff.

[14] Along those lines, RPA and several forms of AI are bundled together eg in World Bank, 'Disruptive technologies' (n 9).

documentation or certificates), will not spot errors in the sources of information (it will simply carry them across databases or domains), and will not be able to balance competing pieces of information (eg in relation to self-cleaning claims, or in relation to information that has not yet been included in the databases from which the 'bot' draws it). RPA will also not change or improve the processes themselves; it will simply replicate them and accelerate them.[15]

The main advantages of RPA thus boil down to time savings and the possibility to improve the regularity, consistency, and completeness of the automated checks. However, the outcome of the RPA will only be as good as the sources of information it uses, and only be truly useful if it is generated in a timely and user-friendly manner. All things considered, RPA is essentially limited to high-volume, non-discretionary, and entirely standardized checks and processes. This reduces the potential for deployment in areas of the procurement process that are not entirely standardized to the last detail across a large volume of procedures. For example, it would be highly implausible to automate technical or economic evaluations without incurring significant costs to tailor the automation to the specific procedure, or without using forms of 'intelligent automation' capable of generating that customization.

Moreover, RPA should not necessarily be seen as a fix for some of the dysfunctionalities or unnecessary complexities resulting from broken up processes or the scattering of information sources. RPA could generate technical debt to the extent that creating the RPA fix required significant maintenance or generated the risk of becoming the basis for the implementation of further layers of technological solutions, which would then build on a sub-optimal underlying data architecture.[16] Moreover, RPA can come with significant cybersecurity risks and the possibility of unplanned actions by bots needs to be carefully considered (see Section 7).[17] There can also be legal constraints on the deployment of RPA, such as issues with permissioned access to information or the need to ensure that a public official is involved in the relevant verifications.[18] This could be overcome by, for example, only deploying 'attended' or 'supervised bots',[19] but that would reduce the potential benefits of some RPA applications. RPA can thus seem like the low hanging fruit for the adoption of digital technologies for procurement governance, but its suitability, viability, and desirability in the medium and long term need to be assessed carefully.

15 ibid 86.
16 For further discussion, see Chapter 8, Section 2.2.
17 World Bank, 'Disruptive technologies' (n 9) 86.
18 See James Boyle, 'A Nondelegation Doctrine for the Digital Age?' (2000) 50(5) Duke Law Journal 5.
19 Deloitte, 'Emerging technologies in public procurement' (n 9) 152 ff.

3. Machine Learning Implementations

ML aims to 'develop systems that learn models from data'[20] or, in other words, 'to acquire skills or knowledge from experience'.[21] ML is the most widely used form of 'narrow' or 'weak' AI.[22] That is, AI that can perform specific tasks, as opposed to ML capable of switching through (very) different tasks, which would require 'general' or 'strong' intelligence.[23] Current ML applications are more advanced than earlier types of narrow AI, such as expert systems,[24] and have the main advantage of avoiding the need to pre-define the rules applicable by a system. ML is a technology that can execute a task without explicitly being programmed to do so,[25] and thus allows moving from input to output without making the rules explicit—and, in some cases, without those rules being susceptible of human comprehension.[26] This opens possibilities to digitalize tasks that cannot be performed through other means, such as RPA (as discussed in the previous section). ML implementations can: (1) classify data on the basis of a trained model (ie categorical classification); (2) generate a prediction or estimate in relation to a data point in a continuous series on the basis of a trained model (through regression); or (3) cluster data points by fitting as close a model as possible to the data (which can functionally be seen as a broader type of classification).[27]

In the context of procurement, potential applications could concern classification of tenderers as at risk of insolvency (or not), or as potentially suitable for a contract (or not);[28] prediction of prices to be used for budget-making purposes, or as a baseline to control for excessive or abnormally low pricing;[29]

[20] Deville, Sergeyssels, and Middag, 'Basic AI Concepts' (n 1) 6.

[21] Tirath Virdee, 'Understanding AI' in Charles Kerrigan (ed), *Artificial Intelligence. Law and Regulation* (Edward Elgar 2022) 37, 40 (hereafter Virdee, 'Understanding AI').

[22] As advanced in Chapter 6, Section 4.

[23] Consideration of 'general' or 'strong' AI is excluded from this chapter. For discussion, see eg Ragnar Fjelland, 'Why General Artificial Intelligence Will Not Be Realized' (2020) 10 Nature Humanities and Social Sciences Communications 7.

[24] See eg Kevin D Ashley, *Artificial Intelligence and Legal Analytics. New Tools for Law Practice in the Digital Age* (CUP 2017) 8 (hereafter Ashley, *Artificial Intelligence and Legal Analytics*).

[25] Tirath Virdee and others, 'Taxonomy of AI' in Charles Kerrigan (ed), *Artificial Intelligence. Law and Regulation* (Edward Elgar 2022) 474, 479 (hereafter Virdee and others, 'Taxonomy of AI').

[26] This raises fundamental issues of explainability, as discussed in Chapter 2, Section 2.

[27] Virdee and others, 'Taxonomy of AI' (n 25) 479. The functionality of skill acquisition is not covered in this chapter.

[28] Manuel J Garcia Rodriguez and others, 'Bidders Recommender for Public Procurement Auctions Using Machine Learning: Data Analysis, Algorithm, and Case Study with Tenders from Spain' (2020) Complexity 8858258 (hereafter Garcia Rodriguez and others, 'Bidders Recommender').

[29] Jong-Min Kim and Hojin Jung, 'Predicting Bid Prices by Using Machine Learning Methods' (2019) 51 Applied Economics 2011.

or clustering of tenderers for the purposes of analysing market trends and screening, for example, for anticompetitive effects.[30]

These are all data-intensive functionalities. It follows that, without data, there are no viable ML implementations, and it has been stressed that '[t]he dominant problem in most projects is still the amount of time that is needed to get data ready for ML'.[31] Therefore, data availability and quality are a huge constraint on the viability of ML implementations. This is not an easily solvable problem in many potential implementations for procurement governance and it may well be that ML projects require several years or even decades of data collection before they can even be piloted, as discussed in more detail in Section 6.

When data is available, algorithms can be developed and trained in three stylized ways: supervised, unsupervised, and reinforcement learning—though these can be combined.[32] Supervised learning requires the data to be 'labelled'. That means that the data used to train the algorithm needs to have been provided with the correct classification so that labelled examples enable the algorithm to associate the correct input (data) with the correct output (classification). For example, if ML was to be applied to detect corrupt tenders, the training data should contain a clear classification of whether each of the previous tenders was corrupt or not. This raises challenges beyond the mere existence of the data, as mislabelled data (eg corrupt transactions that went undetected and are labelled as not corrupt in the database) will undermine the accuracy of the algorithm. Where the data used to train the algorithm is not labelled, the training is unsupervised and, in these applications, the algorithm must discover patterns and structures on its own to cluster the data. In this case, the 'problem definition entails deciding on a particular mathematical measure of similarity'.[33] This will create significant challenges, especially in relation to the interpretability of the results, which could significantly reduce the functionality of the ML solution in practical terms. A third type is reinforcement training, where the data is primarily generated through a feedback loop that indicates to the algorithm whether it had performed the given task in the intended way. For procurement governance purposes, supervised and unsupervised training seem the most relevant techniques, as there is limited scope for

[30] Manuel J Garcia Rodriguez and others, 'Collusion Detection in Public Procurement Auctions with Machine Learning Algorithms' (2022) 133 Automation in Construction 104047 (hereafter Garcia Rodriguez and others, 'Collusion Detection with ML').

[31] Virdee, 'Understanding AI' (n 21) 44.

[32] For discussion, ENISA, 'AI cybersecurity challenges. Threat landscape for artificial intelligence' (2020) 18–19 <https://www.enisa.europa.eu/publications/artificial-intelligence-cybersecurity-challenges> accessed 18 October 2022 (hereafter ENISA, 'AI cybersecurity challenges').

[33] Lehr and Ohm, 'Machine Learning for Legal Scholars' (n 1) 676. See also ENISA, 'AI cybersecurity challenges' (n 32) 19–20.

meaningful trial and error (and the related feedback or reinforcement) in a setting where the rules are open-ended.[34]

Regardless of the specific training technique used, developing and deploying ML implementations involve a sequence of steps that require iteration and repetition.[35] Decisions made at each of those stages can have significant legal and governance implications. Training the algorithm will imply using mathematical methods seeking to minimize or maximize a pre-established goal in relation to an also pre-established variable (eg in/accuracy of classification or prediction of a specific attribute of the data).[36] This means that deploying ML does require not only the existence of (big) training data, but also a clear view of which variable/s are useful to classify or predict for a specific governance outcome, as well as how the algorithmic goal should be specified—for example in relation to the type of errors that can be tolerated.[37] For example, developing an ML implementation to screen tenderers for corruption will look different whether the algorithm is designed to have equal tolerance for false positive and false negative classifications, or the algorithm is geared towards minimizing false negatives over false positives (to catch as many potential instances of corruption as possible).[38] This will in turn have knock-on effects on the workload required to act upon the ML insights, as an overly comprehensive screening tool would generate more work and more complicated due process considerations than a more lenient screening tool. Conversely, deploying an algorithm seeking to minimize false positives to avoid those issues would implicitly require accepting a higher underlying risk of undetected corruption.

Moreover, as mentioned, the development and deployment of ML solutions can be further complicated by difficulties in identifying relevant variables or features in the data.[39] This is important in the context of procurement governance because it can be difficult to identify suitable variables or proxies for complex governance issues.[40] Variables necessarily relate to measurable aspects and some variables can be relatively easier to specify but also generate 'greater risk of mismatch between the predictive goal and the variable's specification'.[41] Moreover, there is generally a difficulty in establishing links between inputs and outputs in relation to contract execution compared to the characteristics

[34] There can, however, be scope for mixed approaches where reinforcement is combined with, eg, unsupervised learning.
[35] Lehr and Ohm, 'Machine Learning for Legal Scholars' (n 1) 655.
[36] ibid 672.
[37] ENISA, 'AI cybersecurity challenges' (n 32) 18–19.
[38] Lehr and Ohm, 'Machine Learning for Legal Scholars' (n 1) 692.
[39] ENISA, 'AI cybersecurity challenges' (n 32) 18.
[40] Lehr and Ohm, 'Machine Learning for Legal Scholars' (n 1) 672–77.
[41] ibid 675.

of a specific procurement process. This can make implementations very procedure-focused, rather than outcomes-focused. This can weigh heavily in implementation design as constrained by the data. Where no contract execution or procurement outcome data exists, ML can be (inadvertently) trained to operate on the basis of governance proxies that are purely procedural (eg ML that assesses the desirability of a specific criterion or process in relation to whether it is likely to lead to a legal challenge) rather than substantive or operational proxies. This can skew procurement governance towards processes rather than outcomes, which is not necessarily desirable.[42]

The further difficulty from a governance perspective is that determining the right variables and features is largely a technical question that can bear little resemblance to choosing a specific variable from a conceptual or intuitive standpoint. It is also important to acknowledge that most ML implementations can establish associations or correlations, but not necessarily causation.[43] This can obviously make ML inadequate in settings where the interpretive problems generated by correlation cannot be technically dealt with. Moreover, there will almost always be unavoidable trade-offs between the available (viable) choices and the effectiveness and knock-on effects of the chosen ML solutions. Similarly, a choice needs to be made on which type of algorithm to deploy, and choices can be constrained in specific settings of relevance for procurement governance purposes, for example 'if the outcome variable contains multiple classes [ie it is not binary] or ordinal classes, an analyst may have fewer algorithms from which to choose'.[44]

Some of these issues will only emerge (to potentially be resolved) through the iterative process of developing a ML implementation. This means that, even where data is available, the likelihood of developing a sufficiently good (ie governance adequate) ML implementation will depend on a number of factors that will only be observable down the line. Establishing the threshold of what is a 'sufficiently good' implementation will also be contentious. This generates a further governance risk in the face of failing or inadequate ML projects, as there can be pressures to deploy suboptimal systems due to the costs already incurred in their development,[45] or the expectations raised.

This overview of the complexities of developing an ML solution should already point out that the scope for successful deployment is likely to be relatively

[42] See eg Oxford Government Outcomes Lab, How to Guide Procurement (2017) <https://golab.bsg.ox.ac.uk/documents/GO_Lab_-_Procurement_Guide_ROe4bJn.pdf> accessed 23 September 2022.

[43] Momiao Xiong, *Artificial Intelligence and Causal Inference* (CRC Press 2022).

[44] Lehr and Ohm, 'Machine Learning for Legal Scholars' (n 1) 690.

[45] Which would be a textbook example of the sunk costs fallacy; for discussion, see Charles A Miller, 'Sunk Costs and Political Decision Making' (2019) Oxford Research Encyclopaedia of Politics <https://doi.org/10.1093/acrefore/9780190228637.013.1022> accessed 23 September 2022.

limited and that ML should not be perceived as an easy fix to deal with procurement complexity. It will, of course, be possible for the public sector to adopt or adapt ML-based solutions developed in relation to issues that are common to the private sector ('ProcureTech'),[46] for example in relation to category management or financial spending analysis,[47] or to develop ML applications for highly-structured (classification) tasks closely related to RPA automation.[48] However, the development of other solutions specifically tailored to the governance needs of the public procurement function will carry its own complications, some of which derive from legal requirements not applicable to the private sector or that create needs for specific information processing.[49] The complexity of developing ML-based solutions can now be further explored in relation to three 'promising' implementations: recommender systems, chatbots, and automated screens (or red flags).

3.1 Recommender Systems

Recommender systems are a specific ML-based solution that seeks to predict user responses to options[50]—for example, they could be used to predict whether a public buyer is interested in engaging a specific tenderer or sourcing a specific product in relation to a specific tender. There are two main types of recommender systems: content-based systems and collaborative filtering systems. Content-based systems examine properties of the objects recommended and make recommendations based on those specific properties, whereas collaborative filtering systems recommend to a user objects preferred by similar users.[51] There could be ways of implementing collaborative filtering recommenders in public procurement, for example in relation to specific products

[46] This could involve a phenomenon of transfer learning that needs careful consideration; ENISA, 'AI cybersecurity challenges' (n 32) 20.

[47] These are, to date, the majority of ML implementations in public procurement, at least on the basis of public information; Deloitte, 'Emerging technologies in public procurement' (n 9) 40. For an overview of private sector procurement applications, see Jan Martin Spreitzenbarth, 'Methods of Artificial Intelligence in Procurement' (2022) 17th International Conference on Wirtschaftsinformatik <https://shorturl.at/jnCFM> accessed 4 October 2022.

[48] eg the prediction of CPV or other procurement classification codes; Deloitte, 'Emerging technologies in public procurement' (n 9) 52.

[49] For related discussion, see Kunmi Ageh, 'When Artificial Intelligence Met Public Procurement: Improving the World Bank's Suspension and Debarment System with Machine Learning' (2019) 48(3) Public Contract Law Journal 565.

[50] Jure Leskovec, Anand Rajaraman, and Jeffrey David Ullman, 'Recommendation Systems' in *Mining of Massive Datasets* (3rd edn, CUP 2020) 307 (hereafter Leskovec, Rajaraman, and Ullman, 'Recommendation Systems').

[51] ibid.

offered within online platforms used only by public buyers.[52] However, it seems that content-based recommenders are better suited for procurement governance, not least because of constraints on the exercise of discretion, objectivity, and case-by-case analysis requirements of procurement decision-making. It should be stressed that most of the private sector recommender systems are consumer-facing and, as such, they do not concern decisions comparable to those of the public buyer as consumers can make entirely subjective decisions without being (legally) accountable to others.

Developing a content-based procurement recommender poses significant challenges,[53] starting by ensuring that the system draws from data that includes all possible options available in the market. This requirement is different from that applicable to the private sector. While there will usually be a business case for private sector (online) recommenders to be as comprehensive as possible,[54] the public sector is under a legal mandate not to exclude potential tenderers or potential (equivalent) solutions and any recommender must thus meet this requirement.[55] This can be problematic where there is no real-time database encompassing, for example, all potential suppliers active in the market, or all products and services capable of satisfying the same need. In that case, using static databases would at the very least exclude new entrants or companies not included in the database where this is built on an opt-in basis.[56] Using databases only collecting data from past procurements would raise additional barriers to participation and exacerbate incumbency advantages. This type of recommender system could thus be developed within legally compliant closed lists of participants in procurement opportunities, but this may be the exception rather than the norm in procurement, and would limit recommender systems to very narrow implementations within dynamic purchasing systems or framework agreements—or even, within those, only in relation to

[52] This would, however, not necessarily be straightforward, as it would need to be coordinated with legal requirements on the rules controlling call-offs within the framework agreements or dynamic purchasing systems that would likely underpin such online platform. A detailed analysis exceeds the scope of this chapter.

[53] See eg Stefan Bensch, 'Recommender Systems for Strategic Procurement in Value Networks' (2012) AMCIS 2012 Proceedings 13 <https://aisel.aisnet.org/amcis2012/proceedings/StrategicUseIT/13> accessed 23 September 2022.

[54] This is usually referred to as the long-tail issue; Leskovec, Rajaraman, and Ullman, 'Recommendation Systems' (n 50) 307.

[55] This is caveated by the fact that some economic operators will not have a legal right to participate in specific tenders, depending on the applicability of international trade rules, in particular the World Trade Organisation Government Procurement Agreement. However, as a general statement, the requirement for universality of the sources of information in this context holds.

[56] It would thus perpetuate, or even increase, barriers to entry and, ultimately, it would replicate and propagate the socio-economic inequalities implicit in the data bias resulting from a less than comprehensive use of the data space.

lists underpinned by electronic catalogues, which could also potentially serve for the deployment of collective screening recommender systems instead.[57]

Beyond that, choosing which features of the potential suppliers to consider in designing and training the algorithm is also challenging, especially as markets may function very differently in relation to any given feature—for example distance between contractor and public buyer, which can be relevant for (some) goods and irrelevant for some (digital or remote) services. This creates a significant challenge in establishing the remit of the recommender system,[58] as it could be that different recommenders need to be developed for different types of objects—which would then create issues for procurement needs that could be satisfied in different ways, or mixed contracts, for example. It is also challenging to establish which level of accuracy a recommender system should have before it is deployed, which can in turn be dependent on the intended use of the recommender system. For example, if the recommender system was solely to be used to target otherwise generally available information (eg a recommender system of potential public tender opportunities addressed to potential tenderers), the requirements, constraints, and practical advantages would be analysed differently than if the recommender system was to be used to determine the scope of the competition for a given contract (eg a recommender system used to select which potential suppliers to invite to a negotiated procedure).

Similar issues would arise in relation to the development of recommender systems for products or services, with the added complexity that the parameters of the recommendation would potentially be either much narrower or much more variable than those concerning a recommender of tenderers or potential providers. The issue of the narrowness and variability of the relevant parameters in product recommendation would stem from the fact that almost each product or service category is likely to have distinguishing features that deviate from those of other products or services—whereas the features that are relevant in comparing tenderers are likely to be more exportable, or at least of relevance at a higher level (eg sector of activity). Products and services are also more likely to generate new features through innovation, while ML models can

[57] But see n 52.

[58] These difficulties are clearly exemplified in Garcia Rodriguez and others, 'Bidders Recommender' (n 28), which develops a general recommender system where the best performance creates about one in ten chances of correctly identifying the most suitable provider, or one in five chances of having it included in a basket of five recommendations. For discussion, see Albert Sanchez-Graells, 'Procurement Recommender Systems: How Much Better Before We Trust Them?' (*howtocrackanut.com*, 10 June 2022) <https://www.howtocrackanut.com/blog/2022/6/10/procurement-recommender-systems-how-much-better-before-we-trust-them> accessed 23 September 2022.

have very limited accuracy in assessing features that were not included in their training data. All of this has an impact on, for example, the volume of data that can be available to train the algorithm, or the need to retrain or adjust algorithms on an ongoing basis, which can be crucial in relation to the viability of the intended recommender system. On this point, it seems worth stressing that most popular private sector recommender systems operate as collaborative filtering systems, and that content-based recommender systems tend to concern single product or single service use cases (eg news or video recommendations). As such, both types of approaches seem rather far removed from applications for complex aspects of procurement governance, which would require a significant development effort. This could only be justified or viable in highly centralized procurement settings, as discussed further in Section 8.

3.2 Chatbots

Virtual assistants, or chatbots, are computer programmes that use NLP to understand user questions and automate responses to them. This necessarily brings all constraints of NLP implementations into play. This is an area of ML that is quickly evolving towards higher levels of performance,[59] at least in relation to widely used languages.[60] Given that the private sector has a major interest in the further development of NLP, further advances can be expected, as demonstrated by most recent developments in generative AI. Nonetheless, there is significant controversy as to the limits of NLP, both technical and regulatory. The future development of NLP and related applications is unclear. However, there is no need to explore those debates or constraints for the purposes of the analysis here, as limitations on the type of information that can be used by chatbots in the procurement context generate their own restrictions.[61]

[59] See eg Diksha Khurana and others, 'Natural Language Processing: State of the Art, Current Trends and Challenges' (2022) Multimedia Tools and Applications <https://doi.org/10.1007/s11042-022-13428-4> accessed 23 September 2022.

[60] This necessarily implies difficulties in developing NLP-based solutions in other languages, and it seems like all languages but English will pragmatically lag behind or be constrained by the workings of automated translation.

[61] cf with some of the views expressed in the panel discussion contained in Institute for Government, 'What does artificial intelligence mean for government procurement?' (2023) <https://www.institutefogovernment.org.uk/event/artificial-intelligence-government-procurement> accessed 12 April 2023. cf also with the broader possibilistic analysis put forward by Tom Whittaker and Ian Tucker, 'Could Machine Learning Be Used to Assist Evaluators in Regulated Public Procurements?' (Lexology, 12 January 2023) <https://www.lexology.com/library/detail.aspx?g=ec7345d2-8892-4c8f-b740-fdd4f13f877c> accessed 12 April 2023.

At their simplest, chatbots can be seen as interactive frequently asked question (FAQ) solutions. Advanced AI chatbots can incorporate ML elements to improve their performance over time. It is also possible to integrate chatbots with RPA, so that either the chatbot can activate an RPA process, or an RPA can activate the chatbot.[62] Chatbots are mainly deployed as a way of simplifying access to information and, as such, chatbots can only be as useful or accurate as the information they can retrieve. They are primarily tools to enhance the user experience of accessing information, while reducing the cost of providing that information for the implementer.

In that regard, chatbots cannot provide any more clarification or guidance than the knowledge base from which they draw. They can pinpoint to information, but not process or analyse it—and it would be extremely risky to use generative AI, for example, to create new information that was not very closely verified by an expert.[63] In the procurement governance setting, chatbots cannot be plugged to open-ended information sources (ie the internet) because the public buyer will hold liability for the information it provides (through the chatbot). In other words, the implementation in procurement governance is likely to be limited to closed domain chatbots.[64] Structurally, then, deploying chatbots for procurement governance will require garden-fencing the information to which the chatbot has access to ensure its reliability, accuracy, etc. In the context of procurement governance, chatbots can thus give access to specific types of information in ways that would save users formulating (more structured) queries in a different manner. This can help reduce initial hurdles to access basic procurement information. But it would not reduce the difficulties and costs of digesting that information, unless the specific type of analysis was pre-produced and the chatbot had access to it. Thus, this would not serve to automate the generation of answers or clarifications.

Tenderer-facing chatbots could deal with some queries on administrative processes, such as how to register as a potential supplier, who to contact about a specific issue, or finding out which contract opportunities are currently

[62] See eg Christian Daase and others, 'Automation of Customer Initiated Back Office Processes: A Design Science Research Approach to Link Robotic Process Automation and Chatbots' (2020) ACIS 2020 Proceedings 15 <https://aisel.aisnet.org/acis2020/15> accessed 23 September 2022.

[63] Council of the European Union, 'ChatGPT in the Public Sector—Overhyped or Overlooked?' (24 April 2023) <https://www.consilium.europa.eu/media/63818/art-paper-chatgpt-in-the-public-sector-overhyped-or-overlooked-24-april-2023_ext.pdf> accessed 3 July 2023; Albert Sanchez-Graells, 'ChatGPT in the Public Sector—Should It Be Banned?' (*howtocrackanut.com*, 3 May 2023) <https://www.howtocrackanut.com/blog/should-we-ban-chatgpt-in-the-public-sector> accessed 3 July 2023.

[64] For further classification, see Eleni Adamopoulou and Lefteris Moussiades, 'An Overview of Chatbot Technology' in Ilias Maglogiannis, Lazaros Iliadis, and Elias Pimenidis (eds), *AIAI 2020, IFIP AICT 584* (Springer 2020) 373, 378.

open in relation to specific goods or services.[65] However, they would not be able to provide clarification on the meaning of a specific tender document, for example, unless that clarification had already been generated and uploaded into the knowledge database. They could also serve to facilitate interactions in relation to, for example, the submission of tenders, where a chatbot could use a pre-defined set of questions to prompt tenderers to check for common errors in tender submission. However, the chatbot would not be able to answer whether something has been correctly done unless an automated (RPA) check was plugged to it and, in that case, the check would need to be strictly formalized and rules-based (see Section 2). Other sorts of qualitative analysis or discretionary elements would not be suitable for this type of automated check. This shows how tenderer-facing chatbots are likely to be useful mostly in relation to types of information-based queries that are high-volume and as such justify the preparation of specific answers, or in relation to clearly pre-established processes. While this can reduce administrative burdens, it would not go much further than that.

Public buyer-facing chatbots would have similar constraints and would not really serve to reduce the need to understand the complexity of procurement rules or to be able to process complex information in relation to the tenders received. Chatbots would mainly be able to help retrieve factual data or pre-prepared (or at the very least pre-existing) knowledge and data. Chatbots could be combined with advanced NLP techniques to undertake tasks like extracting information from specific sources and structuring it (eg in summaries). However, for most purposes, it will not be possible to (solely) assess the relevant documents (eg in tender documentation) by reference to automated summaries, so the practical gains may be limited. Similarly, a chatbot would be able, for example, to point a public buyer to the legal provision, or specific piece of guidance, or case law (if it existed) on which criteria control access to a specific type of procedure, or on which type of criteria are allowed for a specific type of assessment. However, the chatbot would not be able to engage in any assessment of the rationale given for the use of a specific procedure or a specific criterion in the context of a specific tender procedure. In simple terms, chatbots would very quickly reach the limits of their functionality unless they were plugged to a knowledge base created as an expert system.[66] Such a possibility would still have rather limited functionality, particularly in

[65] The YPO study was even more limited than that and showed significant difficulties in attaining levels of performance justifying the deployment of the chatbot even within the limited domain of the organization's own website; see Deloitte, 'Emerging technologies in public procurement' (n 9) 65 ff.

[66] See eg Ashley, *Artificial Intelligence and Legal Analytics* (n 24) 171–209.

relation to aspects of procurement governance involving value judgements, which are the ones where professional public buyers are more likely to face information burdens.

Thus it seems that the practical space for the deployment of chatbots in procurement governance is limited to rather low added value information access tasks. While this could generate administrative savings where the volume of work justified the development, deployment, and maintenance of the chatbot, this technology hardly seems to offer great promise in terms of altering procurement processes or outcomes.

3.3 Automated Screens (or Red Flags)

Red flags can be used to screen procurement procedures from different governance angles. Red flags are quantitative indicators or algorithmic checks based on available procurement data that seek to identify procurement decisions in violation of an identified rule or value.[67] To the extent that the relevant rule or value encapsulates a focus point for suspicious activities, red flags can be useful mechanisms in screening for corruption,[68] anticompetitive behaviour,[69] or other (policy) deviations in procurement practice. For example, a red flag could seek to identify procurement processes where the deadline for the submission of tenders has been very short, which may indicate that the contracting authority had a pre-selected awardee before officially publishing the

[67] Francesco Decarolis and Cristina Giorgiantonio, 'Corruption Red Flags in Public Procurement: New Evidence from Italian Calls for Tenders' (2020) Bank of Italy Economic Research and International Relations Area Occasional Papers No 544 <https://econpapers.repec.org/RePEc:bdi:opques:qef_544_20> accessed 26 September 2022; Mihaly Fazekas and Gabor Kocsis, 'Uncovering High-Level Corruption: Cross-National Objective Corruption Risk Indicators Using Public Procurement Data' (2017) 50 British Journal of Political Science 155; Elizabeth David-Barrett Mihaly and Fazekas, 'Anti-Corruption in Aid-Funded Procurement: Is Corruption Reduced or Merely Displaced?' (2020) 132 World Development 105000 <https://doi.org/10.1016/j.worlddev.2020.105000> accessed 26 September 2022. For discussion, see Albert Sanchez-Graells, 'Procurement Corruption and Artificial Intelligence: Between the Potential of Enabling Data Architectures and the Constraints of Due Process Requirements' in Sope Williams and Jessica Tillipman (eds), *Routledge Handbook of Public Procurement Corruption* (Routledge forthcoming) <https://ssrn.com/abstract=3952665> accessed 30 June 2023 (hereafter Sanchez-Graells, 'Procurement Corruption and Artificial Intelligence').

[68] Open Contracting Partnership, 'RED FLAGS for integrity: Giving the green light to open data solutions' (2016) <https://www.open-contracting.org/resources/red-flags-integrity-giving-green-light-open-data-solutions/> accessed 26 September 2022. For discussion, see Roberto de Michele and Juan Cruz Vieyra, 'From fishing to catching: Developing actionable red flags in public procurement to prevent and control corruption' (2022) Inter-American Development Bank Technical Note No IDB-TN-2598 <http://dx.doi.org/10.18235/0004595> accessed 19 December 2022.

[69] See eg Martin Huber and David Imhof, 'Machine Learning with Screens for Detecting Bid-Rigging Cartels' (2019) 65 International Journal of Industrial Organization 277; Garcia Rodriguez and others, 'Collusion Detection with ML' (n 30).

contract opportunity. In such an implementation, the algorithm could simply require a comparison between the deadline given in the specific procurement documentation and a pre-established benchmark of what is considered 'too short' (eg three working days, or less than half the standard duration of a 'best practice' period for the receipt of tenders), or be trained to identify suspicious cases on the basis of independently established rules and parameters. ML could follow the latter approach and allow for the development of screens without the need to pre-specify abnormality rules. Different approaches reflect different levels of ambition (or complexity, which raises issues of technical feasibility).

3.3.1 Levels of ambition (and complexity) in the use of red flags

At a 'basic level', red flag checks can be deployed 'manually', for example by having a civil servant carry out comparisons between the data derived from a specific procurement exercise against the pre-specified rule or threshold. This could be part of a routine compliance assessment, either in the context of a pre-market approval of tender documentation, for instance, or as a post-award check of legal compliance, either in the context of a procurement challenge, or as a matter of general audit of the procurement function.

At an 'intermediate level', if the adequate procurement data architecture exists, red flags can be automated, so that software carries them out. RPA can be used to cross-check published tender notices against the applicable rules (eg on duration of tender submission periods). This can increase the volume and speed at which the screening takes place. However, by itself, this automation does not alter the inputs of the screening, and thus has no more potential to identify deviations than manual checks (except for the potential reduction in manual check error rates or, conversely, a risk of error increase if the software is faulty). Generally speaking, it can simply reduce gaps in screening where manual checks were either not being carried out, or where it was not possible to screen all procurement exercises due to capacity constraints. Additionally, if there are questions about the integrity of the checks themselves, the automation can also contribute to reducing the corruption risk linked to any discretion (eg not to carry out the check as a result of a corrupt practice). The main advantages of these intermediate level screens are thus their comprehensiveness, objectivity (in the sense of automaticity), and potential repetitiveness of the checks (eg if the parameters of the check are dynamic or susceptible of modification throughout a procedure). But not their 'analytical power', in the sense that they do not offer insights that would not be attainable by a human decision-maker, given sufficient time.

A more 'advanced approach' to red flags would be to use ML to establish the rules (or the underlying benchmarks and parameters) determining the standard of abnormality to be investigated in the checks. In that case, there would be no set rule (eg number of days), but rather, the ML algorithm would be trained to independently calibrate an 'abnormality threshold' that would then allow it to classify procurement exercises as either suspect, or not. This approach would create the potential for a more nuanced (and effective) screening system *if (and only if)* the algorithm was better at setting the relevant benchmarks and/or thresholds than human decision-makers—which would primarily require good access to data, as well as an adequate design of the algorithm itself. Most benchmarks and thresholds for manual or RPA checks are established with a relative degree of arbitrariness, even if that reflects previous expert knowledge on suitable values. The deployment of ML could thus outperform existing approaches if there was enough big data to allow it to generate truly evidence-based thresholds for the required parameter or benchmark—or even to identify parameters or benchmarks not currently used that could however be effective in identifying problematic (potentially corrupt) procurement exercises.[70] The process could be progressively refined through feedback that allowed the ML to fine-tune the parameters. However, it is difficult to find such enabling databases in practice (see also Section 6), and the creation of feedback mechanisms can be difficult. Ultimately, the most advanced approach can be out of reach for a relevant proportion of potential implementations of (theoretical) red flag indicators.

Moreover, depending on the specific type of ML used, this more advanced approach would also generate significant barriers to the explainability of a decision to flag a specific procurement exercise as suspect. While intermediate approaches ensure the ease of interpretability of the red flags (as they are the same that could be deployed manually), the more advanced the approach, the less likely that a human decision-maker will be able to interpret why the flag was triggered, or even what the flag precisely means and how to action the relevant insight. Consequently, the more advanced the approach the more likely it is to breach legal constraints, such as those related to duties of good administration and rights to due process—at least where the algorithms were used for governance functions related to the detection, investigation, and eventual sanction of illegal behaviour.[71] In that regard, the closer the relationship

[70] For related research in relation to the use of ML to identify risks of non-performance and termination for cause, see Tamara Lynn Nall, 'Using Machine Learning to Predict Performance Issues with U.S. Federal Contracts' (PhD thesis, George Washington University ProQuest Dissertations Publishing 2022), 28865868.

[71] Sanchez-Graells, 'Procurement Corruption and Artificial Intelligence' (n 67).

between the red flag and the triggering of procedures potentially leading to the imposition of sanctions (or criminal convictions), the higher the demands in terms of procedural rights—including the explanation of the ML underpinning the red flag.

3.3.2 Breadth and depth of the data underpinning the red flags

In addition to those different levels of technical ambition, there are also variations resulting from the breadth and depth of the information used by the red flags at all levels of sophistication. The narrowest approach to red flags concerns the verification of a single variable (eg duration of the tendering period) against a single rule (eg pre-specified 'too short duration' threshold). A slightly broader approach includes a dynamic element, which implies verifying a single variable (eg contract price) through the development of the procurement process (eg initially against a pre-specified 'expected value' or 'reservation price', or against some market-based benchmark, or, later on, against eg payments effectively made under the contract). Similarly, a slightly broader approach would involve cross-checking information relating to different stages of the procurement process (eg length of the period to receive tenders and procurement challenges, or length of the period to receive tenders and number of tenders received). A more ambitious approach concerns the development of red flags that extract insights from a cross-section or a time series of data (eg to identify entities that are repeatedly awarded contracts by the same contracting authority, or entities that are assigned contracts by different contracting authorities in ways that reflect specific (suspicious) patterns). Finally, perhaps the most ambitious approach concerns developing red flags that also cross-check information spanning different databases or sources of information (eg to check procurement awards against beneficial ownership information of the awardee, and then against a database on donations to political parties, say).

The availability and quality of the (procurement and other) data in the required formats will determine the feasibility of the implementations of any level of ambition in the deployment of red flags. The most plausible implementations of early detection mechanisms under the current state of the art (or, rather, the current state of the data) concern 'intermediate approaches' to the automation of the screens, primarily based on a narrow scope, but progressively including dynamic and systemic checks where the data infrastructure so allows. Importantly, these approaches can either seek to automate checks previously carried out manually or enable checks that were not carried out due to lack of capacity or other operational reasons. In this intermediate approach, it is also likely that the red flags emerge bottom-up, in the sense of being guided by practice and user-centric considerations (eg who should action the insights generated by the red flag), whereas more advanced red flags could follow a top-down approach due to their more limited connection with existing operations (and could require the creation of new job roles in order to action the related insights).

Ultimately, the difficulties in developing this type of ML solutions can primarily concern data availability and data quality, with some recent projects having been abandoned, or significantly pared down, due to data issues.[72] This is a particularly important constraint in this type of ML implementation because it tends to rely on supervised training and there are notorious difficulties in ensuring that the labelling of the training data is accurate.[73] This is discussed further in Section 6.

4. Distributed Ledger Technology Systems and Smart Contracts

4.1 Distributed Ledger Technology Systems

DLT systems allow for new approaches to the storage and exchange of information where 'instead of having one centralised database on which records are stored, this data is stored in a decentralised manner across all of the nodes of the … network'.[74] The advantage of decentralization is that information management does not depend on the decisions of the owner of a traditional database, which is the entity determining what information is contained in the database, and thus establishing the baseline of 'truth'. In centralized systems, what is recorded in the database is true on the authority of the database owner. It is thus necessary to trust the database owner and its information management.

[72] eg the UK's competition watchdog 2017 'Screening for cartels' tool, which was abandoned in early 2020. For discussion of its shortcomings, see Albert Sanchez-Graells, '"Screening for Cartels" in Public Procurement: Cheating at Solitaire to Sell Fool's Gold?' (2019) 10(4) Journal of European Competition Law & Practice 199.

[73] See eg contribution by Mihaly Fazekas to European Parliament, 'Use of big data and AI in fighting corruption and misuse of public funds—good practice, ways forward and how to integrate new technology into contemporary control framework' (Workshop Proceedings) PE 691.722 (2021) <https://www.europarl.europa.eu/RegData/etudes/STUD/2021/691722/IPOL_STU(2021)691722_EN.pdf> accessed 23 September 2022.

[74] As advanced in Chapter 6, Section 3.2; see Deloitte, 'Emerging technologies in public procurement' (n 9) 8.

Conversely, in a decentralized system, such as DLT, there can be a (potentially infinite) multiplicity of agents capable of adding information to the database. In this context, 'truth' is not established by authority, but results from a consensus mechanism (an algorithm)[75] determining whether the agent (network node) seeking to add information is entitled to do so. Once information is added, it will be propagated to all other agents, and it will thus be possible to check whether the information was added following the relevant rules. Once information is added, it cannot be amended or changed (although further transactions can change the state of the 'truth' that results from the ledger). Therefore (some types of) DLTs can be considered trustless mechanisms, in the sense that the 'true state' of the information is determined in a way that does not require trust in any specific agent or entity.[76] Given that agents operate through cryptographic keys that ensure their anonymity, the network can be expected to operate objectively—that is, a decision on whether information should or not be added to the ledger will be made on the basis of pre-defined (rigid) criteria.[77]

However, it should be stressed that the verification that the agent adding information on a DLT can carry out is strictly transactional and formal. This is best understood as checking the origin of the request to add information, as well as (potentially) minimal other checks based on the information already in the ledger. For example, in the context of a cryptocurrency transfer, the verification of the transaction requires validating the origin of the order to transfer an amount of cryptocurrency and checking whether the originator holds sufficient cryptocurrency in its wallet to transfer the required amount. There is no other check, which can lead to well-known problems such as those in relation to the lawfulness of any related transactions, (cryptographic) identity theft, money laundering, etc.

In the context of procurement governance, the functioning of a DLT requires understanding information exchanges as transactions. And, in that

[75] For an accessible description of the different consensus algorithms, see T-Labs, 'Consensus Algorithms: The Essential Forces of the DLT Universe' (*Medium*, 24 April 2018) <https://medium.com/@_tlabs/consensus-algorithms-the-essential-forces-of-the-dlt-universe-e1dd8e049534> accessed 15 September 2022.

[76] In other words, the DLT approach to decentralization is their key feature, and the key challenge to their regulation; see Primavera De Filippi, Morshed Mannan, and Wessel Reijers, 'The Alegality of Blockchain Technology' (2022) 41(3) Policy and Society 358.

[77] See Michel Rauchs and others, 'Distributed Ledger Technology systems. A conceptual framework' (2018) 25–27 <https://www.jbs.cam.ac.uk/wp-content/uploads/2020/08/2018-10-26-conceptualising-dlt-systems.pdf> accessed 7 September 2022 (hereafter Rauchs and others, 'DLT conceptual framework'); see also Chan Yang, 'Is There a Role for Blockchain for Enhancing Public Procurement Integrity?' (2019) Papers of the OECD Global Anti-Corruption & Integrity Forum 1 (hereafter Yang, 'Blockchain for Enhancing Public Procurement Integrity?').

regard, the DLT will usually only be able to ensure that those seeking to add information (whether it is a public buyer publishing a call for tenders, or a tenderer uploading qualification information or a tender, etc) are entitled to do so. However, the DLT will not be able to verify the content or accuracy of the information. The DLT would ensure the provenance of the information and effectively timestamp it and store it (for record permanence). It would also generate a cryptographic mechanism to manage access to the recorded information.

Given the way the DLT operates, it would also generate tamper-proofness. Indeed, the ledger (or chain) is append-only (ie not re-writable) and involves the use of cryptographic keys (hashes) that create a single identifier for every block of information, with any change in the information triggering changes in the key. The DLT chain is created by linking the hashes across data entries (grouped in blocks, whereby the first entry in each block is the hash from the previous block), which means that the addition of new sets of data contributes to ensuring the integrity of data further up the chain.[78] Where already recorded information or data is manipulated (eg modified), the cryptographic linkages down the chain no longer match, the chain of information breaks, and the specific point of discontinuity becomes evident (which makes the system tamper-evident, rather than tamper-proof, strictly speaking).[79]

Ultimately, then, the main advantages of such an approach to information management lie in the permanence and tamper-evidence of the records/data that result from the algorithmically-ruled decentralization and additivity of the system, so that it is not susceptible of control or manipulation by any given party—and, crucially, not susceptible of manipulation by the entity owning a (traditional) database.

However, to gauge the extent of those advantages and their suitability for procurement governance, it is important to drill down in understanding how such qualities can be achieved through a DLT system, and the variety of DLT systems that exist.[80]

[78] This can be further complicated through techniques allowing for DLT structures other than a (linear) chain; see eg Francisco Luis Benítez-Martínez and others, 'Neural Blockchain Technology for a New Anticorruption Token: Towards a Novel Governance Model' (2023) 20(1) Journal of Information Technology & Politics 1.

[79] Law Commission (England and Wales), 'Smart legal contracts. Advice to Government' (2021) 2.22–2.27 <https://www.lawcom.gov.uk/project/smart-contracts/> accessed 19 December 2022 (hereafter Law Commission, 'Smart legal contracts').

[80] See Albert Sanchez-Graells, 'Data-Driven Procurement Governance: Two Well-Known Elephant Tales' (2019) 24 Communications Law 157 (hereafter Sanchez-Graells, 'Data-Driven Procurement Governance').

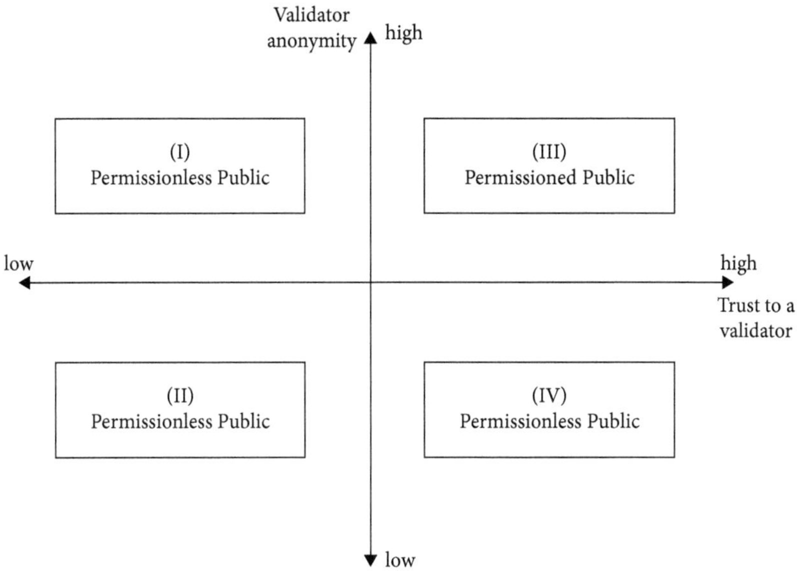

Figure 7.1 Basic classification of DLT technologies
Source: own elaboration, based on further references.

It is possible to classify different DLT solutions according to criteria such as the level of anonymity of transaction validators and the level of trust in validators. Taking these criteria into account, a classification emerges as in Figure 7.1. 'Blockchain' is popularly used to refer to a DLT that operates like bitcoin (a type I blockchain in Figure 7.1), with which it is often confused.[81] In that case, the DLT is permissionless and public, which is understood to mean that anyone can have access to the content of the records (as long as they have the cryptographic keys required to meet cybersecurity) and everyone can potentially participate in the system as a validator of transactions, provided it has access to the computing power required to solve increasingly difficult cryptographic puzzles generated by its consensus mechanism. This creates a strictly rules-based system with minimal scope for collusion or corruption between agents (nodes). It is also relevant to note that most of the advantages derived from commonly discussed DLTs are linked to their 'append-only' design—which means that they are tendentially going to grow indefinitely—and the multiplicity of copies that are kept of the ledger—that is, potentially, an infinite number. See Figure 7.1.

[81] Rauchs and others, 'DLT conceptual framework' (n 77) 15.

From a procurement governance perspective, the premises on which the permanence and tamper-evidence of records held on a DLT are predicated need revisiting. There seems to be an implicit assumption that the DLTs that would be implemented in the procurement setting would be public and permissionless (like those of bitcoin). However, in the public sector, it is very difficult to envisage the adoption of a fully decentralized blockchain solution, not solely due to technical issues of scalability and latency,[82] but also due to the simpler fact that the public sector can hardly be expected to surrender control over the procurement data system.[83] It seems much more plausible that the public sector will consider adopting permissioned DLTs, so that only pre-accredited agents can add information to the ledger. It also seems plausible that, given the need to manage confidential and sensitive information, the DLTs will be private, so that accessing the information also requires pre-accreditation or screening and permissions. It follows that the public sector can plausibly be expected to deploy highly centralized DLTs, where permissions to access and to amend the information are granted by the public sector. It is also possible to think of solutions developed for broad adoption across the public sector, which could keep certain degrees of anonymity and multiplicity of nodes holding records.[84] However, this could create some technical downsides (eg in relation to the network latency of the system, ie the time it takes for the information to be added) and it is plausible to expect public sector organizations to seek to use smaller, private DLTs. If that comes true, and the public sector mainly deploys private permissioned DLTs (type IV blockchain in Figure 7.1),[85] the expected advantages of DLT systems will be significantly eroded. In that scenario, the technical advantages of a DLT would be very close to those of advanced database management with electronic signatures, for example. In some respects, it would also offer limited advantages over systems of automated generation of (open) procurement data.

Emerging evidence on experimentation with blockchain technologies shows precisely this. In some cases, the constraints resulting from the inability of a DLT to hold large volumes of information led to using the DLT simply as a 'tagging' mechanism seeking to ensure the integrity of the information, which

[82] As well as cost and the difficulty of otherwise creating adequate incentives for the mining or processing of the transactions, although this aspect will not be discussed in detail.

[83] This is reflected in the practical implementation of DLT even in most 'blockchain-advanced' countries; see Silvia Semenzin, David Rozas, and Samer Hassan, 'Blockchain-Based Application at a Governmental Level: Disruption or Illusion? The Case of Estonia' (2022) 41(3) Policy and Society 386.

[84] That underpins the European Blockchain Services Infrastructure (EBSI) project; see <https://ec.europa.eu/digital-building-blocks/wikis/display/EBSI/Home> accessed 15 September 2022.

[85] Along the same lines, Yang, 'Blockchain for Enhancing Public Procurement Integrity?' (n 77) 6.

is however stored on off-chain databases,[86] or only using it in relation to specific types of information related to a narrow phase of the procurement process (eg recording evaluation scores).[87] This adds an element of cybersecurity, but one that is probably only marginally different from other types of information security approaches. Emerging implementations are also based on centralized private and permissioned DLTs, initially solely comprising two nodes held by the same public authority[88]—which completely wipes out the expectation of decentralization of the system. To note, some feasibility studies have concluded that the adoption of a DLT would not be cost effective compared to other approaches.[89] Other cases of larger scale experimentation have not gone beyond pilot,[90] or are currently in an uncertain phase of rollout.[91]

4.2 Smart Contracts

Beyond the use of DLTs as information management systems, it is also worth considering them as the data infrastructure capable of enabling the deployment of smart contracts.[92] If smart contracts were to have high potential for procurement governance, developing a (private permissioned) DLT would be a required step[93]—which would then be justified by the more advanced functionality of smart contracts, rather than the inherent (limited) advantages of the DLT as an information management system. In theory, smart contracts could be deployed on a DLT architecture to fully automate (most parts of) the procurement process.[94] However, a detailed analysis of how this would take

[86] eg the Digipolis case study; Deloitte, 'Emerging technologies in public procurement' (n 9) 115 ff.
[87] eg the Glosfer case study; Deloitte, 'Emerging technologies in public procurement' (n 9) 120 ff.
[88] eg the Digipolis case study; Deloitte, 'Emerging technologies in public procurement' (n 9) 115 ff.
[89] eg the Japanese MIC case study; Deloitte, 'Emerging technologies in public procurement' (n 9) 135 ff.
[90] eg the Jalisco case study; Deloitte, 'Emerging technologies in public procurement' (n 9) 126 ff.
[91] eg the US HHS Accelerate case study; Deloitte, 'Emerging technologies in public procurement' (n 9) 109 ff. See also Alex Zhou, 'Tracing HHS Blockchain Adoption' (*Avascent*, 28 April 2021) <https://www.avascent.com/news-insights/healthcare-pulse/tracing-hhs-blockchain-adoption/> accessed 15 September 2022.
[92] Pauline Debono, 'Transforming Public Procurement Contracts into Smart Contracts' (2019) 10 International Journal of Information Technology Project Management 16.
[93] Although, in principle, smart contracts could run on platforms other than DLTs, this is the most common technological deployment; see Law Commission, 'Smart legal contracts' (n 79) 2.30–2.33 and 2.45–2.47. Where smart contracts do not require a DLT infrastructure, their functioning is largely indistinguishable from RPA processes. Therefore, non-DLT smart contracts will not be considered in detail, but most of the issues raised in this section and in relation to the rigidity of RPA processes would be equally applicable.
[94] As mentioned in Chapter 6, Section 3.2.

place shows that the potential for the deployment of smart contracts is rather limited.

Smart contracts are software programs that are triggered, or run, when pre-determined conditions are met. They can be used to automate transactions, as well as workflows, for example triggering the next action when a previous condition is met (such as completion of the previous stage, or the lapse of a pre-specified time period). In that regard their functionality can overlap with other forms of automation.

It is generally suggested that it would be possible to use smart contracts to design self-executable tender procedures leading to the automatic award of the contract to the tender that best satisfied the advertised public sector needs. However, it should be stressed that smart contracts follow a rather simple 'if/when … then' logic that requires setting very clear and rigid rules for each of the relevant statements. Translating procurement processes into that logic is a massive challenge,[95] both in terms of the volume of information that needs to be processed and fit into the programme,[96] but also in terms of the impossibility of reducing all but the simplest of procurement processes into rigid rules (eg concerning tenderer qualification, technical specifications, tender evaluation, or award formulae).[97] By itself, this poses a large question mark around some potential deployments of smart contracts.[98] Even assuming that those challenges could be overcome, the design of a smart contract would only be justified where it could be used on multiple occasions, which would thus limit their likely adoption to highly standardized parts of the procurement procedure, likely to overlap with the practical space that RPA could cover.

The second technical reason pointing at limited potential for smart contracts concerns what is generally seen as their main strength: the automatic generation of (legal) effects. As smart contracts are stored on the DLT, they are deemed irreversible. As soon as the triggering condition is met—usually through the addition of a new transaction to the ledger, or through verification of off-chain information by means of an oracle, potentially an IoT device—the program automatically executes. However, this irreversibility generates

[95] Sanchez-Graells, 'Data-Driven Procurement Governance' (n 80) 165. As is coding smart contracts generally; Eliza Mik, 'Smart Contracts: Terminology, Technical Limitations and Real World Complexity' (2017) 9 Law, Innovation and Technology 269.

[96] A much lauded proof of concept eg stressed that their model could only deal with tenders expressed in up to 700 words; Freya Sheer Hardwick, Raja Naeem Akram, and Konstantinos Markantonakis, 'Fair and Transparent Blockchain based Tendering Framework—A Step Towards Open Governance' (2018) <https://arxiv.org/pdf/1805.05844.pdf> accessed 8 September 2022.

[97] Sanchez-Graells, 'Data-Driven Procurement Governance' (n 80) 164–65.

[98] Kelvin F K Low and Eliza Mik, 'Pause the Blockchain Legal Revolution' (2020) 69 International & Comparative Law Quarterly 135.

significant legal problems and would be particularly problematic in procurement governance, where (administrative) decisions are necessarily open to challenge and (judicial) review. It would also generate problems concerning the need to allow for clarifications of the published information and requirements for example, which could require modifications of the previously uploaded information or code.[99] Moreover, the 'automaticity of irreversible effects' is limited to the on-chain environment. Where the (legal effects) need to manifest off-chain, there is nothing automatic or irreversible about the smart contract. Put together, this also constrains the likely uptake of smart contracts to parts of the procurement process that trigger decisions that are recorded on the DLT, but without further (automatic) legal effectiveness. In other words, this can mainly be applied to exchanges of information, as smart contracts follow the same narrow transactional logic as the DLT itself (as discussed in the previous sub-section).

5. Internet of Things and Oracles

IoT is a technology that automates the collection of information via sensors, as well as facilitating remote interactions by and with the connected things/sensors.[100] It is thus a technology that enables a network of devices or machines to 'exchange information with each other without requiring a human to supervise each action'.[101] IoT can thus be useful in automating the collection of data and this can have benefits in terms of reduction of the data collection burden and the scope of (human) error. It can also potentially speed up the availability of information to (near) real time. That information can then serve as the prompt for an automated process via RPA or a smart contract. Where an IoT sensor feeds information into an automated process, it is usually called an oracle. Oracles not only comprise (IoT) hardware capturing and exchanging data from the 'real world'. They include software oracles delivering data from digital sources such as websites, servers, or databases—which can in turn be fed information either manually or automatically.[102] Oracles can thus be understood as the bridge between the digital and the offline world. However, it should be

[99] Sanchez-Graells, 'Data-Driven Procurement Governance' (n 80) 164–65.
[100] As advanced in Chapter 6, Section 3.1.
[101] Deville, Sergeyssels, and Middag, 'Basic AI Concepts' (n 1) 5.
[102] Niall Roche and Alastair Moore, 'Oracles and Internet of Things in the Internet of Value' in Nikhil Vadgama, Jiahua Xu, and Paolo Tasca (eds), *Enabling the Internet of Value. How Blockchain Connects Global Businesses* (Springer 2022) 157.

stressed that this is mostly a one-way bridge, as the oracles can feed 'real world' information into a database or a DLT, but their ability to generate offline effects is limited to the manipulation of environments through adjustments that can be data led, or digitally activated (eg in the context of a smart heating system, through modifications of a digital thermostat). In other words, oracles are useful to automate the collection of information but, in a procurement governance setting, they can hardly be used to implement any specific environment control mechanisms other than in relation to the execution of public contracts where the mode of delivery is digitally enabled. This largely limits the potential of oracles and IoT implementations to being automated sources of data.[103]

6. The Crucial Relevance of (Big) Data, and the Difficulties in Generating It

The analysis so far has stressed the relevance of data across technological solutions. The outcome of RPA can only be as good as its sources of information (Section 2), and adequate ML solutions can only be trained on high-quality (big) data (Section 3).[104] DLT systems can manage data, but cannot verify its content, accuracy, or reliability (Section 4). IoT and software oracles can automatically capture data, which can alleviate some of the difficulties in generating an adequate data infrastructure. But this is only in relation to the observation of the 'real world' or in relation to digitally available information, which quality raises the same issues as other sources of data (Section 5). These are not solely important technical considerations as, more generally, 'trust in AI is largely based around trust in data'.[105]

Given the crucial relevance of data, it would be hard to overstate how any shortcomings in the enabling data architecture curtail the likelihood of successful adoption of digital technologies. In the absence of adequate data, it may simply be impossible to develop digital solutions at all. And the adoption of digital solutions developed on poor or inadequate data can generate further problems—for example, skewing decision-making on the basis of inadequately derived 'data insights'—which can be compounded by the allure of the digital technologies leading to a lack of critical assessment of such insights,

[103] Which also raises the 'oracle problem' of ensuring that external data sources provide accurate, reliable, and timely data; see Law Commission, 'Smart legal contracts' (n 79) 2.49. This will not be explored in further detail.

[104] Lehr and Ohm, 'Machine Learning for Legal Scholars' (n 1) 676.

[105] Virdee, 'Understanding AI' (n 21) 50.

as discussed in Chapter 6. Ensuring that adequate data is available to develop digital solutions is a challenging but unavoidable requirement.

This section further explores the difficulties in meeting this requirement, despite significant efforts by the European Commission or the OCP, among others. The difficulties are twofold. First, it is proving difficult to generate even a comprehensive system of process-focused (open) procurement (big) data. Second, even if available, such procurement data would be insufficient to enable the deployment of digital technologies, and in particular ML solutions, capable of producing advanced insights beyond the analysis of procurement processes and market interactions explicitly reflected in those processes. A variety of governance-relevant data insights can only be derived from the combination of procurement and other data sources, but creating or accessing the latter also raises big challenges.

6.1 (Open) Procurement (Big) Data

The importance of procurement data is often reflected in high level data strategies, such as the 2020 European strategy for data, which emphasized that:

> Public procurement data are essential to improve transparency and accountability of public spending, fighting corruption and improving spending quality. Public procurement data is spread over several systems in the Member States, made available in different formats and is not easily possible to use for policy purposes in real-time. In many cases, the data quality needs to be improved.[106]

This echoes broader policy statements by the OCP, which is promoting the adoption of its open contracting data standard (OCDS) across the globe.[107]

To address issues of data quality and to facilitate the creation of a data space for the public administration,[108] the EU is in the process of implementing a

[106] European Commission, 'A European strategy for data' (Communication) COM (2020) 66 final, 32.

[107] See <https://standard.open-contracting.org/latest/en/> accessed 26 September 2022.

[108] European Commission, 'A data space to improve public spending, boost data-driven policy-making and improve access to tenders for SMEs' (Communication) [2023] C 98/1. See Albert Sanchez-Graells, 'Digital Procurement, PPDS and Multi-Speed Datafication—Some Thoughts on the March 2023 PPDS Communication' (*howtocrackanut.com*, 28 March 2023) <https://www.howtocrackanut.com/blog/2023/3/28/digital-procurement-ppds-and-multi-speed-datafication> accessed 12 April 2023.

new data standard to control the exchange of information about procurement procedures covered by EU law (eForms).[109] eForms will be mandatory from October 2023. The European Commission has stressed that 'eForms are at the core of the digital transformation of public procurement in the EU. Through the use of a common standard and terminology, they can significantly improve the quality and analysis of data.'[110] eForms are thus the primary initiative at EU level to build big open procurement data as an enabler for the uptake of digital technologies.

The migration towards eForms requires a complete redesign of information exchanges between public buyers and the central publication platform: Tenders Electronic Daily (TED), a supplement of the Official Journal of the European Union (OJEU). Or, rather, the information exchanges between the providers of e-procurement services (acting as e-senders) and TED.[111] eForms are redesigned around universal business language and involve the use of a much more structured information schema compatible with the EU's eProcurement Ontology.[112] eForms are meant to collect a larger amount of information than current TED forms, especially in relation to sub-units within a tender, such as lots, or in relation to framework agreements. eForms are meant to be flexible and regularly revised, specially to add new fields to facilitate data capture in relation to specific EU-mandated requirements.[113]

The implementation of eForms and the related data standard seeks to achieve two goals: first, to ensure the data quality (eg standardization, machine-readability) required to facilitate its automated treatment for the purposes of publication of procurement notices mandated by EU law (ie their primary

[109] Commission Implementing Regulation (EU) 2019/1780 of 23 September 2019 establishing standard forms for the publication of notices in the field of public procurement and repealing Implementing Regulation (EU) 2015/1986 (eForms) [2019] OJ L 272/7 (hereafter 'eForms Implementing Regulation'). eForms are aligned with OCDS, but not identical to it. A previous OCDS schema for TED publications was developed by OCP <https://standard.open-contracting.org/profiles/eu/latest/en/> accessed 28 September 2022.

[110] European Commission, 'eForms' (Website) <https://single-market-economy.ec.europa.eu/single-market/public-procurement/digital-procurement/eforms_en> accessed 26 September 2022.

[111] This distinction is important because in many countries e-procurement services providers compete for the provision of large volume, entirely standardized platform services. Those are markets characterized by small operational margins. This creates incentives for a minimal adaptation of current e-sending systems and disincentives for the inclusion of added-value (data) services unlikely to be used by public buyers. Some optional aspects of the eForms implementation are thus likely to remain unused due to this market structure, as discussed in this section.

[112] European Commission, 'About eProcurement Ontology' (Website) <https://joinup.ec.europa.eu/collection/eprocurement/solution/eprocurement-ontology/about> accessed 27 September 2022.

[113] Such as in relation with the clean vehicles rules. For details, see European Commission, 'Clean Vehicles Directive' (Website) <https://transport.ec.europa.eu/transport-themes/clean-transport-urban-transport/clean-and-energy-efficient-vehicles/clean-vehicles-directive_en> accessed 27 September 2022.

use);[114] and, second, to build a data architecture that can facilitate the accumulation of big data so that advanced data analytics can be deployed by re-users of procurement data.[115] This second(ary) goal is particularly relevant to our discussion.

From an informational point of view, the main constraint remaining despite the adoption of eForms is that their mandatory content is determined by obligations to report and publish tender-specific information under the current EU procurement rules,[116] as well as to meet broader reporting requirements under international and EU law.[117] Ultimately, eForms' main focus is on disseminating details of contract opportunities and capturing different aspects of decision-making by the contracting authorities.[118] Given the process-orientedness and transactional focus of the procurement rules, most of the eForms' mandatory information concerns the scope and design of the tender procedure, some aspects concerning the award and formal implementation of the contract, as well as some minimal data points concerning its material outcome—that is, primarily limited to the winning tender. While some of that information (especially in relation to the winning tender) will be reflective of broader market conditions, and while the accumulation of information across procurement procedures can progressively generate a broader view of the relevant markets,[119] it is worth stressing that *eForms are not designed as a tool of market intelligence*.

eForms do not capture the entirety of information generated by a procurement process and, as mentioned, their mandatory content is rather limited. eForms do include several voluntary or optional fields, and they could be adapted for some voluntary uses, such as in relation to detection of collusion in procurement,[120] or in relation to the beneficial ownership of tenderers and

[114] eForms comprise six standard forms capable of accommodating the 40-plus different types of notice required by EU procurement rules: (1) 'Planning'; (2) 'Competition'; (3) 'Direct award prenotification'; (4) 'Result'; (5) 'Contract modification'; and (6) 'Change; eForms Implementing Regulation (n 109) arts 1(1) and 2.

[115] As well as by the European Commission, as part of the public procurement data space. See n 108.

[116] European Commission, 'eForms: Policy Implementation Handbook' (Guidance) (2020) 11 <https://data.europa.eu/doi/10.2873/646999> accessed 26 September 2022 (hereafter European Commission, 'eForms Handbook').

[117] ibid 16.

[118] In other words, 'eForms only capture a small portion of the information about public procurement (mainly tender and award notices of large contracts)'; Tenders Guru, 'Recommendations for EU procurement' (2021) 12 <https://www.access-info.org/wp-content/uploads/2021-06-28-Tenders-Guru-EU-Recommendations.pdf> accessed 27 September 2022.

[119] In markets where procurement represents most or all demand, that is; for discussion, see Albert Sanchez-Graells, *Public Procurement and the EU Competition Rules* (2nd edn, Hart Publishing 2015) 37–51.

[120] This would be facilitated by capturing details of all tenders received, rather than just the winning tender; European Commission, 'eForms Handbook' (n 116) 24.

subcontractors.[121] However, while eForms are flexible and the schema facilitates the development of additional fields, is it unclear that adequate incentives exist for adoption beyond their mandatory minimum content. This will most likely result in two separate tiers of eForms implementation. Tier 1 would solely concern the collection and exchange of information mandated by EU law. Tier 2 would concern the optional collection and exchange of a much larger volume of information concerning, for example, the entirety of tenders received, as well as qualitative information on things like specific policy goals embedded in a tender process.[122] Of course, in the absence of coordination, a (large) degree of variation within tier 2 implementations can be expected. Tier 2 is potentially very important for (digital) procurement governance, but there is no guarantee that Member States will decide to implement eForms covering it.

One of the major obstacles to the broad adoption of a procurement data model so far, at least in the EU, relates to the slow uptake of e-procurement, discussed in Chapter 6, Section 1. Without an underlying highly automated e-procurement system, the generation and capture of procurement data is a major challenge, as it is a labour-intensive process prone to input error. The entry into force of the eForms could push for the completion of the transition to e-procurement—at least in relation to procurement covered by EU law. However, it is also possible that low e-procurement uptake and generally unsophisticated approaches to e-procurement (eg reduced automation) will limit the future functionality of eForms, with Member States that have so far lagged behind restricting the use of eForms to tier 1. It is also possible that the adoption of eForms may be uneven within a given jurisdiction, with advanced procurement entities (eg central purchasing bodies) adopting tier 2 eForms, and (most) other public buyers limiting themselves to tier 1. While this would not pose legal challenges, it would have a major effect on the utility of the eForms-generated data for the purposes of developing ML solutions, for example, as

[121] Access to beneficial ownership information may, however, be subject to limitations. For discussion, see Chapter 8, Section 2.1.

[122] There are likely also going to be discrepancies in the level of transparency given to the information collected by the eForms, which allow for an advanced level of tailoring of which data fields to publish and which not to publish. This can address concerns of excessive transparency, as well as facilitate adoption across Member States that currently publish widely varying levels of information, as discussed in Kirsi-Maria Halonen, Roberto Caranta, and Albert Sanchez-Graells (eds), *Transparency in EU Procurements: Disclosure within Public Procurement and During Contract Execution* (Edward Elgar 2019). This issue has gained particular prominence following the Court of Justice's judgment in *ANTEA POLSKA and Others* [2022] ECLI:EU:C:2022:888. For discussion, see Albert Sanchez-Graells, 'More Nuanced Procurement Transparency to Protect Competition: Has the Court of Justice Hit the Brakes on Open Procurement Data in Antea Polska (C-54/21)?' (*howtocrackanut.com*, 5 January 2023) <https://www.howtocrackanut.com/blog/2023/1/5/more-nuanced-procurement-transparency-to-protect-competition-in-antea-polska> accessed 12 April 2023.

the data would hardly be representative of important aspects of procurement (markets).[123]

Relatedly, while the data to be captured through eForms could resolve some of the issues with data quality that have been limiting the useability of TED data, and despite the effort to harmonize the underlying data architecture and link it to the Procurement Ontology,[124] 'eForms are not an "off the shelf" product that can be implemented only by IT developers. Instead, before developers start working, procurement policy decision-makers have to make a wide range of policy decisions on how eForms should be implemented'[125] in the different Member States. This poses an additional challenge from the perspective of data quality (and consistency), as there are many fields to be tailored in the eForms implementation process that can result in significant discrepancies in the underlying understanding or methodology to determine them. This adds to the risk of potential further divergence stemming from the domestic interpretation of very similar requirements.[126] This simply extends to the digital data world the current situation, for example in relation to diverging understandings of what is 'recyclable' or what is 'social value' and how to measure them. Whenever open-ended concepts are used, the data may be a poor source for comparative and aggregate analysis. Where there are other sources of standardization or methodology, this issue may be minimized—for example in relation to the green public procurement criteria developed in the EU,[127] if they are properly used. However, where there are no outside or additional sources of harmonization, it seems that there is scope for quite a few difficult issues in trying to develop digital solutions on top of eForms data—except in relation to quantitative issues or in relation to information structured in clearly defined categories, which will mainly link back to the design of the procurement.

Overall, while the implementation of eForms could, in theory, build a big data architecture and facilitate the development of ML solutions, there are many challenges ahead. The generalized adoption of tier 2 eForms implementations seems unlikely, unless Member States make a positive decision in the

[123] See Albert Sanchez-Graells, 'Competition Implications of Procurement Digitalisation and the Procurement of Digital Technologies by Central Purchasing Bodies' (2023) <https://ssrn.com/abstract=4376037> accessed 12 April 2023 (hereafter Sanchez-Graells, 'Digital Tech and CPBs').

[124] See n 112.

[125] European Commission, 'eForms Handbook' (n 116) 19.

[126] For a snapshot of current national divergences, see Open Contracting Partnership, 'How open is public procurement data in the EU?' (2023) <https://www.open-contracting.org/wp-content/uploads/2023/06/OCP2023-EU-OpenData.pdf> accessed 6 July 2023.

[127] European Commission, 'EU GPP criteria' <https://ec.europa.eu/environment/gpp/eu_gpp_criteria_en.htm> accessed 28 September 2022.

process of national adoption. In that regard, it may well be that most of the added functionalities that tier 2 data could enable will only be developed in specific jurisdictions or domains, such as that of centralized procurement. This would not only constrain the broader (re)usability of eForms data, but also generate other governance knock-on effects linked to further procurement centralization pressures, for example, as discussed in Section 8. More generally, that would perpetuate constraints resulting from limited procurement data, which would have a negative effect on the likelihood of successful adoption of digital technologies for procurement governance.

6.2 Other (Big) Data Required to Extract Advanced Insights

A further difficulty in creating an enabling (big) data architecture for procurement governance is that much of the relevant data is not generated within procurement processes, but rather relates to broader market and institutional issues. This ranges from sources of information on beneficial ownership or other sources of potential conflict of interest (eg family relations, or financial circumstances of individuals involved in decision-making), to information on corporate activities and offerings, including detailed information on products, services, and means of production. It also extends to information on levels of utilization of public contracts and satisfaction with the outcomes by those meant to benefit from their implementation, whether they are within the public administration or not.

This challenge is difficult to tackle, as the collection of procurement-related data can have very little value (other than for narrow applications, such as category management) unless it can be cross-checked with those other sources of information. To the extent that the outside sources of information are not digitized, or not in a way that is (easily) compatible or linkable with procurement information, some data-based procurement governance solutions will remain undeliverable. In that regard, some developments in procurement governance will be determined by progress in other policy areas (eg tax data, or data on licensing and standardization of products and services). While these are also receiving increasing attention, for example in the EU, most data-sharing measures are of a voluntary nature,[128] and some recent implementations fall short

[128] eg initiatives concerning access to and the re-use of data held by public sector bodies; Regulation (EU) 2022/868 of the European Parliament and of the Council of 30 May 2022 on European data governance and amending Regulation (EU) 2018/1724 (Data Governance Act) [2022] OJ L 152/1. The latter is likely to be complemented by the Data Act; Proposal for a Regulation of the European Parliament and

of placing procurement-relevant information at the core of the respective regimes, such as in relation to high-value added datasets.[129]

A final issue to consider is that current initiatives only regulate the capture of data for the future. This means that it will take time for big data to accumulate, and accessing historical data would be a way of speeding up the development of digital solutions. Moreover, in some contexts, such as in relation to very infrequent types of procurement, or in relation to decisions concerning previous investments and acquisitions, historical data will be particularly relevant (eg to deploy green policies seeking to extend the life of current assets through programmes of enhanced maintenance or refurbishment). However, there are also significant challenges linked to the creation of backward-looking digital databases, not only due to the digitization cost, but also to difficulties in ensuring the representativeness and adequate labelling of pre-existing information. The lack of availability of such data may continue to constrain developments in data-led procurement governance in the short and medium term, or at least until new measures for the generation of data, such as the eForms discussed above, are fully embedded and facilitate the accumulation of sufficient data.

6.3 Recapitulation of Data Issues

The rollout of an enabling data architecture for the development of digital solutions for procurement governance faces significant challenges. Despite the policy efforts of the European Commission, given the voluntary nature of their most innovative informational aspects, it seems unlikely that the new rules on eForms will generate data other than in relation to limited aspects of the procurement procedure. While this can enable the development of some tools

of the Council on harmonised rules on fair access to and use of data (Data Act), COM (2022) 68 final. The revised guidance on business to government (B2G) data sharing is also of relevance; see High-Level Expert Group on Business-to-Government Data Sharing, 'Towards a European strategy on business-to-government data sharing for the public interest' (2020) <https://op.europa.eu/s/w363> accessed 28 September 2022. For discussion of the latter, see Albert Sanchez-Graells, 'Some Public Procurement Challenges in Supporting and Delivering Smart Urban Mobility: Procurement Data, Discretion and Expertise' in Michele Finck and others (eds), *Smart Urban Mobility—Law, Regulation, and Policy* (Springer 2020) 99, 111–13.

[129] eg in relation to the Directive (EU) 2019/1024 of the European Parliament and of the Council of 20 June 2019 on open data and the re-use of public sector information (recast) (Open Data Directive) [2019] OJ L 172/56, the lack of inclusion of procurement data as a high-value dataset in Commission Implementing Regulation (EU) 2023/138 of 21 December 2022 laying down a list of specific high-value datasets and the arrangements for their publication and re-use [2023] OJ L 19/43. See Chapter 8, Section 2.1.1.

aimed at monitoring and improving decision-making in a narrow sense, it seems unlikely that market intelligence will be significantly boosted, other than under specific circumstances, such as in countries with advanced (automated) e-procurement systems, in relation to the activities of central purchasing bodies, or in sectors where the public buyer is the sole or dominant buyer. This will limit the uses of the data outside those fields and can generate knock-on governance effects, such as pressures for further centralization. Similarly, given the voluntary nature of most measures relating to non-procurement data of relevance for procurement governance, it is also unclear that sufficient data will be available to develop digital solutions providing advanced data insights beyond the narrow confines of the procurement process. The implication of these trends in data generation is that the adoption of digital procurement governance tools will likely either remain slow or not be possible for some applications. This needs to be considered as a foundational part of the feasibility boundary discussed in more detail in Section 8.

7. The Crucial Relevance of Data and Systems Integrity: A Displacement of Governance Risks?

It should also be stressed that big data comes with additional governance risks in relation to the integrity of data and data systems. Once (or to the extent that) procurement governance is data-driven, protecting the integrity of the data becomes an essential part of ensuring adequate governance.[130] Cybersecurity thus becomes a crucial aspect of procurement governance, as discussed in more detail in Chapter 8, Section 3. Moreover, some solutions can generate risks for the integrity of data systems—for example if the deployed digital solutions can rewrite or delete parts of the underlying data architecture, perhaps as a result of their malfunctioning. This requires careful consideration from a technical perspective, and this analysis may be complicated in settings where the new solution is built on top of a legacy or inadequate (part of the) data architecture or requires interoperability with other systems.[131]

[130] See eg UK National Audit Office, Cyber and information security. Good practice guide (2021) <https://www.nao.org.uk/wp-content/uploads/2021/10/Good-practice-guide-Cyber-and-information-security.pdf> accessed 28 September 2022.

[131] This is stressed in the vast majority of studies in the field; see Aristotelis Mavidis and Dimitris Folinas, 'From Public E-Procurement 3.0 to E-Procurement 4.0; A Critical Literature Review' (2022) 14 Sustainability 11252 <https://doi.org/10.3390/su141811252> accessed 28 September 2022.

The functional point to be stressed here is that the feasibility and desirability of the deployment of digital solutions should be assessed not only in relation to their technical characteristics and the existence of adequate data, but also encompassing an analysis of the new governance risks that the digital solution brings. Moreover, in many cases, the digital solution will not resolve, but simply displace, the relevant governance risk. For example, a digital solution seeking to reduce corruption through the implementation of a permissioned DLT to control access to information could just displace the governance risk to those with adequate permissions. A solution based on an oracle would displace the risk from the potential manipulation of the original information to the manipulation of the oracle.[132] In such cases, the displacement of the original governance risk and the addition of technical governance risks could worsen rather than improve the effectiveness of procurement governance. This should raise questions about the desirability of a potential digital solution compared to current, or alternative (less sophisticated) options.[133] It will thus be necessary for the risk assessment to be carried out in relation to the deployment of a digital solution not only to cover new risks, but also (displaced) existing risks, as discussed in Chapter 8.

8. A Feasibility Boundary for Digital Procurement Governance

The major constraint for progress towards digital procurement governance is, and will remain for some time, the underlying (big) data architecture (see Section 6). The absence of adequate data jeopardizes the feasibility of digital procurement governance. To facilitate the unlocking of potential improvements in the adoption of digital technologies, investing in such enabling data architecture should be the priority. In the EU context, it would also require Member States to consider mandating, for example, the adoption of tier 2 eForms implementation, being proactive in generating useable data on other aspects of procurement governance-relevant information, as well as fostering voluntary compliance with data-sharing measures by the private sector. In other jurisdictions, similarly proactive measures should be pursued under the relevant regulatory framework.

[132] See n 103.

[133] This could form part of the assessment of the planned deployment, especially under a principle of AI minimization; see Chapter 2, Section 2.4 and Chapter 5, Section 3.2.

Once (or rather, if) that major data hurdle is cleared, the possibilities realistically brought by the functionality of digital technologies need to be embedded in the procurement governance context, which needs to ensure that technology adoption decisions are grounded on the analysis resulting from a feasibility boundary that can be summarized as follows.

RPA can reduce the administrative costs of managing pre-existing digitized and highly structured information in the context of entirely standardized and repetitive phases of the procurement process. RPA can reduce the time invested in gathering and cross-checking information and can thus serve as a basic element of decision-making support. However, RPA cannot increase the volume and type of information being considered (other than in cases where some available information was not taken into consideration due to things like administrative capacity constraints), and it can hardly be successfully deployed in relation to open-ended or potentially contradictory information points. RPA will also not change or improve the processes themselves (unless they are redesigned with a view to deploying RPA). This generates a clear feasibility boundary for RPA deployment, which will generally have as its purpose the optimization of the time available to the procurement workforce to engage in information analysis rather than information sourcing and basic checks. While this can clearly bring operational advantages, it will hardly transform procurement governance.

Developing ML solutions will pose major challenges, not only in relation to the underlying data architecture (as above), but also in relation to specific regulatory and governance requirements specific to public procurement. Where the operational management of procurement does not diverge from the equivalent function in the (less regulated) private sector, it will be possible to see the adoption or adaptation of similar ML solutions (eg in relation to category spend management). However, where there are regulatory constraints on the conduct of procurement, the development of ML solutions will be challenging.

For example, the need to ensure the openness and technical neutrality of procurement procedures will limit the possibilities of developing recommender systems other than in pre-procured closed lists or environments based on framework agreements or dynamic purchasing systems underpinned by electronic catalogues. Similarly, the intended use of the recommender system may raise significant legal issues concerning, for example, the exercise of discretion, which can limit their deployment to areas of information exchange or to merely suggestion-based tasks that could hardly replace current processes and procedures. Given the limited utility (or acceptability) of collective filtering, there are also constraints on the generality of recommender systems for procurement applications, both at tenderer and at product/service level. This raises a further feasibility issue, as the functional need to develop a multiplicity of different recommenders not only reopens the issue of data sufficiency and adequacy, but also raises questions of (economic and technical) viability. Recommender systems would mostly only be susceptible of feasible adoption in highly centralized procurement settings. This could create a push for further procurement centralization that is not neutral from a governance perspective, and that can certainly generate significant competition issues.[134] This should be carefully considered, as the knock-on effects of the implementation of some ML solutions may only emerge further down the line.

Similarly, the development of chatbots is constrained by regulatory issues, such as the need to deploy closed domain chatbots so that the information they draw from can be controlled and quality assured in line with duties of good administration and other legal requirements concerning the provision of information within tender procedures. Chatbots are suited to types of high-volume information-based queries only. They would have limited applicability in relation to the specific characteristics of any given procurement procedure, as preparing the specific information to be used by the chatbot would be a challenge—with the added functionality of the chatbot being marginal. Chatbots could facilitate access to pre-existing and curated simple information, but their functionality would quickly hit a ceiling as information complexity increased. Chatbots would only be able to perform at a high level if plugged to a knowledge base created as an expert system. But then, again, in that case their added functionality would be marginal. Ultimately, the practical space for the development of chatbots is limited to low added value information access tasks. While this can clearly bring operational advantages, it will hardly transform procurement governance.

ML could facilitate the development and deployment of 'advanced' automated screens, or red flags, which could identify patterns of suspicious behaviour to then be assessed against the applicable rules (eg administrative and criminal law in case of corruption, or competition law, potentially including criminal law, in case of bid rigging) or policies (eg in relation to policy requirements to comply with specific targets in relation to a broad variety of goals). The

[134] For discussion, see Albert Sanchez-Graells, 'Public Procurement by Central Purchasing Bodies, Competition and SMEs: Towards a More Dynamic Model?' in Carina Risvig Hamer and Mario Comba (eds), *Centralising Public Procurement—The Approach of EU Member States* (Edward Elgar 2021) 71; Albert Sanchez-Graells and Ignacio Herrera Anchustegui, 'Impact of Public Procurement Aggregation on Competition: Risks, Rationale and Justification for the Rules in Directive 2014/24' in R Fernandez and P Valcarcel (eds), *Centralizacion de compras publicas* (Civitas 2016) 129. See also Sanchez-Graells, 'Digital Tech and CPBs' (n 123).

trade-off in this type of implementation is between the potential (accuracy) of the algorithmic screening and legal requirements on the explainability of decision-making. Where the screens were not used solely for policy analysis, but acting on the red flag carried legal consequences, the suitability of specific types of ML solutions (eg unsupervised learning solutions tantamount to a 'black box') would be challenging, or altogether excluded. In any case, the development of ML screens capable of significantly improving on RPA-based automation of current screens is particularly dependent on the existence of adequate data, which is still proving an insurmountable hurdle in many an intended implementation.

Other procurement governance constraints limit the prospects of wholesale adoption of DLT (or blockchain) technologies, other than for relatively limited information management purposes. The public sector can hardly be expected to adopt DLT solutions that are not heavily permissioned, and that do not include significant safeguards to protect sensitive, commercially valuable, and other types of information that cannot be in the public domain. This means that the public sector is only likely to implement highly centralized DLT solutions, with the public sector granting permissions to access and amend the relevant information. While this can still generate some (degree of) tamper-evidence and permanence of the information management system, the net advantage is likely to be modest when compared to other types of secure information management systems. This can have an important bearing on decisions about whether DLT solutions meet cost effectiveness or similar criteria of value for money controlling their piloting and deployment. The value proposition of DLT solutions could increase if they enabled significant procurement automation through smart contracts. However, there are massive challenges in translating procurement procedures into a programmable logic. Moreover, smart contracts have limited capability that is not commensurate with the volumes and complexity of procurement information, and their development would only be justified in contexts where a given smart contract (ie specific program) could be used in a high number of procurement procedures. This limits its scope of applicability to standardized and simple procurement exercises, which creates a functional overlap with some RPA solutions. Even in those settings, smart contracts would pose structural problems in terms of their irrevocability or automaticity. Moreover, they would be unable to generate off-chain effects, and this would not be easily sorted out even with the inclusion of IoT solutions or software oracles. This largely restricts smart contracts to an information exchange mechanism, which does not significantly increase the value added by DLT plus smart contract solutions for procurement governance.

To conclude, and to link back to the discussion in Chapter 6, the analysis here has shown that a feasibility boundary emerges whereby the adoption of digital technologies for procurement governance can make contributions in relation to its information intensity, but not easily in relation to its information complexity—at least not in the short to medium term and not in the absence of a significant improvement of the required enabling data architecture. This should be considered in assessing potential use cases. This feasibility boundary should also serve to moderate the expectations that come with the technologies and that can fuel 'policy irresistibility'. However, extracting these insights can be complex and determining whether a deployment is viable may (sometimes) hinge on the views of tech providers. Precisely for this reason, it is appropriate to subject such viability assessment to external verification, as advocated in Chapter 5, Section 3.2. Further, it must be stressed that those advantages do not come without their own additional complexities linked to new governance risks and requirements for their mitigation. Such additional or compounded risks must also be integrated into the decision-making and subject to external oversight. These risks will be explored in detail in Chapter 8, and their management in Chapter 9.

8
Identifying Emerging Risks in Digital Procurement Governance

1. Introduction

Chapter 7 stressed that the potential benefits resulting from the adoption of digital technologies within the feasibility boundary drawn therein need to be assessed holistically and considering new governance risks and requirements for their mitigation.[1] This chapter explores the main governance risks and legal obligations arising from the adoption of digital technologies. These revolve around data governance, algorithmic transparency, technological dependency, technical debt, cybersecurity threats, risks stemming from the long-term erosion of the skills base in the public sector, and difficult trade-offs due to the uncertainty surrounding immature and still changing technologies within an also evolving regulatory framework. The goal is to offer a critical assessment of both the need to recognize the new risks and to factor their assessment into decisions whether to adopt digital technologies. The chapter also makes links with the changing nature (and displacement) of governance risks, which can create opacity and difficulties in the identification of technology-enabled corrupt or anticompetitive practices.

As mentioned in Chapters 6 and 7, the adoption of digital technologies for procurement governance can not only bring improvements and efficiencies in the management of the information intensiveness of procurement (and of its information complexity in a more limited manner), but also new governance risks and challenges. Some of these risks are of a legal nature, such as those concerning compliance with data governance requirements, or the management of Intellectual Property Rights (IPR). Other risks will be of an operational or pragmatic nature, such as the need to manage technical debt, cybersecurity threats, or digital skills shortages. The chapter considers both sources of governance challenges to provide a rounded overview.

[1] That would be the basis for the approval process advocated for in Chapter 5, Section 3.2.

Digital Technologies and Public Procurement. Albert Sanchez-Graells, Oxford University Press.
 DOI: 10.1093/oso/9780198866770.003.0008

It should be acknowledged that the operational challenges can be much more difficult to overcome than most legal issues, and that some operational challenges compound the others—with the issue of the public sector's digital capability gap playing a crucial role. This is not only in relation to the 'policy irresistibility' and risk of capture discussed in Chapter 6, but also in relation to the specific assessment and mitigation of the governance risks discussed here, an understanding of which requires varying degrees of technical expertise (see Section 4). The analysis will show how implementing some of the emerging legal requirements also necessitates detailed technical expertise. Such emerging legal requirements are based on open-ended standards and general principles, and there will be significant challenges in translating them into specific policies, and those policies into practices.[2] As a key to the analysis below, it should be stressed at the outset that a cautious and incremental approach to the adoption of digital technologies is required, given current gaps in public sector digital capability.

2. Data and Technology Risks in Digital Procurement Governance

This section focuses on data governance risks and new types of technology governance risks, paying special attention to technical debt and technological dependency. It is submitted that these are the two sources of governance risks most salient in the development and deployment of digital solutions for procurement governance.

2.1 Data Governance Risks

Chapter 7 highlighted the data dependency of the development and deployment of digital solutions. This places data governance as a core emerging source of governance risks in the transition to digital procurement.[3] Data and data systems integrity are crucial to the proper operation of digital procurement

[2] For discussion, see eg Bob Hudson, David Hunter, and Stephen Peckham, 'Policy Failure and the Policy-Implementation Gap: Can Policy Support Programs Help?' (2019) 2 Policy Design and Practice 1.

[3] OECD, 'Data Governance in the Public Sector' in *The Path to Becoming a Data-Driven Public Sector* (2019) <https://doi.org/10.1787/059814a7-en> accessed 4 October 2022.

governance,[4] not solely in relation to cybersecurity threats (discussed in Section 3), but also in relation to the lawful management of the data used to develop and deploy digital technologies.[5] Some of the procurement data will be subject to disclosure constraints of a statutory or contractual nature.[6] Managing those constraints will be crucial in ensuring a viable and sustainable implementation of digital governance solutions, and minimizing the public buyer's exposure to liability for excessive disclosure of information. It will also be important to avoid (contractual or proprietary) data lock-in, especially in relation to data that is generated during the execution of public contracts and not primarily (or at all) held by the public buyer.[7]

It is worth stressing that public buyers have data governance obligations even if they do not directly engage with the development and deployment of digital technologies. The generation and holding of procurement data creates such data governance obligations.[8] These result in part from the imminent obligation to comply with the rules on eForms in relation to the conduct of procurement and the publication of the associated notices required by EU law,[9] but also go beyond that and concern any other data held by the public buyer.

[4] Rene Abraham, Johannes Schneider, and Jan vom Brocke, 'Data Governance: A Conceptual Framework, Structured Review, and Research Agenda' (2019) 49 International Journal of Information Management 424; Marijn Janssen and others, 'Data Governance: Organizing Data for Trustworthy Artificial Intelligence' (2020) 37 Government Information Quarterly 101493 <https://doi.org/10.1016/j.giq.2020.101493> accessed 4 October 2022.

[5] For broader discussion of the normative underpinnings and implications, see Anke Sophia Obendiek, *Data Governance: Value Orders and Jurisdictional Conflicts* (OUP 2022).

[6] Such contractual arrangements can generate their own data governance issues, such as data lock-in or other issues of data sovereignty. However, their analysis exceeds the scope of this chapter. This can be the case particularly where non-procurement data is sourced to develop specific governance solutions, as it is less likely that the public buyer will have mechanisms to access that data in other ways. In the EU, the proposed Data Act could generate a partial or limited solution to such situations, see n 15. However, this analysis also exceeds the scope of this chapter.

[7] Data lock-in can exacerbate issues of technological or vendor lock-in, as discussed in Section 2.2. Managing this risk will exceed the scope of open data obligations imposed on providers of public transport and utilities services under the Open Data Directive (n 13). However, a detailed analysis exceeds the scope of this chapter. For discussion, see Albert Sanchez-Graells, 'Some Public Procurement Challenges in Supporting and Delivering Smart Urban Mobility: Procurement Data, Discretion and Expertise' in Michele Finck and others (eds), *Smart Urban Mobility—Law, Regulation, and Policy* (Springer 2020) 99 (hereafter Sanchez-Graells, 'Smart Mobility').

[8] Indeed, the EU data governance regime revolves around the position of the data holder (ie the legal person, including public sector bodies, which, in accordance with applicable EU or national law, has the right to grant access to or to share certain data) and a growing set of obligations promoting data access. For discussion, see Peter Georg Picht, 'Caught in the Acts: Framing Mandatory Data Access Transactions under the Data Act, Further EU Digital Regulation Acts, and Competition Law' (2022) Max Planck Institute for Innovation and Competition Research Paper No 22-12 <https://ssrn.com/abstract=4076842> accessed 5 October 2022.

[9] Commission Implementing Regulation (EU) 2019/1780 of 23 September 2019 establishing standard forms for the publication of notices in the field of public procurement and repealing Implementing Regulation (EU) 2015/1986 (eForms) [2019] OJ L 272/7 (hereafter 'eForms Implementing Regulation'). See Chapter 7, Section 6.1.

There are two types of data: (potentially) open data, and data subject to the rights of others. In this context, 'data subject to the rights of others' covers data that might be subject to data protection legislation,[10] IPR, or commercial confidentiality, including business, professional, and company secrets.[11] (Potentially) open data is not constrained by the need to protect such third party rights. (Potentially) open data can however be subject to other types of contractual or statutory rights (eg database rights), which are currently being reshaped under EU law.[12] The governance requirements applicable to (potentially) open data primarily derive from the Open Data Directive,[13] while those applicable to data subject to the rights of others result from the Data Governance Act[14] and can be complemented by the proposed Data Act, if adopted.[15] Each of these sets of requirements will be assessed in turn.

2.1.1 (Potentially) open data

The Open Data Directive establishes minimum rules on practical arrangements to facilitate the re-use of data held by public sector bodies,[16] and requires that information held by public buyers is made available for re-use for commercial or non-commercial purposes in compliance with the specific requirements it lays down.[17] However, the Open Data Directive is aligned with freedom of

[10] It is worth noting that the collection and processing of data in the context of procurement is done under a legal basis other than consent, which reduces the issues that could arise in other contexts; see European Data Protection Supervisor, 'Guidelines on the processing of personal data in the context of public procurement, grants as well as selection and use of external experts' (2013) <https://edps.europa.eu/sites/edp/files/publication/13-06-25_procurement_en.pdf> accessed 5 October 2022.

[11] European Commission, Explanatory Memorandum accompanying the proposal for a Regulation of the European Parliament and of the Council on European data governance, COM (2020) 767 final, 1. See also Regulation (EU) 2022/868 of the European Parliament and of the Council of 30 May 2022 on European data governance and amending Regulation (EU) 2018/1724 [2022] OJ L 152/1, rec (10) and art 3(1) (hereafter 'Data Governance Act').

[12] It will be necessary to assess such constraints on a case-by-case basis, and in relation to transitory regimes under the relevant rules; see eg in relation to data exclusivity agreements (n 33). For broader discussion, see Mireille van Eechoud, 'A Serpent Eating Its Tail: The Database Directive Meets the Open Data Directive' (2021) 52 IIC – International Review of Intellectual Property and Competition Law 375.

[13] Directive (EU) 2019/1024 of the European Parliament and of the Council of 20 June 2019 on open data and the re-use of public sector information (recast) (Open Data Directive) [2019] OJ L 172/56.

[14] Data Governance Act (n 11) rec (10).

[15] European Commission, Proposal for a Regulation of the European Parliament and of the Council on harmonised rules on fair access to and use of data, COM (2022) 68 final (hereafter the 'Data Act'). The obligations stemming from the Data Act would mostly be limited to exceptional circumstances leading to public sector access to private sector data; Data Act, arts 14–22. The primary obligation of relevance for the analysis here would be to not make the accessed data available for re-use under the Open Data Directive (as discussed in Section 2.1.1), which application in this context would be excluded; Data Act, art 17(3).

[16] Open Data Directive (n 13) art 1(1). It should be stressed that the definition of public sector bodies matches the scope of application of the EU procurement rules. See also nn 49 and 144.

[17] Open Data Directive (n 13) art 3(1).

information regimes.[18] Consequently, it does not apply to data[19] excluded from the 'freedom of information' regimes in the Member States, including on grounds of, for example, commercial confidentiality (including business, professional, or company secrets),[20] or due to third parties holding IPR[21]—that is, data subject to the rights of others.[22] In the context of procurement, where public buyers manage and hold significant amounts of commercially sensitive and IPR-protected information,[23] this creates the immediate need to implement adequate governance measures to ensure that information subject to the rights of others is not disclosed as a result of the positive obligations arising from the Open Data Directive. Recent Court of Justice case law has reinforced the duty of contracting authorities to protect the confidentiality of a broad array of information, which cannot be limited to a strict definition of trade secrets.[24] This can, for example, require a strengthening of the institutional and contractual governance of some procurement data, as well as requiring a comprehensive strategy and process to record and classify confidential and other types of information subject to the rights of others throughout the procurement lifecycle.[25]

The main obligation for public sector bodies in relation to disclosable data is to make it available in any pre-existing format or language—and, where possible and appropriate, by electronic means—in formats that are open, machine-readable, accessible, findable, and re-usable. Data must be made available

[18] For discussion, see Kirsi-Maria Halonen, Roberto Caranta, and Albert Sanchez-Graells (eds), *Transparency in EU Procurements: Disclosure within Public Procurement and During Contract Execution* (Edward Elgar 2019).

[19] The Open Data Directive imposes obligations in relation to 'documents', which are defined as any content whatever its medium (paper or electronic form or as a sound, visual, or audiovisual recording), or any part of such content. Therefore, its regime applies to documents, data, or information, indistinctly; see Open Data Directive (n 13) art 2(6).

[20] ibid art 1(2)(d)(iii).

[21] ibid art 1(2)(c).

[22] It also covers personal data and the rights resulting from Regulation (EU) 2016/679 of the European Parliament and of the Council of 27 April 2016 on the protection of natural persons with regard to the processing of personal data and on the free movement of such data, and repealing Directive 95/46/EC (General Data Protection Regulation) [2016] OJ L 119/1 (hereafter 'GDPR'). Personal data can only be made available for re-use where this complies with the GDPR, which can concern the availability of anonymized data; see Open Data Directive (n 13) rec 52. This is largely in line with the regime of the Data Governance Act, see n 65.

[23] The sensitivity of the procurement context to the potential excessive disclosure of commercially confidential information is stressed in Directive (EU) 2016/943 of the European Parliament and of the Council of 8 June 2016 on the protection of undisclosed know-how and business information (trade secrets) against their unlawful acquisition, use and disclosure [2016] OJ L 157/1, rec 18.

[24] *ANTEA POLSKA and Others* [2022] ECLI:EU:C:2022:888. For discussion, see Albert Sanchez-Graells, 'More Nuanced Procurement Transparency to Protect Competition: Has the Court of Justice Hit the Brakes on Open Procurement Data in Antea Polska (C-54/21)?' (*howtocrackanut.com*, 5 January 2023) <https://www.howtocrackanut.com/blog/2023/1/5/more-nuanced-procurement-transparency-to-protect-competition-in-antea-polska> accessed 12 April 2023.

[25] For discussion, see Sanchez-Graells, 'Smart Mobility' (n 7) 104 ff.

together with its metadata—on the understanding that, where possible, both the format and the metadata shall comply with formal open standards;[26] and with emphasis on making the documents 'open by design and by default'.[27]

In other words, the Open Data Directive establishes the default position that data held by public buyers must be made available for re-use. The Open Data Directive also limits the public buyers' ability to claim protection of the information on grounds of the *sui generis* right applicable to databases[28] in order to prevent data re-use or to restrict re-use beyond the limits set by the Directive.[29] It also sets the requirement that data re-use shall be free of charge—with the exception that the recovery of the marginal costs incurred for the reproduction, provision, and dissemination of documents as well as for anonymization of personal data and measures taken to protect commercially confidential information may be allowed.[30] Further to that, data re-use shall not be subject to conditions, unless such conditions are objective, proportionate, non-discriminatory, and justified on grounds of a public interest objective. And when re-use is subject to conditions, those conditions shall not unnecessarily restrict possibilities for re-use and shall not be used to restrict competition.[31] Any applicable conditions for the re-use of documents must be non-discriminatory for comparable categories of re-use, including for cross-border re-use.[32] The Open Data Directive bars public buyers from granting exclusive rights to access the data,[33] except where an exclusive right is necessary for the provision of a service in the public interest.[34]

This general regime falls short of imposing on public buyers the obligation to publish open data, as there is no clear-cut obligation to fully digitize data that is available in other formats.[35] Under the Open Data Directive, such obligation only exists in relation to 'high-value datasets', which must be available free of

[26] Open Data Directive (n 13) art 5(1).

[27] ibid art 5(2). There are additional obligations to facilitate immediate re-use via suitable APIs of 'dynamic data' (ie documents in a digital form, subject to frequent or real-time updates, in particular because of their volatility or rapid obsolescence); ibid arts 2(8) and 5(5). However, most procurement data is unlikely to meet this definition, so this will not be considered in further detail.

[28] Directive (EC) 96/9 of the European Parliament and of the Council of 11 March 1996 on the legal protection of databases [1996] OJ L 77/20, as amended, art 7(1).

[29] Open Data Directive (n 13) art 1(6).

[30] ibid art 6(1). There are other exceptions that are not relevant to the analysis here.

[31] ibid art 8(1).

[32] ibid art 11.

[33] ibid art 12(1). However, there are grace periods running until 2043 and 2049 for exclusivity agreements that were in place by 2013 (public sector bodies) or 2019 (public undertakings); ibid art 12(5) and (6).

[34] In which case a review of the exclusive arrangements should take place every three years. ibid art 12(2).

[35] ibid art 5(1).

charge, in machine-readable format, provided via Application Programming Interfaces (APIs), and provided as a bulk download, where relevant.[36] High-value datasets have been specified by the European Commission in an implementing regulation that does not include procurement data as a high-value dataset.[37] Classifying procurement data as a high-value dataset would clearly have boosted the obligation to publish it as open data,[38] as well as ensuring consistency across the EU. However, the entry into force of the rules on eForms[39] can partly mitigate the non-classification of procurement datasets as high value, as the interaction of the eForms' substantive requirements and the obligation to make data available for re-use under the Open Data Directive[40] may achieve a similar level of open access to procurement data—at least in relation to data subject to mandatory disclosure.

eForms will require public buyers to generate digital information using a structured and machine-readable data format.[41] This information will be published in the Tenders Electronic Daily (TED) supplement of the Official Journal of the European Union (OJEU).[42] However, this information will also be kept on record by the public buyer[43]—and in most cases also be published through national or regional publication portals.[44] It should be stressed that the holding of the information in digital format will trigger the public buyer's obligation to make that data available for re-use 'by electronic means, in formats that are open, machine-readable, accessible, findable and re-usable, together with their metadata'[45]—in addition to TED's publication, which will also be re-usable.

[36] ibid art 14. There are some limited exceptions to the requirement for free access.

[37] Commission Implementing Regulation (EU) 2023/138 of 21 December 2022 laying down a list of specific high-value datasets and the arrangements for their publication and re-use [2023] OJ L 19/43.

[38] Karolis Granickas, 'Open Contracting & the EU: What's the Progress on Contract Transparency?' (*Open Contracting Partnership Blog*, 2 February 2022) <https://www.open-contracting.org/2022/02/02/open-contracting-the-eu-whats-the-progress-on-contract-transparency/> accessed 4 October 2022.

[39] eForms Implementing Regulation (n 9).

[40] Provided the information is held by a covered entity or body, which raises some questions concerning data stored in outsourced eProcurement platforms or systems. However, assessing this issue exceeds the scope of this chapter.

[41] As discussed in Chapter 7, Section 6.1. See also European Commission, 'eForms: policy implementation handbook' (Guidance) (2020) 11 <https://data.europa.eu/doi/10.2873/646999> accessed 4 October 2022 (hereafter European Commission, 'eForms Handbook').

[42] European Commission, 'eForms: governance and life-cycle management' (Guidance) (2020) <https://data.europa.eu/doi/10.2873/185027> accessed 4 October 2022.

[43] There are extensive record-keeping obligations derived from the EU procurement rules; see eg Directive 2014/24/EU of the European Parliament and of the Council of 26 February 2014 on public procurement and repealing Directive 2004/18/EC [2014] OJ L 94/65, art 84. For discussion, see Pedro Cerqueira Gomes, 'Article 84—Individual Reports on Procedures for the Award of Contracts' in Roberto Caranta and Albert Sanchez-Graells (eds), *European Public Procurement. Commentary on Directive 2014/24/EU* (Edward Elgar 2021) 869 (hereafter Caranta and Sanchez-Graells, *Commentary*).

[44] European Commission, 'eForms Handbook' (n 41) 41.

[45] Art 5(1) Open Data Directive (n 13).

Importantly, where the eForms capture information that is not published in TED, the obligation to make the data available for re-use by the public buyer under the Open Data Directive can be more comprehensive than a mere replication of TED publications—for example in relation to optional or voluntary fields captured, but not sent for TED publication,[46] unless it concerns data subject to the rights of others. Moreover, procurement data that is not captured by the eForms, but in other ways (eg within the relevant e-procurement platform) will also be subject to the Open Data Directive regime and, where making that information available for re-use by electronic means involves no 'disproportionate effort, going beyond a simple operation',[47] it is plausible that the obligation of publication by electronic means will extend to such data too.[48] Once the information is published in digital form and in compliance with the data standard underlying the eForms, enabling API access and bulk downloads also seems to require relatively limited effort, especially as the eForms themselves will be underpinned by APIs and the data architecture will thus be easily adaptable. This reinforces the importance of setting up robust data governance mechanisms to ensure that no more (or less) data is published and made available for re-use than needs to be (see Section 2.1.3).

2.1.2 Data subject to the rights of others

As emerges from the previous analysis, as a matter of EU law, public buyers[49] are under no obligation to allow for the re-use of data subject to the rights of others.[50] In fact, they can be *prima facie* prevented from doing so under the relevant procurement rules, at least in relation to: (1) information over which confidentiality requirements were explicitly imposed in the context of the relevant procedure,[51] and (2) information which should be withheld because its

[46] European Commission, 'eForms Handbook' (n 41) 22. This should be covered by the much-delayed procurement data governance framework announced by the European Commission, 'A European strategy for data' (Communication) COM (2020) 66 final, 32 (hereafter European Commission, '2020 data strategy'). There are some additional details in the European Commission, 'Common European data spaces', SWD (2022) 45 final, 30 (hereafter European Commission, 'Common European data spaces').

[47] Open Data Directive (n 13) art 5(3).

[48] As this will be possible and there is no clear reason why it would not be appropriate; see ibid art 5(1).

[49] The obligations under the Data Governance Act apply to public sector bodies, which include bodies governed by public law, which are defined in roughly the same terms as under EU procurement law; see Data Governance Act, art 2(18), cf Directive 2014/24/EU (n 43) art 2(4).

[50] Data Governance Act (n 11) art 1(2). Such obligation is mostly also excluded eg under freedom of information rules, to the extent that the relevant rights of others also exclude the disclosability of the information under that regime. See n 18.

[51] Directive 2014/24/EU (n 43) art 21. For discussion, see Albert Sanchez-Graells, 'Article 21—Confidentiality' in Caranta and Sanchez-Graells, *Commentary* (n 43) 226.

release would impede law enforcement or would otherwise be contrary to the public interest, would prejudice the legitimate commercial interests of a particular economic operator, whether public or private, or might prejudice fair competition between economic operators.[52] This requires setting up a system to manage third party rights and to prevent excessive disclosure of information, as discussed above.[53]

However, from a policy perspective, there is a clear push towards seeking ways of enabling (controlled) access to as much procurement data as possible, including data subject to the rights of others. The Data Governance Act opens the possibility for public buyers to grant access under strictly specified conditions. Ensuring compliance with such conditions generates relevant governance risks that need to be taken into consideration before granting access to third party data.

If public buyers decide to allow for the re-use[54] of procurement data subject to the rights of others,[55] in addition to compliance with the General Data Protection Regulation (GDPR),[56] they must also comply with a set of requirements that largely map onto those of the Open Data Directive (see Section 2.1.1). They must: (1) refrain from entering into exclusive arrangements,[57] with the only exception that 'an exclusive right to re-use data ... may be granted to the extent necessary for the provision of a service or the supply of a product in the general interest that would not otherwise be possible';[58] (2) specify conditions for re-use, which shall be 'non-discriminatory, transparent,

[52] Directive 2014/24/EU (n 43) art 55(3). For discussion, see Albert Sanchez-Graells, 'Article 55—Informing Candidates and Tenderers' in Caranta and Sanchez-Graells, *Commentary* (n 43) 553. See also n 24.

[53] See also European Commission, 'A data space to improve public spending, boost data-driven policy-making and improve access to tenders for SMEs' (Communication) [2023] C 98/1, 8.

[54] It is important to stress that such facilitation of data re-use shall not aim to establish commercial relationships. Otherwise, it will be subject to additional requirements applicable to data intermediation services under the Data Governance Act (art 2(11)(d)).

[55] Non-procurement data held by public buyers could be exempted from these obligations to the extent that its supply was considered to be an activity falling outside the scope of the public task of the body concerned, Data Governance Act (n 11) art 3(2)(e). However, in most cases, it seems plausible that the information held by a public buyer will be linked to its public task of carrying out procurement procedures and/or any other public tasks at the core of the relevant organization.

[56] Data Governance Act (n 11) art 1(3). GDPR compliance may not be the biggest obstacle in this domain, as procurement procedures tend to generate limited amounts of personal data and most of it can be withheld from publication without significantly reducing the value of the disclosure. This contrasts with the need to ensure GDPR compliance where the implementation of a public contract involves the treatment of personal data. For discussion, see Kevin McGillivray, *Government Cloud Procurement. Contracts, Data Protection, and the Quest for Compliance* (CUP 2022) 91 ff.

[57] Data Governance Act (n 11) art 4(1). See also rec 12. There is, however, a grace period until end of 2024; Data Governance Act (n 11) art 4(6).

[58] Data Governance Act (n 11) art 4(2). In that case, the grant of the exclusive right and the reasons therefor will have to 'be made publicly available online, in a form that complies with relevant Union law on public procurement', ibid art 4(5) and rec 12.

proportionate and objectively justified with regard to the categories of data and the purposes of re-use and the nature of the data for which re-use is allowed', as well as 'not be used to restrict competition';[59] (3) advertise the possibility of re-use and the conditions through a single information point created in compliance with the Data Governance Act;[60] and (4) consider granting or refusing access to the data in specific ways and within pre-determined time periods.[61] Crucially, in addition to these requirements,[62] public buyers granting access to data subject to the rights of others must ensure that 'the protected nature of data is preserved',[63] which can require ensuring that the data has been 'modified, aggregated or treated by any other method of disclosure control, in the case of commercially confidential information, including trade secrets or content protected by intellectual property rights'.[64]

This latter requirement seeks to ensure that protected information cannot be associated with specific undertakings. It is reinforced by a prohibition of re-identification and duties to notify the legal persons whose rights and interests may be affected of any unauthorized re-use of their non-personal data,[65] as part of broader confidentiality obligations imposed on the re-user as a condition for data access.[66] Unless the information is subjected to such 'anonymization' treatment, the data can only be accessed with the explicit permission of the data holder.[67] Where the data is covered by IPR, its re-use can only be allowed in compliance therewith.[68] Equally, where the 'data requested is considered to be confidential, in accordance with Union or national law on commercial or statistical confidentiality, the public sector bodies shall ensure that the confidential data is not disclosed as a result of allowing re-use, unless such re-use is allowed' by permission.[69] Additional rules apply to the transfer of such data to a (non-EU) third country.[70]

[59] ibid art 5(2). This should be the object of future guidance by the European Data Innovation Board; ibid art 30(i).
[60] ibid art 8.
[61] ibid art 9.
[62] As well as eg the right to challenge decisions on data access requests; ibid art 9(2).
[63] ibid art 5(3).
[64] ibid art 5(3)(a)(ii). This should be the object of future guidance by the European Data Innovation Board; ibid art 30(d).
[65] ibid art 5(5), which mirrors the rules for personal data and the rights of data subjects.
[66] Such condition can however be excluded where national law provides for specific safeguards on applicable confidentiality obligations relating to the re-use of the data; ibid art 5(5).
[67] ibid art 5(6).
[68] ibid art 5(7). In this case, however, the *sui generis* right over a database 'shall not be exercised by public sector bodies in order to prevent the re-use of data or to restrict re-use beyond the limits set by' ibid art 5(7). This aligns the restriction with that deriving from the Open Data Directive (n 29) art 1(6).
[69] Data Governance Act (n 11) art 5(8).
[70] ibid art 5(9)–(14). Their detailed analysis exceeds the scope of this chapter.

These are important constraints that can altogether exclude the possibility of facilitating access to commercially sensitive data where the data holder does not grant permission, or where data access could generate potential competition impacts. The latter is important, not least because the Data Governance Act explicitly stresses that data access needs to comply with EU competition law.[71]

2.1.3 Balancing data governance risks

The previous two sub-sections have shown that public buyers have an inescapable data governance role that generates tensions in the design of open procurement data mechanisms. On the one hand, the Open Data Directive requires the general facilitation of access to data for re-use. Similarly, the Data Governance Act allows for access to be extended to data subject to the rights of others in a way that would significantly increase material access to procurement data beyond mandatory eForms disclosures and existing freedom of information regimes. On the other hand, the Open Data Directive (largely implicitly) and the Data Governance Act (explicitly) require the public buyer to implement adequate measures to protect data subject to the rights of others from unauthorized or excessive disclosure, including disclosure that could generate anticompetitive effects. This is also established in EU procurement law. It is thus simply not possible to create a system that makes all procurement data open. Data governance requires the careful management of a system of multi-tiered access to different types of information at different times, by different stakeholders, and under different conditions.[72] While the need to balance procurement transparency and the protection of data subject to the rights of others and competition-sensitive data is not a new governance challenge,[73] the digital management of this information creates heightened risks. Such risks arise to the extent that the implementation of data management

[71] ibid art 1(4).

[72] This has long been the case, but the need to ensure granularity in data access has only increased with regulatory developments. See n 53. For discussion, see Albert Sanchez-Graells, 'Centralised Procurement Registers and Their Transparency Implications—Discussion Non-Paper for the European Commission Stakeholder Expert Group on Public Procurement' (2015) <https://www.howtocrackanut.com/blog/2015/09/why-are-public-contracts-registers.html> accessed 18 October 2022.

[73] Albert Sanchez-Graells, 'The Difficult Balance Between Transparency and Competition in Public Procurement: Some Recent Trends in the Case Law of the European Courts and a Look at the New Directives' (2013) University of Leicester School of Law Research Paper No 13-11 <http://ssrn.com/abstract=2353005> accessed 18 October 2022; Kirsi-Maria Halonen, 'Disclosure Rules in EU Public Procurement: Balancing Between Competition and Transparency' (2017) 16 Journal of Public Procurement 528; Albert Sanchez-Graells, 'Transparency and Competition in Public Procurement: A Comparative View on Their Difficult Balance' in Kirsi-Maria Halonen, Roberto Caranta, and Albert Sanchez-Graells (eds), *Transparency in EU Procurements: Disclosure within Public Procurement and During Contract Execution* (Edward Elgar 2019) 33.

solutions is tendentially 'open access' (and could eg reverse presumptions of confidentiality). They also arise in relation to system integrity (ie cybersecurity, see Section 3). Recent case law has rejected the notion that full transparency is by itself a public interest capable of trumping clashing private interests, not only in relation to procurement data, but also other governance-relevant data, such as beneficial ownership data.[74] Therefore, open access is not unconstrained and a system capable of managing differential access to data is a clear legal requirement.[75]

Moreover, the assessment of the potential competition impact of data disclosure can be a moving target, as some exchanges of information may generate varying effects depending on the agents involved and the insights that can be derived from the data in relation to different markets, say, or (future) projects invisible to the disclosing public buyer. This risk is heightened by the possibility to use algorithms to extract insights from that information.[76] It is also raised by new forms of technology-enabled corrupt[77] or collusive behaviour[78]—which can, in turn, become difficult to detect without further changes to the existing governance mechanisms and institutions.[79]

Thus public buyers will have to carefully balance these data governance risks, not solely considering their ability to technically protect the data, but also their ability to manage the complexity that establishing different types of access to data brings. It can well be that most public buyers take a conservative approach to avoid these risks—eg by not facilitating (controlled) data access under the Data Governance Act and by minimizing the data they hold to also

[74] *Luxembourg Business Registers* [2022] ECLI:EU:C:2022:912.

[75] Albert Sanchez-Graells, 'New CJEU Case Law Against Excessive Disclosure: Quid de open data?' (*howtocrackanut.com*, 22 November 2022) <https://www.howtocrackanut.com/blog/2022/11/22/cjeu-case-law-against-excessive-disclosure-quid-de-open-data> accessed 20 December 2022.

[76] As stressed in European Commission, 'Draft Guidelines on the applicability of Article 101 of the Treaty on the Functioning of the European Union to horizontal co-operation agreements' C (2022) 1159, paras 418, 432–33, and 435–36.

[77] Nils Christopher Köbis, Christopher Starke, and Jaselle Edward-Gill, 'The Corruption Risks of Artificial Intelligence' (2022) Transparency International <https://knowledgehub.transparency.org/assets/uploads/kproducts/The-Corruption-Risks-of-Artificial-Intelligence.pdf> accessed 18 October 2022.

[78] See eg OECD, 'Algorithms and collusion. Competition policy in the digital age' (2017) <https://www.oecd.org/daf/competition/Algorithms-and-colllusion-competition-policy-in-the-digital-age.pdf> accessed 18 October 2022. For extended discussion, see Ariel Ezrachi and Maurice E Stucke, *Virtual Competition. The Promise and Perils of the Algorithm-Driven Economy* (Harvard UP 2016) and Maurice E Stucke and Allen P Grunes, *Big Data and Competition Policy* (OUP 2016). cf Thibault Schrepel, *Blockchain + Antitrust. The Decentralization Formula* (Edward Elgar 2021).

[79] Such changes could eg require the adoption of further digital solutions to monitor the functioning of a first layer of digital solutions. This will not be discussed in detail. For analysis in the context of cybersecurity, see eg UK National Cyber Security Centre, 'Intelligent security tools. Assessing intelligent tools for cyber security' (2019) <https://www.ncsc.gov.uk/collection/intelligent-security-tools> accessed 19 October 2022.

minimize their obligations under the Open Data Directive. This would, however, run contrary to the stated policies of seeking to maximize data availability for other (digital industrial policy) purposes.[80] To avoid such a situation, clear guidance on how to digitally manage procurement data is required. Following from the 2020 Data Strategy,[81] the recent communication on the public procurement data space indicates that it will be developed by the end of 2023.[82]

2.2 Technological Dependency Risks

In addition to data governance risks, the development and deployment of digital technologies brings technological dependency risks. There are two main types. The first one refers to technological or vendor lock-in and interoperability. It primarily concerns the increasing need to develop advanced strategies to manage IPR, algorithmic transparency, and technical debt. The second concerns the erosion of the skills base of the public buyer as technology replaces the current workforce, which generates intellectual debt and operational dependency.

2.2.1 Algorithmic transparency, technological lock-in, and technical debt: open source by default?

Relying on proprietary technologies, as opposed to open source and other open standards, will generate risks of technological dependency on specific providers. It will also create limited interoperability with other systems, which can then increase technical debt and raise further barriers to strategies to diversify the technological stock. The problem of technological lock-in is well understood,[83] even if generally inadequately or insufficiently managed.[84] Moreover, the deployment of Artificial Intelligence (AI), and Machine Learning (ML) in particular, raise the additional issue of managing algorithmic transparency in the context of technological dependency. This is closely related to the broader issue of algorithmic transparency discussed in Chapter 2 but generates specific

[80] European Commission, '2020 data strategy' (n 46).

[81] See n 46.

[82] See n 53. This represents a significant delay, compared to earlier announcements; see European Commission, 'Common European data spaces' (n 46).

[83] See eg European Commission, 'Against lock-in: building open ICT systems by making better use of standards in public procurement' (Communication) COM (2013) 455 final, and the accompanying European Commission, 'Guide for the procurement of standards-based ICT—Elements of Good Practice', SWD (2013) 224 final.

[84] PWC, 'Study on best practices for ICT procurement based on standards in order to promote efficiency and reduce lock-in' (2016) <https://ec.europa.eu/newsroom/dae/document.cfm?doc_id=14434> accessed 7 October 2022. See also the report by the UK's Office of Fair Trading, 'Supply of information and communications technology to the public sector' (2014) OFT1533.

challenges in relation to the administration of public contracts and the obligation to create competition in their (re)tendering.[85] Without access to the algorithm's source code, it is nigh impossible to ensure a level playing field in the tender of related services, as well as in the re-tendering of the original contract for the specific ML or AI solution. Source code opacity can thus only entrench incumbent providers.[86]

This was recognized in a recent software procurement case, establishing that, in order to ensure compliance with the general principles of procurement law, contracting authorities must have access to the source code, they must communicate it to potential service providers, and 'access to that source code [must be] in itself a sufficient guarantee that economic operators interested in the award of the contract in question are treated in a transparent manner, equally and without discrimination'.[87] Functionally, under EU law, public buyers are thus under an obligation to ensure that they have access and dissemination rights over the source code, at the very least for the purposes of re-tendering the contract, or tendering ancillary contracts. They must also have adequate licences to facilitate the substitution of the services provider without losing access to the technology. More generally, they need to have a sufficient understanding of the software—or technical documentation enabling that knowledge—so that they can share it with potential tenderers and in that manner ensure that competition is not artificially distorted.

This is highly relevant in the context of emerging practices of AI procurement and can determine the effectiveness of technological governance related to digital procurement going forward. The debates around AI transparency are largely driven by issues of commercial opacity and the protection of business secrets, in particular source code.[88] Preserving such opacity and confidentiality is seen as strategically important.[89] However, opacity makes it difficult to justify and to ensure legal compliance in the deployment of the AI in the public sector (on grounds of eg the duty to provide reasons). It also makes it difficult

[85] Albert Sanchez-Graells, 'Public Procurement and [AI] Source Code Transparency, A (Downstream) Competition Issue (Re C-796/18)' (*howtocrackanut.com*, 20 June 2022) <https://www.howtocrackanut.com/blog/2022/6/20/public-procurement-and-ai-source-code-transparency> accessed 7 October 2022.

[86] For discussion of obligations to neutralize incumbency advantages, see Albert Publishing 2015) 413–18.

[87] *Informatikgesellschaft für Software-Entwicklung* [2020] ECLI:EU:C:2020:395, para 75.

[88] For discussion, see Madalina Busuioc, Deirdre Curtin, and Marco Almada, 'Reclaiming Transparency: Contesting the Logics of Secrecy Within the EU AI Act' (2023) 2(1) European Law Open 79.

[89] eg in free trade agreements. See Kristina Irion, 'Algorithms Off-Limits? If Digital Trade Law Restricts Access to Source Code of Software Then Accountability Will Suffer' (2022) FAccT proceedings 1561.

public buyer.[152] It should be stressed that there is an added difficulty in the fact that the likelihood of materialization of those data, systems integrity, and cybersecurity risks grows with reduced digital capabilities because the organization using digital solutions may be unable to identify and mitigate them. It is not only that the technology carries risks that are either 'known knowns' or 'known unknowns' (as above), but also that the organization may experience them as 'unknown unknowns' due to its limited digital capability.[153] Limited digital skills can, therefore, compound and exacerbate those governance risks.[154]

Further, the implementation of digital solutions not properly backed by the required skills can increase the governance risks faced by the entire organization, which can have a multiplier effect and result in an impact much larger than the advantages the solution can bring. Skills shortages are not merely an issue in ensuring the extraction of the potential benefits of the technologies, but also in minimizing the risk of negative knock-on effects across the organization.[155] Digitalization and the related increase in digital capability requirements can embed an element of (unacknowledged) organizational leverage (or exposure) that mirrors the potential benefits of the technologies. While technology adoption can augment the organization's capability (eg by reducing administrative burdens through automation[156]), this also makes the entire organization dependent on its (disproportionately small) digital capabilities. It also generates increased discretion and potential control of the organization's functioning by those with the relevant digital skills.[157] It is not only the digital solutions that become mission critical, but also those in the workforce tasked with ensuring their proper functioning—who are thus not simply carrying out a 'back office' function. The issue of dependence on scarce knowledge and skills is not unique to the digital technology setting, but it is particularly acute there.[158] It

[152] In relation to cybersecurity risks, see Section 3.

[153] For discussion, Ray Pawson, Geoff Wong, and Lesley Owen, 'Known Knowns, Known Unknowns, Unknown Unknowns: The Predicament of Evidence-Based Policy' (2011) 32 American Journal of Evaluation 518.

[154] Similarly, Merve Hickok, 'Public Procurement of Artificial Intelligence Systems: New Risks and Future Proofing' (2022) AI & Society <https://doi.org/10.1007/s00146-022-01572-2> accessed 27 October 2022.

[155] See eg Brage Fagstad and Knut Andreas Aas, 'Cyber Security in Procurement of Third-Party Suppliers: A Case Study of the Norwegian Power Sector' (Master's thesis, University of Agder 2022) <https://hdl.handle.net/11250/3019797> accessed 7 October 2022.

[156] See Chapter 7, Section 2.

[157] Juho Pääkkönen and others, 'Bureaucracy as a Lens for Analyzing and Designing Algorithmic Systems' (2020) CHI Conference on Human Factors in Computing Systems <https://doi.org/10.1145/3313831.3376780> accessed 21 April 2023.

[158] Sean Boots, '"Charbonneau Loops" and Government IT Contracting' (*Sean Boots blog*, 12 October 2022) <https://sboots.ca/2022/10/12/charbonneau-loops-and-government-it-contracting/>

to manage AI procurement and its propagation within the public sector (eg as a result of initiatives such as 'buy once, use many times' or collaborative and joint approaches to the procurement of AI, which are also seen as strategically significant). While there is increasing regulatory space at an international level,[90] and a movement towards requiring some degree of source code transparency (eg but not necessarily by using open source solutions, or limited disclosure to the public buyer), this is not mainstream policy.[91] Short of future rules demanding source code transparency across the board, which seem unlikely,[92] this issue will remain one for contractual regulation and negotiations. Contracts are likely to follow the approach of the general rules, though.[93] This creates a significant governance risk that requires explicit and careful consideration by public buyers, and which points at the need to embed algorithmic transparency requirements as a pillar of technological governance related to the digitalization of procurement.[94]

Moreover, the development of digital technologies also creates a new wave of lock-in risks, as digital solutions are hardly off-the-shelf and can require a high level of customization or co-creation between the tech provider and the public buyer (eg not only in relation to the role of data in developing the solution, but also in the contribution to testing the implementation). This creates the need for careful consideration of the governance of IPR allocation. Guidance seeking to use procurement to promote innovation tends to adopt the approach of recommending assigning IPR to technology vendors, save in exceptional circumstances.[95] However, this can only perpetuate and exacerbate the risks of lock-in and requires careful consideration,[96] not least in relation

[90] Albert Sanchez-Graells, 'Ensuring Algorithmic Transparency Through Public Contracts?' (*Digital Constitutionalist*, 24 November 2022) <https://digi-con.org/ensuring-algorithmic-transparency-through-public-contracts/> accessed 20 December 2022.

[91] eg, the pilot UK algorithmic transparency standard does not mention source code. See Central Digital and Data Office, 'Algorithmic transparency standard' (2021) <https://www.gov.uk/government/collections/algorithmic-transparency-standard> accessed 21 October 2022.

[92] See eg the approach in the Proposal for a Regulation of the European Parliament and of the Council laying down harmonised rules on Artificial Intelligence (Artificial Intelligence Act) and amending certain union legislative acts, COM (2021) 206 final, art 70.

[93] eg in the Living-In EU, Proposal for standard contractual clauses for the procurement of artificial intelligence by public organisations, version 0.9 (2022), art 6 <https://living-in.eu/sites/default/files/files/Draft%20AI%20Clauses_1.pdf> accessed 21 October 2022.

[94] The reasons why this cannot be sufficiently done via contractual mechanisms mirror those discussed in Part II of this book. They will be revisited in Chapter 9, Section 3.2.

[95] eg European Commission, 'Making the most of the EU's innovative potential. An intellectual property action plan to support the EU's recovery and resilience' (Communication) COM (2020) 760 final, 10. See also PWC, 'The strategic use of public procurement for innovation in the digital economy' (2021) 12 <https://op.europa.eu/s/w6sv> accessed 7 October 2022.

[96] European Commission, 'Guidance on innovation procurement' (Notice) C (2021) 4320 final, Annex I.

to specific transparency obligations in the context of (re)procuring services linked to the digital solutions, as above.

A nuanced approach is needed, as well as coordination with other legal regimes (eg State aid) where IPR are left with the contractor.[97] Some of the considerations determining whether to leave IPR with the technology vendor will be primarily financial (eg concerning the future cost of retaining a digital solution where licensing fees may be payable) and relate to the public buyer's ability to manage legal risks. However, these are also normative choices reflecting specific positions on the relationship between public interest and open source—and could be determined or influenced by broader open source policies.[98] It is arguable that an 'open source by default' approach would be suitable to the context of procurement governance,[99] as there can be high value derived from using and re-using common solutions. Such value can result from interoperability and a reduction of total development costs. There can also be value in enabling the emergence of communities of practice that can contribute to the ongoing improvement of the solutions based on pooled resources, which can help mitigate some of the problems arising from limited to digital skills (see also Section 4).

In addition to the issues of algorithmic transparency and lock-in, from a technical perspective, it should be stressed that most of these technologies are still emergent or immature, which generates additional governance risks. The adoption of such emergent technologies generates technical debt, which 'entails the shortcuts and unsuitable choices made during the development or maintenance of an [information technology (IT)] system, which can result in negative consequences such as inefficiency and instability of the IT system'.[100] Technical debt refers to the long-term costs incurred by moving quickly in software engineering. Such costs can derive from the (future) need to undertake tasks that do not add new functionality, but rather enable future improvements, reduce errors, or improve maintainability, such as refactoring code, improving unit tests, deleting dead code, reducing dependencies, tightening

[97] ibid. See Albert Sanchez-Graells, 'State Aid and EU Public Procurement: More Interactions, Fuzzier Boundaries' in Leigh Hancher and Juan Jorge Piernas López (eds), *Research Handbook on European State Aid Law* (2nd edn, Edward Elgar 2021) 329, 335–36.

[98] See eg European Commission, 'Open source software strategy 2020–2023. Think open' (Communication) C (2020) 7149 final.

[99] See eg European Commission, 'Open source licensing and reuse of Commission software' (Decision) C (2021) 8759 final.

[100] Mille Edith Nielsen and Christian Østergaard Madsen, 'Stakeholder Influence on Technical Debt Management in the Public Sector: An Embedded Case Study' (2022) 39 Government Information Quarterly 101706, 1 (hereafter Nielsen and Madsen, 'Technical Debt Management in the Public Sector').

APIs, or improving technical documentation.[101] Technical debt is not solely a financial issue, but a structural barrier to digitalization.[102] It thus requires strategic management with a view not only on short-term and operational considerations (which are the ones that tend to generate the technical debt in the first instance), as it is crucial for the long-term viability of the implementation of digital technologies, which is not a one-shot but rather an iterative and cumulative process. Technical debt risks stress the importance of carefully considering adopting the open source by default approach mentioned above, as open source can facilitate the progressive collective repayment of technical debt for widely adopted solutions.[103]

2.2.2 Technological dependency and skills base erosion

A second source of technological dependency concerns the erosion of the skills base of the public buyer as technology replaces the current workforce. This is different from dependence on a *given* technology,[104] and concerns dependence on *any technological solutions* to carry out functions that were previously undertaken by human operators. This can generate two specific risks: intellectual debt and operational dependency.

Intellectual debt refers to the implementation of (tech) solutions that work, without knowing or being able to explain why they work.[105] In our context, intellectual debt is the inability to explain a software system, or how it works.[106] Intellectual debt usually has a technical origin, and in the context of digital technologies, it usually refers to the inability to understand complex ML with very low levels of explainability.[107] However, the concept can be easily extended to combine elements of (loss of) institutional knowledge and memory resulting from the participation in the development and deployment of the technological solutions by agents not (longer) involved with the technology as users (eg external providers).

[101] D Sculley and others, 'Hidden Technical Debt in Machine Learning Systems' (2015) <https://papers.nips.cc/paper/2015/file/86df7dcfd896fcaf2674f757a2463eba-Paper.pdf> accessed 7 October 2022.

[102] With further references, see Nielsen and Madsen, 'Technical Debt Management in the Public Sector' (n 100) 1.

[103] However, see some concerns related to excessive transparency discussed in Chapter 2, Section 2.5.

[104] Which was discussed in Section 2.2.1.

[105] Jonathan Zittrain, 'Intellectual Debt. With Great Power Comes Great Ignorance' in Silja Voeneky and others (eds), *The Cambridge Handbook of Responsible Artificial Intelligence. Interdisciplinary Perspectives* (CUP 2022) 176.

[106] Neil D Lawrence, 'Deploying Machine Learning: Intellectual Debt and AutoAI' (*Inverseprobability.com*, 6 October 2020) <http://inverseprobability.com/talks/notes/deploying-machine-learning-systems-intellectual-debt-and-auto-ai.html> accessed 7 October 2022.

[107] This is discussed in more detail in Chapter 2, Section 2.2.

There can be many forms of intellectual debt risk, and some can be mitigated or excluded through, for example, detailed technical documentation. Other forms of intellectual debt risk, however, are more difficult to mitigate. For example, situations where reliance on a technological solution (eg robotic process automation (RPA)) erases institutional knowledge of the reason why a specific process is carried out, as well as how that process is carried out (eg why a specific source of information is checked for the purposes of integrity screening and how that is done). In addition to legal risks related to the need to give reasons for administrative decision-making,[108] and risks of inadequate human-machine interaction where the 'human on the loop' is unable to understand and explain what is being done,[109] this can also generate governance risks of (mal)adaptation to regulatory changes (eg in case of suppression or modification of the legal requirement to carry out the integrity check). Mitigating against this requires keeping additional capability and institutional knowledge (and memory) to be able to explain in full detail what specific function the technology is carrying out, why, how that is done, and how that would be done in the absence of the technology (if it could be done at all). To put it plainly, it requires keeping the ability to 'do it by hand'—or at the very least to be able to explain how that would be done.[110] This is an important consideration in relation to decisions on how to shape the skills base to 'future-proof' procurement governance (Section 4), as there can be no complete replacement of procurement domain expertise with technological expertise.

Where it would be impossible or unfeasible to carry out the digitized task without using technology, digitalization creates absolute operational dependency. Mitigating against technological operational dependency requires an assessment of 'system critical' technological deployments without which it is not possible to carry out the relevant procurement function and, most likely, to deploy measures to ensure system resilience (including redundancy if appropriate) and system integrity (Section 3). It is, however, important to acknowledge that there will always be limits to ensuring system resilience and integrity, which should raise questions about the desirability of generating situations of absolute operational dependency. While this may be less relevant in the context

[108] Albert Sanchez-Graells, 'Procurement Corruption and Artificial Intelligence: Between the Potential of Enabling Data Architectures and the Constraints of Due Process Requirements' in Sope Williams and Jessica Tillipman (eds), *Routledge Handbook of Public Procurement Corruption* (Routledge forthcoming) <https://ssrn.com/abstract=3952665> accessed 30 June 2023.

[109] See eg John Zerilli and others, 'Algorithmic Decision-Making and the Control Problem' (2019) 29 Minds and Machines 555; Simon Chesterman, *We, the Robots? Regulating Artificial Intelligence and the Limits of the Law* (CUP 2021) 166 ff.

[110] The lower the ability to carry out the task without technological support, either through a lack of knowledge or a lack of capacity, the closer this issue is to *de facto* technological operational dependency.

of procurement governance than in other contexts, it can still be an important consideration to factor into decision-making as technological practice can fuel a bias towards (further) technological practice that can then help support unquestioned technological expansion.[111] In other words, it will be important to consider what are the limits of absolute technological delegation.[112]

3. System Integrity Risks: Cybersecurity and Procurement Governance

The previous section hinted at the importance of ensuring the integrity of data systems. Indeed, given that digital solutions build on relatively complicated Information and Communication Technology (ICT) and data infrastructures, from a system integrity perspective, cybersecurity must be a major consideration in their governance.[113] The overarching insight is that digital technologies not only generate *additional* cybersecurity challenges that overlay those of the existing ICT systems, they also generate *different* challenges that are still not completely understood.[114] Moreover, given that the deployment of digital solutions usually involves several external organizations providing a host of interacting ICT and data services,[115] those risks can be located in organizational settings that are beyond the (direct) control of the public buyer using the solutions,[116] and have systemic effects where external providers are used by many organizations.[117] This can be particularly problematic where providers

[111] For discussion, see James B Gerrie, 'Some Ethical and Public Policy Implications of Technological Dependency with Reference to Innis, McLuhan and Grant' (PhD thesis, University of Guelph 1999) <https://hdl.handle.net/10214/21638> accessed 7 October 2022.

[112] For discussion, Albert Sanchez-Graells, 'Can the Robot Procure for You?' (*howtocrackanut.com*, 12 August 2021) <https://www.howtocrackanut.com/blog/can-the-robot-procure-for-you> accessed 21 October 2022

[113] ENISA, 'AI cybersecurity challenges. Threat landscape for artificial intelligence' (2020) <https://www.enisa.europa.eu/publications/artificial-intelligence-cybersecurity-challenges> accessed 18 October 2022 (hereafter ENISA, 'AI cybersecurity challenges').

[114] Andrew J Lohn and Wyatt Hoffman, 'Securing AI. How Traditional Vulnerability Disclosure Must Adapt' (2022) CSET Policy Brief <https://cset.georgetown.edu/publication/securing-ai-how-traditional-vulnerability-disclosure-must-adapt/> accessed 18 October 2022.

[115] For discussion, see Jennifer Cobbe, Michael Veale, and Jatinder Singh, 'Understanding Accountability in Algorithmic Supply Chains' (2023) FAccT proceedings <https://doi.org/10.1145/3593013.3594073> accessed 2 June 2023; Ian Brown, 'Allocating Accountability in AI Supply Chains' (2023) Ada Lovelace Institute Expert Explainer <https://www.adalovelaceinstitute.org/resource/ai-supply-chains/> accessed 30 June 2023.

[116] Derek E Bambauer, 'Cybersecurity for Idiots' (2021) 106 Minnesota Law Review 172.

[117] Jeferson Martinez and Javier M Duran, 'Software Supply Chain Attacks, a Threat to Global Cybersecurity: SolarWinds' Case Study' (2021) 11 International Journal of Safety and Security Engineering 537.

are dominant, or a specific solution becomes the standard or most widely used.[118]

In the end, 'AI and its application to for instance automated decision making ... may expose individuals and organizations to new, and sometimes unpredictable, risks and it may open new avenues in attack methods and techniques, as well as creating new data protection challenges'.[119] Similarly, opening information systems to make data accessible may 'further expose parts of an organisation to digital security threats that can lead to incidents that disrupt the availability, integrity or confidentiality of data and information systems on which economic and social activities rely'.[120] These heightened or new cybersecurity risks require careful management and need to be explicitly included in decisions whether to adopt digital solutions for procurement governance.[121] Leaving cybersecurity as an afterthought would be very problematic indeed.[122] Similarly, relying on cybersecurity policies designed to ensure data integrity in the context of the processing of personal data seems unlikely to suffice in addressing new types of cybersecurity threats unrelated to data access.

This is not solely a matter of 'good tech governance', but a crucial legal compliance issue. In that regard, it is worth noting that cybersecurity regulation is currently being boosted in the EU with a revised Directive on measures for a high common level of cybersecurity (NIS 2 Directive).[123] The NIS 2 Directive will impose a set of procedural and governance obligations seeking to minimize cybersecurity risks and to improve response readiness,[124] as well as extending cybersecurity certification requirements[125] and promoting standardization.[126] It will also create a set of requirements for minimum fines and penalties to strengthen the applicable obligations.[127] Of those obligations,

[118] Dan Geer, Eric Jardine, and Eireann Leverett, 'On Market Concentration and Cybersecurity Risk' (2020) 5 Journal of Cyber Policy 9.

[119] ENISA, 'AI cybersecurity challenges' (n 113) 6.

[120] OECD, 'Enhancing access to and sharing of data. Reconciling risks and benefits for data re-use across societies' (2019) ch 4 <https://doi.org/10.1787/276aaca8-en> accessed 17 October 2022 (hereafter OECD, 'Enhancing access to and sharing of data').

[121] See Chapter 5, Section 3.2.

[122] CIS, NASPO, and NASCIO, 'Buyer be aware. Integrating cybersecurity into the acquisition process' (2021) <https://www.nascio.org/wp-content/uploads/2021/04/NASCIO_NASPO_CIS_CybersecurityAquisition_2021.pdf> accessed 19 October 2022.

[123] See Directive (EU) 2022/2555 of the European Parliament and of the Council of 14 December 2022 on measures for a high common level of cybersecurity across the Union, amending Regulation (EU) No 910/2014 and Directive (EU) 2018/1972, and repealing Directive (EU) 2016/1148 (hereafter 'NIS 2 Directive') [2022] OJ L 333/80.

[124] NIS 2 Directive (n 123) art 1(2). The Directive also creates a set of reporting and collaboration obligations. These will however not be discussed in detail here.

[125] ibid art 24.

[126] ibid art 25.

[127] ibid arts 34 and 36.

the most relevant for digital procurement are cybersecurity risk management obligations.[128]

The NIS 2 Directive will require covered organizations to establish governance mechanisms that ensure training, responsibility, and liability at the highest organizational level for the approval and oversight of the implementation of cybersecurity risk management measures.[129] The core substantive obligation is for those organizations to 'take appropriate and proportionate technical, operational and organisational measures to manage the risks posed to the security of network and information systems which those entities use for their operations or for the provision of their services, and to prevent or minimise the impact of incidents on recipients of their services and on other services'.[130] Those measures 'shall be based on an all-hazards approach aiming to protect network and information systems and their physical environment from incidents'.[131] In establishing measures seeking to ensure a level of security of network and information systems appropriate to the risk presented, organizations can consider 'the state-of-the-art and, where applicable, relevant European and international standards, as well as the cost of implementation',[132] and in 'assessing the proportionality of those measures, due account shall be taken of the degree of the entity's exposure to risks, its size, the likelihood of occurrence of incidents and their severity, including their societal and economic impact'.[133]

Determining the specific scope of the obligations will require detailed case-by-case analysis, which will only be adequately carried out by sufficiently skilled personnel. However, the NIS 2 Directive only includes a soft obligation in that regard, when it establishes that Member States 'shall encourage [covered organizations] to offer ... training to their employees on a regular basis, in order that they gain sufficient knowledge and skills to enable them to identify risks and assess cybersecurity risk-management practices and their impact on the services provided by the entity'.[134] The Directive does not impose any specific requirements for organizations to build internal capabilities, which immediately creates a risk of outsourcing of the cybersecurity risk assessment, as

[128] The NIS 2 Directive is complemented by the Directive on the resilience of critical entities, which establishes additional measures to promote the physical security of critical entities only applicable to the public administration entities of central governments. See Directive (EU) 2022/2557 of the European Parliament and of the Council of 14 December 2022 on the resilience of critical entities and repealing Council Directive 2008/114/EC [2022] OJ L333/164.

[129] NIS 2 Directive (n 123) art 20(1).

[130] ibid art 21(1).

[131] ibid art 21(2).

[132] ibid art 21(1).

[133] ibid.

[134] ibid art 20(2).

well as other measures to comply with the related substantive obligations. This can generate further organizational dependency on outside capability, which can itself be a cybersecurity risk (for further discussion, see Section 4).

Relatedly, given the fact that cybersecurity risks affect the entire organization, the NIS 2 Directive also requires organizations to implement basic computer hygiene practices and cybersecurity training.[135] Moreover, given risks coming from external organizations, the NIS 2 Directive requires measures on 'supply chain security, including security-related aspects concerning the relationships between each entity and its direct suppliers or service providers',[136] as well as the use of contractual cybersecurity requirements. EU Member States thus need to establish policies 'on the inclusion and specification of cybersecurity-related requirements for ICT products and ICT services in public procurement, including in relation to cybersecurity certification, encryption and the use of open-source cybersecurity products'.[137] The limitation here is that the definition of ICT products and services refers to the Cybersecurity Act,[138] which does not comprehensively cover all digital technology solutions. However, further cybersecurity requirements may stem from the proposed Cyber Resilience Act,[139] if adopted.

The NIS 2 Directive thus directly impacts procurement governance in two ways. First, it creates mechanisms of 'regulation by contract' that mirror the use of procurement for broader technological regulation purposes discussed in Part II of this book. Those will be revisited in Chapter 9, Section 3.2, and thus need not be repeated here. Second, the NIS 2 Directive generates obligations for public buyers classed as 'essential entities' under the Directive.[140]

Indeed, the Directive is applicable to 'public administration entities' of central governments, and to those at regional level that provide 'services the disruption of which could have a significant impact on critical societal or economic activities'.[141] It is submitted that this comprises public procurement as

[135] ibid art 21(2)(g).

[136] ibid art 21(2)(d). There is of course a limitation in the requirement to only assess risks related to direct suppliers and providers, although some of them will in turn be covered by the same obligations to the extent that the activities they carry out concern digital infrastructure (eg cloud computing service providers, or data centre service providers). See ibid Annex I.

[137] See ibid art 7(2)(b).

[138] Regulation (EU) 2019/881 of the European Parliament and of the Council of 17 April 2019 on ENISA (the European Union Agency for Cybersecurity) and on information and communications technology cybersecurity certification and repealing Regulation (EU) No 526/2013 (Cybersecurity Act) [2019] OJ L 151/15.

[139] Proposal for a Regulation of the European Parliament and of the Council on horizontal cybersecurity requirements for products with digital elements and amending Regulation (EU) 2019/1020, COM (2022) 454 final (hereafter 'Cyber Resilience Act').

[140] NIS 2 Directive (n 123) art 3(1)(d).

[141] ibid art 2(2)(f).

an enabler of the performance of the general activities of the public administration and the provision of public services. Member States are explicitly allowed to extend the Directive's obligations to the local level,[142] but local entities are not directly covered. Further, while the definition of 'public administration entities'[143] includes most public buyers covered by the EU procurement rules,[144] with the notable exception of those operating at local level,[145] there is a further exception for those 'that carry out their activities in the areas of national security, public security, defence or law enforcement, including the prevention, investigation, detection and prosecution of criminal offences'.[146] This carve-out is broader that the scope of the rules and exceptions for security and defence procurement.[147] Therefore, while most central and regional public buyers will be covered by the NIS 2 Directive, it does not automatically apply to local and some sector-specific buyers, which however carry out a significant volume of total procurement activity.

Moreover, given this incomplete coverage, strict compliance with the NIS 2 Directive would be insufficient to ensure adequate management of the systemic risks created by procurement digitalization. The potential inconsistencies between the scope of application of the NIS 2 Directive and the EU procurement rules are relevant in the context of the broader digitalization of procurement, but also in the narrow context of the entry into force of the new rules on eForms and the related obligations under the Open Data Directive, which will require public buyers to make data collected by eForms available in electronic format (see Section 2.2.1). Given that procurement data systems (including local ones) will be interconnected (via APIs), and that they can provide the data architecture for other AI solutions, cybersecurity risks are a systemic issue that would benefit from a systemic approach. Having most but not all public buyers comply with high standards of cybersecurity may not eliminate significant vulnerabilities if the remaining points of access generate relevant

[142] It is submitted that they would be well-advised to do so, given that the governance risks that arise in the context of procurement are not dependent on the level of government to which the public buyer belongs, as well as given the interconnection of procurement data and other systems across levels of government.

[143] NIS 2 Directive (n 123) art 2(2)(f).

[144] The definition in ibid art 6(35) contains some peculiar elements that raise questions on the coverage of associations between authorities and bodies governed by public law. For discussion, see Albert Sanchez-Graells, 'Will Public Buyers Be Covered by New EU Cybersecurity Requirements?' (*howtocrackanut.com*, 18 October 2022) <https://www.howtocrackanut.com/blog/2022/10/18/will-public-buyers-be-covered-by-new-eu-cybersecurity-requirements> accessed 18 October 2022.

[145] NIS 2 Directive (n 123) art 2(2)(f).

[146] ibid art 2(7). However, there seems to be no good reason not to adopt the same cybersecurity risk management standards, at least in relation to the procurement systems of those entities.

[147] Baudoin Heuninckx, 'Art 15—Defence and Security' in Caranta and Sanchez-Graells, *Commentary* (n 43) 161.

cybersecurity risks. It will therefore be necessary for Member States to ensure comprehensive compliance with substantive obligations of cybersecurity risk management by all public buyers with interconnected systems, even if these do not result from the NIS 2 Directive. This will, of course, ultimately rely on the creation of sufficient capability to identify and manage those risks (Section 4).

Crucially, compliance with general cybersecurity risk management obligations is independent of whether a particular public buyer uses digital solutions. The NIS 2 Directive imposes obligations regardless. However, the specific content of the obligations will significantly change with procurement digitalization because the deployment of digital solutions generates the new and heightened risks discussed above. That will require a proportionate review of the risk management under the NIS 2 Directive. This thus requires embedding cybersecurity analysis in the context of the decision whether to experiment with and adopt digital solutions.[148]

4. 'Future-Proofing' Procurement Governance: The Need for Skills, and Their Continuity

The importance of digital capabilities to manage technological governance risks emerges as a running theme. Some of the general governance risks that arise from the growing gap in the public sector's digital capability have already been discussed.[149] There are also risks of excessive operational dependency where the technology completely replaces institutional knowledge and memory in relation to specific tasks.[150] Further, there are other significant governance risks throughout the digital technologies' lifecycle[151]—as managing their deployment and their interaction with other systems also requires digital capability.

The specific governance risks identified in this chapter in relation to data and systems integrity, including cybersecurity risks, show that skills shortages are problematic in the ongoing use and maintenance of digital solutions, as their implementation does not diminish, but rather expands the scope of technology-related governance challenges. And some of these challenges are not constrained within the scope of the new solutions but can rather have a systemic dimension and affect the operation of all (ICT) systems used by the

[148] See Chapter 5, Section 3.2.
[149] See Chapter 6, Section 5.3.
[150] See Section 2.2.2.
[151] eg as they can exacerbate technical and intellectual debt, see Sections 2.2.1 and 2.2.2.

also spreads beyond the traditional remit of 'ICT departments', as digital skills are required more broadly within the organization as digitalization progresses. Moreover, the possibilities of finding alternative ways of carrying out core activities where the technology or the required support fail are also more limited than in other markets, as the shortage of digital skills is generalized and not unique to the public sector.[159]

From a governance perspective, this places access to digital skills as a crucial element of the critical vulnerabilities and resilience assessment that should accompany all decisions to deploy a digital technology solution.[160] A plausible approach would be to seek to mitigate the risk of insufficient access to in-house skills through, for example, the creation of additional, standby, or redundant contracted capability,[161] but this would come with its own costs and governance challenges. Moreover, the added complication is that the digital skills gap that exposes the organization to these risks in the first place, can also fuel a dynamic of further reliance on outside capabilities (from consultancy firms) beyond the development and adoption of those digital solutions.[162] This has the potential to exacerbate the long-term erosion of the skills base in the public sector. Any decisions to continuously rely on outside capabilities would make the organization particularly vulnerable to external shocks, as well as perpetuating the digital skills gap and potentially worsening it in the long term.[163] Digitalization thus makes the need for the public sector to build up its expertise and skills particularly acute,[164] as that is the only way of slowing down or reducing the widening digital skills gap and ensuring organizational resilience and a sustainable digital transition.

accessed 18 October 2022; see also House of Commons, Public Accounts Committee, *Challenges in Implementing Digital Change* (HC 2021–22, 637).

[159] See eg Carolina Feijao and others, 'The Global Digital Skills Gap. Current Trends and Future Directions' (2021) RAND <https://www.rand.org/pubs/research_reports/RRA1533-1.html> accessed 17 October 2022.

[160] OECD, 'Enhancing access to and sharing of data' (n 120).

[161] As advocated in eg European Parliament, 'The digital single market and the digitalisation of the public sector: GovTech and other innovations in public procurement' (2022) <https://data.europa.eu/doi/10.2861/830794> accessed 17 October 2022.

[162] Vera Weghmann and Kyla Sankey, 'Hollowed out: The Growing Impact of Consultancies in Public Administrations' (2022) EPSU Report <https://www.epsu.org/sites/default/files/article/files/EPSU%20Report%20Outsourcing%20state_EN.pdf> accessed 17 October 2022 (hereafter Weghmann and Sankey, 'Hollowed out'). See also Andrew J Sturdy and others, 'The Management Consultancy Effect: Demand Inflation and Its Consequences in the Sourcing of External Knowledge' (2022) 100 Public Administration 488.

[163] This has been the case of public capability more generally; see Bridget C E Dooling and Rachel Augustine Potter, 'Regulatory Body Shops' (2022) <https://ssrn.com/abstract=4186402> accessed 8 September 2022.

[164] Weghmann and Sankey, 'Hollowed out' (n 162) 30–33 and 41.

This means that any conception that the deployment of digital technologies is a transformative process capable of 'future-proofing' procurement governance (or more generally) must be assessed against the viability of plans to ensure access to and retention of talent commensurate with the operative needs of the new systems. Otherwise, the deployment of the technology can exacerbate pre-existing governance risks in strained institutional and workforce settings and make the organization particularly susceptible to exploitation of its digital capability shortcomings.[165] The difficulty in the implicit approach to making the adoption of digital technologies conditional on having sustainable access to the required digital skills mainly comes from the organizational challenges and time horizons required to build public sector capability. There are two main ways in which the public sector can seek to boost its in-house digital capability: re-skilling and upskilling processes, and changes to recruitment (and retention) strategies.[166] None of these options offers a quick and easy solution. However, given the future (increased) pervasiveness of digital solutions for procurement governance, and public governance more generally, clear plans to plug the public sector digital capability gap and significantly boost it to the level required to ensure adequate (digital) governance should be prioritized,[167] and feature as a key consideration of any decision to deploy technological solutions.[168]

These considerations cannot be left until the stage of deployment of the digital solutions because, in the absence of adequate skills, such an approach would either lead to abandoning the (pilot) project altogether, or lock-in the organization with the services provider that could plug the skills gap—most likely the developer of the solution.[169] This would further reinforce and compound issues of technological dependency discussed in Section 2. Limited access to skills will thus continue to affect the pace of digitalization of procurement governance. It is important for the process of technology adoption not to continue outpacing the accumulation of digital skills in the public sector. Otherwise, there will be widespread governance risks that may become difficult to mitigate or correct.

[165] Nitesh Bharosa, 'The Rise of GovTech: Trojan Horse or Blessing in Disguise? A Research Agenda' (2022) 39 Government Information Quarterly 101692.

[166] Arnauld Bertrand and Julie McQueen, 'How Governments Can Plan for a Future-Fit, Digital Workforce' (*EY blog*, 11 Oct 2022) <https://www.ey.com/en_ch/government-digital-innovation/how-governments-can-plan-for-a-future-fit-digital-workforce> accessed 17 October 2022.

[167] Weghmann and Sankey, 'Hollowed out' (n 162) 41.

[168] See Chapter 5, Section 2.3.

[169] For further discussion on lock-in, see Section 2.2.1.

5. Difficult Trade-Offs and the Risks of Deploying Immature Technologies

The analysis so far has shown that identifying and managing the governance risks that come with the transition to digital procurement requires careful assessment. A final general consideration in that regard is that such assessment will be conditioned by the unavoidable uncertainty that comes with the deployment of immature technologies,[170] as well as with a quickly changing regulatory environment.[171] This will have some implications. First, to the extent that the available information may be limited and based on a series of assumptions to bypass such uncertainty, assessing trade-offs between the potential benefits and the risks created by the technological solutions under consideration will not be straightforward. This makes the framing of the analysis and the methodology used to identify (and quantify) potential benefits and risks particularly susceptible to biases.[172] It also exacerbates the risks of policy entrepreneurship and decision-making capture.[173] These can be mitigated through a reduction in the digital skills gap of the procurement organization,[174] and can be further mitigated through external verification.[175]

Second, the adoption of the technology will itself change the governance framework and will alter and displace some of the relevant governance risks—for example, by creating new possibilities for technology-enabled corrupt or anticompetitive practices,[176] or by creating new opportunities for those in charge of its management (new insiders).[177] Moreover, the technological and regulatory environment will continue to evolve throughout the lifecycle of the technological solutions. These dynamics will thus require periodic reviews to incorporate new information and, potentially, to trigger decisions to pause or abandon projects, at least until the governance framework is further adapted.[178] In other words, the required assessments cannot be undertaken as a one-off exercise. This stresses the importance of continuity in the availability

[170] Joule A Bergerson and others, 'Life Cycle Assessment of Emerging Technologies: Evaluation Techniques at Different Stages of Market and Technical Maturity' (2020) 24 Journal of Industrial Ecology 11.

[171] Jaime Bonnin Roca and Eoin O'Sullivan, 'The Role of Regulators in Mitigating Uncertainty Within the Valley of Death' (2020) 109 Technovation 102157.

[172] Kimberly D Elsbach and Ileana Stigliani, 'New Information Technology and Implicit Bias' (2019) 33 Academy of Management Perspectives 185.

[173] These are discussed in Chapter 3, Section 2.2.2 and in Chapter 6.

[174] See Section 4.

[175] See Chapter 5, Section 3.2.

[176] See nn 77 and 78, and accompanying text.

[177] See Chapter 7, Section 1.2.

[178] See Chapter 5, Section 3.2.

of skills and institutional memory, to mitigate against risks of insufficient understanding of how previous iterations of the relevant assessment were carried out. It also stresses the need for flexibility throughout the technological lifecycle, including organizational flexibility to increase the resources dedicated to its governance.

Third, there will be difficult trade-offs between the speed and the likelihood of success of the deployment of digital solutions. The analysis above and in Chapter 7 has shown that there are many enabling factors and governance requirements that need to be in place ahead of the successful and legally compliant deployment of digital solutions. Meeting some of those technological or regulatory requirements will take time and require potentially significant investments. This could be perceived as slowing down technological adoption. However, sacrificing those elements to speed up the deployment of a particular solution will only generate governance (and operational) problems. This relates partly to the issue of technical debt,[179] but is also a broader consideration, as deploying digital technologies without the adequate governance framework will not be sustainable. Not paying enough attention to these issues could generate well-known problems, such as creating white elephants (ie technological solutions that are too expensive to maintain or that cannot be used for their intended purpose),[180] or generating undesired spillovers that can be either impossible, or difficult, to fix (and which, in an increasingly regulated space, can trigger legal consequences such as penalties or liability). These issues need to be embedded within the broader assessment of digital technologies.

6. Embedding Risk Assessment to Avoid Governance Pitfalls

This chapter has explored the main governance risks and legal obligations arising from the adoption of digital technologies. The analysis has stressed the need to recognize the new governance risks that arise from the adoption of digital technologies, and to factor their management and mitigation in deciding whether to adopt digital technologies.

To be sure, some of the digital governance obligations incumbent on public buyers arise regardless of their active adoption of digital technologies. As data

[179] See Section 2.2.1.
[180] This is developed in Albert Sanchez-Graells, 'Data-Driven Procurement Governance: Two Well-Known Elephant Tales' (2019) 24 Communications Law 157.

holders, public buyers have data governance obligations under the Open Data Directive that will be significantly increased with the entry into force of the eForms (Section 2.1.1), as well as general duties to safeguard data subject to the rights of others and competition sensitive information (Sections 2.1.2 and 2.1.3). This inescapable data governance role generates tensions in the design of open procurement data mechanisms and requires the deployment of a system of multi-tiered access to different types of information at different times, by different stakeholders, and under different conditions, which is not yet the standard approach. Moreover, under the NIS 2 Directive, most public buyers will also have cybersecurity governance obligations, regardless of whether they use digital technologies or not (Section 3).

However, the adoption of digital technologies would increase relevant risks and introduce additional governance requirements, which would in turn require higher levels of compliance with data governance, algorithmic transparency, and cybersecurity obligations. This chapter has stressed the importance of embedding risk assessment in the initial stages of decision-making processes leading to the adoption of digital solutions for procurement governance, and to reiterate the exercise throughout the lifecycle of use of digital technologies. This concerns considerations of algorithmic transparency, technological lock-in, and technical debt that advocate for the adoption of an open source by default approach (Section 2.2.1). It also concerns risks of technological dependency, including risks related to (absolute) operational dependency that could require an assessment of 'system critical' technological deployments, as well as limiting technological delegation to prevent the public buyer and its broader organization from becoming dysfunctional if the technology failed in an irreparable manner (Section 2.2.2). It also concerns an assessment of the cybersecurity risks that would spread across the organization because of the implementation of the digital solution. As the development and deployment of digital solutions generates the new and heightened risks discussed, it will require a proportionate review of the obligations under the NIS 2 Directive, in particular concerning risk management (Section 3).

The chapter has also stressed how an assessment of the mechanisms put in place to ensure sustained access to digital skills needs to be part of the holistic evaluation of any decision to adopt digital solutions because their deployment expands, rather than reduces, the need for those skills. Moreover, the analysis has shown how access to such skills is necessary, not only at an operational level, but also to adequately perform the overarching governance functions. In other words, it has shown how a continued gap in digital capabilities can compound all other risks, as well as operate as an obstacle for a proper risk assessment in the first place (Section 4). This circles back to the conclusion of Chapter 6—which already stressed the need to boost the public sector's digital capabilities[181]—and further reinforces the insight that digitalization exacerbates the need for the public sector to build up its digital expertise and skills. It is important for the process of technology adoption not to continue outpacing the accumulation of digital skills in the public sector. Otherwise, there will be widespread governance risks that may become difficult to mitigate or correct.

Ultimately, to ensure adequate digital procurement governance, it is not only necessary to take a realistic look at the potential of the technology and the required enabling factors (Chapter 7), but also to embed a comprehensive risk assessment of the new risks that come with the technology, which requires enhanced public sector digital capabilities, as stressed in this chapter. Such an approach can mitigate against the 'policy irresistibility' that surrounds these technologies (Chapter 6) and contribute to a gradual and sustainable process of procurement digitalization. However, the ways in which such risk assessment should be carried out require further exploration. This will be the subject of Chapter 9.

[181] This is, more generally, a crucial plank of all recent procurement and public sector digitalization policies. See eg Central Digital and Data Office, 'Transforming for a Digital Future: 2022 to 2025 Roadmap for Digital and Data' (Policy Paper, 9 June 2022) <https://www.gov.uk/government/publications/roadmap-for-digital-and-data-2022-to-2025> accessed 5 September 2022; National Audit Office, *Digital Transformation in Government: Addressing the Barriers to Efficiency* (HC 2022–23, 1171). See also Amanda Clarke and Sean Boots, 'A Guide to Reforming Information Technology Procurement in the Government of Canada' (2022) <https://govcanadacontracts.ca/it-procurement-guide/> accessed 19 October 2022.

9

Governing the Assessment and Taking of Risks in Digital Procurement Governance

1. Introduction

Chapter 8 showed that managing the risks generated by public procurement digitalization requires deploying several risk assessment tools, or at least a tool capable of capturing risks of very different natures and stemming from different sources. Concentrating on data- and technology-related issues only,[1] this already requires assessment of a wide array of issues, such as data hazards,[2] algorithmic harms,[3] technological dependency, and cybersecurity threats.[4] Taking the perspective of the emerging model of risk-based regulation initially discussed in Chapter 1, this chapter furthers the analysis of the specific (sub)model that is emerging in the EU and the UK. Given that this model applies to the acquisition of digital technologies for all types of public sector activity—that is, it is not specific to procurement digitalization—the chapter evidences the shortcomings in the general regulatory approach to public sector

[1] The whole array of issues requiring risk assessment is much wider, encompassing eg human rights, data protection, gender, and environmental impact assessments, etc. The discussion will stay focused on technology-related issues only, but the reasoning can easily be extended to the other issues. For discussion of human rights impact assessments, see eg Brandie Nonnecke and Philip Dawson, 'Human Rights Impact Assessments for AI: Analysis and Recommendations' (2022) Access Now <https://www.accessnow.org/cms/assets/uploads/2022/11/Access-Now-Version-Human-Rights-Implications-of-Algorithmic-Impact-Assessments_-Priority-Recommendations-to-Guide-Effective-Development-and-Use.pdf> accessed 20 December 2022.

[2] See eg Data Hazards, 'Self-Assessment' (2022) <https://datahazards.com/contents/materials/self-assessment.html> accessed 4 November 2022.

[3] See eg National Institute for Standards and Technology, 'Artificial Intelligence Risk Management Framework (AI RMF 1.0)' (2023) <https://www.nist.gov/itl/ai-risk-management-framework> accessed 7 April 2023. See also Dillon Reisman and others, 'Algorithmic Impact Assessments: A Practical Framework for Public Agency Accountability' (2018) AI Now < https://ainowinstitute.org/publication/algorithmic-impact-assessments-report-2> accessed 4 November 2022; and Platform for the Information Society, 'Artificial intelligence impact assessment' (2018) <https://static1.squarespace.com/static/5b7877457c9327fa97fef427/t/5c368c611ae6cf01ea0fba53/1547078768062/Artificial+Intelligence+Impact+Assessment+-+English.pdf> accessed 8 November 2022.

[4] See eg the UK's National Cyber Security Centre, Cyber Assessment Framework v 3.1 (2022) <https://www.ncsc.gov.uk/collection/caf/cyber-assessment-framework> accessed 4 November 2022.

Digital Technologies and Public Procurement. Albert Sanchez-Graells, Oxford University Press.
 DOI: 10.1093/oso/9780198866770.003.0009

digitalization that justify the creation of mechanisms of external oversight and mandatory requirements proposed in Chapter 5.

This chapter is not concerned with the specific form of the tool or tools used to carry out the impact assessment.[5] Rather, it focuses on the governance of the impact assessment process (whichever specific form/s of assessment it relies on), in terms of its design and implementation. It also focuses on the need to embed its results into the decision-making process leading to the adoption of digital technologies for procurement governance, and to iterate it throughout the lifecycle of use of digital technologies. At the time of writing in late Spring of 2023, there are no mandatory rules on these issues, and the adequacy of proposed or emerging risk assessment and related transparency standards is contested.[6] This chapter contributes to that discussion by demonstrating how tackling the risks of regulatory capture and commercial determination identified in Chapters 6 and 7 requires much more robust (institutional) approach to risk-based regulation (see Chapter 5).

The remainder of this chapter will explore in detail the emerging approaches to risk-based regulation in the EU and the UK. The analysis will show that this approach is of limited value in tackling the types of risks related to the adoption of digital solutions. First, the voluntary measures would be too open ended and imprecise. In the absence of clear standards on, for example, data hazards or algorithmic impact assessment, they could potentially impose an unduly high regulatory burden on public buyers with limited digital capabilities. This would probably result in either avoidance or defective compliance (ie box ticking) with the voluntary instruments. Even for more digitally capable public buyers, those instruments would also be undermined by structural institutional conflicts of interest[7] and the general difficulties in generating meaningful mechanisms of information-based governance in the absence of quality controls on the content of such disclosures. Second, the system would also see its effectiveness diminished due to a lack of accountability and contestation mechanisms relating to the self-assessments carried out by tech providers and

[5] There is an important technical discussion to be had on whether 'objective' tools can be developed, given the variety of methodological approaches that are possible. However, those considerations exceed the scope of this chapter, which will thus assume that a satisfactory level of technical consensus is possible.

[6] On the issue of the interaction between risk assessment, its transparency, and the need to empower external actors to replicate them, see Mia Leslie and Tatiana Kazim, 'Executable Versions: An Argument for Compulsory Disclosure (Part 1)' (The Digital Constitutionalist, 3 August 2022) <https://digi-con.org/executable-versions-part-one/> and Mia Leslie and Tatiana Kazim, 'Executable Versions: An Argument for Compulsory Disclosure (Part 2)' (The Digital Constitutionalist, 3 November 2022) https://digi-con.org/executable-versions-part-two/ accessed 4 November 2022.

[7] They are intrinsically linked to the issue of 'policy irresistibility' discussed in Chapters 3 and 6, as well as the unavoidable conflicts inherent to mechanisms of 'second party' assurance, as discussed in Section 3.2.

overseen by public buyers with an interest in the technological deployment. By stressing the weakness of such second party assurance model, the chapter demonstrates how the challenges of digital procurement governance necessitate the regulatory reforms advanced in Chapter 5.

2. Emerging European Approaches: Voluntary Assessment and Largely Unconstrained Risk-Taking

The emerging Artificial Intelligence (AI) risk regulation model in the EU,[8] and the UK's minimalistic approach to AI regulation,[9] are leaving the adoption of digital technologies by public buyers largely unregulated and mostly subject to voluntary measures, or to open-ended obligations in areas without clear impact assessment standards (which reduces the prospect of effective mandatory enforcement).[10] This section provides an overview of these approaches, which will then be critically assessed in the remainder of the chapter.

2.1 Governance of Procurement Digitalization in the EU

Chapter 8 showed how a quickly expanding set of EU digital law instruments is imposing a patchwork of governance obligations on public buyers, whether or not they adopt digital technologies—for example, in relation to data[11] or cybersecurity governance.[12] However, the primary decision whether to adopt digital technologies is not subject to any specific constraints, and the substantive obligations that follow from the diverse EU law instruments tend to refer to open-ended standards that require advanced technical capabilities to operationalize them.

[8] For general discussion and a critical assessment, see Michael Veale, 'A Critical Take on the Policy Recommendations of the EU High-Level Expert Group on Artificial Intelligence' (2020) 11 European Journal of Risk Regulation 1.

[9] Huw Roberts and others, 'Artificial Intelligence Regulation in the United Kingdom: A Path to Global Leadership?' (2022) <https://ssrn.com/abstract=4209504> accessed 21 November 2022. Most recently, see Department for Science, Innovation and Technology and Office for Artificial Intelligence, 'AI regulation: a pro-innovation approach' (CP 815, 2023). For criticism, see Andrew Charlesworth and others, 'Response to the UK's March 2023 White Paper "A pro-innovation approach to AI regulation"' (SSRN, 19 June 2023) <https://ssrn.com/abstract=4477368> accessed 22 June 2023.

[10] Digital Regulation Cooperation Forum, 'Auditing algorithms: the existing landscape, role of regulators and future outlook' (23 September 2022) <https://www.gov.uk/government/publications/findings-from-the-drcf-algorithmic-processing-workstream-spring-2022/auditing-algorithms-the-existing-landscape-role-of-regulators-and-future-outlook> accessed 21 November 2022.

[11] See Chapter 8, Section 2.1.

[12] See Chapter 8, Section 3.

For example, the core cybersecurity obligation under the NIS 2 Directive is to 'take appropriate and proportionate technical, operational and organisational measures to manage the risks posed to the security of network and information systems which [public buyers] use for their operations or for the provision of their services, and to prevent or minimise the impact of incidents on recipients of their services and on other services'.[13] Moreover, in establishing measures seeking to ensure a level of security of network and information systems appropriate to the risk presented, public buyers can consider 'the state-of-the-art and, where applicable, relevant European and international standards, as well as the cost of implementation',[14] and in 'assessing the proportionality of those measures, due account shall be taken of the degree of the entity's exposure to risks, its size, the likelihood of occurrence of incidents and their severity, including their societal and economic impact'.[15] Whether this will result in stringent cybersecurity requirements remains to be seen, at least until clear standards and guidance on the implementation of the NIS 2 Directive emerge as a result of the institutional mechanisms it creates, which is a few years down the line.

Given its focus on AI use,[16] the proposed EU AI Act[17] could *in principle* generate governance requirements applicable to the decision whether to adopt some types of digital solutions for procurement governance. The EU AI Act contains rather specific obligations that concretize minimum requirements for the mechanisms governing the deployment of risk based AI regulation, such as risk management systems,[18] data and data governance requirements,[19] technical documentation,[20] record-keeping,[21] transparency,[22] and accuracy,

[13] See Directive (EU) 2022/2555 of the European Parliament and of the Council of 14 December 2022 on measures for a high common level of cybersecurity across the Union, amending Regulation (EU) No 910/2014 and Directive (EU) 2018/1972, and repealing Directive (EU) 2016/1148 (hereafter 'NIS 2 Directive') [2022] OJ L 333/80, art 21(1).

[14] ibid.

[15] ibid.

[16] There is a relevant definitional issue, as the EU AI Act's definition of AI is contested. However, given the limited obligations that result from the EU AI Act for digital procurement governance, this chapter will not explore the issue in detail. Similarly, minimizing the relevance of the definitional issue other than in relation to high-risk AI, see Lilian Edwards, 'The EU AI Act: A Summary of Its Significance and Scope' (2022) Ada Lovelace Institute Expert Explainer 7 <https://www.adalovelaceinstitute.org/wp-content/uploads/2022/04/Expert-explainer-The-EU-AI-Act-11-April-2022.pdf> accessed 8 November 2022.

[17] Proposal for a Regulation of the European Parliament and of the Council laying down harmonised rules on Artificial Intelligence (Artificial Intelligence Act) and amending certain union legislative acts, COM (2021) 206 final (hereafter 'EU AI Act').

[18] ibid art 9.

[19] ibid art 10.

[20] ibid art 11.

[21] ibid art 12.

[22] ibid art 13.

robustness, and cybersecurity.[23] Compliance with such obligations would be verified through mechanisms of conformity assessment,[24] which could involve third parties (see Section 3), and would be generally overseen by a designated market surveillance authority in each Member State.[25] In trying to follow a technology-neutral and flexible approach to regulation, some of these obligations refer to the state-of-the-art or harmonized standards where these are developed.[26] If sufficiently precise standards were developed,[27] this could reduce the open-endedness of some of the obligations over time. However, it would still generate a risk of shortcomings in implementing risk assessments,[28] as well as bring with them general governance challenges resulting from the EU's 'new approach' to standardization.[29] In general, even if not perfect and still susceptible to change during the legislative process,[30] the set of obligations in the EU AI Act would cover several digital governance risks identified in Chapter 8. However, the EU AI Act will (most likely) not be applicable to public buyers adopting digital solutions for procurement governance, except in a voluntary manner.

The EU AI Act seeks to create a proportionate approach to the regulation of AI by establishing four categories of AI uses: prohibited, high-risk, limited risk requiring transparency measures, and minimal risk. The two categories that carry regulatory constraints or compliance obligations are high-risk,[31] and limited risk requiring transparency measures.[32] Minimal risk AI is unregulated,

[23] ibid art 15.

[24] ibid arts 19 and 43.

[25] ibid art 59.

[26] ibid art 40.

[27] See European Commission, 'Draft standardisation request to the European Standardisation Organisations in support of safe and trustworthy artificial intelligence' (2022) <https://ec.europa.eu/docsroom/documents/52376> accessed 20 December 2022. However, there are important questions on whether standardization can meet the regulatory expectations; Hadrien Pouget, 'The EU's AI Act Is Barreling Toward AI Standards That Do Not Exist' (*Lawfare*, 12 January 2023) <https://www.lawfareblog.com/eus-ai-act-barreling-toward-ai-standards-do-not-exist> accessed 2 February 2023.

[28] See Michael Veale and Frederik Zuiderveen Borgesius, 'Demystifying the Draft EU Artificial Intelligence Act—Analysing the Good, the Dad, and the Unclear Elements of the Proposed Approach' (2021) 22(4) Computer Law Review International 97, 103 (hereafter Veale and Zuiderveen Borgesius, 'Demistifying the EU AI Act').

[29] For discussion, see Pierluigi Cuccuru, 'Regulating by Request: On the Role and Status of the 'Standardisation Mandate' under the New Approach' in Mariolina Eliantonio and Caroline Cauffman (eds), *The Legitimacy of Standardisation as a Regulatory Technique* (Edward Elgar 2020) 48 (hereafter Eliantonio and Cauffman, *Legitimacy of Standardisation as Regulation*); cf Rodrigo Vallejo, 'The Private Administrative Law of Technical Standardization' (2021) 40 Yearbook of European Law 172.

[30] There is widespread criticism of different aspects of the EU AI Act. However, its detailed analysis exceeds the scope of this chapter. Where the criticism relates to some of the measures proposed here, the relevant arguments will be considered.

[31] EU AI Act (n 17) arts 8–15.

[32] ibid art 52, which also applies to some high-risk AI.

although the EU AI Act seeks to promote the development of codes of conduct to foster voluntary compliance with the requirements applicable to high-risk AI systems.[33]

The use of AI for digital procurement governance cannot be classified as prohibited.[34] It is also difficult to see how most digital solutions for procurement governance could fall under the regime applicable to AI uses requiring special transparency because it only applies to AI systems intended to interact with natural persons, which must be 'designed and developed in such a way that natural persons are informed that they are interacting with an AI system, unless this is obvious from the circumstances and the context of use'.[35] It would not be difficult for public buyers using external-facing AI solutions (eg chatbots seeking to guide tenderers through their e-submissions) to make it clear that the tenderers are interacting with an AI solution. And, even if not, the transparency obligations in the EU AI Act are minimal.

Ultimately, the position of AI uses for digital procurement governance under the EU AI Act rests on whether procurement-related AI uses could be classified as high risk.[36] However, procurement-related AI uses are not included in the relevant closed list,[37] and are currently left to the default category of minimal risk subjected only to voluntary self-regulation via codes of conduct—yet to be developed.[38] Such codes of conduct should encourage voluntary compliance with the requirements applicable to high-risk AI uses 'on the basis of technical specifications and solutions that are appropriate means of ensuring compliance with such requirements in light of the intended purpose of the systems'.[39] Despite referring to the specific risk-based regulation mechanisms mentioned above, this seems to introduce a further element of proportionality or 'adaptability' requirement that could well water down the requirements applicable to minimal risk AI uses, along the lines of, for example, the NIS 2 Directive discussed above. Importantly, while it is possible for Member States to draw such

[33] ibid art 69.

[34] ibid art 5.

[35] ibid art 52.

[36] This is regulated in art 6, which cross-refers to ibid Annex III.

[37] ibid Annex III, which is however susceptible of amendment under ibid art 7.

[38] Albert Sanchez-Graells, 'Where Does the Proposed EU AI Act Place Procurement?' (*howtocrackanut.com*, 21 October 2021) <https://www.howtocrackanut.com/blog/2021/10/21/where-does-the-proposed-eu-ai-act-place-procurement> accessed 8 November 2022 (hereafter Sanchez-Graells, 'Procurement in the EU AI Act').

[39] EU AI Act (n 17) art 69. For discussion, see Camilla D'Angelo and others, 'Labelling Initiatives, Codes of Conduct and Other Self-Regulatory Mechanisms for Artificial Intelligence Applications. From Principles to Practice and Considerations for the Future' (2022) RAND <https://www.rand.org/pubs/research_reports/RRA1773-1.html> accessed 8 November 2022.

codes of conduct,[40] in its maximum harmonization approach, the EU AI Act could pre-empt Member States from going further and mandating compliance with specific obligations[41] (eg by imposing a blanket extension of the governance requirements designed for high-risk AI uses) across their public administrations.[42] However, it is submitted that the EU AI Act is unlikely to entirely exclude Member State regulatory activity other than in relation to prohibited, high-risk uses, and transparency requirements—which therefore allows for the development of additional requirements for 'lawful-and-not-high-risk' uses, both in relation to formal checks (eg permissioning or licensing of AI use) and substantive requirements.[43] The emergent EU model is thus clearly limited to the development of voluntary codes of conduct, and their likely content—while yet unknown—seems unlikely to impose the same standards applicable to the adoption of high-risk AI uses.

2.2 Governance of Procurement Digitalization in the UK

The UK is taking a principled light-touch approach to AI regulation,[44] and clearly seeking to deviate from EU regulatory standards (ie lower them). A primary example is the contrast between the UK's laissez faire approach and the proposed EU AI Act.[45] However, given the limited effectiveness of the latter in the field of digital procurement governance (see Section 2.1), the EU and UK approaches converge in this area. Counterintuitively, the UK may even seem more advanced in formulating voluntary standards, as it has developed guidance for the use of AI in the public sector[46] and guidelines for AI

[40] Even if the EU AI Act only mentions that 'the Member States shall encourage and facilitate the drawing up of codes of conduct'; EU AI Act (n 17) art 69(1).

[41] For detailed assessment, see Veale and Zuiderveen Borgesius, 'Demistifying the EU AI Act' (n 28) 108–10. However, the authors stress that it is uncommon for EU regulatory instruments to simply pre-empt domestic legislation, ibid 109. This aligns with the arguments made in Chapter 2, Section 3.2 against considering that the EU AI Act can prevent domestic regulation targeted at disciplining public sector AI adoption. Such issues are also not applicable to other types of digital technology in any case.

[42] For criticism, see Sanchez-Graells, 'Procurement in the EU AI Act' (n 38). See also Chapter 2, Section 3.2.

[43] For further discussion, see Chapter 5, Section 3.

[44] See n 9. See also Department for Digital, Culture, Media and Sport, 'Establishing a pro-innovation approach to regulating AI. An overview of the UK's emerging approach' (CP 728, 2022).

[45] Joël Reland, 'UK-EU Regulatory Divergence Tracker' (5th edn, October 2022) 2–3 <https://ukandeu.ac.uk/wp-content/uploads/2022/10/Divergence-Tracker-5.pdf> accessed 8 November 2022.

[46] Office for Artificial Intelligence, 'A guide to using artificial intelligence in the public sector' (2019) <https://www.gov.uk/government/collections/a-guide-to-using-artificial-intelligence-in-the-public-sector> accessed 8 November 2022 (hereafter OAI, 'AI adoption guidance'). See Lisa Peets and others, 'UK Government's Guide to Using AI in the Public Sector' (2019) 2 The Journal of Robotics, Artificial Intelligence & Law 439.

procurement,[47] and has piloted an algorithmic transparency standard.[48] The UK has also adopted additional guidance in the Digital, Data and Technology Playbook[49] and the Technology Code of Practice.[50] While not specific to procurement digitalization, they do cover technological adoption by public buyers.

These soft law instruments are directly addressed to central government organizations, although they are expected to offer guidance more broadly across the public sector.[51] They do not impose hard obligations, but rather seek to crystallize 'best practice' approaches to the adoption and procurement of technology. The Digital, Data and Technology Playbook is expected to be followed 'on a "comply or explain" basis and, recognising that there is no one-size-fits all model'.[52] The Technology Code of Practice seemingly takes a mixed approach in requiring organizations to 'align [their] project or programme with the mandatory points, and follow as many of the remaining points as is practical'.[53] However, the Code does not explicitly classify requirements as mandatory or optional, which generates some uncertainty where the recommendations are not reflective of legal obligations deriving from other sources.[54]

The interaction between these pieces of guidance and voluntary standards is not always clear. The analysis below will show that, despite the proliferation of this type of document, the substantive assessment of governance risks in

[47] Office for Artificial Intelligence, 'Guidelines for AI procurement' (2020) <https://www.gov.uk/government/publications/guidelines-for-ai-procurement> accessed 8 November 2022 (hereafter OAI, 'AI procurement guidelines').

[48] Central Digital and Data Office, 'Algorithmic Transparency Standard v2.1' (2021) <https://www.gov.uk/government/publications/algorithmic-transparency-template> accessed 3 July 2023 (hereafter CDDO, 'Algorithmic Transparency Standard'). For an update on progress, see Elena Hess-Rheingans and Lara Bird, 'Developing the Algorithmic Transparency Standard in the Open' (*Centre for Data Ethics and Innovation Blog*, 10 October 2022) <https://cdei.blog.gov.uk/2022/10/10/developing-the-algorithmic-transparency-standard-in-the-open/> accessed 8 November 2022. The final version of the standard is available at Central Digital and Data Office and Centre for Data Ethics and Innovation, 'Algorithmic Transparency Recording Standard Hub' (2023) <https://www.gov.uk/government/collections/algorithmic-transparency-recording-standard-hub> accessed 12 April 2023.

[49] Digital, Data and Technology Profession, 'The Digital, Data and Technology Playbook. Government guidance on sourcing and contracting for digital, data and technology projects and programmes' (2022) <https://www.gov.uk/government/publications/the-digital-data-and-technology-playbook> accessed 8 November 2022 (hereafter DDTP, 'DDaT Playbook').

[50] Central Digital and Data Office, 'The Technology Code of Practice' (2021) <https://www.gov.uk/guidance/the-technology-code-of-practice> accessed 8 November 2022 (hereafter CDDO, 'Tech Code of Practice').

[51] The scope of application of the relevant documents is determined by the structure of government in the UK and cannot be seen as an intended feature in the design of the policy instruments. However, it does affect their effectiveness. Where substantive and procedural requirements are developed in such instruments, ways to extend them across the public sector should be sought. However, discussion of this issue exceeds the scope of this chapter.

[52] DDTP, 'DDaT Playbook' (n 49) 9.

[53] CDDO, 'Tech Code of Practice' (n 50).

[54] eg data protection legislation or mandatory accessibility requirements for websites.

digital procurement remains insufficiently addressed and left to undefined risk assessment standards and practices.

2.2.1 AI adoption, digital procurement guidance, and spend controls

2.2.1.1 AI adoption guidance

The AI adoption guidance[55] focuses on Machine Learning (ML) only and includes prompts for public sector adopters to focus on accountability, explainability, and transparency. Most of its recommendations are high level and difficult to operationalize without advanced digital skills or prior experience.[56] For example, the guide recommends 'allocating responsibility and governance for AI projects', but it does not refer to any specific model or tool for doing so. It mentions that it would be useful to consider, for example, whether 'there is a clear testing and monitoring framework in place', or 'the algorithms are robust, unbiased, fair and explainable'. But the guidance ends there.[57] Similarly, the guidance indicates that, by the end of the preparation phase of an AI adoption project, the adopting organization should have 'a data quality assessment using a combination of accuracy, bias, completeness, uniqueness, timeliness/currency, validity or consistency'. But, again, there is no further detail on how to carry this out. The guidance is, however, more specific on cybersecurity, as it refers to the already consolidated guidance of the National Cyber Security Centre.[58]

2.2.1.2 AI procurement guidelines

Similarly, despite setting out to 'provide a set of guiding principles on how to buy AI technology, as well as insights on tackling challenges that may arise during procurement', the AI procurement guidelines[59] provide high-level recommendations that cannot be directly operationalized by inexperienced public buyers, or those with limited digital capabilities. For example,

[55] OAI, 'AI adoption guidance' (n 46).

[56] See Chapter 8, Sections 2–4. This is a common problem with this type of guidance, which sometimes unrealistically intends to enable entities with insufficient data and AI preparedness to adopt AI-based solutions. For a clear example, see World Economic Forum, 'AI procurement in a box' (2020) <https://www.weforum.org/reports/ai-procurement-in-a-box> accessed 9 November 2022.

[57] There is, however, some additional guidance: Centre for Data Ethics and Innovation, 'Review into bias in algorithmic decision-making' (2020) <https://www.gov.uk/government/publications/cdei-publishes-review-into-bias-in-algorithmic-decision-making> accessed 8 November 2022 (hereafter CDEI, 'Algorithmic bias review').

[58] The guidance refers to National Cyber Security Centre, 'Intelligent security tools. Assessing intelligent tools for cyber security' (2019) <https://www.ncsc.gov.uk/collection/intelligent-security-tools> accessed 19 October 2022. Although the reference should probably have been too National Cyber Security Centre, 'Cyber assessment framework v 3.1' (2022) <https://www.ncsc.gov.uk/collection/caf/cyber-assessment-framework> accessed 4 November 2022.

[59] OAI, 'AI procurement guidelines' (n 47).

the recommendation to '[t]ry to address flaws and potential bias within your data before you go to market and/or have a plan for dealing with data issues if you cannot rectify them yourself'.[60] This not only requires a thorough understanding of, for example, the data ethics framework[61] and the (also open-ended) recommendations of the AI adoption guidance (above), but also detailed insights on data hazards.[62] This leads the AI procurement guidelines to stress that it may be necessary 'to seek out specific expertise to support this; data architects and data scientists should lead this process . . . to understand the complexities, completeness and limitations of the data . . . available'.[63]

Relatedly, some of the recommendations are very open ended in areas without clear standards. For example, the effectiveness of the recommendation to '[c]onduct initial AI impact assessments at the start of the procurement process, and ensure that your interim findings inform the procurement. Be sure to revisit the assessments at key decision points'[64] is dependent on the robustness of such impact assessments. However, the guidelines provide no further detail on how to carry out such assessments, other than a list of some generic areas for consideration (eg 'potential unintended consequences') and a passing reference to emerging guidelines in other jurisdictions. Therefore, both the AI adoption guidance and the AI procurement guidelines fail to provide any indication of how the relevant impact assessments need to be conducted, or by reference to which standards and methodologies.

2.2.1.3 Technology and digital spend approval

Interestingly, both the AI adoption guidance and the Digital, Data and Technology Playbook cross-refer to a specific budget approval process for central government organizations[65] planning to 'spend money on AI'. Such approval is required because most AI projects are for the time being classified as 'novel'.[66] This technology and digital spend approval process also applies to all

[60] ibid guideline 3.

[61] Central Digital and Data Office, 'Data ethics framework' (2020) <https://www.gov.uk/government/publications/data-ethics-framework> accessed 9 November 2022.

[62] See eg <https://datahazards.com/index.html >.

[63] OAI, 'AI procurement guidelines' (n 47).

[64] ibid guideline 4.

[65] This covers central government departments and the bodies they sponsor; see Cabinet Office, 'Cabinet Office controls policy: version 6' (2021) <https://www.gov.uk/government/publications/cabinet-office-controls-version-6/cabinet-office-controls-policy-version-6> accessed 9 November 2022.

[66] This points at either a potential for adaptation or a risk of reduced controls as the technology is mainstreamed, depending on the relevant perspective. It is also worth stressing that the classification covers novel or contentious spend indistinctly.

technology service projects (including procurement systems) with a planned spend of over one million pounds, even if they do not involve ML.[67] While the spend approval is triggered by the technology being adopted, it is worth stressing that its main purpose is not to focus on the technology itself or the related use case, but on the alignment of the expenditure with governmental policies. While some of those policies have to do with technological governance, other priorities have to do with centralization and leveraging of procurement expenditure. This is reflected in the relevant guidance. The digital and technology spend control seeks, in particular, to foster '[v]alue for money with suppliers across all public contracts; [u]se of shared services rather than developing new ones; [u]se of procurement frameworks where possible, rather than OJEU procurement[[68]]; [p]rocuring services that may be shared across all public bodies; and [m]oving to common platforms, standards and capability'.[69] It is also worth stressing that the current approach to spend control based on the creation of a pipeline of future projects was developed to provide a lighter-touch approach to expenditure approvals in 2018.[70] This can be expected to impact the interpretation and implementation of the relevant controls towards permissiveness.

The technology and digital spend approval process requires involvement of the Government Digital Service, which will then apply a set of technical checks based on a Service Standard[71] and the Technology Code of Practice. The Technology Code of Practice focuses on avoiding vendor lock-in and on creating interoperable and standards-based procured services, through using common standards across government. It includes requirements on open

[67] Central Digital and Data Office, 'Digital and Technology Spend Controls (Version 5)' (2021) <https://www.gov.uk/guidance/digital-and-technology-spend-controls-version-5> accessed 8 November 2022 (hereafter CDDO, 'Digital and Technology Spend Controls').

[68] 'OJEU procurement' seems to be used here as shorthand for a separate procurement exercise, which would be covered by the UK's international trade commitments in procurement, but not to publication in the Official Journal of the European Union, post-Brexit. Interestingly, there is some indication that significant AI projects are not being procured through existing frameworks (or commercial vehicles more generally), but rather through the direct award of contracts based on the unique expertise or technology of the provider. While this is an issue the spend control seems to want to capture, it is unclear whether commercial vehicles are adequate in a fat-changing technological setting. However, such an assessment exceeds the scope of this chapter.

[69] Cabinet Office, 'Technology and Digital Spend Control Form v3.11' (undated) <https://assets.publishing.service.gov.uk/government/uploads/system/uploads/attachment_data/file/1007387/Spend_control_form_template_-_digital_and_technology_3_11__3_.odt> accessed 3 November 2023.

[70] Anne Laurent, 'Buying as One: Category Management Lessons From the United Kingdom' (2019) IBM Centre for the Business of Government 31 <https://www.businessofgovernment.org/report/buying-one-category-management-lessons-united-kingdom> accessed 9 November 2022.

[71] <https://www.gov.uk/service-manual/service-standard> accessed 8 November 2022. The Service Standard is most relevant for public-facing web services. It will thus not be analysed in detail here.

standards,[72] data and systems security,[73] as well as data governance issues[74]—with the last two referring to the need to carry out risk assessments. However, except for cybersecurity,[75] the Technology Code of Practice does not provide any additional guidance on how such risk assessments should be carried out. It includes instead a series of open-ended questions that can elicit qualitative answers that can be difficult to verify—in particular in the context of a 'comply or explain' approach to the enforcement of the Code (see Section 3.2). In that regard, it should be stressed that the spend control process relies on self-assessment by the organization seeking to adopt the digital technology.

To carry out that self-assessment, the relevant organization must apply pre-determined assessment criteria[76] to establish whether the planned expenditure should be classed as 'assured', 'monitor', or 'control'—which implies different levels of forward-looking oversight.[77] This self-assessment is then validated by the Government Digital Service.[78] An important potential loophole of this process is that organizations can start projects self-assessed as 'assured' even before this assessment is confirmed by the Government Digital Service. This can create perverse incentives in the self-assessment. There is also no clear guidance on how deviations from the applicable standards need to be managed for the expenditure to be classed as 'monitor' (rather than 'control', which requires specific ministerial approval). Moreover, given the embedded reliance on self-assessments, the effectiveness of this spend control ultimately depends on the ability of the Government Digital Service to check the information and evaluations carried out by the organization seeking to adopt the technology, and to impose effective changes or conditions in the planned technological adoption.[79] Unfortunately, there is evidence of systemic failures in that regard,

[72] Central Digital and Data Office, 'Be Open and Use Open Source' (2021) <https://www.gov.uk/guidance/be-open-and-use-open-source> accessed 8 November 2022.

[73] Central Digital and Data Office, 'Make Things Secure' (2021) <https://www.gov.uk/guidance/make-things-secure> accessed 8 November 2022.

[74] Central Digital and Data Office, 'Make Better Use of Data' (2021) <https://www.gov.uk/guidance/make-better-use-of-data> accessed 8 November 2022.

[75] Here, the Code refers again to guidance by the National Cyber Security Centre.

[76] Central Digital and Data Office, 'GDS Spend Controls Pipeline Assessment Criteria' (2018) <https://www.gov.uk/guidance/gds-spend-controls-pipeline-assessment-criteria> accessed 8 November 2022.

[77] CDDO, 'Digital and Technology Spend Controls' (n 67).

[78] The methodology behind these assessments seems patchy, especially the points system used. However, its detailed discussion exceeds the scope of this chapter.

[79] Some of these activities can pose challenges to digital service teams, not least in terms of policy alignment; see Ines Mergel, 'Digital Service Teams in Government' (2019) 36 Government Information Quarterly 101389; Ines Mergel, 'Digital Service Teams: Challenges and Recommendations for Government' (2017) IBM Centre for the Business of Government <https://www.businessofgovernment.org/report/digital-service-teams-challenges-and-recommendations-government> accessed 21 November 2022.

including intervention by the Government Digital Service making things worse in some high-profile projects, especially due to the imposition of specific approaches (eg agile) to technological development,[80] and the lack of continuity in its involvement post-approval.[81]

The lack of clear standards to complete the required self-assessment and the limited analysis of the relevant issues at approval stage—which should be at least fifteen months prior to launching the relevant procurement opportunity[82]—raise some questions about the likely effectiveness of this spend control, as well as broader issues in the institutional design of this governance mechanism, which seems to fall short of ensuring effective external control. Moreover, this process does not apply to public buyers other than those in central government, which severely limits the adequacy of this approach to control the adoption of digital technologies for public procurement governance (and more generally, for public governance) comprehensively. Ultimately, decisions on the adoption of technology in non-central parts of the public administration is thus subject to voluntary compliance with the relevant recommendations as a matter of best practice or simple guidance. This largely aligns the UK position with that of the EU (Section 2.1).

2.2.2 Algorithmic transparency standard

In parallel to the above spend-related guidance and requirements and following a recommendation of a review into algorithmic biases,[83] the UK government developed an algorithmic transparency standard[84] and accompanying guidance.[85] These would apply where the public buyer adopted algorithmic tools and carried out algorithm-assisted decisions. It thus mainly relates to (semi) automated decision-making. The standard is divided into two tiers, with tier 1 aiming to provide succinct information meant for the general public and tier 2 giving more detailed information about the algorithmic tool for a more specialized or professional audience. Tier 2 includes a section dedicated to 'Risks,

[80] Vishanth Weerakkody, 'Identifying the Critical Success Factors for Major Government Projects that Incorporate IT or "Digital" Developments' (2016) Research Background Note <https://bura.brunel.ac.uk/bitstream/2438/13368/1/FullText.pdf> accessed 9 November 2022.

[81] National Audit Office, *The Challenges in Implementing Digital Change* (HC 2021–22, 575) 37.

[82] CDDO, 'Digital and Technology Spend Controls' (n 67).

[83] CDEI, 'Algorithmic bias review' (n 57).

[84] CDDO, 'Algorithmic Transparency Standard' (n 48).

[85] Centre for Data Ethics and Innovation, 'Algorithmic Transparency Standard. Guidance for Public Sector Bodies' (2022) <https://github.com/co-cddo/algorithmic-transparency-standard/blob/320cc8f882e76c0bb29d2477e1608a890a7cb68d/Guidance%20for%20Public%20Sector%20Organisations%E2%80%99%20Use%20of%20the%20Algorithmic%20Transparency%20Standard%20v1.1.pdf> accessed 8 November 2022 (hereafter CDEI, 'Algorithmic Transparency Guidance').

Mitigations and Impact Assessments' that requires listing which impact assessments have been carried out,[86] and to provide a basic 'description of the impact assessment conducted' for each of them—with a link to a full text or summary of the assessment, if available. It also requires a detailed description of the common risks of the tool and the actions taken to mitigate them. However, there is no link or reference to any specific methodology to carry any of this out.

The related guidance only provides slightly additional detail on the categories of risk likely to require consideration, such as risks relating to: 'the data; to the application and use of the tool; to the algorithm, model or tool efficacy; to the outputs and decisions; organisational and corporate risks; or risks relating to public engagement'.[87] The only reference to a model to construct risk assessments (other than for data protection) is to general guidance on risk management in the public sector.[88] This fails to provide clear standards on how to conduct risk assessments and can result in widely varying practice, as shown by the pilot.[89] Moreover, the absence of clear standards makes it more difficult to assess whether the adopting organization has carried out effective risk assessments, or simply engaged in box ticking.[90]

Compliance with the algorithmic standard is voluntary and does not necessarily catch all uses of AI by a public buyer, as its scope of application focuses on 'algorithmic tools that either: [h]ave a significant influence on a decision-making process with significant public effect, or [d]irectly interact with the general public'.[91] This could raise questions on the coverage of AI adoption for some procurement processes that could be seen to constitute strict 'back-office' functions, although voluntary compliance is possible for not-in-scope uses.

A second potential limitation of the transparency standard is in the disclosure of the relevant reports. The guidance makes it clear that '[r]eports for tools in the idea, design, or development phases will be kept internally but not published. Only reports for tools in the production phase will be published

[86] Such as data protection, algorithmic, ethical, or equality impact assessments.

[87] CDEI, 'Algorithmic Transparency Guidance' (n 85) 21.

[88] Government Finance Function, 'The Orange Book. Management of Risk—Principles and Concepts' (2020) <https://www.gov.uk/government/publications/orange-book> accessed 8 November 2022.

[89] For discussion, see Albert Sanchez-Graells, 'Algorithmic Transparency: Some Thoughts on UK's First Four Published Disclosures and the Standards' Usability' (*howtocrackanut.com*, 11 July 2022) <https://www.howtocrackanut.com/blog/2022/7/11/algorithmic-transparency-some-thoughts-on-uk-first-disclosures-and-usability> accessed 8 November 2022.

[90] Albert Sanchez-Graells, 'Written Evidence Submitted to the House of Commons Science and Technology Committee Inquiry on the Governance of artificial intelligence' (2022) GAI0004, paras 12 ff <https://committees.parliament.uk/writtenevidence/113034/pdf/> accessed 20 December 2022.

[91] CDEI, 'Algorithmic Transparency Guidance' (n 85) 6.

in the repository.'[92] This severely limits the functionality of these reports to enable early challenges to the decisions and assessments taken by the public buyer—thus reducing the precautionary value of this regulatory tactic within the context of risk regulation. In fact, the possibility for unpublished algorithmic transparency reports is foreseen more generally where information should be kept from disclosure on grounds of public interest, either completely or partially—for example, information that would reduce the operational effectiveness or enable the gaming of the algorithm, information that would generate cybersecurity risks, or information that would infringe intellectual property rights.[93] Where a public sector body decides that publishing a report for a specific tool is not possible, the guidance suggests that:

> completing a transparency report without making it publicly available ... is a valuable exercise ... to properly think through the relevant risks, impacts, and accountabilities related to a tool. Reports that are not publicly available can still form part of an internal repository, offering important internal visibility into algorithmic tools in use. Filling in a report can also help identify exactly which pieces of information are particularly sensitive and which are not.[94]

This approach highlights two issues. First, it raises questions on the robustness of a self-assessment that is not meant to be disclosed and thus, scrutinized, and which does not need to be based on any clear standards (as above). Second, it points to the need to put further thinking into the possibility of creating a system of algorithmic reporting that is not premised on 'all or nothing' transparency to the public, but rather takes a more nuanced approach and, for example, gives access to relevant information to external organizations entrusted with checking and verifying the soundness of the self-assessment.[95]

2.2.3 Recapitulation

As we have seen, the AI adoption guidance and the AI procurement guidelines do not provide any specific guidance or refer to any specific standards for

[92] ibid 7.

[93] ibid 9–10. This is aligned with the Freedom of Information Act, and thus largely replicates the approach to the protection of data subject to the rights of others discussed in Chapter 8, Section 2.1.2. For an analysis of the complexities in disclosing procurement information under current UK legislation, see Paul Henty and Rory Ashmore, 'Disclosure Rules Within Public Procurement Procedures and During Contract Period in the United Kingdom' in Kirsi-Maria Halonen, Roberto Caranta, and Albert Sanchez-Graells (eds), *Transparency in EU Procurements: Disclosure within Public Procurement and During Contract Execution* (Edward Elgar 2019) 296.

[94] CDEI, 'Algorithmic Transparency Guidance' (n 85) 9.

[95] This links back to the need to develop nuanced approaches to procurement data disclosure, as discussed in Chapter 8, Section 2.1.3.

the conduct of the relevant data and algorithmic risk assessments. Equally, the Digital, Data and Technology Playbook and the Technology Code of Practice do not provide any additional guidance on how such risk assessments should be carried out and instead include a series of open-ended questions that can elicit difficult to verify qualitative answers—especially under a 'comply or explain' approach. The algorithmic transparency standard also fails to provide clear indications on how to conduct risk assessments and can result in widely varying practice.

This shows that, despite the proliferation of this type of guidance documents and voluntary disclosure standards, the substantive assessment of governance risks in digital procurement remains insufficiently addressed and left to undefined risk assessment standards and practices. The only exception concerns cybersecurity assessments, given the consolidated approach and guidance of the National Cyber Security Centre.[96] This lack of precision in the substantive requirements applicable to data and algorithmic impact assessments clearly constrains the likely effectiveness of the UK's approach to embedding technology-related impact assessments in the process of adoption of digital technologies for procurement governance (and, more generally, for public governance). In the absence of clear standards, data and algorithmic impact assessments will lead to inconsistent approaches and varying levels of robustness. The absence of standards will also increase the need to access specialist expertise to design and carry out the assessments. Developing such standards and creating an effective institutional mechanism to ensure compliance therewith thus remain a challenge.

3. The Need for Strengthened Digital Procurement Governance

Section 2 has shown how, both in the EU and the UK, the emerging model of AI risk regulation leaves digital procurement governance to compliance with voluntary measures such as codes of conduct or transparency standards or imposes open-ended obligations in areas without clear standards (which reduces the prospect of effective mandatory enforcement). Most such measures omit

[96] It should be noted that the current Cyber Assessment Framework is, however, not free of shortcomings and implementation challenges. See Ola Michalec, Sveta Milyaeva, and Awais Rashid, 'Regulating Digitisation of Critical Infrastructures: Recommendations to Harmonise Safety and Security of Operational Technologies' (2022) University of Bristol Policy Briefing 120 <https://www.bristol.ac.uk/policybristol/policy-briefings/digitisation-critical-infrastructure/> accessed 9 November 2022.

relevant considerations, such as risks of technological dependency or meta-risks related to the likes of digital skills and capabilities. They also fail to specify requirements for data and algorithmic impact assessments, for example, and, where standards are more specific (notably, in relation to cybersecurity), they are still subjected to proportionality and other considerations (eg state-of-the-art) that make them difficult to specify and implement, with the responsibility for such interpretation and implementation largely left to the adopting organization. This follows general trends of AI risk regulation[97] and evidences the emergence of a (sub)model highly dependent on self-regulation and self-assessment.[98]

This section criticizes this regulatory approach by stressing that the public buyer is not in an adequate position to drive self-regulation—which leads to a very significant risk of regulatory capture in the specification and implementation of the relevant impact assessment standards. The shortcomings in the emerging model also concern a lack of adequate mechanisms for contestability and accountability, which relate to both the intrinsic limitations of information-based governance disclosures, and to the inadequacy of procedure-specific challenges as a regulatory tool to control the adoption of digital technologies for procurement governance.

3.1 Self-Regulation: Outsourcing Impact Assessment Regulation to the Private Sector

The absence of mandatory standards for data and algorithmic impact assessments, as well as the embedded flexibility in the standards for cybersecurity, not only are bound to generate significant costs and barriers to compliance with voluntary standards,[99] but also to outsource the setting of the substantive requirements for those impact assessments to private vendors offering solutions for digital procurement governance. With limited public sector digital capability preventing a detailed specification of the applicable requirements,[100] it is likely that these will be restricted to a general obligation for tenderers to provide an impact assessment plan, perhaps by reference to

[97] Except for the EU AI Act (n 17) in relation to high-risk AI uses.

[98] See Chapter 1, Section 3.

[99] eg due to the need for digital expertise to design and evaluate different approaches, as well as the lack of standardization across procurement procedures carried out by different (or even the same) public buyers.

[100] See Chapter 8, especially Section 4.

emerging (international private) standards.[101] This could be part of the technical compliance assessment, but is more likely to be seen as a quality aspect of tender evaluation, as the absence of standards makes it more difficult to structure the assessment of such plans as a pass/fail criterion.[102] Such an approach would imply the outsourcing of standard-setting for risk assessments to private standard-setting organizations[103] and, in the absence of those standards, to the tenderers themselves.

This generates a clear risk of regulatory capture,[104] whereby private operators can set the threshold of, for example, acceptable data and algorithmic governance practices and can do so to their advantage.[105] Digital governance would then be commercially determined,[106] and limited public sector capability would be no adequate check or balance in a technologically and oftentimes economically unequal relationship.[107] The public buyer would be a norm-taker, which runs opposite to the regulatory function expected of procurement (see Part II).

Moreover, this approach gives tech providers two bites of the cherry. In that regard, it should be stressed that these risk assessments are not only meant to be a technology implementation tool, but also (and primarily) a counterbalance

[101] eg ISO/IEC 23053:2022 Framework for Artificial Intelligence (AI) Systems Using Machine Learning (ML).

[102] Qualitative approaches may be adopted where there is limited awareness or understanding of the existing standards, see DanSense, 'Analysis of Public Sector Procurement Activities—A Report on Referencing Standards in Public Procurement' (2019) <https://www.cencenelec.eu/media/CEN-CENELEC/Areas%20of%20Work/CEN%20sectors/Services/Quicklinks%20General/analysis_publicsector_procurement.pdf> accessed 11 November 2022.

[103] See Sarah Schoenmaekers, 'Standards on the Rise in Procurement Procedures: Are Legitimacy Concerns Justified?' in Eliantonio and Cauffman, *Legitimacy of Standardisation as Regulation* (n 29) 203.

[104] See Chapter 6, Section 6.

[105] For related discussion of recent trends in the cybersecurity field, see Benjamin Farrand and Helena Carrapico, 'Digital Sovereignty and Taking Back Control: From Regulatory Capitalism to Regulatory Mercantilism in EU Cybersecurity' (2022) 31 European Security 435. See also Helena Carrapico and Benjamin Farrand, '"Dialogue, Partnership and Empowerment for Network and Information Security": The Changing Role of the Private Sector from Objects of Regulation to Regulation Shapers' (2017) 67 Crime, Law and Social Change 245.

[106] There is a rich literature on the commercial determinants of health, the insights of which directly transfer to other areas of public policy exposed to an imbalance of power or to contestable approaches to the evidence to be included in cost-benefit analysis. For a general overview, see Nason Maani, Mark Petticrew, and Sandro Galea (eds), *The Commercial Determinants of Health* (OUP 2022). See also Ilona Kickbusch, 'Addressing the Interface of the Political and Commercial Determinants of Health' (2012) 27 Health Promotion International 427; and Ole Petter Ottersen and others, 'The Political Origins of Health Inequity: Prospects for Change' (2014) 383 Lancet 630.

[107] The need for strong internal capabilities to drive similar processes in the GovTech field has been rightly stressed; see Nitesh Bharosa, 'The Rise of GovTech: Trojan Horse or Blessing in Disguise? A Research Agenda' (2022) 39 Government Information Quarterly 101692, and European Parliament, 'The Digital Single Market and the Digitalisation of the Public Sector: GovTech and Other Innovations in Public Procurement' (2022) <https://data.europa.eu/doi/10.2861/830794> accessed 17 October 2022.

to the allure of the potential benefits of digital technologies in the initial stages of decision-making processes leading to their adoption.[108] The vulnerability of the risk assessment process can compound the risk of capture generated by the 'policy irresistibility' of the technology itself, thus exacerbating its potential negative effects under the guise of countervailing governance tools. Incorrect, biased, or insufficient risk assessments can minimize, downplay, or omit relevant risks, thus eschewing the cost-benefit analysis related to the adoption of the technological solution.[109] Given that private vendors stand to benefit from such risk of 'techno optimism',[110] governance mechanisms need to ensure robust checks and balances for decisions on the adoption of digital technologies, not the opposite.

In addition to the general concerns about the way in which private standards are set and the (marginal) place of public interest considerations in that process,[111] there is a further practical consideration that highlights the inadequacy of this approach in procurement governance. Given the public buyer's limited digital competence, it is not best placed to effectively manage a process reliant on private inputs. In any given procurement process, contestation of the specific plans for the implementation of data or algorithmic impact assessments proposed by the tenderers seems unlikely because the public buyer will not generally be in a good position to evaluate them. Given that limited capability to evaluate, there is also a disincentive for tenderers to move beyond (faulty, insufficient) standards and specifications where there are associated costs, or in ways that could open them up to disqualification or lower the evaluation of their tenders, especially if this led to considering their tenders as variants or as non-compliant (with the related, private standard). It is also possible that the evaluation of the impact assessment strategy is itself outsourced to technical consultants brought in to support the process. This would further erode the likelihood of challenge of impact assessment approaches geared towards the interest of private industry, rather than the public buyer (and, more generally, the public interest the latter is meant to pursue).

[108] See Chapters 6 and 8.

[109] Making the same points, in the context of health policy, see Rob Ralston, 'The Informal Governance of Public-Private Partnerships in UK Obesity Policy: Collaborating on Calorie Reduction or Reducing Effectiveness?' (2021) 289 Social Science & Medicine 114451.

[110] For discussion, see Simon Vydra and Bram Klievink, 'Techno-Optimism and Policy-Pessimism in the Public Sector Big Data Debate' (2019) 36 Government Information Quarterly 101383.

[111] For discussion, see Harm Schepel, 'Between Standards and Regulation. On the Concept of "de facto mandatory standards" after Tuna II and Fra.bo' in Panagiotis Delimatsis (ed), *The Law, Economics and Politics of International Standardisation* (CUP 2015) 199.

While this could be seen as only relatively problematic in a setting with strong accountability and challenge mechanisms to scrutinize the decisions made by the public buyer, the following subsection will show that this is not the situation under the emerging model. Consequently, outsourcing the regulation of the impact assessment is concerning.

3.2 Self-Assessment: Inadequacy of Mechanisms for Contestability and Accountability

Section 2 has shown how emerging models primarily rely on self-assessment, as public buyers are expected to carry out risk assessments rather than being subject to external controls.[112] Importantly, public buyers will rarely develop the relevant technological solutions but rather acquire them from technological providers. In that case, the duty to carry out the self-assessment will (or should be) cascaded down to the tech provider through contractual obligations.[113] This would place the tech provider as 'first party' and the public buyer as 'second party' in relation to assuring compliance with the applicable (or voluntary) obligations—that is, it creates a 'second party assurance model'.[114] In a setting of limited public sector digital capability, and in part as a result of a lack of clear standards providing an applicable benchmark, the self-assessment of compliance with risk management requirements will either be *de facto* outsourced to private vendors (through a lack of challenge of their practices), or carried out by public buyers with limited capabilities (eg during the oversight of contract implementation). Even where public buyers have the required digital capabilities to carry out a more thorough analysis, they lack independence.[115] It should be stressed that 'second party' assurance models unavoidably raise questions about their integrity due to the conflicting interests of the assurance provider who wants to use the system (ie the public buyer).[116]

[112] Except for the UK's central government spend control. See Section 2.2.1.

[113] This is clear in the EU's approach; Living-In EU, Proposal for standard contractual clauses for the procurement of artificial intelligence by public organisations, version 0.9 (2022) <https://living-in.eu/sites/default/files/files/Draft%20AI%20Clauses_1.pdf> accessed 21 October 2022. Interestingly, there seems to be an initiative in the UK horizon too; CDEI, 'Algorithmic Transparency Guidance' (n 85) 8.

[114] For broader discussion of the role of the public buyer in reinforcing corporate compliance in the context of procurement, see Pedro Telles and Grith Skovgaard Ølykke, 'Sustainable Procurement: A Compliance Perspective of EU Public Procurement Law' (2017) 12 European Procurement & Public Private Partnership Law Review 239.

[115] See Chapter 3, Section 2.2.

[116] Centre for Data Ethics and Innovation, 'AI assurance guide (beta)' (2022) <https://cdeiuk.github.io/ai-assurance-guide/independence/> access 11 November 2022.

Presumably to try to address this issue, the emerging model also shows a tendency towards promoting the publication of (parts of) the self-assessment to foster accountability. This builds a mechanism of disclosure-based regulation with two shortcomings. First, it fails to tackle the limitations of information-based governance disclosures. Second, it does not create clear mechanisms for contestation.

Indeed, the creation of an assurance model based on open-ended standards largely mimics the approach to self-assessment that is increasingly criticized in the cognate field of AI ethics.[117] In building disclosure mechanisms around such open-ended standards, the model replicates features in the design of information-based governance via (voluntary) disclosure that have consistently been problematic, for example in corporate governance and financial markets.[118] It creates a mediated transparency system that potentially disempowers public buyers by enabling tech providers to set the conditions and content of the relevant disclosures.[119]

In the absence of clearly specified standards, assessing information disclosures is complicated by the lack of a readily available benchmark, which not only reduces comparability across disclosures, but also raises the cost of engaging in the assessment. There is also a clear risk that disclosures become primarily qualitative or provide limited information, in which case assessing the practice underlying the disclosure becomes even more complicated.[120] It also creates fuzziness under a 'comply or explain' approach, as compliance with diffuse standards that need to be interpreted or specified by the disclosing entity (and thus explained) becomes practically indistinguishable from alternative explanations given for (partial) non-compliance. It also tends to equate compliance and the provision of an explanation as equally satisfactory when, in fact, they tend not to be. Given the evolution in other fields towards a system of 'apply and explain' where standards and requirements are open-ended,[121] the

[117] For discussion, see Luke Munn, 'The Uselessness of AI Ethics' (2022) AI and Ethics <https://doi.org/10.1007/s43681-022-00209-w> accessed 11 November 2022.

[118] See Andrew J Charlesworth, 'Regulating Algorithmic Assemblages: Looking Beyond Corporatist AI Ethics' in Uta Kohl and Jacob Eisler (eds), *Data-Driven Personalisation in Markets, Politics and Law* (CUP 2021) 243.

[119] Along the same lines, see Madalina Busuioc, Deirdre Curtin, and Marco Almada, 'Reclaiming Transparency: Contesting the Logics of Secrecy within the EU AI Act' (2023) 2(1) European Law Open 79.

[120] David Seidl, Paul Sanderson, and John Roberts, 'Applying the "Comply-or-Explain" Principle: Discursive Legitimacy Tactics with Regard to Codes of Corporate Governance' (2013) 17 Journal of Management & Governance 791.

[121] For discussion, see Aino Asplund, 'Lost in Accountability. "Comply or Explain", "Apply or Explain" and "Apply and Explain" in a Test: The Barriers to Company Benefit?' (2020) 13 International and Comparative Corporate Law Journal 111.

emerging approach seems both particularly inapt and partly obsolete. This is a limitation to the effectiveness of disclosure mechanisms, as it is unlikely that the information disclosed will enable accountability where it is of poor quality, limited, or difficult to assess.[122]

Even where disclosures are of an adequate quality and provide sufficient detail, they may not generate effective accountability. In the emerging model, the purpose of (voluntary) transparency obligations is not entirely clear, as there is a lack of pre-defined accountability mechanisms or channels, other than informal processes to influence the behaviour of the public buyer (eg through the media or academic publications). This lack of mechanisms to react to disclosures challenges their adequacy as a regulatory tool in this context,[123] as there is no obvious immediate avenue to correct shortcomings, for example in the design or implementation of data and algorithmic impact assessments. While the decisions to adopt digital solutions by a public buyer should be amenable to judicial review, the tests (eg on active standing) applicable to such decisions are not always conducive to broad reviews and the courts can easily refuse to second-guess decisions framed in terms of administrative or technical (or technological) discretion. This largely shields the initial decision from scrutiny.

Moreover, the emergent model delays publication of the (voluntary) disclosures, potentially until after the deployment of the technological solutions.[124] This has the knock-on effect of delaying any external validation (and contestation) of the related risk assessments. In many cases, shortcomings in the risk assessments and the related minimization and mitigation measures will only become observable after the materialization of the underlying harms. For example, the effects of the adoption of a defective digital solution for decision-making support (eg a recommender system) will only emerge in relation to challengeable decisions in subsequent procurement procedures that rely on such solution. At that point, undoing the effects of the use of the tool may be impossible or excessively costly. This makes challenges based on procedure-specific harms, such as the possibility to challenge discrete procurement decisions under the general rules on procurement remedies, inadequate.[125] Not

[122] For discussion, see Andrew Keay, 'Comply or Explain in Corporate Governance Codes: In Need of Greater Regulatory Oversight?' (2014) 34 Legal Studies 279.

[123] Paula J Dalley, 'The Use and Misuse of Disclosure as a Regulatory System' (2007) 34(4) Florida State University Law Review 1089.

[124] See Section 2.2.2 on the UK algorithmic transparency standard.

[125] Arguing for a 'wide angle' perspective on collective harms resulting from governmental use of AI, see Colin Gavaghan and others, 'Government Use of Artificial Intelligence in New Zealand' (2019) 61–62 <https://ourarchive.otago.ac.nz/bitstream/handle/10523/9372/NZLF%20report.pdf> accessed 5 April 2023. The reasoning is the same applicable in relation to data protection risks; see Lilian Edwards and Michael Veale, 'Slave to the Algorithm? Why a "Right to an Explanation" Is Probably Not the

least, because there can be negative systemic harms that are very hard to capture in the challenge to discrete decisions, or for which no agent with active standing has adequate incentives.[126] To avoid potential harms more effectively, *ex ante* external controls are needed instead.[127]

4. Conclusion

This chapter has taken the perspective of risk-based regulation to focus on the governance of impact assessment mechanisms seeking to control risk-taking in the process of adoption of digital technologies for procurement governance. An analysis of emerging regulatory approaches in the EU and the UK has shown that, except for high-risk AI uses, the adoption of digital technologies by public buyers is largely unregulated and only subjected to voluntary measures, or to open-ended obligations in areas without clear standards (which reduces the prospect of effective mandatory enforcement). In the model of the proposed EU AI Act, for most technological deployments, the primary decision whether to adopt digital technologies (and thus take the related risks) is unconstrained and subject only to compliance with voluntary codes of conduct. While there are specific obligations emerging from a patchwork of EU digital law instruments, those refer to open-ended standards that require advanced technical capabilities to operationalize them (see Chapter 8). In the UK, despite a wide range of guidance and a voluntary algorithmic transparency standard, the situation is similar because all guidance refers to undefined impact assessment standards and practices. The only exception concerns cybersecurity impact assessments, which are more developed. A technology and digital spend approval mechanism that could generate *ex ante* scrutiny of the decision to acquire digital solutions by central government organizations is equally limited in its cross-reference to the same guidance. All relevant guidance is ultimately difficult to operationalize without advanced digital skills or prior experience.

Remedy You Are Looking for' (2017) 16(1) Duke Law & Technology Review 18; Margot E Kaminski, 'Binary Governance: Lessons from the GDPR's Approach to Algorithmic Accountability' (2019) 92 Southern California Law Review 1529.

126 For related discussion in the field of green procurement, see Roberto Caranta, 'Opening the Doors to Civil Society Litigation in Public Contracts' (*REALaw blog*, 1 November 2022) <https://realaw.blog/2022/11/01/opening-the-doors-to-civil-society-litigation-in-public-contracts-by-r-caranta/> accessed 15 November 2022.

127 Margot E Kaminski, 'Regulating the Risks of AI' (2023) 103 Boston University Law Review, forthcoming, at 19 <https://ssrn.com/abstract=4195066> accessed 4 November 2022.

Halonen, Kirsi-Maria, Roberto Caranta, and Albert Sanchez-Graells (eds), *Transparency in EU Procurements: Disclosure within Public Procurement and During Contract Execution* (Edward Elgar 2019).

Herrera Anchustegui, Ignacio, *Buyer Power in EU Competition Law* (Concurrences 2017).

Hildebrandt, Mireille, *Smart Technologies and the End(s) of Law* (Edward Elgar 2015).

Janssen, Willem A, *Public Procurement Law and Self-Organisation: A Nexus of Tensions and Reconciliations* (Eleven Publishers 2018).

Kingdon, John W, *Agendas, Alternatives and Public Policies* (HarperCollins 1984).

La Rosa, Stephane de and Patricia Valcarcel Fernandez (eds), *Principles of Public Contracts in Europe* (Bruylant 2022).

Larsson, Anthony and Robin Teigland (eds), *Digital Transformation and Public Services. Societal Impacts in Sweden and Beyond* (Routledge 2020).

Leskovec, Jure, Anand Rajaraman, and Jeffrey David Ullman, *Mining of Massive Datasets* (3rd edn, CUP 2020).

Maani, Nason, Mark Petticrew, and Sandro Galea (eds), *The Commercial Determinants of Health* (OUP 2022).

Maxwell, Jack and Joe Tomlinson, *Experiments in Automating Immigration Systems* (Bristol UP 2022).

Mazzucatto, Mariana, *Mission Economy. A Moonshot Guide to Changing Capitalism* (Allen Lane 2021).

McCrudden, Christopher, *Buying Social Justice. Equality, Government Procurement, & Legal Change* (OUP 2007).

McGillivray, Kevin, *Government Cloud Procurement. Contracts, Data Protection, and the Quest for Compliance* (CUP 2022).

McQuillan, Dan, *Resisting AI. An Anti-Fascist Approach to Artificial Intelligence* (Bristol UP 2023).

Molnar, Christoph, *Interpretable Machine Learning. A Guide for Making Black Box Models Explainable* (2nd edn, 2022) <https://christophm.github.io/interpretable-ml-book/scope-of-interpretability.html> accessed 24 February 2023.

Obendiek, Anke Sophia, *Data Governance: Value Orders and Jurisdictional Conflicts* (OUP 2022).

Pasquale, Frank, *The Black Box Society. The Secret Algorithms that Control Money and Information* (Harvard UP 2015).

Renieris, Elizabeth M, *Beyond Data. Reclaiming Human Rights at the Dawn of the Metaverse* (MIT Press 2023).

Richardson, Jeremy, *Policy-Making in the EU. Interests, Ideas and Garbage Cans of Primeval Soup* (Taylor & Francis 1996).

Sanchez-Graells, Albert, *Public Procurement and the EU Competition Rules* (2nd edn, Hart Publishing 2015).

Sanchez-Graells, Albert (ed), *Smart Public Procurement and Labour Standards. Pushing the Discussion after RegioPost* (Hart Publishing 2018).

Schrepel, Thibault, *Blockchain + Antitrust. The Decentralization Formula* (Edward Elgar 2021).

Steinicke, Michael and Peter L Vesterdorf, *Brussels Commentary on EU Public Procurement Law* (Hart Publishing 2018).

Stucke, Maurice E and Allen P Grunes, *Big Data and Competition Policy* (OUP 2016).

Tan, Evrim and Joep Crompvoets, *The New Digital Era Governance. How New Digital Technologies Are Shaping Public Governance* (Wageningen Academic 2022).

Torfing, Jacob and others, *Public Governance Paradigms. Competing and Co-Existing* (Edward Elgar 2020).

The emerging model of AI risk regulation in the EU and the UK thus follows the more general trends discussed in Chapter 1, and points at the consolidation of a (sub)model of risk-based digital procurement governance that strongly relies on self-regulation and self-assessment. However, given its limited digital capabilities, the public sector is not best placed to control or influence the process of self-regulation, which results in the outsourcing of crucial regulatory tasks to technology vendors and the consequent risk of regulatory capture and suboptimal design of commercially determined governance mechanisms. These risks are compounded by the emerging 'second party assurance' model, as self-assessments by technology vendors would not be adequately scrutinized by public buyers, either due to a lack of digital capabilities or the unavoidable structural conflicts of interest of assurance providers with an interest in the use of the technology, or both. This 'second party' assurance model does not include adequate challenge mechanisms despite efforts to disclose (parts of) the relevant self-assessments. Such disclosures are constrained by general problems with 'comply or explain' information-based governance mechanisms, with the emerging model showing design features that have proven problematic in other contexts (such as corporate governance and financial market regulation) and galvanizing a mediated transparency mechanism that gives tech providers control over the conditions and content of the relevant disclosures. Moreover, there is no clear mechanism to contest the decisions revealed by the disclosures, including in the context of (delayed) specific uses of the technological solutions.

Overall, the chapter has demonstrated how the emerging model is unable to neutralize the risks of regulatory capture and commercial determination identified throughout the case study of procurement digitalization (Chapters 6–8), and that it is a model leading to the privatization of technology regulation. Therefore, in line with the proposal in Chapter 5, this chapter concludes by submitting that a preferable option would be to assign the approval of the decisions to adopt digital technologies and the verification of the relevant risks assessments to a centralized authority also tasked with setting the applicable requirements therefor—the notional 'AI in the Public Sector Authority' (AIPSA). AIPSA would thus be placed as gatekeeper of the process of transition to digital procurement governance, instead of the atomized imposition of this role on public buyers, which this Part III has evidenced as unable to regulate the process of public sector digitalization.

PART IV
CONCLUSION

10
Conclusion

This book has explored the role of public procurement in the 'digital transformation' of the public sector. Such transformation is taking place in a context where fast-paced technological innovation and speedy adoption of immature technologies across the public sector far outstrip progress in digital regulation. Public sector digitalization will continue to accelerate, as governments seek both to use the public sector as a source of funding and a site of experimentation to boost domestic tech industries, and to deploy technology as the next stage of 'streamlining' or modernization of their public services. In contrast, even if further advances in digital regulation follow from the current prominence in political agendas of digital technologies—and Artificial Intelligence (AI) in particular—the regulatory framework will be slow to settle around a new model of public digital governance.

Now, and for the foreseeable future, there is a regulatory gap that leaves the adoption of digital technologies by the public sector largely unregulated, as well as exposed to regulatory capture and commercial determination. This creates significant risks of privatization of regulatory power. The adoption of digital technologies also implies the acceptance of risks and harms. This jeopardizes fundamental and other individual rights and social interests affected by the functioning of an increasingly tech-dependent public sector and by the digitalized provision of public services. Mounting evidence of the discrimination, exclusion, and other violations of fundamental rights that can result from unregulated technological deployments by the public sector fuels calls for effective regulation of the 'digital public sector'. However, such regulation is proving slow to emerge. Meanwhile, the public sector keeps acquiring and deploying digital technology.

In this context, there is an emerging regulatory intuition or consensus that, being the entry point for digital technologies into the public sector, public procurement could act as a regulatory gatekeeper. By mobilizing the public sector's buying power, procurement could ensure that the public sector acted as a 'responsible buyer' and that the adopted digital technologies met public interest goals such as trustworthiness, responsibility, explainability, transparency,

Digital Technologies and Public Procurement. Albert Sanchez-Graells, Oxford University Press.
 DOI: 10.1093/oso/9780198866770.003.0010

safety, or high levels of robustness, interoperability, and cybersecurity. This intuition frames public procurement as a 'regulatory fix' or stopgap in the absence of more general regulation of the 'digital public sector'. Public procurement could 'regulate by contract' the process of public sector digitalization and, in doing so, it could emerge as a beacon of standards and best practices that could then be propagated to the entire economy. The public buyer would be a gatekeeper and digital regulator. This would be an appealing regulatory strategy, as it would not require the development of new institutions or rules. It would also be appealing in its apparent simplicity and flexibility. It is thus likely to be a regulatory strategy advocated for, or pursued, in many jurisdictions. Focusing on the EU and the UK to allow for detailed analysis, the book has tested this intuition or regulatory strategy against the basic requirements of effective regulation and gatekeeping: skills, independence, and effective enforcement tools.

The book has stressed how the existing and growing gap in the public sector's digital skills undermines the ability of public procurement to act as an effective gatekeeper and regulator. A digitally unskilled public buyer is a weak buyer unable to critically scrutinize claims around the offered digital technologies, and thus exposed to the 'policy irresistibility' of 'tech fixes' for governance problems. An unskilled buyer can give excessive weight to techno-solutionist claims based on a shallow understanding of different digital technologies and their functionality. The book explored this issue in the context of procurement digitalization, where governance depends on the public sector's ability to face the challenges of information intensity and information complexity underpinning decision-making. This makes procurement digitalization particularly suited to claims that digital technologies can generate significant governance gains. The analysis has shown how, despite the seemingly endless possibilities for digital technologies to transform public procurement, a closer look at their limited functionalities and the significant enablers required to harness them evidences that their likely contribution is incremental rather than transformational. This insight reshapes the narratives surrounding procurement digitalization policymaking. Crucially, only a public buyer capable of plotting such a feasibility boundary and able to tame the expectations around digital technology deployment could avoid commercial capture and the related engagement in excessive experimentation with immature technologies ultimately incapable of providing desired functional improvements to procurement governance. Moreover, the book showed that a digitally unskilled public buyer can be captured and out-negotiated by tech providers. A digitally unskilled public buyer is also unable to design contractual mechanisms to effectively harness tools of 'regulation by contract'. Limited digital skills hamper public buyers' ability to comply with the growing thicket of requirements and obligations arising from new digital laws and to cascade them down to tech providers through contractual requirements. A public buyer overwhelmed by such digital governance requirements is likely to use its discretion and the flexibility of the procurement rules in ways that do not necessarily protect the public interest. A digitally unskilled public buyer is also likely to be over-reliant on tech consultants to try to plug its digital skills gap, but this will generate additional regulatory challenges and further erode the public buyer's ability to avoid commercial capture. A digitally unskilled public buyer cannot be an effective gatekeeper.

The book has also shown that the regulatory challenge is not 'merely practical' and would not be solved through adequate resourcing to provide the public sector with the digital talent it requires. There is an unavoidable limitation stemming from institutional design and embeddedness that undermines procurement's digital regulation role. The book has shown how the role assigned to procurement puts it in the position of a two-sided gatekeeper needing to discipline not only the behaviour of tech providers but also, and crucially, that of the public sector entities seeking to deploy the technology. Procurement must not only ensure that the technology is trustworthy, but also that it is deployed responsibly by the public sector user. There is no guarantee that public sector entities will be committed to goals of digital regulation due to operational imperatives and their own risks of capture. Given current pressures and political priorities around public sector digitalization, there is a 'window of opportunity' for policy formulation and implementation that can be exploited not only by tech companies, but also by internal 'policy entrepreneurs'. These agents may not be committed to goals of digital regulation which are not aligned with their own interests. This increases the importance of robust regulatory controls and mechanisms such as impact assessments for the adequate identification, mitigation, and management of the risks and harms inherent in the adoption of digital technologies. However, such controls and mechanisms cannot be effective where they depend on self-assessments by the entities seeking to adopt the technologies, or on self-assessments by the tech companies seeking to provide them. In that context, procurement is expected to oversee and ensure the adequacy of those assessments, but it lacks the independence to do so. And, even if procurement were to take an independent view of the planned technological deployments, it would not be able to impose requirements or to prevent specific technology uses by entities that hold a position of hierarchical superiority within the public sector, or that can veto procurement procedures. Procurement is undermined by its institutional embedding and lacks the independence required to act as a gatekeeper and regulator. Moreover, procurement is not necessarily involved in the entire lifecycle of deployment of digital technologies by the public sector. Procurement's attempts to regulate such deployment by contract could easily be side-lined and rendered ineffective where the interests of the adopting public sector entity and the tech provider aligned in ways that deviate from the contractual regime designed by procurement. The book has shown that a regulatory contract whose implementation depends on the decisions of those whose behaviour it seeks to constrain cannot be an effective regulatory mechanism. A dependent or subordinated public buyer cannot be an effective gatekeeper.

Further, the book has shown that even if the public buyer could be (sufficiently) independent, it would not have adequate tools to regulate public sector digitalization by contract. Procurement procedures are meant to be geared towards generating competition for public contracts. This market-like design prevents technological determinism and requires public buyers to consider functional equivalents in all cases. The logic and purpose of procurement rules thus prevents or significantly complicates the setting of strict mandatory requirements that would put specific technological solutions at a disadvantage. Moreover, public buyers are not in a good position to fully describe the technology they seek to buy and frequently refer to technical standards or to the industry's state-of-the-art. Such standards tend to be used to facilitate comparability across tenders submitted by competing tech providers and, where relevant, to specify the way in which regulatory requirements need to be discharged. However, the book has shown how there are significant difficulties in translating the goals of digital regulation into technical standards, in part due to the fuzziness of those goals, and in part due to their contested nature. Differently from other areas of technical standardization, there are currently no accepted metrics or methodologies to test for specific regulatory goals. The book has shown how, for example, it is nigh impossible to come up with a standard, simple, and deployable understanding of what 'explainability' means in the context of public sector AI adoption. However, technical standards on AI explainability are emerging. If a public buyer relies on such standards, it will also be relying on the (invisible) 'hard choices' embedded in them without necessarily interrogating the extent to which the standard captures and leads towards implementing the requirements of explainability in the relevant context of use by the public sector. This could eventually result in breaches of fundamental guarantees, such as the duty to give reasons in administrative decision-making. Ultimately, in the digital technology space, reliance on immature and still evolving standards and solutions is problematic. It is also problematic that emerging standards are not developed in ways that ensure the public interest is sufficiently considered and protected. Technical standards are largely private standards in the sense of advancing the industry's views and interests in the contested space of digital regulation. If procurement was to rely on those standards, rather than acting as a gatekeeper and rule-setter, it would be acting as a rule-taker and a facilitator of the diffusion of industry-determined norms of digital regulation. Procurement would be creating a second-party assurance mechanism unable to guarantee that technological deployments met the goals of digital regulation it is meant to be enforcing. Even if third-party certification mechanisms were to be developed, for example in the context of AI safety, for as long as they relied on the same industry-led (and procurement-endorsed) standards, the same issues would arise. Moreover, in relation to procurement digitalization, the book has shown how the increasing complexity of data and technology governance requirements faced by public buyers raises the difficulty of designing tender and contract requirements to ensure compliance, even where the relevant goals are not contested. A public buyer that cannot entirely prescribe the characteristics of the technology it buys and that relies on industry-led conceptual and technical standards and assessments cannot be an effective gatekeeper.

Both by reference to theoretical analysis and the detailed case study of procurement digitalization as a site of unregulated public sector technological experimentation, the book has thus shown that the intuition that procurement can act as an effective gatekeeper of the public interest in the process of public sector digitalization is misleading and cannot achieve the regulatory goals it seeks. It has demonstrated that 'regulation by contract' is a strategy incapable of closing the regulatory gap left by the absence of general legislation and rules controlling the accelerating process of public sector digitalization. The primary conclusion of the book is thus that public procurement cannot, by itself, ensure the trustworthy digital transformation of the public sector. In view of this, the book has put forward a stylized proposal for a different regulatory strategy to address the skills, independence, and enforcement mechanisms lacking in the 'regulation by contract' approach. Through a proposal to create a notional 'AI in the Public Sector Authority' (AIPSA), the book has stressed the need to create an independent regulatory body tasked with monitoring the process of public sector digitalization. AIPSA would need to be designed and implemented in a way that ensured it had the required digital skills and political independence, as the mechanisms most likely to reduce the risks of regulatory capture and commercial determination stemming from the shortcomings in the institutional design of the procurement function. To address the additional risks stemming from procurement's exposure to commercial determination and excessive reliance on industry's understandings and specification of regulatory goals through technical standards and best practices, AIPSA's main role would be twofold. First, it would be tasked with certifying technical standards to ensure they adequately encapsulated and protected the public interest. Second, it would be tasked with licensing or permissioning the adoption of digital technologies by the public sector. There would be additional benefits in such a change of regulatory strategy, including a systematic increase of the transparency surrounding public sector digitalization. It would also slow down the process of adoption of digital technologies by the public sector, which would reduce the likelihood that the acquisition of digital technologies under the current deregulatory framework will lead to the accumulation of a stock of technological solutions that cannot be brought into compliance with the stated goals of digital regulation.

The book has provided a detailed technology-centred legal analysis of the regulatory context in which the public sector is 'digitally transforming' at pace. It has shown the flaws in the intuition or regulatory strategy of placing procurement as a digital regulation gatekeeper tasked with 'regulating by contract' public sector digitalization. It has advanced an alternative regulatory strategy based on core elements of regulatory theory, such as the need to ensure capability, independence, and effective enforcement in regulatory design. The book has thus contributed to current policymaking debates surrounding digital technology regulation and ruled out a regulatory strategy that was gaining traction. It has also contributed to broader debates of digital constitutionalism to the extent that it is focused on the ways in which the transition towards a new model of digital public governance needs to be regulated if the process is to be led by public interest considerations. The detailed case study in the book has also provided actionable insights into the more specific regulation and policymaking related to procurement digitalization. While the details of the case study are likely to lose relevance as time goes by and technology and governance frameworks continue to evolve, the author hopes that the way it fleshes out the more abstract challenges discussed in the theoretical part of the book will remain relevant.

Bibliography

Books

Arrowsmith, Sue, *The Law of Public and Utilities Procurement. Regulation in the EU and UK*, vol 1 (3rd edn, Sweet & Maxwell 2014).

Arrowsmith, Sue and Peter Kunzlik (eds), *Social and Environmental Policies in EC Procurement Law. New Directives and New Directions* (CUP 2009).

Ashley, Kevin D, *Artificial Intelligence and Legal Analytics. New Tools for Law Practice in the Digital Age* (CUP 2017).

Bradford, Anu, *The Brussels Effect. How the European Union Rules the World* (OUP 2020).

Caranta, Roberto and Martin Trybus (eds), *The Law of Green and Social Procurement in Europe* (DJØF Publishing 2010).

Caranta, Roberto and Albert Sanchez-Graells (eds), *European Public Procurement. Commentary on Directive 2014/24/EU* (Edward Elgar 2021).

Cerqueira Gomes, Pedro, *EU Public Procurement and Innovation. The Innovation Partnership Procedure and Harmonization Challenges* (Edward Elgar 2021).

Chesterman, Simon, *We, the Robots? Regulating Artificial Intelligence and the Limits of the Law* (CUP 2021).

Chinen, Mark, *The International Governance of Artificial Intelligence* (Edward Elgar 2023).

Coffee, John C, *Gatekeepers: The Professions and Corporate Governance* (OUP 2006).

Cohen, Julie, *Between Truth and Power: The Legal Constructions of Informational Capitalism* (OUP 2019).

Collingridge, David, *The Social Control of Technology* (Pinter 1980).

Collins, Hugh, *Regulating Contracts* (OUP 1999).

Cooter, Robert D and Michael D Gilbert, *Public Law and Economics* (OUP 2022).

Davies, Anne C L, *The Public Law of Government Contracts* (OUP 2008).

Dawson McGuinness, Tara and Hana Schank, *Power to the Public: The Promise of Public Interest Technology* (Princeton UP 2021).

De Gregorio, Giovanni, *Digital Constitutionalism in Europe. Reframing Rights and Powers in the Algorithmic Society* (CUP 2022).

Dunleavy, Patrick and others, *Digital Era Governance: IT Corporations, the State, and E-Government* (OUP 2006).

Eliantonio, Mariolina and Caroline Cauffman (eds), *The Legitimacy of Standardisation as a Regulatory Technique* (Edward Elgar 2020).

Ezrachi, Ariel and Maurice E Stucke, *Virtual Competition. The Promise and Perils of the Algorithm-Driven Economy* (Harvard UP 2016).

Fahey, Elaine, *The EU as a Global Digital Actor. Institutionalising Global Data Protection, Trade, and Cybersecurity* (Hart Publishing 2022).

Fountain, Jane E, *Building the Virtual State: Informational Technology and Institutional Change* (Brookings Institution 2001).

Groussot, Xavier, Jörgen Hettne, and Sanja Bogojevic (eds), *Law and Discretion in EU Public Procurement* (Hart Publishing 2019).

Trepte, Peter, *Regulating Procurement. Understanding the Ends and Means of Public Procurement Regulation* (OUP 2004).
Turpin, Colin, *Government Contracts* (Penguin 1972).
Vincent-Jones, Peter, *The New Public Contracting: Regulation, Responsiveness, Relationality* (OUP 2006).
Xiong, Momiao, *Artificial Intelligence and Causal Inference* (CRC Press 2022).
Zerilli, John and others, *A Citizen's Guide to Artificial Intelligence* (MIT Press 2021).

Contributions to Edited Books

Adamopoulou, Eleni and Lefteris Moussiades, 'An Overview of Chatbot Technology' in Ilias Maglogiannis, Lazaros Iliadis, and Elias Pimenidis (eds), *AIAI 2020, IFIP AICT 584* (Springer 2020) 373.
Auby, Jean-Bernard, 'Contracting out and "Public Values": A Theoretical and Comparative Approach' in Susan Rose-Ackerman, Peter L Lindseth, and Blake Emerson (eds), *Comparative Administrative Law* (2nd edn, Edward Elgar 2017) 552.
Charlesworth, Andrew J, 'Regulating Algorithmic Assemblages: Looking Beyond Corporatist AI Ethics' in Uta Kohl and Jacob Eisler (eds), *Data-Driven Personalisation in Markets, Politics and Law* (CUP 2021) 243.
Coglianese, Cary, 'Performance-Based Regulation: Concepts and Challenges' in Francesca Bignami and David Zaring (eds), *Comparative Law and Regulation* (Edward Elgar 2016) 403.
Coglianese, Cary and Evan Mendelson, 'Meta-Regulation and Self-Regulation' in Robert Baldwin, Martin Cave, and Martin Lodge (eds), *The Oxford Handbook of Regulation* (OUP 2010) 146.
Deville, Rembrandt, Nico Sergeyssels, and Catherine Middag, 'Basic Concepts of AI for Legal Scholars' in Jan De Bruyne and Cedric Vanleenhove (eds), *Artificial Intelligence and the Law* (Intersentia 2021) 1.
Dunleavy, Patrick, 'Governance and State Organization in the Digital Era' in Chrisanthi Avgerou and others (eds), *The Oxford Handbook of Information and Communication Technologies* (OUP 2009) 404.
Finck, Michèle, 'Automated Decision-Making and Administrative Law' in Peter Cane and others (eds), *The Oxford Handbook of Comparative Administrative Law* (OUP 2020) 656.
Grabosky, Peter, 'Meta-Regulation' in Peter Drahos (ed), *Regulatory Theory. Foundations and Applications* (ANU Press 2022) 149.
Gunningham, Neil and Darren Sinclair, 'Trust, Culture and the Limits of Management-Based Regulation: Lessons from the Mining Industry' in Peter Drahos (ed), *Regulatory Theory. Foundations and Applications* (ANU Press 2022) 711.
Hirsch Ballin, Ernst, 'Critical Angles in Legal Research' in *Legal Research Methods* (Edward Elgar 2020) ch 2.
Holzinger, Andreas and others, 'Explainable AI Methods—A Brief Overview' in Andreas Holzinger and others (eds), *xxAI—Beyond Explainable AI* (Springer 2022) 13.
Kohl, Uta, 'Blockchain Utopia and Its Governance Shortfalls' in Oreste Pollicino and Giovanni De Gregorio (eds), *Blockchain and Public Law. Global Challenges in the Era of Decentralisation* (Edward Elgar 2021) 13.
Koivisto, Ida, 'Thinking Inside the Box: The Promise and Boundaries of Transparency in Automated Decision-Making' in Deirdre Curtin and Mariavittoria Catanzariti (eds), *Data at the Boundaries of European Law* (OUP 2023) 66.

Maas, Matthijs M, 'Aligning AI Regulation to Sociotechnical Change' in Justin Bullock and others (eds), *The Oxford Handbook of AI Governance* (OUP 2022) <https://doi.org/10.1093/oxfordhb/9780197579329.013.22> accessed 7 March 2023.

Madan, Rohit and Mona Ashok, 'A Public Values Perspective on the Application of Artificial Intelligence in Government Practices: A Synthesis of Case Studies' in Jose Ramon Saura and Felipe Debasa (eds), *Handbook of Research on Artificial Intelligence in Government Practices and Processes* (IGI Global Publishing 2022) 162.

Miller, Charles A, 'Sunk Costs and Political Decision Making' (2019) Oxford Research Encyclopaedia of Politics <https://doi.org/10.1093/acrefore/9780190228637.013.1022> accessed 23 September 2022.

Mintrom, Michael, 'Policy Entrepreneurs and Dynamic Change' in M Ramesh and others (eds), *Cambridge Elements in Public Policy* (CUP 2020) <http://www.cambridge.org/9781108461467> accessed 7 September 2022.

Mohungoo, Idah, Irwin Brown, and Salah Kabanda, 'A Systematic Review of Implementation Challenges in Public E-Procurement' in Marie Hattingh and others (eds), *Responsible Design, Implementation and Use of Information and Communication Technology* (Springer 2020) 46.

Pacces, Alessio M, 'A Law and Economics Perspective on Normative Analysis' in Sanne Taekema, Bart van Klink, and Wouter de Been (eds), *Facts and Norms in Law. Interdisciplinary Reflections on Legal Method* (Edward Elgar 2016) 171.

Petit, Nicolas and Jerome De Cooman, 'Models of Law and Regulation for AI' in Anthony Elliott (ed), *The Routledge Social Science Handbook of AI* (Routledge 2022) 199.

Roche, Niall and Alastair Moore, 'Oracles and Internet of Things in the Internet of Value' in Nikhil Vadgama, Jiahua Xu, and Paolo Tasca (eds), *Enabling the Internet of Value. How Blockchain Connects Global Businesses* (Springer 2022) 157.

Sanchez-Graells, Albert, 'Public Procurement and "Core" Human Rights: A Sketch of the EU Legal Framework' in Olga Martin-Ortega and Claire M O'Brien (eds), *Public Procurement and Human Rights: Risks, Dilemmas and Opportunities for the State as a Buyer* (Edward Elgar 2019) 96.

Sanchez-Graells, Albert, 'Some Public Procurement Challenges in Supporting and Delivering Smart Urban Mobility: Procurement Data, Discretion and Expertise' in Michele Finck and others (eds), *Smart Urban Mobility—Law, Regulation, and Policy* (Springer 2020) 99.

Sanchez-Graells, Albert, 'Public Procurement by Central Purchasing Bodies, Competition and SMEs: Towards a More Dynamic Model?' in Carina Risvig Hamer and Mario Comba (eds), *Centralising Public Procurement—The Approach of EU Member States* (Edward Elgar 2021) 71.

Sanchez-Graells, Albert, 'State Aid and EU Public Procurement: More Interactions, Fuzzier Boundaries' in Leigh Hancher and Juan Jorge Piernas López (eds), *Research Handbook on European State Aid Law* (2nd edn, Edward Elgar 2021) 329.

Sanchez-Graells, Albert, 'Competition and Procurement Regulation' in Carina Risvig Hamer and others (eds), *Into the Northern Light—In Memory of Steen Treumer* (Ex Tuto Publishing 2022) 65.

Sanchez-Graells, Albert, 'Procurement Corruption and Artificial Intelligence: Between the Potential of Enabling Data Architectures and the Constraints of Due Process Requirements' in Sope Williams and Jessica Tillipman (eds), *Routledge Handbook of Public Procurement Corruption* (Routledge forthcoming) <https://ssrn.com/abstract=3952665> accessed 30 June 2023.

Sanchez-Graells, Albert and Ignacio Herrera Anchustegui, 'Impact of Public Procurement Aggregation on Competition: Risks, Rationale and Justification for the Rules in Directive

2014/24' in R Fernandez and P Valcarcel (eds), *Centralizacion de compras publicas* (Civitas 2016) 129.

Schepel, Harm, 'Between Standards and Regulation. On the Concept of "de facto mandatory standards" after Tuna II and Fra.bo' in Panagiotis Delimatsis (ed), *The Law, Economics and Politics of International Standardisation* (CUP 2015) 199.

Scott, Colin, 'Standard-Setting in Regulatory Regimes' in Robert Baldwin, Martin Cave, and Martin Lodge (eds), *The Oxford Handbook of Regulation* (OUP 2010) 104.

Simons, Helen, 'Case Study Research: In-Depth Understanding in Context' in Patricia Leavy (ed), *The Oxford Handbook of Qualitative Research* (2nd edn, OUP 2020) 676.

Telles, Pedro, 'Reflecting on 18 Years of Competitive Dialogue' in Carina Risvig Hamer and others (eds), *Into the Northern Light—In Memory of Steen Treumer* (Ex Tuto Publishing 2022) 193.

Telles, Pedro and Luke A Butler, 'Public Procurement Award Procedures in Directive 2014/24/EU' in François Lichere, Roberto Caranta, and Steen Treumer (eds), *Modernising Public Procurement: The New Directive* (DJØF Publishing 2014) 131.

Virdee, Tirath, 'Understanding AI' in Charles Kerrigan (ed), *Artificial Intelligence. Law and Regulation* (Edward Elgar 2022) 37.

Whalen, Ryan, *Computational Legal Studies. The Promise and Challenge of Data-Driven Research* (Edward Elgar 2020).

Whittlestone, Jess and Samuel Clarke, 'AI Challenges for Society and Ethics' in Justin Bullock and others (eds), *The Oxford Handbook of AI Governance* (OUP 2022) <https://doi.org/10.1093/oxfordhb/9780197579329.013.3> accessed 7 March 2023.

Wren-Lewis, Liam, 'Regulatory Capture: Risks and Solutions' in Antonio Estache (ed), *Emerging Issues in Competition, Collusion, and Regulation of Network Industries* (CEPR 2011) ch 7.

Yeung, Karen, Andrew Howes, and Ganna Pogrebna, 'AI Governance by Human Rights-Centered Design, Deliberation, and Oversight: An End to Ethics Washing' in Markus D Dubber and others (eds), *The Oxford Handbook of Ethics of AI* (OUP 2020) 76.

Zittrain, Jonathan, 'Intellectual Debt. With Great Power Comes Great Ignorance' in Silja Voeneky and others (eds), *The Cambridge Handbook of Responsible Artificial Intelligence. Interdisciplinary Perspectives* (CUP 2022) 176.

Journal Articles

Abbot, Carolyn and Maria Lee, 'Economic Actors in EU Environmental Law' (2015) 34(1) Yearbook of European Law 26.

Abraham, Rene, Johannes Schneider, and Jan vom Brocke, 'Data Governance: A Conceptual Framework, Structured Review, and Research Agenda' (2019) 49 International Journal of Information Management 424.

Adler, Matthew, 'Law and Incommensurability: Introduction' (1998) 146(5) University of Pennsylvania Law Review 1169.

Ageh, Kunmi, 'When Artificial Intelligence Met Public Procurement: Improving the World Bank's Suspension and Debarment System with Machine Learning' (2019) 48(3) Public Contract Law Journal 565.

Ahmed, Nur, Muntasir Wahed, and Neil C Thompson, 'The Growing Influence of Industry in AI Research' (2023) 379 Science 884.

Almada, Marco, 'Regulation by Design and the Governance of Technological Futures' (2023) European Journal of Risk Regulation, First View <https://doi.org/10.1017/err.2023.37> accessed 17 May 2023.

Alvial-Palavicino, Carla, 'The Future as Practice: A Framework to Understand Anticipation in Science and Technology' (2015) 6(2) Tecnoscienza 135.

Anderson, Robert D, Alison Jones, and William E Kovacic, 'Preventing Corruption, Supplier Collusion and the Corrosion of Civic Trust: A Procompetitive Program to Improve the Effectiveness and Legitimacy of Public Procurement' (2019) 26 George Mason Law Review 1233.

Arrowsmith, Sue, 'Horizontal Policies in Public Procurement: A Taxonomy' (2010) 10 Journal of Public Procurement 149.

Arrowsmith, Sue, 'The Purpose of the EU Procurement Directives: Ends, Means and the Implications for National Regulatory Space for Commercial and Horizontal Procurement Policies' [2012] Cambridge Yearbook of European Legal Studies 1.

Aspey, Eleanor and Richard Craven, 'Regulating Complex Contracting: A Socio-Legal Study of Decision-Making under EU and UK Law' (2018) 81 Modern Law Review 191.

Asplund, Aino, 'Lost in Accountability. "Comply or Explain", "Apply or Explain" and "Apply and Explain" in a Test: The Barriers to Company Benefit?' (2020) 13 International and Comparative Corporate Law Journal 111.

Auby, Jean-Bernard, 'Administrative Law Facing Digital Challenges' (2020) 1(1) European Review of Digital Administration & Law 7.

Bambauer, Derek E, 'Cybersecurity for Idiots' (2021) 106 Minnesota Law Review 172.

Baraggia, Antonia and Matteo Bonelli, 'Linking Money to Values: The New Rule of Law Conditionality Regulation and Its Constitutional Challenges' (2022) 23(2) German Law Journal 131.

Bastianin, Andrea and Chiara F Del Bo, 'Public Procurement in Big Science: Politics or Technology? The Case of CERN' (2021) 30(3) Industrial and Corporate Change 740.

Bauhr, Monika and others, 'Lights on the Shadows of Public Procurement: Transparency as an Antidote to Corruption' (2020) 33 Governance 495.

Beigang, Fabian, 'Reconciling Algorithmic Fairness Criteria' (2023) 51(2) Philosophy & Public Affairs 166.

Ben Dor, Lavi M, and Cary Coglianese, 'Procurement as AI Governance' (2021) 2(4) IEEE Transactions on Technology and Society 192.

Bench-Capon, Trevor, 'Thirty Years of Artificial Intelligence and Law: Editor's Introduction' (2022) 30 Artificial Intelligence and Law 475.

Benítez-Martínez, Francisco Luis and others, 'Neural Blockchain Technology for a New Anticorruption Token: Towards a Novel Governance Model' (2023) 20(1) Journal of Information Technology & Politics 1.

Bennett Moses, Lyria, 'Recurring Dilemmas: The Law's Race to Keep Up With Technological Change' (2007) 2 University of Illinois Journal of Law, Technology & Policy 239.

Beraja, Martin and others, 'AI-tocracy' (2023) 138 (3) The Quarterly Journal of Economics 1349.

Bergerson, Joule A and others, 'Life Cycle Assessment of Emerging Technologies: Evaluation Techniques at Different Stages of Market and Technical Maturity' (2020) 24 Journal of Industrial Ecology 11.

Beuve, Jean, Marian W Moszoro, and Stephane Saussier, 'Political Contestability and Public Contract Rigidity: An Analysis of Procurement Contracts' (2019) 28(2) Journal of Economics & Management Strategy 316.

Bharosa, Nitesh, 'The Rise of GovTech: Trojan Horse or Blessing in Disguise? A Research Agenda' (2022) 39 Government Information Quarterly 101692.

Binns, Reuben, 'Data Protection Impact Assessments: A Meta-Regulatory Approach' (2017) 7 International Data Privacy Law 22.

Black, Julia, 'Decentring Regulation: Understanding the Role of Regulation and Self-Regulation in a "Post-Regulatory" World' (2001) 54(1) Current Legal Problems 103.

Black, Julia, 'Constructing and Contesting Legitimacy and Accountability in Polycentric Regulatory Regimes' (2008) 2(2) Regulation & Governance 137.

Black, Julia and Robert Baldwin, 'Really Responsive Risk-Based Regulation' (2010) 32(2) Law & Policy 181.

Black, Julia and Robert Baldwin, 'When Risk-Based Regulation Aims Low: Approaches and Challenges' (2012) 6(1) Regulation & Governance 2.

Black, Julia and Robert Baldwin, 'When Risk-Based Regulation Aims Low: A Strategic Framework' (2012) 6(2) Regulation & Governance 131.

Black, Julia and Andrew Douglas Murray, 'Regulating AI and Machine Learning: Setting the Regulatory Agenda' (2019) 10(3) European Journal of Law and Technology 1.

Blanc, Florentin, 'Tools for Effective Regulation: Is "More" Always "Better"?' (2018) 9(3) European Journal of Risk Regulation 465.

Bleda, Mercedes and Julien Chicot, 'The Role of Public Procurement in the Formation of Markets for Innovation' (2020) 107 Journal of Business Research 186.

Bodo, Balazs and Heleen Janssen, 'Maintaining Trust in a Technologized Public Sector' (2022) 41(3) Policy and Society 414.

Boffa, Federico and others, 'Industry Dynamics in Digital Markets' (2022) 49(3) Journal of Industrial and Business Economics 401.

Bonnin Roca, Jaime and EoinO'Sullivan, 'The Role of Regulators in Mitigating Uncertainty Within the Valley of Death' (2020) 109 Technovation 102157.

Borodina, Marina and Mari-Ann Simovart, 'A Qualitative Step from E-Communication to E-Procurement: The Estonian E-Procurement Model' (2017) 2 Ius Publicum 6 <http://www.ius-publicum.com/repository/uploads/09_05_2022_22_14_06_Simovart_Borodina_2017_IUSPUB1.pdf> accessed 7 September 2022.

Boyle, James, 'A Nondelegation Doctrine for the Digital Age?' (2000) 50(5) Duke Law Journal 5.

Braithwaite, John, 'Enforced Self-Regulation: A New Strategy for Corporate Crime Control' (1982) 80(7) Michigan Law Review 1466.

Broomfield, Heather and Lisa Marie Reutter, 'Towards a Data-Driven Public Administration: An Empirical Analysis of Nascent Phase Implementation' (2021) 25(2) Scandinavian Journal of Public Administration 73.

Buckley, Ross P and others, 'The Road to RegTech: The (Astonishing) Example of the European Union' (2020) 21 Journal of Banking Regulation 26.

Buiten, Miriam C, 'Towards Intelligent Regulation of Artificial Intelligence' (2019) 10(1) European Journal of Risk Regulation 41.

Busuioc, Madalina, Deirdre Curtin, and Marco Almada, 'Reclaiming Transparency: Contesting the Logics of Secrecy within the EU AI Act' (2023) 2(1) European Law Open 79.

Calo, Ryan, 'Artificial Intelligence Policy: A Primer and Roadmap' (2017) 51(2) UC Davis Law Review 399.

Calo, Ryan, 'Modeling Through' (2022) 71(6) Duke Law Journal 1391.

Calo, Ryan and Danielle Keats Citron, 'The Automated Administrative State: A Crisis of Legitimacy' (2021) 70(4) Emory Law Journal 797.

Carrapico, Helena and Benjamin Farrand, '"Dialogue, Partnership and Empowerment for Network and Information Security": The Changing Role of the Private Sector from Objects of Regulation to Regulation Shapers' (2017) 67 Crime, Law and Social Change 245.

Carvalho, Raquel, 'Blockchain and Public Procurement' (2019) 6 European Journal of Comparative Law and Governance 187.

Cobbe, Jennifer, 'Administrative Law and the Machines of Government: Judicial Review of Automated Public-Sector Decision-Making' (2019) 39(4) Legal Studies 636.

Coglianese, Cary and David Lazer, 'Management-Based Regulation: Prescribing Private Management to Achieve Public Goals' (2003) 37(4) Law & Society Review 691.

Coglianese, Cary and Daniel E Walters, 'Agenda-Setting in the Regulatory State: Theory and Evidence' (2016) 68 Administrative Law Review 93.

Coglianese, Cary, 'The Limits of Performance-Based Regulation' (2017) 50(3) University of Michigan Journal of Law Reform 525.

Coglianese, Cary, 'Administrative Law in the Automated State' (2021) 105(3) Daedalus 104.

Coglianese, Cary and Erik Lampmann, 'Contracting for Algorithmic Accountability' (2021) 6 Administrative Law Review Accord 175.

Coglianese, Cary and Alicia Lai, 'Algorithm vs. Algorithm' (2022) 71(6) Duke Law Journal 1281.

Cohen, Michael D, James G March, and Johan P Olsen, 'A Garbage Can Model of Organizational Choice' (1972) 17 Administrative Science Quarterly 1.

Collington, Rosie, 'Disrupting the Welfare State? Digitalisation and the Retrenchment of Public Sector Capacity' (2022) 27(2) New Political Economy 312.

Coyle, Diane and Adrian Weller, '"Explaining" Machine Learning Reveals Policy Challenges' (2020) 368(6498) Science 1433.

Criado, Juan Ignacio and others, 'Chief Information Officers' Perceptions About Artificial Intelligence. A Comparative Study of Implications and Challenges for the Public Sector' (2020) 26(1) First Monday <https://doi.org/10.5210/fm.v26i1.10648> accessed 12 April 2023.

Crocker, Keith J and Scott E Masten, 'Regulation and Administered Contracts Revisited: Lessons from Transaction-Cost Economics for Public Utility Regulation' (1996) 9(1) Journal of Regulatory Economics 5.

Daintith, Terence, 'Regulation by Contract—The Third Prerogative' (1979) 32(1) Current Legal Problems 41.

Dalley, Paula J, 'The Use and Misuse of Disclosure as a Regulatory System' (2007) 34(4) Florida State University Law Review 1089.

Debono, Pauline, 'Transforming Public Procurement Contracts into Smart Contracts' (2019) 10 International Journal of Information Technology Project Management 16.

De Filippi, Primavera, Morshed Mannan, and Wessel Reijers, 'The Alegality of Blockchain Technology' (2022) 41(3) Policy and Society 358.

De Gregorio, Giovanni and Pietro Dunn, 'The European Risk-Based Approaches: Connecting Constitutional Dots in the Digital Age' (2022) 59(2) Common Market Law Review 47.

Derave, Charly, Nathan Genicot, and Nina Hetmanska, 'The Risks of Trustworthy Artificial Intelligence: The Case of the European Travel Information and Authorisation System' (2022) 13(3) European Journal of Risk Regulation 389.

Dobbe, Roel, Thomas Krendl Gilbert, and Yonatan Mintz, 'Hard Choices in Artificial Intelligence' (2021) 300 Artificial Intelligence 103555.

Domenech-Pascual, Gabriel, 'Thought Experiments in Law' (2021) Law and Method <https://doi.org/10.5553/REM/.000053> accessed 7 November 2022.

Dunleavy, Patrick and others, 'New Public Management Is Dead—Long Live Digital-Era Governance' (2006)16(3) Journal of Public Administration Research and Theory 467.

Edwards, Lilian and Michael Veale, 'Slave to the Algorithm? Why a "Right to an Explanation" Is Probably Not the Remedy You Are Looking for' (2017) 16(1) Duke Law & Technology Review 18.

Elsbach, Kimberly D and Ileana Stigliani, 'New Information Technology and Implicit Bias' (2019) 33 Academy of Management Perspectives 185.

Fabra, Natalia and Juan-Pablo Montero, 'Technology-Neutral Versus Technology-Specific Procurement' (2023) 133 (650) The Economic Journal 669.

Farrand, Benjamin and Helena Carrapico, 'Digital Sovereignty and Taking Back Control: From Regulatory Capitalism to Regulatory Mercantilism in EU Cybersecurity' (2022) 31 European Security 435.

Fazekas, Mihaly and Gabor Kocsis, 'Uncovering High-Level Corruption: Cross-National Objective Corruption Risk Indicators Using Public Procurement Data' (2017) 50 British Journal of Political Science 155.

Ferk, Petra, 'Can the Implementation of Full E-Procurement into Real Life Address the Real Challenges of EU Public Procurement?' (2016) 11 European Procurement & Public Private Partnership Law Review 327.

Fink, Melanie and Michele Finck, 'Reasoned A(I)administration: Explanation Requirements in EU law and the Automation of Public Administration' (2022) 47(3) European Law Review 376.

Fjelland, Ragnar, 'Why General Artificial Intelligence Will Not Be Realized' (2020) 10 Nature Humanities and Social Sciences Communications 7.

Floridi, Luciano, 'Establishing the Rules for Building Trustworthy AI' (2019) 1 Nature Machine Intelligence 261.

Floridi, Luciano, 'The Fight for Digital Sovereignty: What It Is, and Why It Matters, Especially for the EU' (2020) 33 Philosophy & Technology 369.

Freedland, Mark, 'Government by Contract and Public Law' [1994] Public Law 86.

Frydlinger, David and Oliver Hart, 'Overcoming Contractual Incompleteness: The Role of Guiding Principles' (2023) Journal of Law, Economics, and Organization, forthcoming <https://doi.org/10.1093/jleo/ewac027> accessed 2 February 2023.

Gabryelczyk, Renata, 'Has COVID-19 Accelerated Digital Transformation? Initial Lessons Learned for Public Administrations' (2020) 37(4) Information Systems Management 303.

Galaz, Victor and others, 'Artificial Intelligence, Systemic Risks, and Sustainability' (2021) 67 Technology in Society 101741.

Garcia Rodriguez, Manuel J and others, 'Bidders Recommender for Public Procurement Auctions Using Machine Learning: Data Analysis, Algorithm, and Case Study with Tenders from Spain' (2020) Complexity 8858258.

Garcia Rodriguez, Manuel J and others, 'Collusion Detection in Public Procurement Auctions with Machine Learning Algorithms' (2022) 133 Automation in Construction 104047.

Geer, Dan, Eric Jardine, and Eireann Leverett, 'On Market Concentration and Cybersecurity Risk' (2020) 5 Journal of Cyber Policy 9.

Genus, Audley and Andy Stirling, 'Collingridge and the Dilemma of Control: Towards Responsible and Accountable Innovation' (2018) 47(1) Research Policy 61.

Giacomini, Davide and Caterina Muzzi, 'Promoting Digital Innovation in the Public Sector: Managerial and Organisational Insights from a Case Study' (2021) 8(3) International Journal of Public Sector Performance Management 236.

Goldberg, Victor P, 'Regulation and Administered Contracts' (1976) 7(2) Bell Journal of Economics 426.

Gu, Hongfei, 'Data, Big Tech, and the New Concept of Sovereignty' (2023) Journal of Chinese Political Science <https://doi.org/10.1007/s11366-023-09855-1> accessed 12 June 2023.

Hagemann, Ryan, Jennifer Huddleston Skees, and Adam Thierer, 'Soft Law for Hard Problems: The Governance of Emerging Technologies in an Uncertain Future' (2018) 17(1) Colorado Technology Law Journal 37.

Halonen, Kirsi-Maria, 'Disclosure Rules in EU Public Procurement: Balancing Between Competition and Transparency' (2017) 16 Journal of Public Procurement 528.

Halonen, Kirsi-Maria, 'Is Public Procurement Fit for Reaching Sustainability Goals? A Law and Economics Approach to Green Public Procurement' (2021) 28(4) Maastricht Journal of European and Comparative Law 535.

Hamilton, Sandra G, 'Public Procurement—Price-Taker or Market-Shaper?' (2022) 18(4) Critical Perspectives on International Business 574.

Hart, Oliver D, 'Incomplete Contracts and the Theory of the Firm' (1988) 4(1) Journal of Law, Economics, & Organization 119.

Hart, Oliver D, 'Incomplete Contracts and Control' (2017) 107(7) American Economic Review 1731.

Hermalin, Benjamin E and Michael L Katz, 'Information and the Hold-Up Problem' (2009) 40(3) The RAND Journal of Economics 405.

Hickok, Merve, 'Public Procurement of Artificial Intelligence Systems: New Risks and Future Proofing' (2022) AI & Society <https://doi.org/10.1007/s00146-022-01572-2> accessed 27 October 2022.

Hildebrandt, Mireille, 'Privacy as Protection of the Incomputable Self: From Agnostic to Agonistic Machine Learning' (2019) 20(1) Theoretical Inquiries in Law 83.

Huber, Martin and David Imhof, 'Machine Learning with Screens for Detecting Bid-Rigging Cartels' (2019) 65 International Journal of Industrial Organization 277.

Hudson, Bob, David Hunter, and Stephen Peckham, 'Policy Failure and the Policy-Implementation Gap: Can Policy Support Programs Help?' (2019) 2 Policy Design and Practice 1.

James, Alexandra and others, 'From Access and Transparency to Refusal: Three Responses to Algorithmic Governance' (2023) 12(2) Internet Policy Review <https://doi.org/10.14763/2023.2.1691> accessed 12 June 2023.

Janssen, Marijn and others, 'Data Governance: Organizing Data for Trustworthy Artificial Intelligence' (2020) 37 Government Information Quarterly 101493 <https://doi.org/10.1016/j.giq.2020.101493> accessed 4 October 2022.

Johal, Sukhdev, Michael Moran, and Karel Williams, 'Breaking the Constitutional Silence: The Public Services Industry and Government' (2016) 87 Political Quarterly 389.

Kaminski, Margot E, 'Binary Governance: Lessons from the GDPR's Approach to Algorithmic Accountability' (2019) 92 Southern California Law Review 1529.

Kaminski, Margot E, 'Regulating the Risks of AI' (2023) 103 Boston University Law Review, forthcoming <https://ssrn.com/abstract=4195066> accessed 4 November 2022.

Keay, Andrew, 'Comply or Explain in Corporate Governance Codes: In Need of Greater Regulatory Oversight?' (2014) 34 Legal Studies 279.

Kempeneer, Shirley and Frederik Heylen, 'Virtual State, Where Are You? A Literature Review, Framework and Agenda for Failed Digital Transformation' (2023) Big Data & Society <https://doi.org/10.1177/20539517231160528> accessed 12 April 2023.

Khorana, Sangeeta, Kirsten Ferguson-Boucher, and William A Kerr, 'Governance Issues in the EU's e-Procurement Framework' (2015) 53 Journal of Common Market Studies 292.
Khurana, Diksha and others, 'Natural Language Processing: State of the Art, Current Trends and Challenges' (2022) Multimedia Tools and Applications <https://doi.org/10.1007/s11042-022-13428-4> accessed 23 September 2022.
Kickbusch, Ilona, 'Addressing the Interface of the Political and Commercial Determinants of Health' (2012) 27 Health Promotion International 427.
Kim, Jong-Min and Hojin Jung, 'Predicting Bid Prices By Using Machine Learning Methods' (2019) 51 Applied Economics 2011.
Kleizen, Bjorn and Wouter Van Dooren, 'Is Everything Under Control? An Experimental Study on How Control Over Data Influences Trust in and Support for Major Governmental Data Exchange Projects' (2023) 28(2) Information Polity 277.
Kleizen, Bjorn and others, 'Do Citizens Trust Trustworthy Artificial Intelligence? Experimental Evidence on the Limits of Ethical AI Measures in Government' (2023) Government Information Quarterly, forthcoming <https://doi.org/10.1016/j.giq.2023.101834> accessed 12 June 2023.
Kolt, Noam, 'Algorithmic Black Swans' (2023) 101 Washington University Law Review 31.
Kraakman, Reiner H, 'Gatekeepers: The Anatomy of a Third-Party Enforcement Strategy' (1986) 2 Journal of Law, Economics and Organization 53.
Kunzlik, Peter, 'Neoliberalism and the European Public Procurement Regime' [2013] Cambridge Yearbook of European Legal Studies 283.
Kuziemski, Maciej and Gianluca Misuraca, 'AI Governance in the Public Sector: Three Tales from the Frontiers of Automated Decision-Making in Democratic Settings' (2020) 44(6) Telecommunications Policy 101976.
Kuzniacki, Blazej and others, 'Towards eXplainable Artificial Intelligence (XAI) in Tax Law: The Need for a Minimum Legal Standard' (2022) 14(4) World Tax Journal 573.
Laby, Arthur B, 'Differentiating Gatekeepers' (2006) 1 Brooklyn Journal of Corporate, Financial & Commercial Law 119.
Leese, Matthias, 'Staying in Control of Technology: Predictive Policing, Democracy, and Digital Sovereignty' (2023) Democratization <https://doi.org/10.1080/13510347.2023.2197217> accessed 19 April 2023.
Lehr, David and Paul Ohm, 'Playing with the Data: What Legal Scholars Should Learn About Machine Learning' (2017) 51 UC Davis Law Review 653.
Lewis, Gregory and Patrick Bajari, 'Procurement Contracting with Time Incentives: Theory and Evidence' (2011) 126(3) Quarterly Journal of Economics 1173.
Li, Wendy Y, 'Regulatory Capture's Third Face of Power' (2023) 21(2) Socio-Economic Review 1217.
Low, Kelvin F K and Eliza Mik, 'Pause the Blockchain Legal Revolution' (2020) 69 International & Comparative Law Quarterly 135.
Maciejewski, Mariusz, 'To Do More, Better, Faster and More Cheaply: Using Big Data in Public Administration' (2016) 83(1) International Review of Administrative Sciences 120.
Margetts, Helen and Patrick Dunleavy, 'The Second Wave of Digital Era Governance: A Quasi-Paradigm for Government on the Web' (2013) 371(1987) Philosophical Transactions of the Royal Society 1.
Markus, Aniek F, Jan A Kors, and Peter R Rijnbeek, 'The Role of Explainability in Creating Trustworthy Artificial Intelligence for Health Care: A Comprehensive Survey of the Terminology, Design Choices, and Evaluation Strategies' (2021) 113 Journal of Biomedical Informatics 103655.

Martinez, Jeferson and Javier M Duran, 'Software Supply Chain Attacks, a Threat to Global Cybersecurity: SolarWinds' Case Study' (2021) 11 International Journal of Safety and Security Engineering 537.

Mavidis, Aristotelis and Dimitris Folinas, 'From Public E-Procurement 3.0 to E-Procurement 4.0; A Critical Literature Review' (2022) 14 Sustainability 11252 <https://doi.org/10.3390/su141811252> accessed 28 September 2022.

Mazzucato, Mariana and Gregor Semieniuk, 'Public Financing of Innovation: New Questions' (2017) 33(1) Oxford Review of Economic Policy 24.

McCarl, Ryan, 'The Limits of Law and AI' (2022) 90 University of Cincinnati Law Review 923.

Mergel, Ines, 'Digital Service Teams in Government' (2019) 36 Government Information Quarterly 101389.

Mik, Eliza, 'Smart Contracts: Terminology, Technical Limitations and Real World Complexity' (2017) 9 Law, Innovation and Technology 269.

Miller, Fiona A and Pascale Lehoux, 'The Innovation Impacts of Public Procurement Offices: The Case of Healthcare Procurement' (2020) 49(7) Research Policy 104075.

Milward, H Brinton and Keith Provan, 'Managing the Hollow State. Collaboration and Contracting' (2003) 5 Public Management Review 1.

Mitchell, Shira and others, 'Algorithmic Fairness: Choices, Assumptions, and Definitions' (2021) 8 Annual Review of Statistics and Its Application 141.

Mokander, Jakob and others, 'Conformity Assessments and Post-market Monitoring: A Guide to the Role of Auditing in the Proposed European AI Regulation' (2022) 32 Minds and Machines 241.

Moniruzzaman, Mohammad, 'Risk of Regulatory Failure of "Risk-Based Regulation" While Using Enterprise Risk Management as a Meta-Regulatory Toolkit' (2022) 6(1) Asian Journal of Economics and Banking 103.

Morvillo, Marta and Maria Weimer, 'Who Shapes the CJEU Regulatory Jurisprudence? On the Epistemic Power of Economic Actors and Ways to Counter It' (2022) 1 European Law Open 510.

Moszoro, Marian W, Pablo T Spiller, and Sebastian Stolorz, 'Rigidity of Public Contracts' (2016) 13(3) Journal of Empirical Legal Studies 396.

Mühlhoff, Rainer, 'Predictive Privacy: Collective Data Protection in the Context of Artificial Intelligence and Big Data' (2023) Big Data & Society <https://doi.org/10.1177/20539517231166886> accessed 19 April 2023.

Mulligan, Deirdre K and Kenneth A Bamberger, 'Procurement as Policy: Administrative Process for Machine Learning' (2019) 34(3) Berkeley Technology Law Journal 773.

Munn, Luke, 'The Uselessness of AI Ethics' (2022) AI and Ethics <https://doi.org/10.1007/s43681-022-00209-w> accessed 11 November 2022.

Nielsen, Mille Edith and Christian Østergaard Madsen, 'Stakeholder Influence on Technical Debt Management in the Public Sector: An Embedded Case Study' (2022) 39 Government Information Quarterly 101706.

Nin Sanchez, Sergi, 'The Implementation of Decentralised Ledger Technologies for Public Procurement: Blockchain-based Smart Public Contracts' (2019) 14 European Procurement & Public Private Partnership Law Review 180.

Nowicki, Pawel, 'Deus Ex Machina? Some Remarks on Public Procurement in the Second Machine Age' (2020) 15 European Procurement & Public Private Partnership Law Review 53.

Ottersen, Ole Petter and others, 'The Political Origins of Health Inequity: Prospects for Change' (2014) 383 Lancet 630.

Papakonstantinou, Vagelis and Paul De Hert, 'The Regulation of Digital Technologies in the EU: The Law-Making Phenomena of "Act-Ification", "GDPR Mimesis" and "EU Law Brutality"' (2022) Technology and Regulation <https://doi.org/10.26116/techreg.2022.005> accessed 7 March 2023.

Paul, Regine, 'Can Critical Policy Studies Outsmart AI? Research Agenda on Artificial Intelligence Technologies and Public Policy' (2022) 16(4) Critical Policy Studies 497.

Pawson, Ray, Geoff Wong and Lesley Owen, 'Known Knowns, Known Unknowns, Unknown Unknowns: The Predicament of Evidence-Based Policy' (2011) 32 American Journal of Evaluation 518.

Peets, Lisa and others, 'UK Government's Guide to Using AI in the Public Sector' (2019) 2 The Journal of Robotics, Artificial Intelligence & Law 439.

Posner, Eric A and E Glen Weyl, 'An FDA for Financial Innovation: Applying the Insurable Interest Doctrine to Twenty-First-Century Financial Markets' (2015) 107 Northwestern University Law Review 1307.

Pöysti, Tuomas, 'Trust on Digital Administration and Platforms' (2018) 65 Scandinavian Studies in Law 321

Prins, Johnny, Jean-Paul Van Belle, and Marita Turpin, 'Using Information and Distributed Ledger Technologies to Combat Public Procurement Corruption: A South African Perspective' (2022) 32 Annals of Computer Science and Information Systems 223.

Ralston, Rob, 'The Informal Governance of Public-Private Partnerships in UK Obesity Policy: Collaborating on Calorie Reduction or Reducing Effectiveness?' (2021) 289 Social Science & Medicine 114451.

Ranchordas, Sofia, 'Experimental Regulations and Regulatory Sandboxes—Law Without Order?' (2021) Law and Method <https://doi.org/10.5553/REM/.000064> accessed 7 November 2022.

Ranchordas, Sofia, 'Empathy in the Digital Administrative State' (2022) 71(6) Duke Law Journal 1341.

Roberts, Huw and others, 'Artificial Intelligence Regulation in the United Kingdom: A Path to Good Governance and Global Leadership?' (2023) 12(2) Internet Policy Review <https://policyreview.info/articles/analysis/artificial-intelligence-regulation-united-kingdom-path-good-governance> accessed 15 June 2023.

Rubenstein, David S, 'Acquiring Ethical AI' (2021) 73(4) Florida Law Review 747.

Rubin, Edward L, 'Law and the Methodology of Law' (1997) 3 Wisconsin Law Review 521.

Rueda, Jon and others, '"Just" Accuracy? Procedural Fairness Demands Explainability in AI-Based Medical Resource Allocations' (2022) AI & Society <https://link.springer.com/article/10.1007/s00146-022-01614-9> accessed 22 February 2023

Ryan, Mark, 'In AI We Trust: Ethics, Artificial Intelligence, and Reliability' (2020) 26 Science and Engineering Ethics 2749.

Saltelli, Andrea and others, 'Science, the Endless Frontier of Regulatory Capture' (2022) 135 Futures 102860

Sanchez-Graells, Albert, 'Truly Competitive Public Procurement as a Europe 2020 Lever: What Role for the Principle of Competition in Moderating Horizontal Policies?' (2016) 22(2) European Public Law Journal 377.

Sanchez-Graells, Albert, 'Regulatory Substitution between Labour and Public Procurement Law: The EU's Shifting Approach to Enforcing Labour Standards in Public Contracts' (2018) 24(2) European Public Law Journal 229.

Sanchez-Graells, Albert, '"Screening for Cartels" in Public Procurement: Cheating at Solitaire to Sell Fool's Gold?' (2019) 10(4) Journal of European Competition Law & Practice 199.

Sanchez-Graells, Albert, 'Data-Driven Procurement Governance: Two Well-Known Elephant Tales' (2019) 24 Communications Law 157.

Sanchez-Graells, Albert, 'The Emergence of Trans-EU Collaborative Procurement: A 'Living Lab' for European Public Law' (2020) 29(1) Public Procurement Law Review 16.

Santiso, Carlos, 'Govtech Against Corruption: What Are the Integrity Dividends of Government Digitalization?' (2022) 4 Data & Policy e39.

Sava, Nadia-Ariadna and Dacian Dragos, 'The Legal Regime of Smart Contracts in Public Procurement' (2022) 66 Transylvanian Review of Administrative Sciences 99.

Schuett, Jonas, 'Risk Management in the Artificial Intelligence Act' (2023) European Journal of Risk Regulation <https://doi.org/10.1017/err.2023.1> accessed 12 April 2023.

Seidl, David, Paul Sanderson, and John Roberts, 'Applying the "Comply-or-Explain" Principle: Discursive Legitimacy Tactics with Regard to Codes of Corporate Governance' (2013) 17 Journal of Management & Governance 791.

Scherer, Matthew U, 'Regulating Artificial Intelligence Systems: Risks, Challenges, Competencies and Strategies' (2016) 29(2) Harvard Journal of Law & Technology 353.

Schlaufer, Caroline and others,' The Narrative Policy Framework: A Traveler's Guide to Policy Stories' (2022) 63 Politische Vierteljahresschrift 249.

Schooner, Steven L, 'Desiderata: Objectives for a System of Government Contract Law' (2002) 11 Public Procurement Law Review 103.

Scott, Colin, 'Private Regulation of the Public Sector: A Neglected Facet of Contemporary Governance' (2002) 29(1) Journal of Law and Society 56.

Semenzin, Silvia, David Rozas, and Samer Hassan, 'Blockchain-based Application at a Governmental Level: Disruption or Illusion? The Case of Estonia' (2022) 41(3) Policy and Society 386.

Shanahan, Elizabeth A, Michael D Jones, and Mark K McBeth, 'Policy Narratives and Policy Processes' (2011) 39 Policy Studies Journal 535.

Smuha, Nathalie A, 'The EU Approach to Ethics Guidelines for Trustworthy Artificial Intelligence. A Continuous Journey Towards an Appropriate Governance Framework for AI' (2019) 20(4) Computer Law Review International 97.

Smuha, Nathalie A, 'From a "Race to AI" to a "Race to AI Regulation": Regulatory Competition for Artificial Intelligence' (2021) 13 Law, Innovation and Technology 57.

Sofka, Wolfgang, Pedro de Faria, and Edlira Shehu, 'Protecting Knowledge: How Legal Requirements to Reveal Information Affect the Importance of Secrecy' (2018) 47(3) Research Policy 558.

Stahl, Bernd Carsten and others, 'A European Agency for Artificial Intelligence: Protecting Fundamental Rights and Ethical Values' (2022) 45 Computer Law & Security Review 105661.

Stokes, Elen, 'Beyond Evidence: Anticipatory Regimes in Law' (2021) 43(1) Law & Policy 73.

Sturdy, Andrew J and others, 'The Management Consultancy Effect: Demand Inflation and Its Consequences in the Sourcing of External Knowledge' (2022) 100 Public Administration 488.

Synyutka, Nataliya, Oksana Kurylo, and Mariya Bondarchuk, 'Digitalisation of Public Procurement: The Case Study of Ukraine' (2019) 53(3) Annales Universitatis Mariae Curie-Skłodowska 61.

Telles, Pedro, 'Existing and Potential Use Cases for Blockchain in Public Procurement' (2022) 17(3) European Procurement & Public Private Partnership Law Review 179.

Telles, Pedro and Grith Skovgaard Ølykke, 'Sustainable Procurement: A Compliance Perspective of EU Public Procurement Law' (2017) 12 European Procurement & Public Private Partnership Law Review 239.

Tirole, Jean, 'Socially Responsible Agencies' (2023) 7(4) Competition Law & Policy Debate 171.

Trittin-Ulbrich and others, Hannah, 'Exploring the Dark and Unexpected Sides of Digitalization: Toward a Critical Agenda' (2020) 28(1) Organization 3.

Truby, Jon and others, 'A Sandbox Approach to Regulating High-Risk Artificial Intelligence Applications' (2022) 13 European Journal of Risk Regulation 270

Tutt, Andrew, 'An FDA for Algorithms' (2017) 69 Administrative Law Review 83.

Ulbricht, Lena and Karen Yeung, 'Algorithmic Regulation: A Maturing Concept for Investigating Regulation of and Through Algorithms' (2022) 16(1) Regulation & Governance 3.

Uyarra, Elvira and others, 'Barriers to Innovation Through Public Procurement: A Supplier Perspective' (2014) 34(10) Technovation 631.

Vallejo, Rodrigo, 'The Private Administrative Law of Technical Standardization' (2021) 40 Yearbook of European Law 172.

Vandercruysse, Laurens, Caroline Buts, and Michael Dooms, 'Public Procurement as a Safeguard for Competition: The Case of Smart City Services' (2021) 5 European Competition and Regulation Law Review 102.

Van der Veer, Sabine N and others, 'Trading off Accuracy and Explainability in AI Decision-Making: Findings from 2 Citizens' Juries' (2021) 28(10) Journal of the American Medical Informatics Association 2128.

Van der Voort, H G and others, 'Rationality and Politics of Algorithms. Will the Promise of Big Data Survive the Dynamics of Public Decision Making?' (2019) 36 Government Information Quarterly 27.

Van Eechoud, Mireille, 'A Serpent Eating Its Tail: The Database Directive Meets the Open Data Directive' (2021) 52 IIC – International Review of Intellectual Property and Competition Law 375.

Veale, Michael, 'A Critical Take on the Policy Recommendations of the EU High-Level Expert Group on Artificial Intelligence' (2020) 11 European Journal of Risk Regulation 1.

Veale, Michael and Frederik Zuiderveen Borgesius 'Demystifying the Draft EU Artificial Intelligence Act—Analysing the Good, the Bad, and the Unclear Elements of the Proposed Approach' (2021) 22(4) Computer Law Review International 97.

Veale, Michael, Kira Matus, and Robert Gorwa, 'AI and Global Governance: Modalities, Rationales, Tensions' (2023) 19 Annual Review of Law and Social Science <https://doi.org/10.1146/annurev-lawsocsci-020223-040749> accessed 5 June 2023.

Vecht, Joost Jacob, 'Open Texture Clarified' (2020) Inquiry <https://doi.org/10.1080/0020174X.2020.1787222> accessed 23 February 2023.

Vida Fernandez, Jose, 'Artificial Intelligence in Government: Risks and Challenges of Algorithmic Governance in the Administrative State' (2023) 30(1) Indiana Journal of Global Legal Studies 65.

Vincent-Jones, Peter, 'Citizen Redress in Public Contracting for Human Services' (2005) 68 Modern Law Review 887.

Vincent-Jones, Peter, 'The New Public Contracting: Public Versus Private Ordering?' (2007) 14(2) Indiana Journal of Global Legal Studies 259.

Voda, Oana P and Carolien Jobse, 'Rules and Boundaries Surrounding Market Consultations in Innovation Procurement' (2016) 11(3) European Procurement & Public Private Partnership Law Review 179.

Vydra, Simon and Bram Klievink, 'Techno-Optimism and Policy-Pessimism in the Public Sector Big Data Debate' (2019) 36 Government Information Quarterly 101383.

Williams, Rebecca, 'Rethinking Administrative Law for Algorithmic Decision Making' (2022) 42(2) Oxford Journal of Legal Studies 468.

Yeung, Karen, 'Algorithmic Regulation: A Critical Interrogation' (2018) 12(4) Regulation & Governance 429.

Yeung, Karen, 'Recommendation of the Council on Artificial Intelligence (OECD)' (2020) 59(1) International Legal Materials 27.

Yeung, Karen, 'The New Public Analytics as an Emerging Paradigm in Public Sector Administration' (2022) 27(2) Tilburg Law Review 1.

Yukins, Christopher R, 'A Versatile Prism: Assessing Procurement Law Through the Principal-Agent Model' (2010) 40(1) Public Contract Law Journal 63.

Zerilli, John and others, 'Algorithmic Decision-Making and the Control Problem' (2019) 29 Minds and Machines 555.

Zerilli, John and others, 'Transparency in Algorithmic and Human Decision-Making: Is There a Double Standard?' (2019) 32 Philosophy & Technology 661.

Zuiderwijk, Anneke, Yu-Che Chen, and Fadi Salem, 'Implications of the Use of Artificial Intelligence in Public Governance: A Systematic Literature Review and a Research Agenda' (2021) 38 Government Information Quarterly 101577.

Züger, Theresa and Hadi Asghari, 'AI for the Public. How Public Interest Theory Shifts the Discourse on AI' (2022) AI & Society <https://doi.org/10.1007/s00146-022-01480-5> accessed 3 February 2023.

Conference, Discussion, and Working Papers

Almada, Marco, 'Regulating Machine Learning by Design' (2023) CPI TechREG Chronicle <https://ssrn.com/abstract=4367025> accessed 7 March 2023.

Andhov, Marta and others, 'Sustainability Through Public Procurement: The Way Forward—Reform Proposals' (2020) <https://ssrn.com/abstract=3559393> accessed 23 February 2023.

Behr, Timo von and Pekka Abrahamsson, 'AI Governance and Ethics in Public Procurement: Bridging the Gap Between Theory and Practice' (2022) IEEE 28th ICE/ITMC & 31st IAMOT Joint Conference <https://ieeexplore.ieee.org/document/10033173> accessed 1 June 2023.

Bender, Emily M and others, 'On the Dangers of Stochastic Parrots: Can Language Models Be Too Big?' (2021) FAccT proceedings 610.

Bensch, Stefan, 'Recommender Systems for Strategic Procurement in Value Networks' (2012). AMCIS 2012 Proceedings 13 <https://aisel.aisnet.org/amcis2012/proceedings/StrategicUseIT/13> accessed 23 September 2022.

Black, Julia, 'Constitutionalising Regulatory Governance Systems' (2021) LSE Law, Society and Economy Working Papers 02/2021 <http://eprints.lse.ac.uk/id/eprint/113670> accessed 7 April 2023.

Bordt, Sebastian and others, 'Post-Hoc Explanations Fail to Achieve their Purpose in Adversarial Contexts' (2022) FAccT proceedings 891.

Brown, Ian, 'Allocating Accountability in AI Supply Chains' (2023) Ada Lovelace Institute Expert Explainer <https://www.adalovelaceinstitute.org/resource/ai-supply-chains/> accessed 30 June 2023.

Calo, Ryan, 'The Scale and the Reactor' (SSRN, 15 April 2022) <https://ssrn.com/abstract=4079851> accessed 7 September 2022.

Charlesworth, Andrew and others, 'Response to the UK's March 2023 White Paper "A pro-innovation approach to AI regulation"' (SSRN, 19 June 2023) <https://ssrn.com/abstract=4477368> accessed 22 June 2023.

Cobbe, Jennifer, Michael Veale, and Jatinder Singh, 'Understanding Accountability in Algorithmic Supply Chains' (2023) FAccT proceedings <https://doi.org/10.1145/3593013.3594073> accessed 2 June 2023.

Daase, Christian and others, 'Automation of Customer Initiated Back Office Processes: A Design Science Research Approach to link Robotic Process Automation and Chatbots' (2020) ACIS 2020 Proceedings 15 <https://aisel.aisnet.org/acis2020/15> accessed 23 September 2022.

Desouza, Kevin C, 'Artificial Intelligence in the Public Sector: A Maturity Model' (2021) IBM Centre for the Business of Government <https://businessofgovernment.org/report/artificial-intelligence-public-sector-maturity-model> accessed 8 September 2022.

Dooling, Bridget C E and Rachel Augustine Potter, 'Regulatory Body Shops' (2022) <https://ssrn.com/abstract=4186402> accessed 8 September 2022.

Edwards, Lilian, 'The EU AI Act: A Summary of Its Significance and Scope' (2022) Ada Lovelace Institute Expert Explainer <https://www.adalovelaceinstitute.org/wp-content/uploads/2022/04/Expert-explainer-The-EU-AI-Act-11-April-2022.pdf> accessed 8 November 2022.

Filer, Tanya, 'Thinking about GovTech. A Brief Guide for Policymakers' (2020) Bennett Institute for Public Policy <https://www.bennettinstitute.cam.ac.uk/publications/thinking-about-govtech-brief-guide-policymakers/> accessed 7 September 2022.

Floridi, Luciano and others, 'capAI—A Procedure for Conducting Conformity Assessment of AI Systems in Line with the EU Artificial Intelligence Act' (2022) <https://artificialintelligenceact.eu/assessment/> accessed 15 November 2022.

Hardwick, Freya Sheer, Raja Naeem Akram, and Konstantinos Markantonakis, 'Fair and Transparent Blockchain based Tendering Framework—A Step Towards Open Governance' (2018) <https://arxiv.org/pdf/1805.05844.pdf> accessed 8 September 2022.

Hamon, Ronan and others, 'Impossible Explanations? Beyond Explainable AI in the GDPR from a COVID-19 Use Case Scenario' (2021) <https://ssrn.com/abstract=3774114> accessed 9 March 2023.

Irion, Kristina, 'Algorithms Off-limits? If Digital Trade Law Restricts Access to Source Code of Software then Accountability Will Suffer' (2022) FAccT proceedings 1561.

Köbis, Nils Christopher, Christopher Starke, and Jaselle Edward-Gill, 'The Corruption Risks of Artificial Intelligence' (2022) Transparency International <https://knowledgehub.transparency.org/assets/uploads/kproducts/The-Corruption-Risks-of-Artificial-Intelligence.pdf> accessed 18 October 2022.

Laurent, Anne, 'Buying as One: Category Management Lessons From the United Kingdom' (2019) IBM Centre for the Business of Government <https://www.businessofgovernment.org/report/buying-one-category-management-lessons-united-kingdom> accessed 9 November 2022.

Laux, Johann, Sandra Wachter, and Brent Mittelstadt, 'Three Pathways for Standardisation and Ethical Disclosure by Default under the European Union Artificial Intelligence Act' (SSRN, 20 February 2023) <https://ssrn.com/abstract=4365079> accessed 7 April 2023.

Lohn, Andrew J and Wyatt Hoffman, 'Securing AI. How Traditional Vulnerability Disclosure Must Adapt' (2022) CSET Policy Brief <https://cset.georgetown.edu/publication/securing-ai-how-traditional-vulnerability-disclosure-must-adapt/> accessed 18 October 2022.

Malgieri, Gianclaudio and Frank Pasquale, 'From Transparency to Justification: Toward Ex Ante Accountability for AI' (2022) Brooklyn Law School Legal Studies Paper No. 712<https://ssrn.com/abstract=4099657> accessed 4 November 2022.

McBride, Keegan and others, 'Towards a Systematic Understanding on the Challenges of Procuring Artificial Intelligence in the Public Sector' (2021) <https://doi.org/10.31235/osf.io/un649> accessed 7 March 2023.

Mergel, Ines, 'Digital Service Teams: Challenges and Recommendations for Government' (2017) IBM Centre for the Business of Government <https://www.businessofgovernment.org/report/digital-service-teams-challenges-and-recommendations-government> accessed 21 November 2022.

Pääkkönen, Juho and others, 'Bureaucracy as a Lens for Analyzing and Designing Algorithmic Systems' (2020) CHI Conference on Human Factors in Computing Systems <https://doi.org/10.1145/3313831.3376780> accessed 21 April 2023.

Peters, B Guy, 'Governance: A Garbage Can Perspective' (2002) Vienna Institute for Advanced Studies, Political Science Series Num 84 <https://aei.pitt.edu/347/1/wp_84.pdf> accessed 8 September 2022.

Picht, Peter Georg, 'Caught in the Acts: Framing Mandatory Data Access Transactions under the Data Act, further EU Digital Regulation Acts, and Competition Law' (2022) Max Planck Institute for Innovation and Competition Research Paper No. 22-12 <https://ssrn.com/abstract=4076842> accessed 5 October 2022.

Raji, Inioluwa Deborah and others, 'The Fallacy of AI Functionality' (2022) FAccT proceedings 959.

Rauchs, Michel and others, 'Distributed Ledger Technology Systems. A Conceptual Framework' (2018) <https://www.jbs.cam.ac.uk/wp-content/uploads/2020/08/2018-10-26-conceptualising-dlt-systems.pdf> accessed 7 September 2022.

Roberts, Huw and others, 'Artificial Intelligence Regulation in the United Kingdom: A Path to Global Leadership?' (2022) <https://ssrn.com/abstract=4209504> accessed 21 November 2022.

Rosenbaum, Howard, 'Algorithmic Neutrality, Algorithmic Assemblages, and the Lifeworld' (2020) AMCIS 2020 Proceedings 6 <https://aisel.aisnet.org/amcis2020/philosophical_is/philosophical_is/6> accessed 9 March 2023.

Sanchez-Graells, Albert, 'The Difficult Balance between Transparency and Competition in Public Procurement: Some Recent Trends in the Case Law of the European Courts and a Look at the New Directives' (2013) University of Leicester School of Law Research Paper No 13-11 <http://ssrn.com/abstract=2353005> accessed 18 October 2022.

Sanchez-Graells, Albert, 'Centralised Procurement Registers and their Transparency Implications—Discussion Non-Paper for the European Commission Stakeholder Expert Group on Public Procurement' (2015) <https://www.howtocrackanut.com/blog/2015/09/why-are-public-contracts-registers.html> accessed 18 October 2022.

Sanchez-Graells, Albert, 'Competition Implications of Procurement Digitalisation and the Procurement of Digital Technologies by Central Purchasing Bodies' (2023) <https://ssrn.com/abstract=4376037> accessed 12 April 2023.

Schooner, Steven L, Daniel I Gordon, and Jessica Lynn Wherry, 'Public Procurement Systems: Unpacking Stakeholder Aspirations and Expectations' (2008) GWU Legal Studies Research Paper No 1133234 <https://ssrn.com/abstract=1133234> accessed 6 September 2022.

Schrepel, Thibault, 'Law + Technology' (2022) VU University Amsterdam Legal Studies Research Paper Series <https://ssrn.com/abstract=4115666> accessed 13 September 2022.

Sculley, D and others, 'Hidden Technical Debt in Machine Learning Systems' (2015) <https://papers.nips.cc/paper/2015/file/86df7dcfd896fcaf2674f757a2463eba-Paper.pdf> accessed 7 October 2022.

Shaikh, Maha and Tony Cornford, 'Strategic Drivers of Open Source Software Adoption in the Public Sector: Challenges and Opportunities' (2012) ECIS 2012 Proceedings 237.

Somasundaram, Ramanathan and S M Quamrul Hasan, 'Regional: Development of a Global e-Government Procurement Architecture using Blockchain Technology' (2018) Asian Development Bank Technical Assistance Consultant's Report <https://www.adb.org/sites/default/files/project-documents/47192/47192-001-tacr-en_4.pdf> accessed 8 September 2022.

Spreitzenbarth, Jan Martin, 'Methods of Artificial Intelligence in Procurement' (2022) 17th International Conference on Wirtschaftsinformatik <https://shorturl.at/jnCFM> accessed 4 October 2022.

Ubaldi, Barbara and others, 'State of the Art in the Use of Emerging Technologies in the Public Sector' (2019) OECD Working Papers on Public Governance, No 31 <https://doi.org/10.1787/932780bc-en> accessed 7 September 2022.

Vita, Viorica, 'The Rise of Spending Conditionality in the EU: What Can EU Learn from the U.S. Conditional Spending Doctrine and Policies?' (2017) EUI Working Papers LAW 2017/16 <https://cadmus.eui.eu/handle/1814/48644> accessed 6 February 2023.

Weerakkody, Vishanth, 'Identifying the Critical Success Factors for Major Government Projects that Incorporate IT or "Digital" Developments' (2016) Research Background Note <https://bura.brunel.ac.uk/bitstream/2438/13368/1/FullText.pdf> accessed 9 November 2022.

Widder, David Gray and others, 'Limits and Possibilities for "Ethical AI" in Open Source: A Study of Deepfakes' (2022) FAccT proceedings 2035.

Williams, Sope, 'Public Procurement, Corruption and Blockchain Technology: A Preliminary (Legal) Inquiry' (2018) Inaugural Lecture at Stellenbosh University <https://www.sun.ac.za/english/Documents/newsclips/InauguralLecture_ProfSopeWilliamsElegbe_23Oct2018.pdf> accessed 8 September 2022.

Yang, Chan, 'Is there a Role for Blockchain for Enhancing Public Procurement Integrity?' (2019) Papers of the OECD Global Anti-Corruption & Integrity Forum 1.

Yeung, Karen and Adam Harkens, 'How Do "Technical" Design Choices Made When Building Algorithmic Decision-Making Tools for Criminal Justice Authorities Create Constitutional Dangers?' Parts I and II (2023) Public Law forthcoming <https://ssrn.com/abstract=4319307> and <https://ssrn.com/abstract=4319319> accessed 8 March 2023.

Research Degree Theses

Fagstad, Brage and Knut Andreas Aas, 'Cyber Security in Procurement of Third-Party Suppliers: A Case Study of the Norwegian Power Sector' (Master's thesis, University of Agder 2022) <https://hdl.handle.net/11250/3019797> accessed 7 October 2022.

Gerrie, James B, 'Some Ethical and Public Policy Implications of Technological Dependency with Reference to Innis, Mcluhan and Grant' (PhD thesis, University of Guelph 1999) <https://hdl.handle.net/10214/21638> accessed 7 October 2022.

Gutierrez Gaviria Carlos Ignacio, 'The Unforeseen Consequences of Artificial Intelligence (AI) on Society. A Systematic Review of Regulatory Gaps Generated by AI in the U.S.' (2020) RAND <https://www.rand.org/pubs/rgs_dissertations/RGSDA319-1.html> accessed 8 March 2023.

Nall, Tamara Lynn, 'Using Machine Learning to Predict Performance Issues with U.S. Federal Contracts' (PhD thesis, George Washington University ProQuest Dissertations Publishing 2022), 28865868.

Sjoerdstra, Bianca, 'Dealing with Vendor Lock-in' (2016) 7th IBA Bachelor Thesis Conference <https://essay.utwente.nl/70153/1/Sjoerdstra_BA_BMS.pdf> accessed 9 March 2023.

Szilagyi, Katie, 'Artificial Intelligence & the *Machine*-ation of the Rule of Law' (PhD thesis, University of Ottawa 2022) <http://dx.doi.org/10.20381/ruor-28401> accessed 15 June 2023.

Canadian Policy Documents

Clarke, Amanda and Sean Boots, 'A Guide to Reforming Information Technology Procurement in the Government of Canada' (2022) <https://govcanadacontracts.ca/it-procurement-guide/> accessed 19 October 2022.

EU Policy Documents

European Commission, 'Green Paper on public procurement in the European Union: exploring the way forward' (Communication) COM (96) 583 final.

European Commission, 'Action plan for the implementation of the legal framework for electronic public procurement' (Communication) COM (2004) 841 final.

European Commission, 'Green Paper on expanding the use of e-Procurement in the EU' (Communication) COM (2010) 571 final.

European Commission, 'A strategy for e-procurement' (Communication) COM (2012) 179 final.

European Commission, 'Against lock-in: building open ICT systems by making better use of standards in public procurement' (Communication) COM (2013) 455 final.

European Commission, 'Guide for the procurement of standards-based ICT—Elements of Good Practice', SWD (2013) 224 final.

European Data Protection Supervisor, 'Guidelines on the processing of personal data in the context of public procurement, grants as well as selection and use of external experts' (2013) <https://edps.europa.eu/sites/edp/files/publication/13-06-25_procurement_en.pdf> accessed 5 October 2022.

PWC, 'e-Procurement Golden Book of Good Practice. Final report' (2013) <https://ec.europa.eu/docsroom/documents/15443/> accessed 7 September 2022.

PWC, 'e-Procurement uptake. Final report' (2015) <https://ec.europa.eu/docsroom/documents/10050/> accessed 12 September 2022.

PWC, 'Study on best practices for ICT procurement based on standards in order to promote efficiency and reduce lock-in' (2016) <https://ec.europa.eu/newsroom/dae/document.cfm?doc_id=14434> accessed 7 October 2022.

Time.lex and others, 'Legal review on industrial design protection in Europe', Annex 3 '3D printing' (2016) <https://ec.europa.eu/docsroom/documents/18921/> accessed 15 September 2022.

European Commission, 'Making public procurement work in and for Europe' (Communication) COM (2017) 572 final.

European Commission, 'Public procurement guidance for practitioners on avoiding the most common errors in projects funded by the European Structural and Investment

Funds' (2018) <https://ec.europa.eu/regional_policy/sources/wikiguidance/brochure_public_procurement_guidance_for_practitioners.pdf> accessed 6 February 2023.

European Parliament, 'Systems and e-procurement—improving access and transparency of public procurement' (Briefing) PE 618.990 (2018) <https://www.europarl.europa.eu/RegData/etudes/BRIE/2018/618990/IPOL_BRI(2018)618990_EN.pdf> accessed 7 September 2022.

European Commission, 'Artificial Intelligence: A European perspective' (2018) <https://ec.europa.eu/futurium/en/system/files/ged/ai-flagship-report_online.pdf> accessed 7 March 2023.

High-Level Expert Group on AI, 'Ethics guidelines for trustworthy AI' (2019) <https://digital-strategy.ec.europa.eu/en/library/ethics-guidelines-trustworthy-ai> accessed 7 March 2023.

Deloitte, 'Study on up-take of emerging technologies in public procurement. Final report' (2020) <https://ec.europa.eu/docsroom/documents/40102> accessed 7 September 2022.

European Commission, 'ProcurCompEU. European competency framework for public procurement professionals (2020) <https://ec.europa.eu/info/sites/default/files/procurcompeu-ecf_for_pp_en.pdf> accessed 8 September 2022.

European Commission, 'A European strategy for data' (Communication) COM (2020) 66 final.

European Commission, 'Making the most of the EU's innovative potential. An intellectual property action plan to support the EU's recovery and resilience' (Communication) COM (2020) 760 final.

European Commission, 'eForms: policy implementation handbook' (Guidance) (2020) <https://data.europa.eu/doi/10.2873/646999> accessed 4 October 2022.

European Commission, 'eForms: governance and life-cycle management' (Guidance) (2020) <https://data.europa.eu/doi/10.2873/185027> accessed 4 October 2022.

European Commission, 'Open source software strategy 2020–2023. Think open' (Communication) C (2020) 7149 final.

ENISA, 'AI cybersecurity challenges. Threat landscape for Artificial Intelligence' (2020) <https://www.enisa.europa.eu/publications/artificial-intelligence-cybersecurity-challenges> accessed 18 October 2022.

European Commission, 'AI Watch, overview of the use and impact of AI in public services in the EU' (2020) <https://data.europa.eu/doi/10.2760/039619> accessed 7 March 2023.

European Commission, 'Fostering a European approach to Artificial Intelligence' (Communication) COM (2021) 205 final.

PWC, 'The strategic use of public procurement for innovation in the digital economy' (2021) <https://op.europa.eu/s/w6sv> accessed 7 October 2022.

European Commission, 'Guidance on innovation procurement' (Notice) C (2021) 4320 final.

European Parliament, 'Use of big data and AI in fighting corruption and misuse of public funds—good practice, ways forward and how to integrate new technology into contemporary control framework' (Workshop Proceedings) PE 691.722 (2021) <https://www.europarl.europa.eu/RegData/etudes/STUD/2021/691722/IPOL_STU(2021)691722_EN.pdf> accessed 23 September 2022.

European Parliament, 'Challenges and limits of an open source approach to Artificial Intelligence' (2021) <https://www.europarl.europa.eu/RegData/etudes/STUD/2021/662908/IPOL_STU(2021)662908_EN.pdf> accessed 9 March 2023.

European Data Protection Board and European Data Protection Supervisor, Joint Opinion 5/2021 on the proposal for a Regulation of the European Parliament and of the Council laying down harmonised rules on artificial intelligence (Artificial Intelligence Act) (18

June 2021) <https://edpb.europa.eu/system/files/2021-06/edpb-edps_joint_opinion_ai_regulation_en.pdf> accessed 21 November 2022.

European Parliament, 'The digital single market and the digitalisation of the public sector: GovTech and other innovations in public procurement' (2022) <https://data.europa.eu/doi/10.2861/830794> accessed 17 October 2022.

European Commission, 'AI Watch, European landscape on the use of artificial intelligence by the public sector' (2022) <https://data.europa.eu/doi/10.2760/39336> accessed 5 September 2022.

Living-In EU, Proposal for standard contractual clauses for the procurement of artificial intelligence by public organisations, version 0.9 (2022) <https://living-in.eu/sites/default/files/files/Draft%20AI%20Clauses_1.pdf> accessed 21 October 2022.

European Commission, 'Common European data spaces', SWD (2022) 45 final.

European Commission, 'Draft Guidelines on the applicability of Article 101 of the Treaty on the Functioning of the European Union to horizontal co-operation agreements' C (2022) 1159.

European Commission, 'Digital procurement' <https://single-market-economy.ec.europa.eu/single-market/public-procurement/digital-procurement_en> accessed 7 September 2022.

European Commission, 'Draft standardisation request to the European Standardisation Organisations in support of safe and trustworthy artificial intelligence' (2022) <https://ec.europa.eu/docsroom/documents/52376> accessed 20 December 2022.

European Data Protection Board, 2022 Coordinated enforcement action, use of cloud-based services by the public sector (2023) <https://edpb.europa.eu/system/files/2023-01/edpb_20230118_cef_cloud-basedservices_publicsector_en.pdf> accessed 7 March 2023.

European Court of Auditors, 'e-Government actions targeting businesses' (2022) Special Report 24/2022 <https://www.eca.europa.eu/Lists/ECADocuments/SR22_24/SR_e-Government_EN.pdf> accessed 10 March 2023.

European Commission, 'AI Watch: Artificial Intelligence standardisation landscape update' (2023) <https://publications.jrc.ec.europa.eu/repository/handle/JRC131155> accessed 7 April 2023.

European Commission, 'A data space to improve public spending, boost data-driven policy-making and improve access to tenders for SMEs' (Communication) [2023] C 98/1.

Council of the European Union, 'ChatGPT in the public sector—overhyped or overlooked?' (24 April 2023) <https://www.consilium.europa.eu/media/63818/art-paper-chatgpt-in-the-public-sector-overhyped-or-overlooked-24-april-2023_ext.pdf> accessed 3 July 2023.

OECD Policy Documents

OECD, 'Recommendation on Fighting Bid Rigging in Public Procurement' (2012) <https://legalinstruments.oecd.org/en/instruments/OECD-LEGAL-0396> accessed 7 February 2023.

OECD/SIGMA, 'Organising Central Public Procurement Functions' (2013) <https://www.sigmaweb.org/publications/Brief26_CentralPPFunctions_2013.pdf> accessed 6 February 2022.

OECD, Recommendation on Digital Government Strategies (2014) <https://www.oecd.org/gov/digital-government/Recommendation-digital-government-strategies.pdf> accessed 12 June 2023.

OECD, 'Recommendation on Public Procurement' (2015) <https://www.oecd.org/gov/public-procurement/recommendation/> accessed 7 February 2023.

OECD, 'Algorithms and Collusion. Competition Policy in the Digital Age' (2017).

OECD, 'Preventing Policy Capture. Integrity in Public Decision Making' (2017).

OECD, 'Regulatory Consultation. A MENA-OECD practitioners' guide for engaging stakeholders in the rule-making process (2017) <https://www.oecd.org/mena/governance/MENA-Practitioners-Guide-%20EN.pdf> accessed 22 February 2023.

OECD, 'Data governance in the public sector' in *The Path to Becoming a Data-Driven Public Sector* (2019) <https://doi.org/10.1787/059814a7-en> accessed 4 October 2022.

OECD, 'The Path to Becoming a Data-Driven Public Sector' (2019) OECD Digital Government Studies <https://doi.org/10.1787/059814a7-en> accessed 7 March 2023.

OECD, 'Enhancing Access to and Sharing of Data. Reconciling Risks and Benefits for Data Re-use across Societies' (2019).

OECD, 'Government at a Glance 2021' (2021).

OECD, 'OECD Regulatory Policy Outlook 2021' (2021).

OECD, 'Tackling Policy Challenges Through Public Sector Innovation: A Strategic Portfolio Approach' (2022) <https://oecd-opsi.org/> accessed .

OECD, 'AI Language Models: Technological, Socio-Economic and Policy Considerations' (2023) OECD Digital Economy Papers, No. 352 <https://doi.org/10.1787/13d38f92-en> accessed 14 April 2023.

OECD, 'The Governance of Regulators. Creating a Culture of Independence' (undated).

UK Policy Documents

Office of Fair Trading, 'Supply of Information and Communications Technology to the Public Sector' (2014) OFT1533.

House of Lords Committee on Artificial Intelligence, *AI in the UK: Ready, Willing and Able?* (HL 2017–19, 100).

Central Digital and Data Office, 'GDS spend controls pipeline assessment criteria' (2018) <https://www.gov.uk/guidance/gds-spend-controls-pipeline-assessment-criteria> accessed 8 November 2022.

Central Digital and Data Office, 'Managing technical lock-in in the cloud' (2019) <https://www.gov.uk/guidance/managing-technical-lock-in-in-the-cloud> accessed 9 March 2023.

National Cyber Security Centre, 'Intelligent security tools. Assessing intelligent tools for cyber security' (2019) <https://www.ncsc.gov.uk/collection/intelligent-security-tools> accessed 19 October 2022.

Office for Artificial Intelligence, 'A guide to using artificial intelligence in the public sector' (2019) <https://www.gov.uk/government/collections/a-guide-to-using-artificial-intelligence-in-the-public-sector> accessed 8 November 2022.

Government Finance Function, 'The Orange Book. Management of Risk—Principles and Concepts' (2020) <https://www.gov.uk/government/publications/orange-book> accessed 8 November 2022.

Office for Artificial Intelligence, 'Guidelines for AI Procurement' (2020) <https://www.gov.uk/government/publications/guidelines-for-ai-procurement> accessed 8 November 2022.

Central Digital and Data Office, 'Data ethics framework' (2020) <https://www.gov.uk/government/publications/data-ethics-framework> accessed 9 November 2022.

Centre for Data Ethics and Innovation, 'Review into bias in algorithmic decision-making' (2020) <https://www.gov.uk/government/publications/cdei-publishes-review-into-bias-in-algorithmic-decision-making> accessed 8 November 2022.

Law Commission (England and Wales), 'Smart legal contracts. Advice to Government' (2021) <https://www.lawcom.gov.uk/project/smart-contracts/> accessed 19 December 2022.

National Cyber Security Centre, 'Cyber Assessment Framework v 3.1' (2022) <https://www.ncsc.gov.uk/collection/caf/cyber-assessment-framework> accessed 4 November 2022.

National Audit Office, 'Good practice guidance. Principles of effective regulation' (2021) <https://www.nao.org.uk/wp-content/uploads/2021/05/Principles-of-effective-regulation-SOff-interactive-accessible.pdf> accessed 7 April 2023.

National Audit Office, 'The challenges in implementing digital change' (HC 2021-22, 575).

House of Commons Committee of Public Accounts, *Challenges in implementing digital change* (HC 2021–22, 637).

National Audit Office, 'Digital transformation in government: addressing the barriers to efficiency' (HC 2022-23, 1171).

Central Digital and Data Office, 'The Technology Code of Practice' (2021) <https://www.gov.uk/guidance/the-technology-code-of-practice> accessed 8 November 2022.

Central Digital and Data Office, 'Be open and use open source' (2021) <https://www.gov.uk/guidance/be-open-and-use-open-source> accessed 8 November 2022.

Central Digital and Data Office, 'Make things secure' (2021) <https://www.gov.uk/guidance/make-things-secure> accessed 8 November 2022.

Central Digital and Data Office, 'Make better use of data' (2021) <https://www.gov.uk/guidance/make-better-use-of-data> accessed 8 November 2022.

Cabinet Office, 'Cabinet Office controls policy: version 6' (2021) <https://www.gov.uk/government/publications/cabinet-office-controls-version-6/cabinet-office-controls-policy-version-6> accessed 9 November 2022.

Central Digital and Data Office, 'Digital and technology spend controls (version 5)' (2021) <https://www.gov.uk/guidance/digital-and-technology-spend-controls-version-5> accessed 8 November 2022.

Central Digital and Data Office, 'Algorithmic Transparency Standard v2.1' (2021) <https://www.gov.uk/government/publications/algorithmic-transparency-template> accessed 3 July 2023

Department for Digital, Culture, Media and Sport, 'National AI Strategy' (CP 525, 2021).

Office for Artificial Intelligence, 'Understanding UK Artificial Intelligence R&D commercialisation and the role of standards' (2022) <https://www.gov.uk/government/publications/understanding-uk-ai-rd-commercialisation-and-the-role-of-standards> accessed 7 April 2023.

Centre for Data Ethics and Innovation, 'Algorithmic Transparency Standard. Guidance for public sector bodies' (2022) <https://github.com/co-cddo/algorithmic-transparency-standard/blob/320cc8f882e76c0bb29d2477e1608a890a7cb68d/Guidance%20for%20Public%20Sector%20Organisations%E2%80%99%20Use%20of%20the%20Algorithmic%20Transparency%20Standard%20v1.1.pdf> accessed 8 November 2022.

Digital, Data and Technology Profession, 'The Digital, Data and Technology Playbook. Government guidance on sourcing and contracting for digital, data and technology projects and programmes' (2022) <https://www.gov.uk/government/publications/the-digital-data-and-technology-playbook> accessed 8 November 2022.

Central Digital and Data Office, 'Transforming for a digital future: 2022 to 2025 roadmap for digital and data' (Policy Paper, 9 June 2022) <https://www.gov.uk/government/publications/roadmap-for-digital-and-data-2022-to-2025> accessed 5 September 2022.

Digital, Data and Technology Profession, 'The Digital, Data and Technology Playbook' (2022) <https://www.gov.uk/government/publications/the-digital-data-and-technology-playbook/the-digital-data-and-technology-playbook> accessed 6 September 2022.

Department for Digital, Culture, Media and Sport, 'Establishing a pro-innovation approach to regulating AI. An overview of the UK's emerging approach' (CP 728, 2022).

Ben Goldacre and Jess Morley, 'Better, broader, safer: Using health data for research and analysis. A review commissioned by the Secretary of State for Health and Social Care' (2022) <https://www.goldacrereview.org/> accessed 12 September 2022.

Centre for Data Ethics and Innovation, 'AI assurance guide (beta)' (2022) <https://cdeiuk.github.io/ai-assurance-guide/independence/> access 11 November 2022.

Digital Regulation Cooperation Forum, 'Auditing algorithms: the existing landscape, role of regulators and future outlook' (23 September 2022) <https://www.gov.uk/government/publications/findings-from-the-drcf-algorithmic-processing-workstream-spring-2022/auditing-algorithms-the-existing-landscape-role-of-regulators-and-future-outlook> accessed 21 November 2022.

Digital Regulation Cooperation Forum, 'The benefits and harms of algorithms: a shared perspective from the four digital regulators' (23 September 2022) <https://www.gov.uk/government/publications/findings-from-the-drcf-algorithmic-processing-workstream-spring-2022/the-benefits-and-harms-of-algorithms-a-shared-perspective-from-the-four-digital-regulators> accessed 22 November 2022.

Department for Science, Innovation and Technology and Office for Artificial Intelligence, 'AI regulation: a pro-innovation approach' (CP 815, 2023).

Information Commissioner's Office, 'Guidance on AI and data protection' (2023) <https://ico.org.uk/for-organisations/guide-to-data-protection/key-dp-themes/guidance-on-ai-and-data-protection/> accessed 12 April 2023.

Central Digital and Data Office and Centre for Data Ethics and Innovation, 'Algorithmic Transparency Recording Standard Hub' (2023) <https://www.gov.uk/government/collections/algorithmic-transparency-recording-standard-hub> accessed 12 April 2023.

Central Digital and Data Office and Centre for Data Ethics and Innovation, 'Algorithmic Transparency Reports' (last updated 13 January 2023) <https://www.gov.uk/government/collections/algorithmic-transparency-reports> accessed 12 April 2023.

United Nations Policy Documents

UNCITRAL, 'United Nations Convention against Corruption: implementing procurement-related aspects' (2008) <https://digitallibrary.un.org/record/623202> accessed 7 February 2023.

UNESCO/EQUALS, 'I'd blush if I could: closing gender divides in digital skills through education' (2019) <https://unesdoc.unesco.org/ark:/48223/pf0000367416> accessed 7 March 2023.

UNESCO, 'AI and education: guidance for policy-makers' (2021) <https://unesdoc.unesco.org/ark:/48223/pf0000376709.locale=en> accessed 12 June 2023.

UN Environment Programme, 'How digital technology and innovation can help protect the planet' (17 August 2022) <https://www.unep.org/news-and-stories/story/how-digital-technology-and-innovation-can-help-protect-planet> accessed 12 June 2023.

US Policy Documents

CIS, NASPO and NASCIO, 'Buyer be aware. Integrating cybersecurity into the acquisition process' (2021) <https://www.nascio.org/wp-content/uploads/2021/04/NASCIO_NASPO_CIS_CybersecurityAquisition_2021.pd> accessed 19 October 2022.

National Institute of Standards and Technology, 'AI Risk Management Framework Concept Paper' (13 December 2021) <https://www.nist.gov/system/files/documents/2021/12/14/AI%20RMF%20Concept%20Paper_13Dec2021_posted.pdf> accessed 4 November 2022.

National Institute for Standards and Technology, 'Artificial Intelligence Risk Management Framework (AI RMF 1.0)' (2023) <https://www.nist.gov/itl/ai-risk-management-framework> accessed 7 April 2023.

World Bank Policy Documents

World Bank, 'GovTech: The New Frontier in Digital Government Transformation' (2020) <https://documents.worldbank.org/curated/en/898571612344883836/GovTech-The-New-Frontier-in-Digital-Government-Transformation> accessed 8 September 2022.

World Bank, 'Disruptive Technologies in Public Procurement' (2021) <http://documents.worldbank.org/curated/en/522181612428427520/Disruptive-Technologies-in-Public-Procurement> accessed 8 September 2022.

Cem Dener and others, *GovTech Maturity Index: The State of Public Sector Digital Transformation* (World Bank 2021).

Other Policy Documents

appliedAI, 'AI Act: Risk Classification of AI Systems from a Practical Perspective' (2023) <https://aai.frb.io/assets/files/AI-Act-Risk-Classification-Study-appliedAI-March-2023.pdf> accessed 14 April 2023.

BILETA, 'Written Evidence Submitted to the House of Commons Science and Technology Committee Inquiry on the Governance of artificial intelligence' (2022) GAI0082 <https://committees.parliament.uk/writtenevidence/113846/pdf/> accessed 7 March 2023.

Chinn, David and others, 'The future is now: Closing the skills gap in Europe's public sector' (2020) McKinsey <https://www.mckinsey.com/industries/public-and-social-sector/our-insights/the-future-is-now-closing-the-skills-gap-in-europes-public-sector> accessed 9 March 2023.

DanSense, 'Analysis of Public Sector Procurement Activities—A Report on Referencing Standards in Public Procurement' (2019) <https://www.cencenelec.eu/media/CEN-CENELEC/Areas%20of%20Work/CEN%20sectors/Services/Quicklinks%20General/analysis_publicsector_procurement.pdf> accessed 11 November 2022.

Data Hazards, 'Self-Assessment' (2022) <https://datahazards.com/contents/materials/self-assessment.html> accessed 4 November 2022.

D'Angelo, Camilla and others, 'Labelling initiatives, codes of conduct and other self-regulatory mechanisms for artificial intelligence applications. From principles to practice and considerations for the future' (2022) RAND <https://www.rand.org/pubs/research_reports/RRA1773-1.html> accessed 8 November 2022.

De Michele, Roberto and Juan Cruz Vieyra, 'From Fishing to Catching: Developing Actionable Red Flags in Public Procurement to Prevent and Control Corruption' (2022) Inter-American Development Bank Technical Note Nº IDB-TN-2598 <http://dx.doi.org/10.18235/0004595> accessed 19 December 2022.

Digital Catapult, 'Challenges to Responsible AI Adoption in Industry' (2021) <https://www.digicatapult.org.uk/wp-content/uploads/2021/11/Digital_Catapult_Challenges_to_Responsible_AI_Adoption_Report_Juy_2021.pdf> accessed 9 March 2023.

European eGovernment Services, 'Guideline on public procurement of Open Source Software' (2010) <https://joinup.ec.europa.eu/sites/default/files/document/2011-12/OSS-procurement-guideline%20-final.pdf> accessed 9 March 2023.

Feijao, Carolina and others, 'The global digital skills gap. Current trends and future directions' (2021) RAND <https://www.rand.org/pubs/research_reports/RRA1533-1.html> accessed 17 October 2022.

Gavaghan, Colin and others, 'Government Use of Artificial Intelligence in New Zealand' (2019) <https://ourarchive.otago.ac.nz/bitstream/handle/10523/9372/NZLF%20report.pdf> accessed 5 April 2023.

Hamon, Ronan, Henrik Junklewitz and Ignacio Sanchez, 'Robustness and Explainability of Artificial Intelligence – From technical to policy solutions' (2020) <https://data.europa.eu/doi/10.2760/57493> accessed 9 March 2023.

Hasselbalch, Gry, Birgitte Kofod Olsen and Pernille Tranberg, 'White Paper on Data Ethics in Public Procurement of AI based services and solutions' (2021) <https://www.nist.gov/system/files/documents/2021/08/23/ai-rmf-rfi-0043.pdf> accessed 9 March 2023.

ICAEW, 'Digitalisation of tax: international perspectives' (2022) <https://www.icaew.com/technical/technology/technology-and-the-profession/digitalisation-of-tax-international-perspectives> accessed 12 June 2023.

IEEE, 'GET Program for AI Ethics and Governance Standards' (undated) <https://ieeexplore.ieee.org/browse/standards/get-program/page/series?id=93> accessed 20 April 2023.

Institute for Government, 'What does artificial intelligence mean for government procurement?' (2023) <https://www.instituteforgovernment.org.uk/event/artificial-intelligence-government-procurement> accessed 12 April 2023.

Interreg Europe, 'GovTech and digitalising the public sector' (2022) <https://www.interregeurope.eu/find-policy-solutions/webinar/govtech-and-digitalising-the-public-sector> accessed 7 March 2023.

Kavanagh, Camino, 'New Tech, New Threats, and New Governance Challenges: An Opportunity to Craft Smarter Responses?' (2019) Carnegie Endowment for International Peace <https://carnegieendowment.org/files/WP_Camino_Kavanagh___New_Tech_New_Threats1.pdf> accessed 7 March 2023.

Leslie, David, 'Understanding artificial intelligence ethics and safety: A guide for the responsible design and implementation of AI systems in the public sector' (2019) Alan Turing Institute <https://doi.org/10.5281/zenodo.3240529> accessed 9 March 2023.

Leslie, David and others, 'Artificial Intelligence, Human Rights, Democracy, and the Rule of Law. A Primer' (2021) Council of Europe and Alan Turing Institute <https://rm.coe.int/primer-en-new-cover-pages-coe-english-compressed-2754-7186-0228-v-1/1680a2fd4a> accessed 9 March 2023.

Liberty, 'Written Evidence Submitted to the House of Commons Science and Technology Committee Inquiry on the Governance of artificial intelligence' (2022) GAI0081 <https://committees.parliament.uk/writtenevidence/113845/pdf/> accessed 7 March 2023.

Mazzucato, Mariana, 'Mission-oriented public procurement: lessons from international examples. UCL Institute for Innovation and Public Purpose' (2020) Policy Report IIPP 2020-20 <https://www.ucl.ac.uk/bartlett/public-purpose/pr2020-20> accessed 7 March 2023.

McFadden, Mark and others, 'Harmonising Artificial Intelligence: The role of standards in the EU AI Regulation' (2021) Oxford Commission on AI & Good Governance <https://oxil.uk/publications/2021-12-02-oxford-internet-institute-oxil-harmonising-ai/Harmonising-AI-OXIL.pdf> accessed 7 April 2023.

Mergel, Ines and others, 'Study on the Impact of Digital Transformation on Democracy and Good Governance' (2021) Council of Europe CDDG(2021)4 Final <https://rm.coe.int/study-on-the-impact-of-digital-transformation-on-democracy-and-good-go/1680a3b9f9> accessed 12 June 2023.

Michalec, Ola, Sveta Milyaeva and Awais Rashid, 'Regulating digitisation of critical infrastructures: recommendations to harmonise safety and security of Operational Technologies' (2022) University of Bristol Policy Briefing 120 <https://www.bristol.ac.uk/policybristol/policy-briefings/digitisation-critical-infrastructure/> accessed 9 November 2022.

Mosey, David and others, 'White Paper on Procurement Strategies for Incentivizing Collaborative Delivery to Optimize Whole-Life Outcomes' (2022) <https://www.cdbb.cam.ac.uk/files/white_paper_on_procurement_strategies.pdf> accessed 21 February 2023.

Nonnecke, Brandie and Philip Dawson, 'Human rights impact assessments for AI: analysis and recommendations' (2022) Access Now <https://www.accessnow.org/cms/assets/uploads/2022/11/Access-Now-Version-Human-Rights-Implications-of-Algorithmic-Impact-Assessments_-Priority-Recommendations-to-Guide-Effective-Development-and-Use.pdf> accessed 20 December 2022.

Open Contracting Partnership 'RED FLAGS for integrity: Giving the green light to open data solutions' (2016) <https://www.open-contracting.org/resources/red-flags-integrity-giving-green-light-open-data-solutions/> accessed 26 September 2022.

Open Contracting Partnership, 'How Open is Public Procurement Data in the EU?' (2023) <https://www.open-contracting.org/wp-content/uploads/2023/06/OCP2023-EU-OpenData.pdf> accessed 6 July 2023.

Oxford Government Outcomes Lab, 'How to Guide Procurement' (2017) <https://golab.bsg.ox.ac.uk/documents/GO_Lab_-_Procurement_Guide_ROe4bJn.pdf> accessed 23 September 2022.

Oxford Insights, 'Government AI Readiness Index 2022' (2022) <https://www.oxfordinsights.com/government-ai-readiness-index-2022> accessed 10 March 2023.

Perera, Kapila, 'Buying better technology in government' (*doteveryone*, 22 May 2020) <https://doteveryone.org.uk/wp-content/uploads/2020/05/Buying-better-technology-in-government.pdf> accessed 9 March 2023.

Platform for the Information Society, 'Artificial Intelligence Impact Assessment' (2018) <https://static1.squarespace.com/static/5b7877457c9327fa97fef427/t/5c368c611ae6cf01ea0fba53/1547078768062/Artificial+Intelligence+Impact+Assessment+-+English.pdf> accessed 8 November 2022.

Policy Connect, 'An Ethical AI Future: Guardrails & Catalysts to make Artificial Intelligence a Force for Good' (2023) <https://www.policyconnect.org.uk/research/ethical-ai-future-guardrails-catalysts-make-artificial-intelligence-force-good> accessed 22 June 2023.

Public Law Project, 'The Tracking Automated Government register. A new tool lifting the lid on secretive government algorithms' (2023) <https://publiclawproject.org.uk/resources/the-tracking-automated-government-register/> accessed 9 March 2023.

Reisman, Dillon and others, 'Algorithmic Impact Assessments: A Practical Framework for Public Agency Accountability' (2018) AI Now < https://ainowinstitute.org/publication/algorithmic-impact-assessments-report-2> accessed 4 November 2022.

Reland, Joël, 'UK-EU Regulatory Divergence Tracker' (5th edn, October 2022) 2-3 <https://ukandeu.ac.uk/wp-content/uploads/2022/10/Divergence-Tracker-5.pdf> accessed 8 November 2022.

Royal Society, 'Explainable AI: the basics' (2019) Policy briefing <https://royalsociety.org/-/media/policy/projects/explainable-ai/AI-and-interpretability-policy-briefing.pdf> accessed 9 March 2023.

Sanchez-Graells, Albert, 'Written Evidence Submitted to the House of Commons Science and Technology Committee Inquiry on the Governance of artificial intelligence' (2022) GAI0004 <https://committees.parliament.uk/writtenevidence/113034/pdf/> accessed 20 December 2022.

Siegmann, Charlotte and Markus Anderljung, 'The Brussels Effect and Artificial Intelligence' (2022) Centre for the Governance of AI <https://www.governance.ai/research-paper/brussels-effect-ai> accessed 10 March 2023.

Sloane, Mona and others, 'AI and Procurement. A Primer' (2021) NYU <https://archive.nyu.edu/bitstream/2451/62255/2/AI%20and%20Procurement%20Primer%20Summer%202021.pdf> accessed 9 March 2023.

Tenders Guru, 'Recommendations for EU procurement' (2021) <https://www.access-info.org/wp-content/uploads/2021-06-28-Tenders-Guru-EU-Recommendations.pdf> accessed 27 September 2022.

Timmers, Paul, 'Digital Industrial Policy for Europe' (2022) CERRE <https://cerre.eu/wp-content/uploads/2022/12/Digital-Industrial-Policy-for-Europe.pdf> accessed 7 March 2023.

Tussell, 'Artificial Intelligence & the Public Sector: Trends, Growth & Opportunities' (2022) <https://www.tussell.com/insights/ai-and-the-public-sector> accessed 9 March 2023.

Weghmann, Vera and Kyla Sankey, 'Hollowed out: The growing impact of consultancies in public administrations' (2022) EPSU Report <https://www.epsu.org/sites/default/files/article/files/EPSU%20Report%20Outsourcing%20state_EN.pdf> accessed 17 October 2022.

World Economic Forum, 'AI Procurement in a Box' (2020, updated May 2022) <https://www.weforum.org/reports/ai-procurement-in-a-box> accessed 9 March 2023.

World Economic Forum, 'Adopting AI Responsibly: Guidelines for Procurement of AI Solutions by the Private Sector' (June 2023) <https://www3.weforum.org/docs/WEF_Adopting_AI_Responsibly_Guidelines_for_Procurement_of_AI_Solutions_by_the_Private_Sector_2023.pdf> accessed 22 June 2023.

Yeung, Karen, 'A study of the implications of advanced digital technologies (including AI systems) for the concept of responsibility within a human rights framework' (2019) Council of Europe DGI(2019)05 <https://rm.coe.int/a-study-of-the-implications-of-advanced-digital-technologies-including/168096bdab> accessed 12 June 2023.

Blogs and Other Online Resources

Almada, Marco, 'What Do We Talk About When We Talk About AI Regulation?' (*RAILS blog*, 9 April 2023) <https://blog.ai-laws.org/what-do-we-talk-about-when-we-talk-about-ai-regulation/> accessed 11 April 2023.

Aneja, Urvashi, 'Public Sector Procurement of AI Must Take a Principled Approach' (*mint*, 4 December 2022) <https://www.livemint.com/opinion/online-views/public-sector-procurement-of-ai-must-take-a-principled-approach-11670173999072.html> accessed 9 March 2023.

Ben Dor, Lavi M and Cary Coglianese, 'The Procurement Path to AI Governance' (*Regulatory Review*, 27 June 2022) <https://www.theregreview.org/2022/06/27/ben-dor-coglianese-procurement-path-to-ai-governance/> accessed 7 March 2023.

Bertrand, Arnauld and Julie McQueen, 'How Governments Can Plan for a Future-Fit, Digital Workforce' (*EY blog*, 11 Oct 2022) <https://www.ey.com/en_ch/government-digital-innovation/how-governments-can-plan-for-a-future-fit-digital-workforce> accessed 17 October 2022.

Boots, Sean, '"Charbonneau Loops" and Government IT Contracting' (*Sean Boots blog*, 12 October 2022) <https://sboots.ca/2022/10/12/charbonneau-loops-and-government-it-contracting/> accessed 18 October 2022.

Burrell, Jenna, 'Artificial Intelligence and the Ever-Receding Horizon of the Future' (*Tech Policy Press*, 6 June 2023) <https://techpolicy.press/artificial-intelligence-and-the-ever-receding-horizon-of-the-future/> accessed 15 June 2023.

Caranta, Roberto, 'Opening the Doors to Civil Society Litigation in Public Contracts' (*REALaw blog*, 1 November 2022) <https://realaw.blog/2022/11/01/opening-the-doors-to-civil-society-litigation-in-public-contracts-by-r-caranta/> accessed 15 November 2022.

Chenok, Dan, 'How Can Governments Use AI to Improve Procurement?' (*Regulatory Review*, 30 June 2022) <https://www.theregreview.org/2022/06/30/chenok-how-can-governments-use-ai-to-improve-procurement/> accessed 7 March 2023.

Clement-Jones, Tim, 'Government AI Procurement Needs Ethical and Data Compliance Obligation' (blog, 30 July 2022) <https://www.lordclementjones.org/2022/07/30/government-ai-procurement-needs-ethical-and-data-compliance-obligation/> accessed 9 March 2023.

Cocciolo, Serena, Hunt La Cascia and Maria Arnal Canudo, 'Strengthening Public Procurement Through Data Analytics' (*Governance for Development*, 20 October 2022) <https://blogs.worldbank.org/governance/strengthening-public-procurement-through-data-analytics-0> accessed 20 December 2022.

Coyle, Diane, 'The Tensions Between Explainable AI and Good Public Policy' (*Tech Stream*, 15 September 2020) <https://www.brookings.edu/techstream/the-tensions-between-explainable-ai-and-good-public-policy/> accessed 9 March 2023.

Croker, John, 'Law, Artificial Intelligence and Human Rights; Connecting the Dots' (*Law That Shapes Us*, 2 March 2023) <https://www.law.ox.ac.uk/content/article/law-shapes-us-law-artificial-intelligence-and-human-rights-connecting-dots> accessed 7 March 2023.

Demetzou, Katerina, 'Introduction to the Conformity Assessment under the Draft EU AI Act, and How It Compares to DPIAs' (Future of Privacy Forum, 12 August 2022) <https://fpf.org/blog/introduction-to-the-conformity-assessment-under-the-draft-eu-ai-act-and-how-it-compares-to-dpias/> accessed 15 November 2022.

Dotan, Ravit and others, 'How to Manage AI Procurement in Public Administration' (*World Economic Forum blog*, 5 July 2023) <https://www.weforum.org/agenda/2023/07/how-to-manage-ai-procurement-in-public-administration/> accessed 6 July 2023.

Granickas, Karolis, 'Open Contracting & the EU: What's the Progress on Contract Transparency?' (*Open Contracting Partnership Blog*, 2 February 2022) <https://www.open-contracting.org/2022/02/02/open-contracting-the-eu-whats-the-progress-on-contract-transparency/> accessed 4 October 2022.

Gutierrez, Carlos Ignacio, 'Procurement as an AI Governance Change Agent' (*Regulatory Review*, 6 July 2022) <https://www.theregreview.org/2022/07/06/ignacio-gutierrez-procurement-as-an-ai-governance-change-agent/> accessed 7 March 2023.

Hess-Rheingans, Elena and Lara Bird, 'Developing the Algorithmic Transparency Standard in the Open' (*Centre for Data Ethics and Innovation Blog*, 10 October 2022) <https://cdei.blog.gov.uk/2022/10/10/developing-the-algorithmic-transparency-standard-in-the-open/> accessed 8 November 2022.

Jimenez Arandia, Pablo, 'What to Expect from Europe's First AI Oversight Agency' (*Algorithm Watch*, 1 February 2023) <https://algorithmwatch.org/en/what-to-expect-from-europes-first-ai-oversight-agency/> accessed 7 April 2023.

Kim, Song-Hee and Hummy Song, 'How Digital Transformation Can Improve Hospitals' Operational Decisions' (*Harvard Business* Review, 18 January 2022) <https://hbr.org/2022/01/how-digital-transformation-can-improve-hospitals-operational-decisions> accessed 12 June 2023.

Lawrence, Neil D, 'Deploying Machine Learning: Intellectual Debt and AutoAI' (*Inverseprobability.com*, 6 October 2020) <http://inverseprobability.com/talks/notes/deploying-machine-learning-systems-intellectual-debt-and-auto-ai.html> accessed 7 October 2022.

Leslie, Mia and Tatiana Kazim, 'Executable Versions: An Argument for Compulsory Disclosure (Part 1)' (The Digital Constitutionalist, 3 August 2022) <https://digi-con.org/executable-versions-part-one/> accessed 4 November 2022.

Leslie, Mia and Tatiana Kazim, 'Executable Versions: An Argument for Compulsory Disclosure (Part 2)' (The Digital Constitutionalist, 3 November 2022) <https://digi-con.org/executable-versions-part-two/> accessed 4 November 2022.

McQuillan, Dan, 'Predicted Benefits, Proven Harms. How AI's Algorithmic Violence Emerged from Our Own Social Matrix' (*Sociological Review*, 6 June 2023) <https://thesociologicalreview.org/magazine/june-2023/artificial-intelligence/predicted-benefits-proven-harms/> accessed 15 June 2023.

Morozov, Evgeny, 'The True Threat of Artificial Intelligence' (*New York Times*, 30 June 2023) <https://www.nytimes.com/2023/06/30/opinion/artificial-intelligence-danger.html> accessed 2 July 2023.

Mutagi, Girish, 'Digital Transformation: Next Gen Procurement and Supply Chain' (*IBM Supply Chain and Blockchain Blog*, 25 April 2018) <https://www.ibm.com/blogs/blockchain/2018/04/digital-transformation-next-gen-procurement-and-supply-chain/> accessed 12 September 2022.

Narayanan, Arvind, 'Twitter Showed Us Its Algorithm. What Does It Tell Us?' (*Knight Institute blog*, 10 April 2023) <https://knightcolumbia.org/blog/twitter-showed-us-its-algorithm-what-does-it-tell-us> accessed 12 April 2023.

O'Shaughnessy, Matt and Matt Sheenan, 'Lessons From the World's Two Experiments in AI Governance' (*Carnegie Endowment for International Peace*, 14 February 2023) <https://carnegieendowment.org/2023/02/14/lessons-from-world-s-two-experiments-in-ai-governance-pub-89035> accessed 6 April 2023.

Pouget, Hadrien, 'The EU's AI Act Is Barreling Toward AI Standards That Do Not Exist' (*Lawfare*, 12 January 2023) <https://www.lawfareblog.com/eus-ai-act-barreling-toward-ai-standards-do-not-exist> accessed 2 February 2023.

Pouget, Hadrien, 'What Will the Role of Standards Be in AI Governance? Why Standards Are at the Centre of AI Regulation Conversations and the Challenges They Raise' (*Ada Lovelace Institute blog*, 5 April 2023) <https://www.adalovelaceinstitute.org/blog/role-of-standards-in-ai-governance/> accessed 7 April 2023.

Rubenstein, David S, 'Retooling the Acquisition Gateway for Responsible AI' (*Regulatory Review*, 28 June 2022) <https://www.theregreview.org/2022/06/28/rubenstein-retooling-the-acquisition-gateway-for-responsible-ai/> accessed 7 March 2023.

Sanchez-Graells, Albert, 'Using "Cultural Fitness" as Evaluation Criteria Breaches EU and UK Public Procurement Law' (*howtocrackanut.com*, 1 March 2017) <https://www.howtocrackanut.com/blog/2017/3/1/using-cultural-fitness-as-evaluation-criteria-breaches-eu-and-uk-public-procurement-law> accessed 23 February 2023.

Sanchez-Graells, Albert, 'How to Rethink the Role of Procurement to Foster Economic Recovery and the Green Transition—Re Mazzucato (2021, 2020)' (*howtocrackanut.com*, 6 August 2021) <https://www.howtocrackanut.com/blog/how-to-rethink-procurement-for-economic-and-green-transition-re-mazzucato> accessed 7 March 2023.

Sanchez-Graells, Albert, 'Can the Robot Procure for You?' (*howtocrackanut.com*, 12 August 2021) <https://www.howtocrackanut.com/blog/can-the-robot-procure-for-you> accessed 21 October 2022.

Sanchez-Graells, Albert, 'Where Does the Proposed EU AI Act Place Procurement?' (*howtocrackanut.com*, 21 October 2021) <https://www.howtocrackanut.com/blog/2021/10/21/where-does-the-proposed-eu-ai-act-place-procurement> accessed 8 November 2022.

Sanchez-Graells, Albert, 'Procurement Recommender Systems: How Much Better Before We Trust Them?' (*howtocrackanut.com*, 10 June 2022) <https://www.howtocrackanut.com/blog/2022/6/10/procurement-recommender-systems-how-much-better-before-we-trust-them> accessed 23 September 2022.

Sanchez-Graells, Albert, 'Public Procurement and [AI] Source Code Transparency, A (Downstream) Competition Issue (Re C-796/18)' (*howtocrackanut.com*, 20 June 2022) <https://www.howtocrackanut.com/blog/2022/6/20/public-procurement-and-ai-source-code-transparency> accessed 7 October 2022.

Sanchez-Graells, Albert, 'Algorithmic Transparency: Some Thoughts on UK's First Four Published Disclosures and the Standards' Usability' (*howtocrackanut.com*, 11 July 2022) <https://www.howtocrackanut.com/blog/2022/7/11/algorithmic-transparency-some-thoughts-on-uk-first-disclosures-and-usability> accessed 8 November 2022.

Sanchez-Graells, Albert, 'Interesting Legislative Proposal to Make Procurement of AI Conditional on External Checks' (*howtocrackanut.com*, 2 September 2022) <https://www.howtocrackanut.com/blog/interesting-proposal-procurement-ai-gatekeeping-external-checks> accessed 15 November 2022.

Sanchez-Graells, Albert, 'Interoperable Europe Act: Quick Procurement Annotation' (*howtocrackanut.com*, 5 January 2023) <https://www.howtocrackanut.com/blog/2023/1/5/interoperable-europe-act-quick-procurement-annotation> accessed 9 March 2023.

Sanchez-Graells, Albert, 'Will Public Buyers Be Covered by New EU Cybersecurity Requirements?' (*howtocrackanut.com*, 18 October 2022) <https://www.howtocrackanut.com/blog/2022/10/18/will-public-buyers-be-covered-by-new-eu-cybersecurity-requirements> accessed 18 October 2022.

Sanchez-Graells, Albert, 'New CJEU Case Law Against Excessive Disclosure: Quid de Open Data?' (*howtocrackanut.com*, 22 November 2022) <https://www.howtocrackanut.com/blog/2022/11/22/cjeu-case-law-against-excessive-disclosure-quid-de-open-data> accessed 20 December 2022.

Sanchez-Graells, Albert, 'Ensuring Algorithmic Transparency Through Public Contracts?' (*Digital Constitutionalist*, 24 November 2022) <https://digi-con.org/ensuring-algorithmic-transparency-through-public-contracts/> accessed 20 December 2022.

Sanchez-Graells, Albert, 'More Nuanced Procurement Transparency to Protect Competition: Has the Court of Justice Hit the Brakes on Open Procurement Data in

Antea Polska (C-54/21)?' (*howtocrackanut.com*, 5 January 2023) <https://www.howtocrackanut.com/blog/2023/1/5/more-nuanced-procurement-transparency-to-protect-competition-in-antea-polska> accessed 12 April 2023.

Sanchez-Graells, Albert, 'Some Further Thoughts on Setting Procurement up to Fail in "AI Regulation by Contract"' (*howtocrackanut.com*, 27 January 2023) <https://www.howtocrackanut.com/blog/2023/1/27/setting-procurement-up-to-fail-in-ai-regulation-by-contract> accessed 8 February 2023.

Sanchez-Graells, Albert, 'Digital Procurement, PPDS and Multi-Speed Datafication—Some Thoughts on the March 2023 PPDS Communication' (*howtocrackanut.com*, 28 March 2023) <https://www.howtocrackanut.com/blog/2023/3/28/digital-procurement-ppds-and-multi-speed-datafication> accessed 12 April 2023.

Sanchez-Graells, Albert, 'UK's "Pro-Innovation Approach" to AI regulation Won't Do, Particularly for Public Sector Digitalisation' (*howtocrackanut.com*, 31 March 2023) <https://www.howtocrackanut.com/blog/2023/3/31/uk-pro-innovation-ai-regulation-wont-do> accessed 6 April 2023.

Sanchez-Graells, Albert, 'Procuring AI Without Understanding It. Way To Go?' (*howtocrackanut.com*, 4 April 2023) <https://www.howtocrackanut.com/blog/2023/3/31/uk-pro-innovation-ai-regulation-wont-do> accessed 7 April 2023.

Sanchez-Graells, Albert, 'ChatGPT in the Public Sector—Should It Be Banned? (*howtocrackanut.com*, 3 May 2023) <https://www.howtocrackanut.com/blog/should-we-ban-chatgpt-in-the-public-sector> accessed 3 July 2023.

Sanchez-Graells, Albert and Michael Lewis, 'Digital Technologies, Hype, and Public Sector Capability' (*howtocrackanut.com*, 13 July 2022) <https://www.howtocrackanut.com/blog/2022/7/13/digital-technologies-hype-and-public-sector-capability> accessed 12 September 2022.

Santiso, Carlos, 'Artificial Intelligence in the Public Sector: An Engine for Innovation in Government... If We Get It Right!' (OPSI blog, 6 July 2022) <https://oecd-opsi.org/blog/ai-an-engine-for-innovation/> accessed 9 March 2023.

Telles, Pedro, 'Applying Tirole's Socially Responsible Agencies Thesis to Public Procurement' (*telles.eu*, 11 May 2023) <http://www.telles.eu/blog/2023/5/11/applying-tiroles-socially-responsible-agencies-thesis-to-public-procurement> accessed 11 May 2023.

Tillipman, Jessica, 'Using AI to Reduce Performance Risk in U.S. Procurement' (*Regulatory Review*, 29 June 2022) <https://www.theregreview.org/2022/06/29/tillipman-using-ai-to-reduce-performance-risk-in-u-s-procurement/> accessed 15 September 2022.

T-Labs, 'Consensus Algorithms: The Essential Forces of the DLT Universe' (*Medium*, 24 April 2018) <https://medium.com/@_tlabs/consensus-algorithms-the-essential-forces-of-the-dlt-universe-e1dd8e049534> accessed 15 September 2022.

Whittaker, Tom and Ian Tucker, 'Could Machine Learning Be Used to Assist Evaluators in Regulated Public Procurements?' (Lexology, 12 January 2023) <https://www.lexology.com/library/detail.aspx?g=ec7345d2-8892-4c8f-b740-fdd4f13f877c> accessed 12 April 2023.

Yu, Howard, 'GDPR Isn't Enough to Protect Us in an Age of Smart Algorithms' (*The Conversation*, 29 May 2018) <https://theconversation.com/gdpr-isnt-enough-to-protect-us-in-an-age-of-smart-algorithms-97389> accessed 21 November 2022.

Zhou, Alex, 'Tracing HHS Blockchain Adoption' (*Avascent*, 28 April 2021) <https://www.avascent.com/news-insights/healthcare-pulse/tracing-hhs-blockchain-adoption/> accessed 15 September 2022.

Index

For the benefit of digital users, indexed terms that span two pages (e.g., 52–53) may, on occasion, appear on only one of those pages.

Figures are indicated by *f* following the page number